ruited
nmi
ndi
re

RACE AND LABOUR IN LONDON TRANSPORT

The Institute of Race Relations was founded as an
independent body in 1958. The main aims are to
promote the study of the relations between groups
racially defined, to make available information on
race to different groups, and to give advice on
proposals for improving relations. In its work, the
subject of 'race relations' is regarded as primarily
referring to the social relationships between groups
that are influenced by prejudice and beliefs about race,
but 'race' is inevitably related to the many factors
affecting group relations, including the major problems
of political and economic relationships. The Institute
has responded to a changing situation by extending its
work and services to members of minority groups.
The Institute cannot itself hold a corporate opinion:
the opinions expressed in this work are those of the
author.

The Acton Society Trust was founded in
1948 as an independent agency researching
into social, political, and economic issues.

CE

RACE AND LABOUR IN LONDON TRANSPORT

DENNIS BROOKS

PUBLISHED FOR THE
INSTITUTE OF RACE RELATIONS
and the
ACTON SOCIETY TRUST *by*

OXFORD UNIVERSITY PRESS
LONDON   NEW YORK   TORONTO
1975

Universitas
BIBLIOTHECA
ttaviensis

312464

Oxford University Press, Ely House, London W1

GLASGOW   NEW YORK   TORONTO   MELBOURNE   WELLINGTON
CAPE TOWN   IBADAN   NAIROBI   DAR ES SALAAM   LUSAKA   ADDIS ABABA
DELHI   BOMBAY   CALCUTTA   MADRAS   KARACHI   LAHORE   DACCA
KUALA LUMPUR   SINGAPORE   HONG KONG   TOKYO

ISBN 0 19 218408 3

© Institute of Race Relations 1975

*All rights reserved. No part of this publication may be reproduced,
stored in a retrieval system, or transmitted, in any form or by any means,
electronic, mechanical, photocopying, recording or otherwise, without
the prior permission of the Institute of Race Relations*

HD
4903.5
.G7B76
1975

Printed in Great Britain by
Ebenezer Baylis and Son Limited,
The Trinity Press, Worcester, and London.

BIBLIOTHECA

For Marjorie

For Marlene

CONTENTS

LIST OF DIAGRAMS

ACKNOWLEDGEMENTS

More so than most writers, the author of a report of a large field study owes a debt of gratitude to those who have made the study possible or have assisted him in many and varied ways. Names too numerous to mention spring to mind as deserving thanks; perhaps they will forgive me if they do not receive specific mention.

First I am indebted to the London Transport Board for permitting the study to be made, to its Chairman at that time, Sir Alec Valentine, and more particularly to Mr. Anthony Bull, the Board member with responsibility for personnel and industrial relations.

The main burden of London Transport's co-operation in the project fell on Mr. F. H. Spratling, and to him I owe a special debt of gratitude. Likewise Mr. C. C. Gomm, who was very much involved at most stages of the study. Others outside the operating or engineering departments deserving my thanks are Mr. J. E. Ager, for producing much statistical data, and Messrs. F. E. Wilkins and F. Baker.

In Railway Operating the major burden was shouldered by Mr. H. P. Steele to whom I owe a special word of thanks. I am indebted to Mr. F. G. Maxwell, to the Divisional Superintendents (particularly Messrs. A. E. Dowton and C. M. Cray), and to their Assistants (particularly Mr. G. C. Pearse). Similarly to Mr. R. Potter and his colleagues at the Railway Training Centre.

In Permanent Way the heaviest task fell to Mr. W. A. S. Anderson, and I am grateful for his help at all times. I must thank too Mr. A. C. Edrich, Mr. H. Chanter, and the Divisional Assistants (particularly Messrs. J. G. O'Callaghan and C. S. Cole).

In Central Buses my thanks are due particularly to Mr. M. J. McCoy, and Mr. F. E. Smith. The Divisional Garage Managers also deserve my thanks, as do the staff at the Chiswick Training Centre.

A study of this kind would not be possible without the active co-operation of the trade unions concerned, and I am indebted to the following: the Associated Society of Locomotive Engineers and Firemen (particularly its General Secretary Mr. Ray Buckton), the National Union of Railwaymen (particularly Mr. G. W. Brassington, then an Assistant General Secretary), and the Transport and General Workers' Union. Here a special word of thanks is owed to Mr. E. B. G. ('Terry') Allen, but I am also indebted to Mr. Jack Jones, Mr. V. S. Collier, Mr. C. A. Young, and the divisional officers in the No. 1 Passenger Group. The Central Bus Committee and the Railway Sectional Councils also deserve my appreciation, and from amongst the latter my particular thanks are due to Mr. Don James, who acted as our 'guide' and gave us some insights into permanent way.

The Barbados Government co-operated fully in that part of the study concerned with its recruitment scheme and for this help I am grateful, particularly to Mr. Harold Brewster in London and Mr. Frank King in Bridgetown.

Financial backing was provided by the Social Science Research Council, supplemented by a grant from the Institute's 'Survey of Race Relations in Britain'; subsequently the Joseph Rowntree Social Service Trust stepped in to assist with the cost of writing the report. To them all I am indebted, as I am to the Acton Society and its trustees (especially Mr. Edward Goodman) for sponsoring the study.

Mrs. Susan Rayner assisted at most stages of the fieldwork, with the preliminary analysis, and wrote the first draft of Chapter 12; for all this I am indeed grateful. To Professor John Vaizey for his ever-willing counsel, to Mr. Graham Massey for his help with the pilot study, to Mr. Roy Manley for assistance during the early months, and to Mr. Trevor Smith for help in the later stages, my thanks are due. To Mrs. Sheila Patterson, consultant to the study, I owe a special debt of gratitude for her guidance and encouragement.

I am indebted too to the project's advisory committee and especially to its chairman, Professor Meyer Fortes; to the School of Social Sciences at Brunel University for taking the project under its wing during the difficult months of 1966; to the Institute of Community Studies for its punch-card facilities; to the numerous typists who have worked on the various drafts.

I owe a particular debt to my wife Marjorie for her assistance with the data, with proof-reading (that most boring of tasks), and for much else besides.

Perhaps in some ways most important of all, my thanks are due to the busmen and railwaymen—and women—who agreed to be interviewed. I hope that they will recognize something of their own situations in the following pages. I would like to thank too the managers and supervisors at the locations visited for their assistance and particularly for arranging the timing of the interviews.

It is customary for the writer to accept sole responsibility for his work; in many cases this is but a ritual—here, though, it is very relevant. Drafts of this work have been widely circulated and I know that officials of London Transport in particular disagree with some of its conclusions. This disagreement does not, however, make my gratitude for their assistance any less warm.

Industrial Relations Research
Unit of the Social Science Research Council   Dennis Brooks
University of Warwick   February 1972.

INTRODUCTION

The research project which has resulted in this volume has had a long and at times tortuous history. It was first suggested by me in the summer of 1963 during a review of the Acton Society Trust's future research activities. No action was taken at that time, but interest was revived by the announcement in the autumn of 1963 that the Institute of Race Relations (I.R.R.) proposed to establish a 'Survey of Race Relations in Britain'.

After discussions with its Director and the submission of outline proposals, the 'Survey' provided a small sum of money for the preparation of a comprehensive research design. This was done in the closing months of 1964.

At the same time we sought agreement in principle to the study from the London Transport Board (L.T.B.),[1] since it was obvious that it could only be undertaken with the active co-operation of that body. After discussions the L.T.B. agreed to co-operate in the project, subject to certain safeguards[2] and provided, too, that the three trade unions whose members would be involved also gave their

---

[1] Most of this report was written before the London Transport Board's title was changed to the London Transport Executive (1 January 1970). I have throughout referred to the 'Board' or 'L.T.B.' and have not attempted to update the designation: it was correct at the time of the study.

[2] The understanding between the Acton Society Trust and the L.T.B. concerning the publication resulting from the study was that: (i) L.T.B. 'would see in draft form the completed manuscript for comment'; (ii) that it 'would have a veto right on the publication of any confidential information it had supplied'; and (iii) 'the identity of garages, depots, etc. studied in detail would be disguised and the anonymity of individuals maintained'. It must be added that London Transport did not attempt in any way to exercise this veto right.

agreement. The Board also provided us with some documentary and statistical data to enable us to complete the research design.

We next approached the three trade unions: the Associated Society of Locomotive Engineers and Firemen (A.S.L.E.F.) and the National Union of Railwaymen (N.U.R.) for the railwaymen, the Transport and General Workers' Union (T.G.W.U.) for the busmen and the canteen workers.[1] After discussions, the two railway unions agreed in principle to the study. The T.G.W.U., whilst not unsympathetic at headquarters level, felt bound to refer the matter to its Regional Passenger Transport Group for decision.

A further complication at this stage was that the 'Survey of Race Relations' was prepared to provide only part of the financial backing necessary for the project and consequently we applied to the Human Sciences Committee of the Department of Scientific and Industrial Research (D.S.I.R.) for a grant to cover most of the costs. This body agreed to provide a grant, subject to formal assurances of co-operation from L.T.B. and the three trade unions.

The T.G.W.U. then referred the question of its co-operation to its Central Bus Committee.[2] This body took the view that whilst progress had been made in the absorption of Commonwealth immigrants in Central Buses, the situation was still delicate and could easily be worsened by the proposed study. It could not, therefore, give its agreement.

Following this decision, we amended our proposals to make the study a two-stage one: the first part would cover the railway departments, the second part Central Buses. We reasoned that if the field work of the railway part could be completed without any observable adverse repercussions, a second approach to the Central Bus Committee would be more likely to be successful. This proved to be prophetic: the Committee agreed to co-operate with the study in July 1966.

The field work was uneventful. Many, perhaps most, of the L.T.B. managers and supervisors met during the course of the study feared that it would have adverse consequences in worsening relations between native and immigrant staff, but no effects of this kind have been reported.

---

[1] The proposal to include canteen workers in the study had to be later abandoned owing to a lack of time.

[2] See below, p. 58n.

WHY THE STUDY WAS UNDERTAKEN

At the time of its conception, there appeared to be a number of reasons why a study of Commonwealth immigrants in London Transport would be valuable. Very little research had been done on coloured immigrants in industry; indeed there were few published works available on coloured immigrants in Britain in the post-war period.

There was, in our approach, both a strong problem and policy orientation, coupled with a wish to further our understanding of the processes of absorption of minority groups which would have value at a more theoretical level. We assumed that *harmonious* relations between racial groups were desirable.[1] From this standpoint, it appeared that much of value could be learnt from the London Transport situation. L.T.B. had employed considerable numbers of Commonwealth immigrants for a relatively long period of time. From outside the organization it appeared to us that it had in its employment policies been more successful than had some other employers, in that there had been few reports of large-scale or organized resistance from the native work force.

There was, too, at that time, considerable interest in the Barbados recruitment scheme: it seemed at least possible that it could serve as a 'blueprint' for future immigration policy. This was of course during the 'optimistic' phase of Commonwealth immigration: after the 1962 Commonwealth Immigrants Act, but before the White Paper of August 1965,[2] two race relations acts, and the advent of what has been popularly termed 'Powellism'. Finally, the public transport industry, and indeed most of the service sector, had been largely neglected by sociologists in Britain.

There were other reasons of less immediate relevance which spurred us on. It was clear from such work as had been published or was then under way that further detailed work was necessary for any significant advance in developing an adequate theoretical framework of race relations, particularly in their industrial context. It is hoped that this report does advance our knowledge in this area and will contribute towards such a theoretical framework. Most of the generalizations of the sociology of industry have been

Se[1] I accept John Rex's point 'that there is no such thing as "good race relations" '.
19e John Rex, *Race Relations in Sociological Theory* (London, Weidenfeld & Nicolson, 70), p. 124.

[2] *Immigration from the Commonwealth* (Cmnd. 2739) (London, H.M.S.O., August 1965).

derived from studies of manufacturing industry. Again it is hoped that something of value emerges from this examination of part of the service sector. In some respects, then, this is two studies: one of the sociology of public transport, and one of race relations and immigrant absorption within the context of that industry. Yet they are complementary: it would not be possible to understand and explain the race relations of the industry without reference to the sociology of work; any attempt at explaining the sociology of public transport in urban Britain today must take account of the presence of coloured immigrants.

THE PROBLEMS OF THE INVESTIGATOR OF RACE RELATIONS

More so than most, the student of race relations faces problems arising from his own beliefs and values. Differences of race and colour divide mankind, and it is idle to pretend that the social scientist can remain aloof from this conflict—he is a citizen too. He cannot, in his role as a social scientist, be objective: in the data he chooses to collect, in his presentation and interpretation of such data, he is *selective*; and the notion of objectivity is unreal. He can, though, *try* to be objective; he can to some extent present the evidence and let it speak for itself. This has been my approach here. The striving for objectivity is not to be confused with neutrality: in relation to racialism there can be no sitting on the fence. As a citizen I reject the less favourable treatment of people based on differences of ethnicity, colour, or any other irrelevant criteria.

I am perhaps required to declare my position on one other issue which is likely to become increasingly important during this decade: that of absorption versus pluralism. If a minority group seeks to maintain its own cultural identity or some degree of separateness, then it is that group's own affair. It would be arrogant of me to argue that it should not do so. To that extent I am a pluralist.

On the other hand, I am impressed by the weight of evidence of intolerance shown towards ethnic minorities throughout recorded history. Whilst I accept that contemporary Western racialism is largely a product of capitalist colonial expansion, intolerance of minorities existed before capitalism and will probably outlive it. This suggests to me therefore that the less that groups are seen to be different, the less likelihood there is of persecution of minorities. To that extent I am an assimilationist.

These are my biases, if that is the appropriate word, but I re-emphasize that I have tried to be objective. I cannot invite you, the reader, to judge how successful I have been in this respect, as you have your biases too. I can only make you aware of mine, and invite you to be conscious of your own.

My aim throughout this study has been to *understand*; my aim in this volume is to *explain*. It is no part of my role to criticize, or for that matter to praise, though I am aware that some passages can probably be interpreted as containing either criticism or praise.

SOME GENERAL CONSIDERATIONS

I have spelled out the research findings in considerable detail, indeed some may think there is too much detail. I believe, though, that this amount of detail is necessary for an adequate understanding of the subject matter of this volume. A problem of some importance here is how much previous knowledge the writer assumes on the part of the reader—that is, knowledge of the social sciences, of public transport, and specifically of London's public transport system. Clearly, individual readers' knowledge of these areas will vary widely. I have assumed some familiarity with both, though I hope not too much for the majority of readers. To those who find they are covering all too familiar territory, I can only apologize.

The situation described is usually as we found it at the time of our study, from mid-1965 to mid-1967. It has seldom been possible to take account of subsequent changes, though some are recorded. It is likely, though, that there have been a number of changes since our study which have relevance for the subject matter of this report.

The passage of time is also relevant in one other respect. Most of the events recorded here that concerned coloured immigrants have taken place in the past twenty years or so. Yet so much has happened in race relations in Britain over this period that it is sometimes a little difficult to make the mental adjustment required to understand fully the racial tempo of the early to mid-fifties. The terms of the 'immigration debate' have moved in a more overtly racial direction. Restriction—and repatriation—has increasingly become the password of the bigot.

On the other hand, there has been a growth of specialist agencies concerned with race in Britain and, more important, of our knowledge of problems arising from racial and ethnic differences. The relevance of this is that many of the events recorded here took place at a time when there was little published information available and few specialist agencies capable of proffering advice. The decision-makers—whatever their intentions—had to learn by experience.

Finally, the field work was carried out at a time when the language of public debate was far less vitriolic than it subsequently became, and this has relevance for the behaviour and attitudes reported. Overt racialism was less respectable then.

I

THE THEORETICAL APPROACH AND RESEARCH METHODS

SOME THEORETICAL CONSIDERATIONS

Whilst this is not intended as a major theoretical work, it does, I believe, have something of value to contribute to the development of an adequate race relations theory, particularly one which is applicable to the British scene. Empirical work ought, in any case, to have a sound theoretical framework. It is necessary then to explain the theoretical considerations which appeared important when the study was designed, and to take account of some contributions to theory which have appeared since that time.

This is a study of the absorption of coloured immigrant workers within one organization.[1] As such it attempts to draw on the concepts and theoretical strengths of immigration studies, of race relations, and of the sociology of industry. My own predisposition is certainly not to regard race relations as a separate discipline, but rather as an area of study amenable to the theoretical approaches, skills, and techniques of a wide variety of specialists—sociologists, anthropologists, economists, geographers, and so on. We cannot look at race relations in isolation. The emphasis of this study is very much on understanding the tasks, beliefs, values, and behavioural norms of a single organization, and immigration and race relations are examined both within the context of that organization and as a part of this structure.

[1] Throughout this volume I have used the terms 'coloured' and 'immigrant' interchangeably, unless specifically stated. I do not particularly like the term 'coloured' and I realize that some find it offensive. However, it is used colloquially by many—including some who regard themselves as coloured—and is used in that sense here. The problem is that there is no completely satisfactory alternative term which would cover those of diverse origins with which we are concerned: some certainly did not consider themselves 'black'; and 'non-white' is clumsy and has the same value connotations as 'coloured'. As is seen below (Chapter 3, p. 34), most of those described as coloured are of West Indian origin. White immigrants are described as such, or in terms of their ethnic origins, e.g., Irish, Polish, and so on.

Whilst I am not unwilling to cross the rather indistinct boundaries separating the various social science disciplines if this is warranted by the data and consistent with my own competence, the approach adopted here is largely sociological.

The student of immigration and race in contemporary Britain is faced with a problem of some magnitude which arises from the fact that coloured immigrants in Britain *are* immigrants and *are* coloured. Is the situation one in which immigration variables are paramount, or is it one which is dominated by race?[1] The answers given in the past have depended in part on the questions posed, in part on the predispositions of the investigator, and in part on when the investigation was carried out and reported.

If one looks for immigration factors in the contemporary British situation, they can certainly be found, and similarly with those of race. More so than most areas of study, race relations has attracted students with strong personal commitments, and this has influenced both the selection and interpretation of data. There has also been something of a 'pendulum swing' between the race and immigration approaches over the past quarter century or so in Britain. Early postwar investigators emphasized the importance of colour and race.[2]

With the development of larger-scale Commonwealth immigration in the fifties the pendulum swung towards the immigration perspective.[3] This reflected some dissatisfaction with earlier approaches and, of course, the fact that the coloured immigrants were recent arrivals. More recently, there has been a movement in the opposite direction: the immigrant-host framework has been rejected as inadequate.[4]

[1] As used here the term 'race' refers to 'a group that is *socially* defined but on the basis of *physical* criteria'. Pierre van den Berghe, *Race and Racism* (London, Wiley, 1967), p. 9 (italics in original text). For our purposes this definition is satisfactory, but for others it is not: it would, for example, exclude anti-Semitism. The controversy over the scope of 'race relations' is outside the province of this present work. See ibid.; John Rex, 'The Concept of Race in Sociological Theory', in Sami Zubaida (ed.), *Race and Racialism* (London, Tavistock, 1970); and Rex, *Race Relations in Sociological Theory*.

[2] For example, K. L. Little, *Negroes in Britain* (London, Kegan Paul, 1947.)

[3] Most notably in the works of Sheila Patterson: *Dark Strangers* (London, Tavistock, 1963); and *Immigrants in Industry* (London, Oxford University Press, for Institute of Race Relations, 1968). Peter Wright, *The Coloured Worker in British Industry* (London, Oxford University Press, for Institute of Race Relations, 1968) uses the concept of 'integration', but his is also basically an 'immigration' approach.

[4] For example, see John Rex and Robert Moore, *Race, Community, and Conflict*, (London, Oxford University Press, for Institute of Race Relations, 1967); Sheila

This argument over the primacy of race or immigration variables is, I believe, largely sterile; the dichotomy posed is a false one. Rather than seeking to establish which set of variables is of paramount importance, it is more appropriate to ask in *which areas* each operates. By themselves both race and immigration explanations are inadequate, and it is necessary to develop a theoretical framework which can incorporate both. This I have attempted to do.

The starting-point for this study was very much in the immigration tradition, and it is true to say that my own position has shifted considerably since that time. Before developing the theoretical framework of the study, I shall outline some existing theories of immigration and race, indicating the extent to which I have drawn on them in my approach.

First, the 'immigrant-host' framework.[1] This stresses the essentially 'immigration' aspects of group interaction. The two key concepts of this framework are *adaptation* on the part of the immigrants and *acceptance* on the part of the host or receiving society.

On the one hand, there are the immigrants with their motives for migration, their expectations and images of the receiving or host society, their own beliefs, value systems, behavioural norms, and so on. On the other hand, the host society has its images of and attitudes towards the immigrants, as well as a set of expectations about their behaviour; and that society has its own beliefs, value systems, and behavioural norms.

It is unlikely that these two sets of expectations, beliefs, values, and norms will be completely in accord, and from this premise stem two processes. On the part of the immigrants there is the process of *adaptation* which is best seen as a form of re-socialization or acculturation: learning new skills, new roles, new values, new behavioural norms, new expectations. Aside from the learning of new technical skills which may be involved, there is the much more complex and subtle process of learning social skills, the perception of cues, including, for English-speaking immigrants to England, subtle differences in the use of the language, voice inflexions, and the like.

Allen, 'Immigrants or Workers', in Zubaida; E. J. B. Rose and associates, *Colour and Citizenship* (London, Oxford University Press, for Institute of Race Relations, 1969); and T. B. Rees, 'Accommodation, Integration, Cultural Pluralism and Assimilation: Their Place in Equilibrium Theories of Society' *Race* (Vol. XI, No. 4, April 1970), pp. 481–90.

[1] I have drawn heavily here on Patterson, *Dark Strangers* and S. N. Eisenstadt, *The Absorption of Immigrants* (London, Routledge & Kegan Paul, 1954). The reader is referred to both these works for a fuller explanation.

As Banton has written, 'the stranger is not only uncertain of the norms: he cannot read the signals'.[1] Eisenstadt has written similarly: 'The immigrant enters a society relatively unknown to him and constituting for him an unstructured field of behaviour. Only rarely does reality in the society correspond to his picture of it.'[2] This, briefly, is the adaptation the immigrants are required to make if they are to be *absorbed* into the society. Specific aspects of adaptation as they apply to the empirical data are elaborated in later chapters, here it is sufficient to state that a complete adaptation of an immigrant group is unlikely to be made in the life span of one generation.

Acceptance, on the part of the receiving society, has been described as a 'more passive process ... adaptation [by the receiving society], where it takes place at all, is largely unconscious. It consists in an enlargement or modification of the receiving society's organizational framework or cultural pattern, so as to include certain elements retained by the minority or immigrant group.'[3]

Absorption, then, is the term which covers both these processes: adaptation on the part of the immigrants and acceptance on the part of the host society. It refers both to the dynamic aspects implied by 'processes' and to the ideal 'end product'. This may be defined as complete adaptation by the immigrants, either on a group or individual basis, accompanied by complete acceptance by the host society.

Whilst conceptually the 'immigrant-host' framework is an orderly one, the actual processes are likely to be anything but orderly. Adaptation does not necessarily synchronize with acceptance and may even precede it; acceptance itself is likely to be greater in some areas of interaction than in others.

We have seen that one important variable in the interaction between immigrants and the host society is the image—or images—that this society has of the newcomers, its preconceptions, beliefs, and attitudes towards the migrants. Here we move from the more general aspects of immigrant-host relationships to the specific situation: that of Britain in relation to its various groups of immigrants, and particularly coloured immigrants.

A number of students of the British scene have noted that a degree of antipathy to outsiders, and particularly coloured outsiders, is a cultural norm. Both the extent and degree of this antipathy appear to depend in part on the amount of competition for

---

[1] Michael Banton, *White and Coloured*, (London, Cape, 1959), p. 97.
[2] Eisenstadt, pp. 139–40.   [3] Patterson, *Dark Strangers*, p. 10.

scarce resources: housing, employment, and so on. British history between the two World Wars provides numerous examples of antipathy towards 'outsiders' from other parts of the country who were competing for employment.

There is then a common element of antipathy towards outsiders, but it appears to be both far wider in extent and more deeply felt towards coloured than other outsiders. Given the present state of knowledge, it is doubtful if a complete explanation for this can yet be advanced. It is clearly a complex phenomenon; views and emotions run deep. There are two hypotheses which have been postulated by other investigators of British race relations and which have explanatory value in the present context.

Little has argued that there is a tendency for British society to identify coloured people with the lowest social class and that this stems largely from the country's colonial history. Superficial observation by members of the host society tends to confirm the low status of coloured people in that they *are* often found in roles which are low in the status hierarchy. This can and does become a circular process in that coloured people are *allocated* to these low status roles. This, briefly, is the 'colour-class' hypothesis. Its relevance to our data will become apparent in later chapters.

In his recent theoretical work on race relations, Rex has argued that:

in those countries which use skin colour as a means of discriminating between men ... colour is taken as the indication that a man is only entitled to colonial status, and this means that he has to be placed outside the normal stratification system. The stratification system thus becomes extended to take account of additional social positions marked by a degree of rightlessness not to be found amongst the incorporated workers.[1]

This is very close to Little's position, though the 'degree of rightlessness' is an empirical question. It will be demonstrated that again and again white native workers were very much concerned with considerations of status in their relationships with coloured immigrant workers, and that some accorded the coloured immigrant fewer rights *because* of his colour. We can then apply the colour-class hypothesis and at the same time incorporate Rex's thesis without doing violence to either viewpoint: for our purposes they are sufficiently close.

To introduce a personal note, anyone whose school years in

---

[1] Rex, *Race Relations in Sociological Theory*, pp. 107–8.

Britain were wholly or partly before the Second World War will recall perhaps some of what was taught about Britain and its relations with the rest of the world, and particularly the colonial Empire. I do not recall being *told* that 'British is best', but certainly this was assumed and in that sense one did not need to be explicitly told. Much of a map of the world was coloured red, and the 'heroic deeds' of the empire builders were told: Wolfe at Quebec, Clive at Plassey, Livingstone taking 'the word' to darkest Africa. The 'black hole of Calcutta' was an event of some historical importance. 'Empire Day', if my memory can be relied on, was a school holiday —but only after a religious service. Certainly, inhabitants of other parts of the world were regarded as being 'less fortunate', and in that sense being British was undoubtedly seen to be 'best'. This cultural tradition does, I believe, go some way towards explaining typical British attitudes towards outsiders, particularly coloured outsiders, and is consistent with the 'colour-class' viewpoint.

The other hypothesis found useful has been Banton's 'stranger' hypothesis, which postulates that 'in Britain, the coloured man is not seen as a different sort of being but as the furthest removed of strangers—the archetypal stranger'.[1] There are, as our data show, two aspects of 'strangeness'. On the one hand, the 'coloured stranger' is perceived as such by members of the host society. On the other, he *is* strange to that society or, rather, that society is strange to him. Again and again the evidence shows that the newcomers have problems in their perceptions of behavioural cues and so on; that they have not fully developed an adequate framework in which to interpret various aspects of natives' behaviour; that they cannot, as Banton puts it, 'read the signals'.[2] This aspect of 'strangeness' is of course very akin to that postulated by Eisenstadt which is quoted above.[3] It is one which decreases both on the part of the immigrants and the natives, over time, given interaction between the two groups in a wide range of social situations.

With one major exception, these are the more important theoretical concepts and hypotheses used which have been developed in previous works on immigration and race relations. The applicability of the 'immigrant-host' approach has been questioned by a number of writers and it is perhaps necessary to meet these criticisms.

First, it has been argued that this approach implies a 'unitary concept of the host society'[4] with an emphasis on *shared* values, *shared*

---

[1] Banton, *White and Coloured*, p. 84.   [2] Ibid., p. 97.
[3] See p. 4.   [4] Rex and Moore, p. 14. See also Allen.

norms, and so on; that, in other words, it necessarily requires a Parsonian 'social system' approach.[1] It is possible to reject both the Parsonian approach and this criticism. All I need argue here is that within that section of the native population with whom the coloured immigrants are in frequent and prolonged interaction during their working hours,[2] namely, the native workforce, there *are* shared values and norms. These have to be learnt, in the sense that the coloured immigrant—or any immigrant—will not necessarily share them or even be aware of them. Members of the native workforce have the power to grant or withhold acceptance: both in the formal sense as fellow-employees and in the less formal sense as work*mates*. Both aspects are important, the latter particularly so. As Everett and Helen Hughes have written: 'industry . . . considers its people not merely as technical help, but as actual or potential participants in a struggle for power within industry and society, and as potentially close colleagues (or unfit to be such)'.[3] It will be demonstrated in some detail in later chapters that these shared norms and values do exist and that the closer the coloured immigrant is *seen* to conform to them and accept them, the more likely he is to be accepted by members of the native workforce. Conformity does not, it must be emphasized, guarantee acceptance, and it is here that racial factors become important. These shared norms and values are explored in some detail in later chapters, as are those of management, which are not necessarily identical with those of the native workforce. At this level, then, it is possible to analyse much of the data in terms of the immigrant-host approach without subscribing to a non-conflictual view of society.

The second major criticism made of the immigrant-host approach has been that it implies a static view of society.[4] Again, this is not necessarily the case. In an investigation of the type reported here we necessarily focus on attitudes and behaviour in one comparatively short period of time, but it is possible to take account of changing behavioural norms, changing values, and changing power positions. Our conception of the host society—or rather that section

[1] Talcott Parsons, *The Social System* (Glencoe, The Free Press, and London, Routledge, 1951).

[2] This, of course, disregards the contact of transport workers with passengers, as mostly the interaction is of short duration.

[3] Everett Cherrington and Helen McGill Hughes, *Where Peoples Meet: Racial and Ethnic Frontiers* (Glencoe, The Free Press, 1952), p. 82.

[4] Rex and Moore, p. 13.

of it with which we are principally concerned here—is not necessarily a static one.

The third criticism has been that the immigrant-host approach implies a one-way process: 'the immigrant is seen as altering his own patterns of behaviour until they finally conform to those of the host society'.[1] Again, this is not necessarily a part of the immigrant-host approach. Theoretically, the values and behaviour of the host society—or a segment of it—could change at least as much as those of the immigrants; and the change would be compatible with this approach. Empirically, though, the situation will be seen as rather different: the native workforce showed a marked tendency to emphasize that the immigrants *should* conform to prevailing behavioural patterns. This is summed up in that piece of folk wisdom 'when in Rome. . . .' The extent to which behavioural norms *had* changed in the direction of those of the immigrants was limited but not completely absent. The 'one-way process' implication can then be rejected.

To sum up this part of the argument, there are accepted values and norms within the native workforce, as well as both technical and social skills, all of which have to be acquired by the coloured immigrants—or by any newcomer. It is preferable to treat this aspect of coloured immigrant/white native interaction in a systematic way, and the immigrant-host approach provides a means of doing this. The dimension is, of course, a cultural one, but it cannot be ignored —or, rather, it ought not to be ignored. I do not need to argue that the absorption process—seen in these terms—is irreversible. Nor do I need to argue that race is irrelevant; clearly, it is not. In some areas of interaction, race factors will be seen as paramount; in others cultural and hence immigration variables appear to be the salient ones.

The one remaining thread in my race relations–immigration theoretical approach I have drawn from the theory of pluralism. Modern theories of pluralism begin with the works of Furnivall on South-east Asia.[2] In his oft-quoted passage, Furnivall writes:

[1] Ibid.

[2] J. S. Furnivall, 'Some Problems of Tropical Economy', in Rita Hinden, (ed)., *Fabian Colonial Essays* (London, Unwin, 1945), and *Colonial Policy and Practice* (Cambridge, Cambridge University Press, 1948; and New York, New York University Press, 1956). On pluralism, see also David Lockwood, 'Race, Conflict and Plural Society', in Zubaida; M. G. Smith, *The Plural Society in the British West Indies* (Berkeley and Los Angeles, University of California Press, 1965); van den Berghe; and *Race* (Vol. XII, No. 4, April 1971).

In Burma, as in Java, probably the first thing that strikes the visitor is the medley of peoples—European, Chinese, Indian and native. It is in the strictest sense a medley, for they mix but do not combine. Each group holds by its own religion, its own culture and language, its own ideas and ways. As individuals they meet, but only in the market-place, in buying and selling. There is a plural society, with different sections of the community living side by side, but separately, within the same political unit.[1]

Whilst Furnivall was concerned with colonial situations—both British and Dutch—and particularly with the effects of economic forces, his analysis has relevance for the situation of immigrants from ex-colonial territories in the metropolitan countries. In Furnivall's South-east Asia, the members of the different racial and ethnic groups met 'in the market-place'; in the situation described here, they meet on the bus or station platform. This is an over-simplification, but it provides a clue to the relevance of the theory of pluralism.

We can now draw together these various themes: from immigration theory, from race relations, and specifically from pluralism. There were in the situation reported here some tendencies operating towards greater absorption, but there were also some operating in a pluralistic direction. Conceptually, we can see the situation as a 'tug of war', but one in which there are forces *pushing* as well as pulling. The 'receiving' society demands conformity by the newcomers in some areas of behaviour, and the lack of visible conformity occasions considerable resentment. This, then, is one force pulling towards absorption. Another force pushing in the same direction is the immigrants' own predispositions to conform: they want to be accepted. Whilst the receiving society demands conformity as the price for acceptance, it is not willing to grant this acceptance on an equal basis in all areas of interaction. To that extent, there are forces in the host society pushing towards pluralism. The immigrants' own ties, both with their countries of origin and with their fellow-countrymen in the 'new' country, pull also towards pluralism. This total situation is shown diagrammatically in Diagram 1.1.

This diagram is an over-simplification to the extent that it could be made both more comprehensive and more specific. It does, though, provide us with the outlines of a useful framework within which to analyse the empirical data. Moreover, within this framework it is possible to incorporate both 'race' and 'immigration' variables without commitment to one or the other viewpoint. Both sets of variables can be identified. Similarly, we shall see that it is

[1] Furnivall (1956), p. 304.

DIAGRAM I.I.

The Absorption-Pluralism Framework

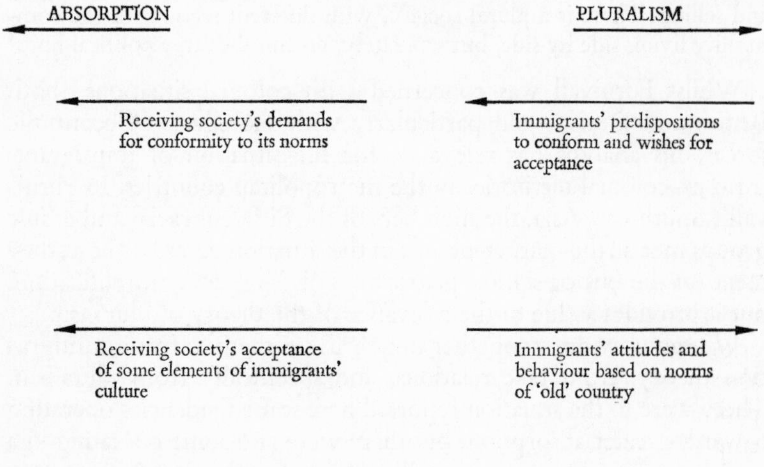

ABSORPTION	PLURALISM
←	→

| ← Receiving society's demands for conformity to its norms | ← Immigrants' predispositions to conform and wishes for acceptance → |

| ← Receiving society's acceptance of some elements of immigrants' culture | Immigrants' attitudes and behaviour based on norms of 'old' country → |

| Receiving society's refusal to accept immigrants on an equal basis in some areas of interaction → | ← Immigrants' adaptation to behavioural and attitudinal norms of 'new' country |

| | Immigrants' ties with 'old' country and own community in 'new' country[1] → |

[1] The immigrants' ties with their own community in the new country can assist absorption if the immigrant community – and particularly its leaders – is motivated to work towards absorption.

possible to identify the forces pulling and pushing towards absorption on the one hand, and pluralism on the other. The 'outcome'—or, more realistically in the short-term, the direction of change—will depend on this complex interaction of forces. Conceptually, the situation is one of tension.

In the next section of this chapter, the operational indices of absorption and to a lesser extent of pluralism are discussed in some detail. Here it might be useful to outline briefly ideal type models of both absorption and pluralism.

Our ideal type absorption model can be defined as complete adaptation by the minority group(s) and the 'host' society[1] to commonly accepted systems of values and norms, coupled with complete acceptance of the minority group(s) by the host society. This acknowledges the possibility that norms and values in the host society may change and thus overcomes the 'one-way process' criticism discussed above. Applied to a whole society, this 'complete' absorption would imply a *random* residential, industrial, and occupational distribution of the minority group(s). If applied to one employing organization, the implication would be that occupational and internal geographical or spatial distribution would be random.

Turning to pluralism, van den Berghe has written that:

societies are pluralistic insofar as they are *segmented into corporate groups* that frequently, although not necessarily, have different cultures or sub-cultures and insofar as their *social structure is compartmentalized into analogous, parallel, noncomplementary but distinguishable sets of institutions.*[2]

An ideal type pluralistic society might then be defined as one in which two or more culturally and possibly racially distinct groups coexist within one political unit, with no contact between the groups other than purely market relationships and participation in, or subservience to, the same political authority. Between the groups there will be a complete lack of value consensus and a maximum of cultural heterogeneity. Occupational distribution will be related to racial or ethnic group membership.

These ideal types provide the polar points of continua: most societies will be located at some point between the two extremes. It might be argued that the two ideal types are different *in kind* and, therefore, not on the same scale. This clearly is debatable, but it need

---

[1] Or, more accurately, that section of it which is the focus of attention—in our case, the native workforce.
[2] van den Berghe, p. 34.

not affect our analysis here. We are concerned here very much with the 'middle ground': the ideal type models are relevant only as hypothetical polar points of the theoretical framework.

This completes the theoretical discussion at this level. We can now turn to the theory which I have drawn from industrial sociology.

Whilst in much of the analysis we shall be concerned with values, behavioural norms, and so on, I have also adopted a 'task' approach. Specifically, I have examined the work tasks performed by individuals, work teams, and to a lesser extent departments, and related these tasks to patterns of behaviour and attitudes. This has some features in common with the Tavistock Institute's 'socio-technical systems' approach,[1] and also the 'technological implications' approach developed by Woodward.[2] However, I have not attempted a full analysis of the 'socio-technical system' implied in that approach, but only of some aspects which appear most relevant. In any case, I share most of Brown's reservations about the Tavistock approach.[3] Similarly, I have not undertaken a detailed 'technological implications' analysis, and again I have some reservations.[4] My own attempt is more modest, and some of its differences from the two approaches cited will become apparent in this and following chapters. There are also differences in the orientation of the research, and technical variables are explored for different reasons.

Superficial observation at the planning stage of the project—before a conceptual framework had been devised—suggested that technical variables were likely to prove important in the patterns of relationship between members of work groups, for example, between a bus driver and conductor, a train motorman and guard, and these workers and their first-line supervisors. That the movement of railway rolling-stock is controlled by an impersonal signal system, whilst the movement of road rolling-stock is controlled by supervisors in face-to-face interaction with crews, appeared to be a factor that ought to be taken

[1] See numerous publications of the work of the Tavistock Institute of Human Relations, for example, E. L. Trist, et al., Organisational Choice (London, Tavistock, 1963).

[2] Joan Woodward, Management and Technology (London, H.M.S.O., 1958), and Industrial Organization: Theory and Practice (London, Oxford University Press, 1965).

[3] Richard K. Brown, 'Research and Consultancy in Industrial Enterprises', Sociology (Vol. 1, No. 1, January 1967), pp. 33–60.

[4] On both the Tavistock and Woodward's approaches, see John H. Goldthorpe, et al., The Affluent Worker: Industrial Attitudes and Behaviour (Cambridge, Cambridge University Press, 1968), especially pp. 181–3; and David Silverman, The Theory of Organisations (London, Heinemann, 1970), Chapter 5.

into account. It was obvious that my investigation would have to explore the 'technical organization of work' of the production system.

To designate my own approach, I have used the phrase the 'technical organization of work'. In the appropriate chapters, I have described this technical organization of work and analysed its consequences for relationships between members of work teams and between them and supervisors and passengers. This does not imply a strictly 'determinist' approach; it means that technical factors impinge on the patterns of interaction and act as constraints on behaviour. It is less clear that these technical factors influence attitudes on racial matters, as they influence other issues, for example, the differences in their attitudes of busmen and railwaymen towards women workers, discussed later in the text.

Thus, whilst this is a study of the absorption of coloured immigrants within one organization, it was clear from the very beginning that it would require a full and detailed analysis of many aspects of that organization. This led us to attempt to understand the sociology of the public transport industry. In that sense this volume is two studies. Whilst this understanding of the sociology of public transport was very necessary for the strictly race or immigration aspects, it is also something of a bonus, as it were. It does, I believe, contribute something of value in its own right. Service industries have been largely neglected by social scientists in Britain and to a lesser extent in the United States. This volume does, it is hoped, make some modest contribution towards filling this void.

Having sketched the theoretical considerations which appeared important and relevant, I now turn to their specific application to the area of study.

THE APPLICATION OF THEORY TO THE RESEARCH AREA

We made a number of assumptions which were derived from a specifically race relations approach. First we assumed that 'antipathy' towards outsiders, and particularly coloured outsiders, was a cultural norm amongst the native British population and specifically, for our purposes, the native workforce.[1] 'Antipathy' is used here in the sense of the Banton definition:[2] as the opposite of 'sympathy'.

[1] For purposes of convenience, I have grouped in the 'native British population' and 'native workforce' some who are not strictly speaking 'British', the largest group numerically being citizens of the Republic of Ireland. Also included are small groups of continental European origins.

[2] Banton, *White and Coloured*, p. 30.

Second, we assumed that 'prejudice', that is, a hostile attitude which is not amenable to modification as a result of learning, was confined to a relatively small proportion of the native workforce.

This distinction between antipathy and prejudice is of some importance. The cause of prejudice is seen as lying in the individual. It is an essentially psychological, irrational phenomenon, originating in individual inadequacies. On the other hand, antipathy 'as an attitude . . . is arrived at in a rational way, and the cause lies in the object of the aggression or *in the subject's image of the object*; attitudes of this kind are culturally and socially transmitted, whereas prejudice . . . is not'.[1] We rejected the 'prejudice-discrimination axis', which holds that discrimination is the behavioural manifestation of prejudiced attitudes.[2]

Whether prejudice is a *sociological* or *psychological* phenomenon is a question which is hotly debated. I have assumed it is the latter. If there is a meaningful difference between what we might term 'sociological prejudice', and 'psychological prejudice', then it is misleading to give both the same designation. I have overcome this problem by using the term 'antipathy' for the sociological variety and 'prejudice' for the psychological. From a purely scientific point of view this is satisfactory, but sociologists have to recognize that their works are likely to be misinterpreted, both intentionally and unintentionally. In popular usage 'prejudice' has different connotations from 'antipathy'. It must then be emphasized that the behavioural manifestations of prejudice and antipathy can be very similar, and that the difference between the two lies solely in their origins and in the possibility of modification by experience. Antipathy can be so modified; prejudice cannot.

Whilst these assumptions on antipathy and prejudice were our premises and we did not intend to test them as hypotheses, the data in the event supported them, with the reservation that our sociological approach precluded an exploration of prejudice. We met, though, a small number of individuals who expressed *very* hostile attitudes towards coloured immigrants and it seemed not unreasonable to *assume* that they were prejudiced.

Thus far we have outlined the 'race relations' assumptions about the native British population. On the part of the coloured immigrants, we assumed that the West Indians—and most of the coloured population we dealt with were West Indian—came from very

---

[1] Ibid., p. 30. (My italics.)   [2] See Patterson, *Dark Strangers*, pp. 20–3.

'colour-conscious' societies.[1] This assumption is of far less relevance than the assumptions about the native population. We will see that many of the West Indians expected to be *immediately and fully accepted* in Britain and that they were *surprised* as well as hurt when these expectations were not realized. We will see too that some were reluctant to discuss the difficulties they had encountered and tended to play down or explain away hostile behaviour on the part of the native population. A variable here was very probably the fact that the interviewers were white.[2]

Turning to the 'immigration' approach, Eisenstadt has found three main indices of *full* immigrant absorption in the literature on immigration. Whilst we are here concerned with partial absorption, these three indices are nevertheless useful to our analysis. They are: '(a) acculturation; (b) satisfactory and integral personal adjustment of the immigrants; and (c) complete dispersion of the immigrants as a group'.[3] In the application of these indices, our focus of attention is, of course, the interaction between the immigrants and the industrial organization, rather than the wider host society, but on occasions we will cross the border between the two.

Eisenstadt has defined 'acculturation' as being 'concerned principally with the extent to which the immigrant learns the various roles, norms, and customs of the absorbing society'.[4] In our case, we must substitute 'organization' for 'absorbing society'. We cover these various aspects of acculturation in some detail and, as Eisenstadt points out,[5] this is not only a question of acquiring new values, norms, and so on, but also of 'internalising' them.

Before we could examine the acculturation of the immigrants, it was necessary to explore in some detail the society—in our case the industrial organization—into whose norms, skills, values, and so on the immigrant was being acculturated. There are a number of areas to consider here.

At the macro-level we explored particularly the methods and procedures by which the organization sought to carry out its tasks and here Weber's concept of bureaucracy was found to be useful. That the organization is a bureaucratic one was found to be of considerable significance for the immediate focus of our study.

Turning to the micro-level, we found it necessary to explore in

[1] On colour in the British Caribbean, see M. G. Smith, especially pp. 60–6 and 307–8.
[2] This is discussed in more detail on p. 23.   [3] Eisenstadt, p. 11.
[4] Ibid., p. 12.   [5] Ibid.

some depth the technical and social organization of work, and again structural factors were found to be of considerable significance.

These tasks and structural variables were found to be important for the administrative practices adopted, the conflict which was built into the organization of work, and the value systems which buttressed and sustained them. We will return to these structural variables in a moment, but first it might be useful to consider in more detail the application of the acculturation theory to our research area and data.

As Eisenstadt has noted, 'the assumption underlying all three [indices of absorption] is that the less the immigrant stands out within his new society as having a separate identity, the more fully he is merged into it and the more complete is his absorption'.[1] The coloured immigrant *does* stand out, and this visibility has important consequences which are explored in later chapters. Generally, though, the more closely the immigrants are perceived by the natives to conform to the latter's norms and values, the more likely they are to be accepted. We have explored the implications of this in a number of areas.

In terms of obtaining entry to the organization through recruitment, the more closely the immigrant is perceived to accord to the 'ideal type' British recruit, the more likely he is to be accepted by the organization.[2] The framework suggests, then, that cultural differences are likely to make the selection of immigrants more difficult, and indeed this was found to be the case. In practice there appeared to be a range of characteristics which made a recruit 'acceptable': a perceived deficiency in one area might be compensated for by perceived 'strengths' in other characteristics.

I have analysed the various aspects of training in terms of acculturation, specifically the teaching of skills and spoken English in the Barbados pre-recruitment training and the teaching of technical skills in England. Aside from the teaching of these technical skills some effort is also made to inculcate behavioural norms and influence attitudes. Again, as with the recruitment data, it is useful to analyse 'failures' in the training courses as ʲdeviations from the norms. Training difficulties are also examined in terms of cultural differences, and the concept of 'strangeness' was found to be particularly useful in the analysis.

[1] Eisenstadt, pp. 11–12.
[2] This is an over-simplification to the extent that there are a number of ideal types. See Chapter 12.

The acculturation approach to the recruitment and training data does not, of course, exclude consideration of deliberate discrimination on racial grounds.[1] Indeed, by isolating other variables it is more likely to locate this type of discrimination.

The concept of acculturation was again useful in our analysis of relationships between natives and immigrants in the work situation. For example, we examined the perceptions that both groups had of their occupational roles; in the railway departments, I found it useful to compare these with ideal types. Generally, though, it was the natives' perceptions and definitions which were regarded as the norm. The similarities and differences give an indication of how far the process of acculturation had progressed or, rather, how far it had to go.

Most of the occupations with which we were concerned formed part of a work team: a train or bus crew, a permanent way work group, the staff of a station. There was a degree of interdependence among members of these work teams. The extent of this interdependence varied considerably as, for example, between train and bus crews, and this is explored in later chapters. Its relevance here, though, is that it is important that, for example, a bus driver has what he considers to be a 'good' conductor. This suggested that the 'adequate' performance by the immigrants of their occupational roles was likely to be an important factor in their acceptance by native workers. I have defined 'adequate' as the expectations that others have of the performance of a specific role: that is, the bus driver's expectations of his conductor, the conductor's of his driver, and so on. Thus in addition to comparing the perceptions that both groups had of their roles, we explored the natives' perceptions and

[1] For the purposes of this study I have defined 'discrimination' as 'less favourable treatment because of racial or ethnic group membership'. This stresses the *act* of discrimination, and the general motives for it, but so far as possible I have also tried to establish specific motivations. The problem of a completely satisfactory definition of discrimination is a very real one, and has not been solved in the literature on the subject. To illustrate the problem: are West Indians discriminated against when they do not apply for promotion because they fear discrimination? By my definition they would not be, but clearly it could be argued that they are and a definition of discrimination ought to encompass this kind of situation. My definition is, though, adequate for my purposes here; fears of discrimination I have described as such. See Simon Abbott, 'Defining Racial Discrimination', *Race* (Vol. XI, No. 4, April 1970), pp. 477–80.; Hubert M. Blalock, Jr., *Towards a Theory of Minority-Group Relations* (New York, Wiley, 1967); and George Eaton Simpson and J. Milton Yinger, *Racial and Cultural Minorities* (New York, Harper, 1958).

evaluations of the immigrants in their own roles and—where applicable—their crew partner's role.

This brings us back to various structural factors, which are important in the relationships between crew partners, between crews, and between crews and first line supervisors. There are, as has been indicated, varying degrees of interdependence at the work team level between crew partners. This suggested the notion of 'co-operation', and this was found to be important: between crew partners, between crews, and between crews and supervisors. Similarly, there is a potential for 'conflict', again between crew partners and between crews. For our purposes, I have defined 'conflict' as 'a *perceived* difference of interest', the perception being that of the actor concerned. Insofar as this perception is not reflected in behaviour, the conflict is latent. When it does affect behaviour, conflict is manifest. These potentials for co-operation and conflict exist irrespective of racial or cultural differences.

Whilst, then, both racial and immigration variables were found to be important for explaining both behaviour and attitudes, they are not the sole factors involved. I have hypothesized that conflict is built into the social and technical organization of work and that racial and cultural differences *exacerbate*, rather than cause, this conflict, though this does not deny their importance as independent variables for attitudes and behaviour. A major variable in the avoidance of conflict is the adequate performance of occupational roles, as defined above. This hypothesis is of a fairly high order of generality and, perhaps inevitably, there are exceptions to it. We will see that in two areas—specifically, the relationships between white native workers and coloured superordinates, and between passengers and coloured workers—a condition of acceptance of coloured staff by some was that they did *not* perform their roles in the management-prescribed manner.

The second of the indices of absorption noted by Eisenstadt was the 'satisfactory and integral personal adjustment of the immigrants'.[1] This Eisenstadt has defined as being 'concerned . . . with the point of view of the individual immigrant and the ways in which the new country affects his personality, his satisfaction, his ability to cope with the various problems arising out of his new situation'.[2] It is in this area that the data are weakest. There are some data on satisfaction, particularly job satisfaction, and also on ability, and inability, to cope with various problems. On personality there is

[1] Eisenstadt, p. 11.   [2] Eisenstadt, p. 12.

little or nothing, nor, it ought to be added, did we set out to collect data in this area.

The last of Eisenstadt's three indices of full absorption was the 'complete dispersion of the immigrants as a group'.[1] I have applied this index in a way appropriate to the research area; that is, I have examined the occupational distribution of the immigrants and the factors which have assisted and impeded dispersion. Most of the data collected are from the period of the field work, but this has been supplemented in a number of key areas by later information. I am thus able to examine the dynamic as well as static aspects. I have also explored the immigrants' occupational aspirations and their expectations on how far these aspirations are likely to be realized.

To conclude this section, we have seen the assumptions derived from a race relations approach, the indices of absorption derived from immigration theory, and the importance I have attached to various structural variables. It now remains in this chapter to explain the research methods employed.

RESEARCH METHODS

A number of methods of data collection were employed. Some are spelled out in detail in the appropriate chapters, but it is perhaps useful here to give an outline of the research techniques used.

Logically, we begin with the Barbados pre-recruitment training and the recruitment scheme. Here I interviewed members and officials of the Barbados Government, lecturers engaged in pre-recruitment training, and L.T.B. recruitment staff. Documentary and statistical data were collected and analysed. The Barbados-recruited staff who appeared in the main interview samples were asked a number of questions on the recruitment scheme specifically. Additionally, we asked managers and supervisors for their opinions on the scheme and its value.

Turning to recruitment in London, we again interviewed recruitment staff. We carried out a detailed analysis of all applicants for employment during one typical week, that is, a week outside the troughs and peaks of numbers of applicants, which appear to be related largely to seasonal factors. This analysis made it possible to compare the relative acceptance and rejection rates of various groups of applicants and to examine the reasons given by recruitment interviewers for rejections.

[1] Ibid., p. 11.

For training we used a number of methods. In total we spent nearly four weeks observing training sessions. Staff engaged in training were interviewed and documentary and statistical material analysed, though there was less of the latter available than we would have wished. All those in our interview samples were asked questions on their training experiences and difficulties.

The largest single source of data was the interview samples, and their selection posed some problems. So far as was practical, we wanted matched samples of coloured immigrant and white native workers, as we intended to compare the patterns of answers to a number of questions. The immigrants were, however, found to be over-represented in a number of occupations and under-represented in others. Amongst the bus drivers and motormen, for example, immigrants were under-represented. Some reasons for this will become apparent in later chapters. Had we taken the coloured population as our sampling population and as one to be matched with the native population, motormen and drivers would have formed a smaller part of our interview samples than guards and conductors. Yet we were obviously interested in the attitudes and experiences of native motormen and drivers. Given that motormen and guards are roughly similar in numbers, we decided to select equal numbers of immigrant and native motormen and guards, and almost the same with drivers and conductors. This meant that amongst the coloured immigrants those whose occupational achievement was greatest were somewhat over-represented. Had the samples been larger it would have been useful to weight them, but this was not attempted here. When significant differences have been found between different grades, this has been stated in the text.

A further complication was the presence of women in some grades. This only posed a problem in the selection of the conductor and women conductor samples. Their relative representation in the samples was determined by the ratio of coloured women conductors to coloured conductors in our population. Given that there was a great disparity between the numbers of white native and coloured immigrant women conductors, the former were *very* much under-represented in the interview samples.

The sampling fractions varied, then, in a number of ways: between white natives and coloured immigrants, between occupational grades, between men and women in the bus samples. Given that the coloured proportions of the total populations varied somewhat between locations, the sampling fractions varied also. Again, the sampling fractions differed between departments, but this is of no consequence as they are only totalled if there are no significant differences between the departments. Generally, then, answers of different samples have only been combined if the patterns are broadly similar, though in a few cases they have been combined and possibly significant differences noted in the text.

Over-all, that is, combining natives and immigrants, the sampling fractions were one in ten in the bus department, one in five of trainmen, and between one in two and one in three of both station and permanent way staff. (In all cases these figures refer to the staff at the locations included in the main study.) The main study was preceded by pilot studies in the three departments and the data obtained have been included in the results shown.

The compositions of the samples, together with their refusal rates, are shown in Table 1.1.

TABLE 1.1
*Interview Samples.**

	Native					Immigrant				
	Bus-men	Train-men	Station staff	Per. Way	Total	Bus-men	Train-men	Station staff	Per. Way	Total
Selected	86	61	41	29	217	88	63	41	27	219
Refused	13	8	10	2	33	6	2	4	1	13
Not available and not replaced	3	—	1	6	10	4	1	1	5	11
Interviewed	70	53	30	21	174	78	60	36	21	195
Refusals as percentage of those selected†	15%	13%	24%	7%	15%	7%	3%	10%	4%	6%

* The samples *selected* were intended to have equal numbers of natives and immigrants; there were, however, one or two cases of mistaken identity. In some grades the busmen and station staff included women.

† In all tables percentages have been rounded to the nearest whole number, unless otherwise stated, and may therefore not total 100.

It will be seen that the refusal rates differed as between the native and immigrant samples and among the occupational groupings. Some reasons for these occupational differences are advanced in later chapters. The most significant difference, though, was that between native and immigrant staff, and we return to this below. So far as possible, we replaced those interviewees who were not available for reasons of illness and the like.

The methods of sample selection were as follows. We obtained lists of names of all the staff in the grades which we wished to include in our interview samples at the locations selected. These lists did not usually distinguish between staff in terms of origins, so these were marked in for us, usually by a supervisor. (This method was not foolproof, because one or two selected in the 'native' samples turned out to be coloured immigrants and one 'conductor' selected was a woman conductor.) From each list we selected random samples: of native drivers, of immigrant drivers, and so on.

Those selected for interview were then sent a letter which explained the purposes of the study, stated that we would like to interview them, and promised confidentiality and anonymity. Interviews of railway staff were held during working hours. As their duty schedules did not allow for a similar arrangement, busmen were interviewed in their own time and paid an interview fee. (Some came in for the interview on their rest day.) Interviews were held in private, they lasted on average from forty-five minutes to one hour, though some were shorter and some considerably longer. (Some interviews had to be shortened owing to operating requirements, and some questions were omitted: if a man being interviewed was required to take out a train, we could hardly detain him. This explains some of the 'no answers' recorded; others resulted from accidental omissions on the part of the interviewers.)

The interviews were structured to a questionnaire, which used mostly open-ended questions. Answers were as far as possible recorded verbatim and were subsequently coded into a number of categories; the data were then transferred to punch cards for counting. The text makes considerable use of direct quotations for illustrative purposes. The interview data have mostly been presented in terms of frequency of mention, though the explanations offered seldom rest completely on the statistical data.

A further source of data was roughly eighty interviews of managers, supervisors, trade union officials, and local representatives. These interviews were unstructured; though a check list was often used. Additionally, we had a large number of informal discussions at all stages of the field work.

A considerable amount of documentary and statistical material was collected. Unfortunately, there was less statistical material available than we would have wished which distinguished between employees in terms of their countries of origin, or even in terms of a coloured immigrant/white native breakdown. We inherited the 'liberal tradition': i.e., that the keeping of records, statistics, and the like, which distinguished according to origins, was in itself a discriminatory act. Fortunately, both for social scientists and for public policy, this belief appears to be fading. Some statistical data which did make a coloured immigrant/white native breakdown were specifically produced for us, and this has been a great help. Often, though, the basic records did not permit this kind of analysis.

A problem met by researchers in the sensitive area of race relations is that some interviewees are reluctant to be completely frank when discussing attitudes and experiences. We encountered this reluctance most noticeably amongst the coloured immigrant samples, though it was by no means confined to them. Consequently, the immigrants' experiences of overt hostility tend to be understated, as, to a lesser extent, do natives' hostile attitudes.

There was no easy answer to this problem. To have employed a West Indian interviewer would have reduced the flexibility of the research team and prolonged the interviewing programme—and time was not on our side. Moreover, a West Indian would possibly have been less acceptable than an Englishman to some West Indians from other islands. To other coloured immigrants he would almost certainly have been less acceptable.

Sometimes it was suggested to us that those who refused to be interviewed included some natives known to hold opinions very hostile to coloured immigrants. This appears a tenable hypothesis, and again the extent of native hostility tends to be understated. It appeared possible, too, that the sex of the interviewer was a variable in native responses: natives were less willing to report hostile attitudes and behaviour to a female interviewer.[1] The total effect of the reluctance of some to speak frankly and of others to be interviewed is to understate the extent of behaviour and attitudes perceived as hostile to the coloured immigrants. It does not affect the validity of the analysis made to any significant degree.

The sensitivity of the research area was important, too, in one other respect. In our preliminary discussions, it was continually stressed that the situation was 'delicate'. Consequently, we tended to be cautious in, for example, the phrasing of our questionnaire, using some indirect questions when a direct one might have been

[1] See Chapter 17.

more valuable. In retrospect, it may be that we were over-cautious, that, for example, more direct questions could have been used with no adverse reactions. In the light of our knowledge at that time, we were clearly right to err on the side of caution: we could not afford *any* adverse reactions, and it can be stated that absolutely none have been reported.

When interviewing managers, we sometimes experienced initially a 'public relations' response: that is, the interviewee was reluctant to admit of problems or of the existence of documentary or statistical data. Eventually, though, the word got around that we could be trusted with such material and the problem was overcome. We had in any case agreed in writing with London Transport the precise conditions under which confidential data were made available to us, and this agreement was helpful in giving us access to such data.

The relationship of the social investigator to managers in the organization being studied poses problems. In this case some assumed that we identified with the coloured immigrants and were therefore 'looking for trouble'; others that we shared managerial beliefs and values; but these were in the minority.[1] We carefully avoided commitment to any particular viewpoint. To the rarely asked question,'Would you let your daughter . . .?', I had to reply, 'I don't have a daughter'.

A final source of data was nonparticipant observation. Public transport lends itself to this technique, in that the observer makes no impact on the situation other than as a passenger. In this sense, every public transport journey I have made in the past few years has been nonparticipant observation. This has been useful, more for the general sociology of public transport than the narrower focus of this study. In the Permanent Way Department, too, the technique was useful; and again, it is unlikely that it made any impact on behaviour.[2]

CONCLUSIONS

The major themes of this study can be stated quite simply. First, it is argued that the situation of coloured immigrants in Britain, and their relationships with the 'host' society, can be best understood in terms of the absorption-pluralism framework. Whilst the post-war immigration from the Commonwealth is too recent for us to be very certain of trends, it will be argued that in many respects the pluralis-

---

[1] This suggests a consensus of managerial opinions which is perhaps misleading.
[2] See below, Chapter 10.

tic model is more appropriate to the situation found than is the absorption one.

Within the absorption-pluralism framework both race and immigration variables will be identified, as will the areas in which each appear to be of paramount importance. To say which of these two sets of variables is most important *over-all* raises problems of aggregation and cannot be answered at this stage.

Finally, it is argued that both race and immigration factors can only be understood in the context of the industrial organization: the tasks, norms, values etc., which constitute the industrial culture. Throughout this volume, then, I will be concerned to identify and evaluate the importance of these variables on the more immediate focus of the study.

We began with a systematic and 'tidy' theoretical framework. When we reached the stage of data collection and analysis problems arose: some data required were not available, and our resources were limited. Thus, there are gaps in our information, and some explanations offered must be very tentative. With these reservations, though, the theoretical framework and concepts are appropriate to the data. In that sense, they have explanatory value. Whilst some explanations are offered with more certainty than others, all must be regarded to a greater or lesser degree as tentative. Race relations are very complex, particularly so in the relatively fluid British situation.

2

LONDON TRANSPORT: THE INDUSTRIAL ORGANIZATION

LONDON TRANSPORT: A BRIEF HISTORY AND INTRODUCTION
The origins of the organization are to be found well back in the nineteenth century.[1] The London General Omnibus Company, later to become one of its major constituent parts, was founded in Paris in 1855 and began operating in London the following year. Another company, the Metropolitan Railway Company, later to become an important part of London Transport, opened the world's first underground railway in 1863. The first electric-powered 'tube' railway, the City and South London, began operating in 1890. With evidence of the potentialities of the electric motor as a viable form of underground traction, a spate of deep-level tube schemes was promoted in the closing years of the nineteenth century and the early years of the twentieth.

The process of concentration of ownership and control of public transport services in London began in earnest in the early years of the twentieth century and by the time of the First World War most bus, tram, and underground railway companies in the capital were effectively controlled by the Underground Group.[2] The major exceptions were the Metropolitan Railway Company, some municipal tram undertakings, and, of course, the main line railway companies.

This process of consolidation was completed in 1933 by the creation of the London Passenger Transport Board (L.P.T.B.) which became responsible for public transport in an area of nearly 2,000 square miles and with a population of over nine million people.[3] In all, some 170 railway, bus, coach, and trolleybus undertakings were

---

[1] For a history of transport in London in the nineteenth century, see T. C. Barker and Michael Robbins, *A History of London Transport, Vol. 1 The Nineteenth Century*, (London, Allen & Unwin, for London Transport Board, 1963).

[2] For a history of the development of the 'tube' railways, see Alan A. Jackson and Desmond F. Croome, *Rails Through the Clay* (London, Allen & Unwin, 1962).

[3] Ibid., p. 242

acquired by the L.P.T.B.,[1] but the greater part of the system had already been under unified control for a number of years. The L.P.T.B. was a form of public ownership, but lacked effective ministerial control over, for instance, the appointment of Board members, which has been a characteristic of nationalized bodies created since. In the folklore of the organization, 'nationalization' dated from 1948, when 'the system became the responsibility of the British Transport Commission and was managed on behalf of the Commission by the London Transport Executive [L.T.E.]'.[2]

The period from 1933 to the outbreak of the Second World War saw plans for a considerable expansion of the system, and much did take place. Some plans were delayed by the War and implemented later; some were abandoned. In the folklore of the organization, particularly at management level, the years from the formation of the L.P.T.B. to the Second World War were a 'golden age': the system was expanding and demand increasing. Again in management folklore, the period 1948–62 represented the 'lean years' when, for example, capital expenditure was controlled by the Transport Commission and London Transport's autonomy was much reduced. In 1963, the system passed into the hands of the London Transport Board and autonomy was largely restored, but with close ministerial financial control. Further changes in control and ownership were, however, not long in coming and on 1 January 1970 the railway and Central Bus systems became the responsibility of the Greater London Council (G.L.C.), the Country Bus and Coach network became London Country Bus Services, a subsidiary of the National Bus Company. The Central Bus and railway systems were managed for the G.L.C. by a London Transport Executive from the beginning of 1970.

Until 1948, demand for public transport in the capital grew steadily, but since that time changes in public behaviour and habits, particularly increased use of the private car, have caused it to fall considerably. The private car, too, has been responsible for much of the traffic congestion which has delayed bus services, causing them to be less predictable and encouraging further the drift to private transport.

The more notable developments in the post-war years have been the withdrawal of tram and trolleybus services in 1952 and 1962

[1] London Transport, *Basic Facts* (London, L.T.B. Press Office, 1965).
[2] Ibid.

respectively, on the one hand, and the opening of a new tube railway, the Victoria Line, in 1968, on the other.

The size of the organization, in terms of numbers employed, has changed considerably since the formation of the L.P.T.B. From roundly 75,000 in 1933–4, they grew to 100,000 in 1948,[1] then falling to 73,000 at the end of 1966[2] (which was roughly mid-way through our fieldwork) and to about 60,000 at the beginning of 1970.[3] These variations reflected in part the changes in demand and in productivity; and the final figure reflects in addition the transfer of some staff to London Country Bus Services.[4]

Detailed descriptions of the three departments in which most of the fieldwork was carried out are given in later chapters, but it is perhaps useful at this stage to give a brief outline.

Preliminary enquiries indicated that most coloured immigrants were to be found in the Central Bus, Railway Operating, Permanent Way, and Catering Departments. The first two were (along with Country Buses and Coaches) the *operating* departments of London Transport; Permanent Way was a major engineering department.

Together the three departments[5] employed nearly 40,000 operatives and supervisors, of whom some 7,000 were coloured immigrants.

The important points to emerge from this brief historical survey are: that the organization has a comparatively long history and tradition of 'service'; that in spite of changes of ownership and control there has been continuity running through it; and that in recent years it has faced a declining market. Some aspects of the organization are explored in greater detail in the next section.

SOME CHARACTERISTICS OF THE ORGANIZATION

In many respects the organization shares the characteristics of bureaucracy postulated by Weber.[6] The organization, a hierarchical one, operates on a largely functional basis. The common link between its departments, in terms of formal responsibility, is often at

[1] H. A. Clegg, *Labour Relations in London Transport* (Oxford, Blackwell, 1950), p. 171.

[2] London Transport Board, *Annual Report and Accounts,* 1966 (London, H.M.S.O. 1967), p. 30.

[3] London Transport Board, *Annual Report and Accounts,* 1969 (London, H.M.S.O. 1970), p. 31.

[4] Ibid.

[5] The Catering Department was later excluded from the study, see Introduction.

[6] See H. H. Gerth and C. Wright Mills, *From Max Weber: Essays in Sociology* (London, Routledge & Kegan Paul, 1948), Chapter VIII.

board level. Whilst there are common 'service' departments for 'labour relations', 'establishments', and the like each department is primarily responsible for its own industrial relations and staff matters. Managers responsible for these functions in the operating and maintenance departments tend to be busmen, railwaymen, or engineers, in terms of their experience and possibly their orientation, rather than personnel specialists. Within the hierarchical structure, each level is designated in terms of grade, responsibilities,[1] salary scale, and so on.

Management of the organization is on the basis of 'the rules' in the sense of formal procedures. The operation of a complex transport network requires a high degree of *predictability*, and this is probably one important variable affecting the extent and complexity of formal procedures, others possibly include the laws relating to public transport operations and the 'public accountability' of the organization. Size, too, is of course relevant here. Various aspects of these formal procedures are discussed in later chapters, but here it is useful to note their importance in two areas: discipline and promotion.

There are formal disciplinary procedures which allow for representation of the 'accused', and there are appeals systems.[2] No employee can be dismissed without a formal disciplinary hearing. Whilst this is a safeguard for all employees, it is of particular importance for coloured immigrants: the threat of one type of discriminatory behaviour is largely removed.

Formal promotion procedures are less of a safeguard against discrimination. In Railway Operating, though, promotion, or rather the opportunity to qualify for promotion to grades up to the supervisory level, is on a seniority basis. Seniority is an impersonal mechanism in that it does not discriminate, and it is objective in the sense that it can be measured.[3] Again, then, a threat of discriminatory behaviour is largely removed.[4] This is, however, subject to the following qualifications: that there are not separate seniority lists for

---

[1] Detailed job descriptions, however, appear to be a fairly recent innovation.

[2] These disciplinary procedures are outlined in Appendix 2. For a detailed study of appeals systems, see William G. Scott, *The Management of Conflict: Appeals Systems in Organizations* (Homewood, Illinois, Richard D. Irwin, and Dorsey Press, 1965).

[3] I am not suggesting that seniority is necessarily the most appropriate criterion of suitability for promotion.

[4] It might be argued that there is a conflict between the bureaucratic ideal of fitness for office and the principle of seniority. In this case, though, seniority is a necessary but not sufficient qualification for promotion. It is in any case *largely* equated with fitness. See Chapter 7.

white and coloured workers, and that the latter are not formally barred from some lines of promotion. In the United States railroad industry, seniority systems have had the opposite effect to that described here. 'Seniority systems have had a tragic impact on the opportunities for advancement by Negro employees ... [and have] "frozen" Negro employees into historically, discriminatory employment patterns.'[1] Whilst the existence of formal procedures and rules is conducive to the absorption of minority groups by an organization in that a tendency not to discriminate is built into the system, there are some disadvantageous aspects. Some West Indians, in particular, found it hard to accept the requirements of these formal procedures, insofar as they affected them.

There is a career structure in the organization: that is, there is movement of personnel upwards through the various levels of the hierarchy. This has implications for the culture of the organization, to which I return in a moment. At the lower levels in Railway Operating, 'seniority' is an important mechanism in the career pattern, but as I will show, the whole notion of a career pattern is becoming less relevant at these lower levels. The vocational aspects of railway work are less important than they apparently once were. At management and supervisory levels many staff have spent all or most of their working lives in the organization. Promotion to senior levels has largely been from within the organization, but there have been recent indications that this policy is changing.[2] Increasingly, senior posts are being filled by people from outside and, in this sense, immigrants have joined the organization at the wrong time, so far as their own career prospects are concerned.

One consequence of the emphasis on internal promotion is the preservation of the culture of the organization. I use culture in Jaques's sense: 'the culture of the factory is its customary and traditional way of thinking and of doing things. ...'[3] This culture tends to be reinforced and sustained by internal promotion. That staff in various

[1] Howard W. Risher, Jr., *The Negro in the Railroad Industry* (Philadelphia, University of Pennsylvania, 1971), p. 130.

[2] Appointments from outside the organization have been made to the Board (now Executive) and to the officer grade. (Officer has a specific meaning in London Transport: it includes the two top tiers immediately below Board level; and some in the third tier are also officers.) See also *Report from the Select Committee on Nationalised Industries: London Transport* (London, H.M.S.O., 1965), Vol. I, p. 129, paragraph 501; and Vol. II, p. 373, Appendix 27, paragraph 1.

[3] Elliott Jaques, *The Changing Culture of a Factory* (London, Tavistock, 1951), p. 251.

personnel roles in the organization—industrial relations, recruitment, and so on—are busmen, railwaymen, and engineers[1] in terms of their experience rather than personnel specialists, tends further to sustain this culture to the extent that these staff members influence recruitment and promotion. Second, given that all supervisors and some managers are promoted from the lower levels of the hierarchy, there is a strong likelihood that this culture, to a lesser or greater extent, pervades the whole organization.

The values of the organization are largely those of British industrialism, though perhaps in a more pronounced form than is found in some organizations.[2] There is an emphasis on *time* in the sense of services operating to schedule or tasks being completed in a predetermined time period. Likewise, *punctuality* in attendance for work. *Smartness* in appearance, in a conventional sense, is seen as important, as is *neatness* in work. Remaining both *alert* and *calm* is highly valued, particularly in the railway departments. Again, especially in the Railway Operating Department, we detected a quasi-militaristic discipline: here instructions were to be obeyed promptly and without question. Finally, there was a considerable emphasis on the safety of both passengers and staff.

Most of these values are functional as they facilitate the performance of the tasks of the organization, and their importance will become apparent in later chapters. Some immigrants, and the West Indians in particular, found them difficult to accept and internalize. The over-all emphasis is very much on *service* as the organization is, of course, a service organization. If, though, one can draw a distinction between a service and a marketing orientation—the emphasis of the one being on providing a *public service*, that of the other on *selling* a product—then the service orientation appears uppermost. There are indications, though, that this is changing: services appear to be subject to a closer scrutiny in terms of their cost-revenue balance, and recent appointments suggest a greater emphasis on marketing than there has been hitherto. The organization has apparently for many years been very public relations conscious.

In behaviour, deference appeared to be accorded those of higher rank in a more pronounced form than I have observed in some other

---

[1] This does not apply to the whole organization, only to the operating departments and those concerned with the wages grades.

[2] I am not suggesting that there is a unitary system of values throughout the organization: those discussed here were primarily those of management, but they were largely shared by supervisors and to some extent by operatives also.

organizations. 'Sir' was a fairly common form of address, though there were differences between the departments in this respect. This behavioural pattern is consistent with the somewhat traditional system of values.

There is a sense of continuity in the undertaking. Whilst there have been changes in its formal ownership and accountability, these appear in many respects to have left it unscathed. There has been a continuity of staff throughout these changes, and this is doubtless an important factor here. There is, too, a tendency to think long term rather than short term. Civil engineering projects may affect the pattern of operations for a hundred years or more; railway rolling-stock may remain in service thirty or forty years.[1] Percentage changes in demand, whilst considerable in the long term, tend to be quite low in any given year. All these factors appear to contribute to this perceived sense of continuity.

The changing pattern of demand for public transport has made some considerable impact. Until very recently it appeared to be widely accepted—that is, outside the organization—that public transport *was* a declining industry and there was relatively little interest in reviving its fortunes. The fall in demand, coupled with the apparent lack of interest generally in public transport, appeared to lead to pessimism within the organization. More recently, however, it appears to be more widely understood that the private car is not the most socially desirable or efficient form of transport in large urban areas, and the future for public transport looks brighter than it did. This revival in the fortunes has perhaps been symbolized for London Transport by the commissioning of a new tube line, and there now appears to be a greater optimism, though possibly some clouds remain.

One other component of the set of beliefs and values ought perhaps to be mentioned at this stage. We saw earlier that there was comparatively little information readily available which distinguished staff according to ethnic origins. A possible consequence of this was the prevalence of folklore, particularly at management level, about the coloured immigrant staff. It appeared to be widely believed, for example, that their turnover rate was higher than that of white native staff. Whilst we have not been able to establish whether or not this was so, it does seem somewhat unlikely. In this and other respects the lack of statistical and documentary information

---

[1] At the time of writing some passenger rolling-stock commissioned in 1923 was still in service, as was some engineering stock built before the turn of the century.

served to buttress a number of beliefs which otherwise might have been dispelled.

Other beliefs about the coloured immigrants varied widely, and these are spelled out in detail in later chapters. There was, though, a very widespread set of beliefs about another group of 'outsiders'—the Irish. The image of the Irish amongst many managers and supervisors was not a favourable one, particularly in the two operating departments. Perhaps the most commonly met stereotype was that of the unreliability of the Irish in respect of attendance, and particularly of their perceived tendency to 'disappear to help with the farm at home'. I have no evidence on how far this image was based on a myth.

It might be concluded that London Transport—with its long traditions, its policies of internal promotion, a somewhat 'closed' culture, and the freedom to choose whom it employed which it enjoyed until the late 1940s—would be unreceptive to coloured newcomers. In some respects this conclusion would be correct, but there were important variables operating in the opposite direction. That it was a bureaucratic organization was very important. The relevance of bureaucracy to race and ethnic relations is far wider than London Transport and can usefully be elaborated here.

First, bureaucratic rules and procedures may be deliberately discriminatory. Second, they may in practice be discriminatory, without this being their author's intention; they may though be *maintained* because they are discriminatory. Apart from these two types, bureaucratic rules and procedures are conducive to the equal treatment of ethnic or racial minorities. Much depends on how comprehensive and detailed rules are; and on how rigidly they are applied and monitored. Generally, the more detailed rules are, and the more rigidly they are applied, the less likelihood there is of discriminatory behaviour. Similarly, centralization reduces the opportunity for individuals to behave in a discriminatory manner, especially at lower levels in an organization. Another important aspect of bureaucracy is the reliance on formal, written job rules. In two departments the work content of roles was prescribed in some detail in writing. These rules were taught, and considerably reduced the area of ambiguity in others' expectations of the actor's performance. They serve to reduce the area of potential conflict arising from cultural strangeness.[1] Finally, London Transport's technical and social organization of work was conducive to conflict minimization.

[1] For a contrasting situation see Malcolm Rimmer, *Race & Industrial Conflict* (London, Heinemann, 1972).

3

SOME CHARACTERISTICS OF THE INTERVIEW SAMPLES

THE COUNTRIES OF ORIGIN OF THE IMMIGRANTS
Table 3.1 shows the countries of origin of our samples.

TABLE 3.1
Countries of Origin of the Immigrants, in Percentages.★

	Busmen	Operating Railwaymen	Permanent Way	All
Barbados, direct recruit	18	30	14	24
Other Barbados	5	11	24	10
Total Barbados	23	42	38	34
Jamaica	45	30	29	36
Trinidad	1	2	5	2
Guyana	8	8	—	7
Other West Indies	9	11	29	12
Total Caribbean	86	94	100	91
India, Anglo-Indian	—	5	—	3
Other India	1	—	—	0·5
Pakistan	8	1	—	4
Other countries	5	—	—	2
Total	100	100	100	100
(Sample)	(78)	(96)	(21)	(195)

★ The terms 'busmen' and 'railwaymen' include the women in these grades unless otherwise stated. Any definition of 'Anglo-Indian' is inexact: those so classified here (including one Anglo-Sinhalese) were regarded as 'Anglo-Indians'. The Pakistanis included some from Kashmir who had travelled with Pakistani documents.

Overwhelmingly, the immigrants were from the Caribbean. The Barbadians and Jamaicans in almost equal numbers constituted over two-thirds of the samples.

When we compare all our immigrant samples with the 'New

Commonwealth' population of Greater London, as enumerated in the 1966 10 per cent sample census, it is clear that immigrants from the Caribbean are considerably over-represented in public transport.[1] Some important variables here are the direct recruitment by London Transport in the Caribbean,[2] its requirements concerning 'good' spoken English, discrimination by other employers, and the educational and pre-migration occupational attainments of the various immigrant groups. Given a pattern of job discrimination, an employer who is known to employ large numbers of coloured immigrants will attract more, as appears to be the case with London Transport. From the immigrant's point of view, there is the sheer necessity of obtaining employment and the wish to avoid exposure to possible discrimination in this quest.

Whilst then, 'the majority of West Indians are not transport workers',[3] the majority of London Transport's coloured immigrants are West Indian.

WHY THE IMMIGRANTS CAME TO BRITAIN

The major underlying reason for the movement of Commonwealth immigrants to Britain has, of course, been economic: the pull of labour-hungry industry, on the one hand; the push of relatively low earnings and unemployment or under-employment, on the other. Yet this analysis, whilst not false, is too simple. Though seemingly explaining everything, it nonetheless fails to tell us anything about why those who came did so—when the majority of their countrymen stayed at home. It was not evident that those immigrants we interviewed were amongst the most economically oppressed in their home countries; many clearly were not. Nor would we expect this to be so: at the very least they required access to enough money to pay their passages, as only the Barbados-recruited immigrants had this problem made relatively easy for them.

More important is the fact that many were in sought-after occupations in their home countries. The West Indian recruits were more likely to have been carpenters, mechanics, clerks, or policemen than cane cutters. In these terms, they were in the upper strata of the working class and the lower strata of the middle class in their home countries. It is then useful to examine the reasons *they* gave for coming to Britain. One problem here is that some of the interviewees had

---

[1] See the *Commonwealth Immigrant Tables* from the *Sample Census, 1966* (London, H.M.S.O., 1969), and the census data presented in Rose, *et al.*

[2] See Chapter 13. [3] Rose, *et al.*, p. 155.

been here several years: what appears to them *now* to have been important might not have seemed so at the time of migration. It was not obvious, though, that this distorted the picture: the answers given did at least appear realistic to us. Table 3.2 summarizes these answers.

TABLE 3.2
*Why the Immigrants Came to Britain, in Percentages.**

No special reason/to see the world/ to see the 'mother country'/ travel/experience/adventure	35
Advancement/a better job	27
To study	14
Friends came	12
Unemployed/previous job insecure	11
Relatives came	8
Other answer	3
No answer	2

* More than one answer was recorded and the percentage total may therefore exceed 100. The size of the samples was 195 respondents.

The table shows that a wish to see the world or gain experience was the most frequently given reason for coming to Britain.

I'd heard all about the 'mother country'—I thought it would be a good place to come to. [Barbadian Motorman.]

There was 'England fever' in the West Indies. [West Indian Motorman.]

Clearly the wish to see the world was an important immediate motive for migration.

Next there were those who were apparently more concerned with economic advancement: ambition, to better oneself.

My main purpose was to earn money and get a better living. [Pakistani Conductor.]

Ambition—to better myself. When you were young you wish you were this and had this. [Barbadian Motorman.]

A number wished to study: full time or, more frequently, to combine study with work. Some had commenced study courses, mostly evening classes, but few had found attendance at these classes compatible with the hours of work of public transport.

I wanted to go to an evening course. I did mechanical engineering at a technical college, but I gave it up when I went to Birmingham. I will take it up again. [Pakistani Conductor.]

I wanted to work and study. But I cannot afford to [study]. [Jamaican Conductor.]

Those who told us that their friends came sometimes mentioned that they were at that time reluctant.

My friends were all coming here—I was half pushed into it. [Jamaican Guard.]

The number who told us that they were unemployed, or that their home jobs were threatened or 'insecure', was relatively small.

To work: Kashmir is a disputed territory and no one wants to develop it. [Pakistani Conductor.]

[There was] no work at home. [Barbadian Motorman.]

The influence of relatives coming to Britain as a factor in migration was felt mostly by those whose parents came and in this respect they often had little choice. The influence of relatives was not, however, confined to parents.

My wife came before me and I came to join her. [Jamaican Conductor.]

Whilst the contrasts in economic conditions and prospects between Britain and the home countries provide the basic conditions which made migration possible, the economic explanation is not adequate for individual motivation. For some, the economic motivation was apparently paramount, but they were not the majority, though for most, perhaps, there was the prospect of a better life in terms of economic well-being.

The relatively large number who came out of a wish to see the world, to gain experience, or out of a sense of adventure is impressive. Some of the countries of origin, notably Barbados, have a tradition of migration, and a rough parallel here might be with Ireland. In both, there have not been the necessary economic conditions to sustain a population at the standard of living which the people desired and some sought a better life through migration.

At least as far as our samples are concerned, those who migrated were by no means at the lowest level of the economic strata. In their own countries, the *relative* occupational and economic positions of many, possibly most, were better than those of many of their fellow-citizens. They perhaps differed from the majority of their fellow-citizens in three respects: their higher level of aspirations; their readiness to travel in order to satisfy these aspirations; and their ability to raise sufficient money to pay their passages. To that extent, our data appear to support the traditional migration hypothesis that the more adventurous individuals migrate. Time and again I was impressed by this sense of adventure and the optimism that had managed to survive the rebuffs experienced by coloured immigrants in Britain, as well as the rigours of a cold Northern clime.

THE LENGTH OF TIME THE IMMIGRANTS HAD SPENT IN BRITAIN

TABLE 3.3
Length of time spent in Britain.★

Years	%
Less than 1	1
1–2	7
3–4	11
5–6	28
7–8	16
9–10	17
11–12	15
13 or more	5

★ As it is *reported* length of time in Britain, there is the possibility of some inaccuracy due to error of recall. The samples totalled 195.

The majority (81 per cent) had at the time of our fieldwork been in Britain five years or more. As the fieldwork was during the period mid-1966 to mid-1967, most arrived before the operation of the Commonwealth Immigrants Act 1962. Over half had been in Britain seven or more years, which dates their arrival in the 1950s, mostly in the second half of that decade. The important point here is that most had spent some years in Britain; few were 'straight off the boat'.

We have seen where the immigrants came from, the motivations that brought them here, and how long they had been here. What jobs did they leave behind?

OCCUPATIONS OF THE IMMIGRANTS BEFORE MIGRATION

TABLE 3.4
*Occupations of the Immigrants Before Migration, in Percentages.**

Unskilled or semi-skilled manual	24
Skilled manual	32
Non-manual	17
Supervisory	2
Teaching	5
Agricultural/fishing	6
Not employed	6
At school	8
Insufficient information	1

* The samples totalled 195.

First, a word on the coding categories used: the breakdown is a fairly crude one as the material did not lend itself to a more refined classification, such as the Registrar-General's. Our informants were sometimes a little vague on their previous occupations, and as this aspect of the interview was not central to our enquiry we did not wish to spend much time on it. The Registrar-General's classification is in any case perhaps more appropriate to a complex industrial society.

The skilled manual category included such occupations as carpenter, plumber, motor mechanic—in other words, mostly artisan occupations. The non-manual category consisted mostly of clerks of various types. The other categories are self-explanatory. It ought, perhaps, to be added that few, if any, of the teachers were formally qualified for this occupation. The sample did include two graduates, both from the Indian subcontinent.

The table shows that roughly one-third of the immigrants were previously in skilled manual occupations and nearly one-fifth in clerical jobs.[1] What jobs did they expect to find in Britain, what jobs had they sought, and how successful had they been?

[1] For data from other studies on the pre-migration occupations of West Indian immigrants, see Rose, *et al.*, Chapter 5.

JOB EXPECTATIONS OF THE IMMIGRANTS AND THEIR EXPERIENCES OF
SEEKING EMPLOYMENT

TABLE 3.5
*Job Expectations of the Immigrants, in Percentages.**

No idea/anything	35
Previous occupation (skilled or white collar)†	24
Direct recruit L.T.B.	24
Unskilled/semi-skilled	9
Nursing (women)	3
Other/school	4
Direct recruit (not L.T.B.)	1

* The samples totalled 195.

† The white-collar category here consists of non-manual, supervisory, and teaching staff. (Over one-half of the teachers shown in Table 3.4 had been recruited by L.T.B. in Barbados, and hence are not included here.)

The largest single group had no firm ideas about the type of work they expected to be able to obtain in Britain. It was often evident in the interviews that there had been an almost complete lack of information about employment opportunities and conditions, and we return to this below.[1]

In some respects the most interesting group are those who expected to find skilled or white-collar work. Some who had been employed in these occupations in their home countries had joined London Transport in Barbados. Others did not expect to find work in their own occupations and had not sought it. Of the forty-seven immigrants who had worked in these occupations in their home countries, and expected to find such work here, thirty-eight had sought similar employment in Britain. Less than one-third (eleven) had been successful. The problems experienced in these searches can be illustrated from the interview material.

They [the Ministry of Labour] sent me, but it was no good. I have tried again but they said I must have experience in this country. [West Indian ex-Shoemaker.]

I went for a printing job, but the man told me it wasn't for non-Europeans and I'd better go to Euston and try the railways. . . . I felt like going straight home that week, I was so upset. [West Indian ex-Printer.]

[1] See Chapter 16.

Clearly, job discrimination at that time was widespread, and this has been confirmed by other studies.[1] It was evident, too, that much distress was caused to those adversely affected. It is sometimes argued that levels of skill are generally lower in the West Indies than in Britain; and there may be something in this argument, but we have no evidence. What is clear is that most of those who applied for skilled or white-collar employment were given no opportunity to *prove* their abilities: they were turned away at the door.

The question of different levels of skill is also relevant when we consider the possible occupational down-grading of immigrant workers. Using the Registrar-General's criteria, we can see some down-grading, but there has also been some upgrading. Our skilled manual category is roughly similar to the Registrar-General's socio-economic group 9; 32 per cent of our sample came under this category. But 48 per cent of our sample are now in socio-economic group 9. Those who have been occupationally down-graded are then those who were previously in non-manual, supervisory, or teaching employment.[2]

There was some recognition that levels of skill do vary. The following comment, from a West Indian panel beater, illustrates this:

I have had a job as a panel beater in the U.K. but I found out that what I'd learnt was not the beginning: these men here are so good you'd think it [the repaired car body] was off the assembly line.

Whilst, then, by the Registrar-General's criteria there has been both down-grading and upgrading, we cannot establish how far skills are under-used. (There may indeed be some under-utilization of skills in the native part of the workforce.) The Registrar-General's classification is in any case a relatively crude instrument for the kind of complex analysis that would be required. We do know that a number tried and failed to find employment comparable to that which they had previously held. It appeared too that others had been deterred from seeking such employment by their fears of discrimination.

We collected data on the employment our immigrant interviewees had held in Britain before joining London Transport.

[1] Notably, the P.E.P. report; Political and Economic Planning and Research Services Ltd., *Racial Discrimination* (London, P.E.P., 1967). It is not suggested that discrimination has lessened since the P.E.P. report.

[2] In our immigrant samples the immigrants whose occupational attainment has been highest were over-represented. See Chapter I.

TABLE 3.6
*Number of Jobs held in Britain by Immigrants Before Joining L.T.B., in Percentages.**

None	44
One	19
Two	19
Three	11
Four or more	7

* The samples totalled 195.

Whilst comparable data on other occupational groups are lacking, and a detailed analysis would require that we relate the number of jobs to the period of time spent in Britain, the evidence does not suggest that the immigrants have been rapidly changing jobs: over 80 per cent had had one, two, or no previous jobs in Britain before they joined London Transport. (The Barbadian direct recruits account for slightly over half of those who had had no other jobs in Britain.) The pattern, then, is one of stability.

WHY WORKERS HAD JOINED LONDON TRANSPORT
We asked both native and immigrant workers why they had joined London Transport.

With the exception of the Barbadian recruits who said that they had joined London Transport because it provided the easiest way to get to Britain, and the small number of immigrants who told us that they knew London Transport employed coloured staff, the pattern of answers from the two groups is broadly similar. There are, however, some differences of emphasis which will become apparent as we elaborate on the various answers given.

It is difficult to say how far answers to this type of question reflect the considerations which were uppermost in the minds of our respondents at the time they joined. It might be argued that the answers reflect the satisfactions which workers have subsequently found in their employment. Such an argument would, though, find little supporting evidence in our data. Often the contrast was made between conditions prevailing at the time workers joined London Transport and those of today. This came out with particular force from those who spoke of the attractions of job security, especially

TABLE 3.7
*Why Workers Had Joined London Transport, in Percentages.**

Reasons	Native	Immigrant
A good, regular, or secure job	25	21
Unemployed/could not get work in own trade/jobs scarce/ sent by Ministry of Labour	25	18
Pay/fringe benefits	17	11
To get to the U.K.†	—	16
No particular reason/discontent with previous job	12	15
Wanted clean work/open-air work/ to meet people	12	6
Wanted driving/bus/railway work	11	10
Wanted shift/night work	6	4
Knew L.T. employed coloured immigrants	—	4
Other answer	4	3

* More than one answer was recorded and the percentage totals may therefore exceed 100. The samples totalled 174 natives and 195 immigrants.

† Barbadian direct recruits only.

from those natives who had joined at a time of widespread unemployment.

Most of those who spoke of security mentioned that London Transport employment was thought to be good, regular, permanent, or secure. The emphasis appeared to be very much on the likelihood that one would not be dismissed. It is not clear whether they had in mind the security of employment in an organization whose employment levels were relatively unaffected by variations in trading conditions; or whether they knew something of the security derived from the formal disciplinary procedures; or whether in the more recent past they were aware of the staff shortage which made it unlikely that a worker would be dismissed. The security resulting from the existence of formal disciplinary procedures is of particular importance to the coloured immigrant workers, and it is possible that this aspect of security, summed up by the phrase 'they've got to prove you are wrong before they sack you', is part of London Transport's image amongst the coloured immigrant working population of London. It is possible too that the very fact that London Transport was a *large, public service* organization, gave it an

3

image of an employer providing secure employment. The importance of security is illustrated by the interview material.

I was unemployed and wanted a *secure* job. There is more money in building, but it is less secure. [West Indian Driver.]

Security: in those days jobs were scarce and it was a lasting job, a steady job. [U.K. Motorman.]

In those answers which referred to 'job security' the most noticeable difference of emphasis was between those who had joined pre-war and the more recent recruits. The former often stressed that security 'was worth something then' or 'this was a good job then', with the clear implication that security is now less important and that 'the job is not what it was'. Whilst with a high level of employment security may be a less salient consideration for some, its appeal is still powerful and it provides one of the major attractions of employment in the public service sector.[1]

Security may be seen as having a positive appeal in a society in which some unemployment is always present. Related to this is the need for the individual to find *any* employment when he is out of work, and this may be seen as a negative reason for joining an organization. Whilst amongst both immigrant and native workers there were some who merely said that they were 'unemployed' or that they were 'sent by the Ministry of Labour'—and here London Transport's reputation as a large employer of coloured immigrants is obviously relevant—there was some difference of emphasis between the immigrant and native workers who could not get work in their own trades. Most of the coloured immigrants here appeared to have experienced job discrimination by potential employers. Amongst the natives were some whose trades were becoming less important providers of employment owing to technical change, for example, french-polishers whose skills were becoming obsolete with the widespread use of cellulose and polyurethane finishes. For those who joined before the War, the Depression was the dominant influence.

The Depression—I was pleased to get any job. [U.K. Ticket Collector.]

It was a job: I was out of work after the War. [U.K. Motorman.]

[1] This came out very clearly in an unpublished attitude survey of Post Office workers: Dennis Brooks, Tom Davies, and Bob Fryer, 'Attitudes to Employment on the Postal Side of the G.P.O.' (London, Imperial College Industrial Sociology Unit, 1968).

Some interviewees gave the level of pay as a reason for joining London Transport; others mentioned various fringe benefits, notably, the free travel pass and free uniform provided.

It paid more than most: forty-two shillings a week. [U.K. Ticket Collector.]

A friend said the wages were O.K. [Pakistani Conductor.]

Numerically, the next most important group were those Barbadians who said that they had joined London Transport as a means of 'getting to the U.K.' For all, the provision of a loan to pay their passage and the guarantee of a job on arrival was probably important, particularly the loan. For those who had travelled since the Commonwealth Immigrants Act 1962 there was the additional benefit—if that is the word—of obtaining an entry voucher. (Seventy per cent of the Barbadian direct recruits mentioned entry into the U.K. as a reason for joining London Transport.)

The [recruitment] scheme. It is difficult to come to England except by the scheme: it is a question of cash. The job was said to be worth having—a rosy picture was painted of English life. [Barbadian Stationman.]

These answers must of course be related to those given for wanting to come to England.[1] The London Transport recruitment scheme provided the means which made immigration possible and for some, it appeared to furnish an incentive for immigration.

Some, immigrants and natives alike, were discontented with their previous jobs. In a sense, this may be seen as a negative incentive, except that employment in London Transport was presumably seen to be better in some respect. It was the discontent with their previous employment which provided the motivation, and for this reason it is legitimate to group these workers with those who joined London Transport for no particular reason.

I decided to have a change: my previous job was permanent nights and I met friends who worked for London Transport. [Pakistani Conductor].

I wasn't settled in my previous trade after the Navy: [It was an] indoor job and didn't suit me at all. [U.K. Conductor.]

The last quotation provides a link to the next group of answers: those for whom the prospect of a clean, open air job, or one in which they could meet people, was attractive.

[1] See above, pp. 35–8.

I wanted a fresh air job. [U.K. Guard.]

I like to meet people—this is the best [job] for that. You come across every type of people. [Pakistani Conductor.]

The division between those who wanted 'open air work' and those who specifically mentioned driving, bus, or railway work is to some extent an artificial one, in that we do not know *why* they wanted public transport work. Some had experience of work in the public transport sector, and its attractions may have included some of those listed. The appeal of railways to some appears to have an almost romantic content—the magic of the iron road, as it were. Again, some of the answers straddle two coding categories, particularly the first one quoted, from an 'old platelayer':

I was on the —— railway and when the holiday period came they put you off—to save the two weeks holiday pay. [U.K. Relayer.]

I wanted driving and I wanted to give up long distance driving. [U.K. Driver.]

I wanted to work on the railways. [West Indian Motorman.]

Finally, there were those, few in number, who specifically wanted shift or night work, and those immigrants who went to London Transport because they knew it employed coloured workers. It is highly probable that the size of this last group considerably under-states the number for whom this was a relevant factor, given the extent of job discrimination by other employers and a reluctance on the part of some coloured immigrants to discuss their experiences and disappointments with a white interviewer.

We have seen that the reasons given for joining London Transport varied considerably. How far these answers reflected the considera-tions salient at the time of joining probably differs between the type of answer. Those who reported that they were unemployed, or that they wanted a secure job, were probably accurately recalling their dominant motives. One problem in this analysis is that we are comparing the answers of native workers who had joined in a period of up to forty-five years with those of immigrants who had joined in only a third of that time. This difference does provide one important common factor: those natives who joined in the inter-war years shared with the immigrants a situation where jobs were scarce —so far as *they* were concerned—but scarce for different reasons and with a different degree of scarcity.

We have seen that a number of both immigrant and native

workers were to some extent pushed into the organization by a lack of other available employment opportunities. These natives had clearly stayed some years. Once in, they had found some rewards in their employment; the skills of railwaymen are, in any case, largely nontransferable. It seems likely that many of the immigrants will follow this path, particularly the railwaymen. This will happen, I believe, largely irrespective of any reduction in job discrimination elsewhere, and a *marked* reduction in this discrimination is unlikely. We shall return to this theme of the permanency of the coloured immigrant sector of the workforce in later chapters.

THE AGE AND LENGTH OF SERVICE PATTERNS OF THE SAMPLES

To round out the picture of our samples, we shall now consider two further topics: their age and length of service patterns.

TABLE 3.8
Age Structure of the Samples as at 1 January 1967, in Percentages.

Years	Native				Immigrant			
	Bus-men	Train-men	Station staff	Per. Way	Bus-men	Train-men	Station staff	Per. Way
Under 20	4	4	7	—	1	—	—	—
20–24	9	4	10	14	15	13	11	—
25–29	11	6	3	10	27	20	25	19
30–34	7	4	7	10	31	30	19	10
35–39	11	15	—	10	13	23	22	29
40–44	11	9	7	—	10	5	11	29
45–49	10	9	17	10	1	5	3	14
50–54	11	11	17	29	1	2	8	—
55–59	16	15	17	10	—	2	—	—
60–64	7	19	17	10	—	—	—	—
65 and over	1	4	—	—	—	—	—	—
(Sample)	(70)	(53)	(30)	(21)	(78)	(60)	(36)	(21)

It will be seen that the age distribution of the native samples was fairly even, though in each sample more than 50 per cent were in the 40 and over age groups. By contrast, the immigrants were mostly in the under 40 age groups, in some samples overwhelmingly so. This is the first important difference between the two groups: the immigrants were on average considerably younger than the natives.[1]

TABLE 3.9
Length of Service Pattern as at 1 January 1967, in Percentages.*

Years	Native Bus-men	Native Train-men	Native Station staff	Native Per. Way	Immigrant Bus-men	Immigrant Train-men	Immigrant Station staff	Immigrant Per. Way
Under 1	20	—	3	14	23	—	11	14
1–2	10	15	40	24	19	17	31	5
3–4	11	6	3	14	22	10	17	—
5–9	9	8	7	5	35	53	36	57
10–14	14	8	3	5	1	18	6	24
15–19	11	26	23	10	—	2	—	—
20–24	13	4	7	14	—	—	—	—
25–29	3	17	7	14	—	—	—	—
30 and over	9	17	7	—	—	—	—	—
Total	100	100	100	100	100	100	100	100
Previous L.T. service	20	6	7	10	5	5	—	5
(Sample)	(70)	(53)	(30)	(21)	(78)	(60)	(36)	(21)

* For those with previous service, the length of service shown dated from the last re-engagement.

The coloured immigrants are of course almost all concentrated in the under fifteen years' service groups. Between the native samples it is the trainmen who are most heavily represented in the groups having the longest length of service. This reflects both the pattern of promotion in the Railway Operating Department and the lower wastage rate of railwaymen as compared with busmen.

One final comparison is the length of service of the operating railwaymen before they achieved their present grades.

[1] This concentration of the Immigrants in the 25 to 44 age groups reflects a general pattern. See the *Commonwealth Immigrant Tables* from the *Sample Census 1966* (London H.M.S.O., 1969).

TABLE 3.10
Length of L.T. Service Before Promotion to Present Grade (Operating Railwaymen Only), in Percentages.

Years	Native		Immigrant	
	Trainmen	Station staff	Trainmen	Station staff
None	19	43	17	47
Under 1	6	7	25	11
1–2	9	10	8	11
3–4	4	—	20	19
5–9	34	15	28	11
10–14	15	7	2	—
15–19	8	—	—	—
20–24	2	—	—	—
25 and over	2	—	—	—
Demotion	2	17	—	—
(Sample)	(53)	(30)	(60)	(36)

The main contrast is between the two samples of trainmen: 60 per cent of the native trainmen had five or more years' service in the Department before they reached their present grade, compared with 30 per cent of the immigrant trainmen. Promotion has been much more rapid in recent years, which accounts for the difference between the two samples: the immigrants had all joined during this period of relatively rapid promotion. This change in the speed of promotion is one of some importance and its relevance will become apparent when we consider the reactions of native railwaymen to the introduction of coloured immigrants to the Department. Those native railwaymen listed as having been demoted had been downgraded for health reasons; most were former trainmen who became ticket collectors.

To conclude, we have seen that most of the immigrants were West Indian, that many came from skilled manual or white-collar occupations, and had but vague ideas of employment prospects in Britain. This is largely an immigration factor, though clearly race is important in the forces which have shaped West Indian history, and West Indians' image of the 'Mother Country'. Race is important too in the job discrimination reported. The similarities in the reasons given for joining London Transport conceal differences: the two groups face different—but overlapping—labour markets.

4

CENTRAL BUSES, I:
BUSES AND BUSMEN

THE STRUCTURE OF THE DEPARTMENT

The structure of Central Buses was undergoing radical change at the time of the field work, so it is necessary to describe it as it existed before and after the change. The major functional distinction is between *traffic* management (control of the operation of vehicles on the road) and *garage* management (provision of vehicles and crews).[1]

Our focus of interest is the lower level of the two charts, that is, the bus crews and their superordinates both at the garages and on the road. It will be seen that crews receive instructions from two sources: garage inspectors and road or 'point' inspectors.[2] The broad distinction here is that the allocation of duties and so on is the responsibility of garage inspectors, control on the road is the responsibility of point inspectors.[3]

The fleet consisted of roundly 6,500 vehicles. Most were double-decked, rear-entrance vehicles, with seating capacities of up to seventy-two passengers. Some single-deck vehicles were also in service, either crew or driver operated. One-man operation (O.M.O.) was relatively new, but the number of O.M.O. vehicles has since grown considerably. Almost all the busmen in our study operated double-decked vehicles, none were on one-man operation. The analysis here, particularly of the driver-conductor relationship, applies only to those operating double-decked rear-entrance vehicles. The social situation of crews operating front-entrance vehicles is probably very different, given the ease of communication between driver and conductor afforded by that type of vehicle. The

[1] Vehicle maintenance is the responsibility of an engineering department and as such is quite separate from garage or traffic management.
[2] 'Point' is the busmen's term for a bus stop.
[3] The tasks of point inspectors are spelled out in greater detail below.

fleet operated from some 70 garages. These varied in the numbers of drivers and conductors employed: from less than 200 to 8–900. Most were in the 250–500 range; few had more than 650 men.

THE TECHNICAL AND SOCIAL ORGANIZATION OF WORK

The road—which will be central to our discussion—is where busmen spend most of their working hours; it is here that the work is done and the possibilities of both co-operation and conflict occur. In most respects the garage is less important. Crews book on and off at the garage, receive instructions on duties, and so on. A crew may pick up or leave a bus at the garage, but many crew changes take place on the road. Meal breaks—'meal reliefs'—may be taken at the garage canteen, but many busmen go home. A busman may see his friends at the garage, but most busmen will either be out on the road or off duty.

Two underlying values are functionally all-important in bus operation: time and safety. About safety little need be said: its necessity is self-evident and there are sanctions available to management and the courts for failure to comply with the rules.[1] There is also a small cash

[1] 'Rules' is used here to include those laid down by management, the public service licensing authority, and the laws relating to the use of vehicles on the highway.

DIAGRAM 4.1.
Structure of a Central Bus Division

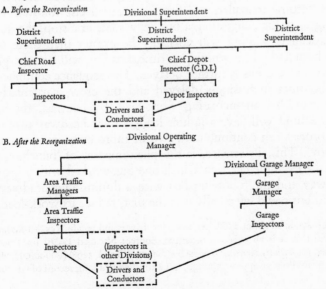

incentive based on the number of years without 'blame-worthy' accident.[1] Various aspects of safety are referred to below, but we can now turn to the question of 'time'. Time is so important in bus work that it is necessary to explain it in some detail.

Each journey is scheduled to take a definite time. Moreover, the journey time is broken up in that a bus is due to arrive at and depart from points along the route—the 'road' in bus parlance—at specified times. Arrival and departure times are checked at some of the points along the route either by an inspector on 'point' duty or, less commonly, by a machine which records the time on a card carried by the conductor. On each route there is a scheduled time interval between consecutive buses, the 'headway'. This headway varies considerably during the day, and again on Saturdays, Sundays, and public holidays. Likewise, the allowed journey time varies according to time of day and direction.

Bus operations are best explained by means of a simple model. In our model we see a number of buses on a route. The time interval between them—the 'headway'—is similar for all the buses. If we assume that the route does not vary at all in its road characteristics, other traffic, or passenger demand, then the distances between the buses will also be equal.

If we introduce an irregular movement of other vehicular traffic into our model, together with congestion at various points along the route, we take a step towards reality. The intervals between the buses become irregular, and from this much else follows. When, owing to traffic congestion, a bus arrives late at a stop, the number of passengers waiting will normally be greater than there would have been had it been running to time. Loading will take marginally longer and the bus is further delayed. This sequence continues; the bus becomes increasingly delayed and the crew, particularly the conductor, has an increasing work-load. By contrast, the bus or buses behind will have a lighter load as their headway is reduced. The process can continue until two or more buses are running 'in convoy'. This, in essence, is the phenomenon of 'bunching'.

In the example cited, in which one bus worked with a growing headway and the following bus with a diminishing headway, the second bus could eventually pass the first, reduce its work-load, and

[1] This averaged about 2/6d. per week for drivers and conductors in 1967 and it is doubtful that it is an effective incentive. Source: National Board for Prices and Incomes, *Productivity Agreements in the Bus Industry* (Cmnd. 3498) (London, H.M.S.O., 1967), p. 12. Prestige appears, though, to be attached to a long record of safe driving.

help it to 'make up time'. This represents co-operation between the crews; however, the extra work-load for the 'passing' crew would fall more on the conductor than on the driver. (It is likely that the driver would have to make some additional stops. The conductor, however, would have to issue more tickets, give more change, make more journeys along both decks and up and down the stairs, and count and pay in more cash at the end of the day.) The example leads us to a conflict situation: that of a bus 'running early', that is, ahead of its scheduled time. By running early a crew ensures that it is working with a reduced headway, assuming the previous bus is running to time, and thus has a lighter work-load. The following bus, however, will be working with an extended headway and hence the crew will have a heavier work-load. These factors also apply when two or more routes operate over the same stretch of road: the 'first' bus will pick up the majority of the 'short-riding' passengers, and the following buses will be running light. Similarly, one of the following buses can pass the first bus and reduce its work-load. Moreover, on a multi-route section of road a crew can 'hang back' in order not to be the first bus of a 'bunch' to reach a stop. Hanging back can also be practised where the terminal point of one route is on the road of another route: again, a number of short-riding passengers can be avoided. In short, there is in the work situation an area of possible conflict or co-operation between crews over the allocation of the work-load. There is, moreover, an area of possible conflict between the driver and the conductor, again over the work-load to be carried. There are also areas of possible co-operation between driver and conductor, and to these we now turn.

Given the importance of 'running to time' in bus operation, there are a number of ways in which a crew can co-operate to ensure that the bus does run to schedule:[1] for example, quick loading and un-loading by the conductor. Here it can be noted that helping pas-sengers on and off, especially elderly people, women with children, push-chairs, and the like, is not *only* a matter of courtesy: it speeds up loading and unloading. Similarly, knowing the number of vacant places on the bus before the stop is reached helps the conductor to load quickly. Likewise signalling to the driver not to stop when the

---

[1] Both driver and conductor are held responsible for failure to run to time with-out an acceptable reason. Both carry time cards showing the times the bus is due at a number of points along the route. In practice, the driver is usually blamed more than the conductor for 'time offences'.

bus is full helps to maintain time.[1] Being quick to give the starting signal—'quick on the bell'—is a further means of helping to keep to time. Conversely, slowness in giving starting signals is important when there is a possibility of running early: passengers, moreover, tend to resent a bus *waiting* at a stop because it is running ahead of schedule.

Quick collection of fares by the conductor enables him to spend more time on the platform, to control unloading and loading, to prevent boarding at unauthorized stops when the bus is full, and thus to assist in running to schedule. Avoiding arguments with passengers prevents possible delay and contributes to the same aim. Hand signals from the platform to other traffic at road junctions is another means whereby a conductor assists the driver in the safe performance of his job, as is waiting for a 'gap' in the traffic before giving the starting signal from a stop. These are the more important ways in which the conductor can assist in achieving the goal of running to time. It follows that failure to behave in these ways is liable to interfere with running to time and to produce conflict between driver and conductor. We now examine the ways in which the driver can assist his conductor.

Keeping to time is an important part of the driver's task. We have noted the effect on the conductor's work-load of late running, and we have also noted that by running early the driver can lighten the conductor's work-load—an 'easy ride' for the conductor, or 'fiddling' in busmen's terminology.[2] Ensuring a longer meal break, or more 'stand time' for tea or a smoke, provides further incentives for crews to run early. Careful control of the vehicle—avoiding harsh acceleration, braking and cornering—enables the conductor to move about the bus more easily and collect his fares. Likewise, it reduces the risk of accidents to passengers. It also reduces the likelihood of passengers complaining to the conductor about the *driver's* conduct. The conductor, in face-to-face contact with passengers, is the major butt of passengers' criticism of *all* aspects of the service: the conduct of the driver, the frequency of buses and delays in the service, the actions of other crews, rises in fare charges, and almost anything else.

---

[1] The all but universal 'three rings' bell signal, used to indicate to the driver that the bus is full, is not recognized in L.T. Central Buses *Rule Book for Drivers and Conductors* (London, L.T.B., 1964) (afterwards referred to as the Central Buses *Rule Book* or *Rules*).

[2] Fiddling is often used loosely to cover any means by which a crew lightens the work-load on the road, but mostly it refers to early running.

A driver can help his conductor in other ways. When a bus is full and carrying mostly short-riding passengers, some drivers will drive slightly slower than normal to give the conductor more time to collect his fares, with the intention of making up any lost time later on the route. This is quite important: a conductor with a bus full of short-riding passengers has some considerable difficulty in collecting *all* his fares in the time available.[1]

Using the nearside rear view mirror to check that the platform is clear of passengers and that none are about to board when the conductor gives the starting signal from upstairs is another way in which the driver can assist the conductor. Again, safety and keeping to time are involved. Whilst the *Rule Book*[2] lays down a definite code for bell signals, practices vary considerably, as do the expectations of one crew member regarding the behaviour of the other in respect of signals. It is enough at this stage to say that there must be a *clear* understanding between the driver and conductor about the use and meaning of signals. Some drivers will sound the horn to attract the conductor's attention when he is upstairs and too many passengers are boarding. Helping to 'persuade' passengers to leave the bus when it is over-full is done by some drivers, but again expectations and practices vary considerably.[3] Other ways in which a driver can help his conductor are: helping to count the day's takings before the conductor pays in and collecting the conductor's equipment box if he signs on first.

A driver and conductor are then very much dependent on each other. Each can ease or aggravate the task of the other. To attain the twin goals of running to time and with safety, the two must co-operate. It is also vital that there should be clear *understanding* between them about the expectation that each has of the performance of the other: there is little room for ambiguity. Finally, in the event of an accident, it is important that both report a similar version of the event.[4]

Relations between bus crews and inspectors are covered fully below.[5] Here it is only necessary to give a brief description of the

[1] This problem is most acute with the R.M. type vehicle (sixty-four seats) and the R.M.L. type vehicle (seventy-two seats). The latter would appear to have reached, if not passed, the optimum capacity for one conductor to conduct efficiently with conventional methods of fare collection and ticket issuing.

[2] Central Buses, *Rule Book*.

[3] The aim here is to outline the major areas of possible co-operation and conflict. Actual practices are covered more fully below, in Chapter 5.

[4] This can be something of a sanction, see Chapter 5.   [5] See Chapter 6.

inspectors' duties. These are of two types: 'revenue' and 'point'.

The task of the inspector on revenue duty is to deter fraudulent travel and to ensure that conductors issue the correct tickets for the type of passenger and the journey. The major part of this task is the inspection of passengers' tickets. The conductor is then far more likely than the driver to come into contact—and possibly conflict—with the inspector on revenue duty.

Inspectors on point duty supervise the operation of bus services. For this purpose they are located at points on the road. Major parts of this task are checking that buses run to time and with the prescribed headway, 'turning' buses short of their destinations to cover gaps in the service, supervising the loading of vehicles at busy points, and assisting crews with 'difficult' passengers. The point inspector interacts, then, with both driver and conductor, but given the importance of 'time', he is more likely to be in contact with the driver than the conductor.

In the analysis of the railway departments it was both possible and useful to construct ideal type 'traditional' railwaymen and platelayers, but this was not possible for busmen. One key difference was that managers and supervisors in the railway departments who were important sources of information mostly had long service, which began in the inter-war years. By contrast, a number of bus managers and supervisors, including some fairly senior managers, had joined post-war. There is a folklore on the 'good types' who worked the buses before the Second World War, but it was not possible to establish with any precision the characteristics of the 'old busman'. Possibly there never was an expectation that busmen should conform so closely to a type, such as in the railway departments. The traditional old busman was a bus*man*. He was thought to be of a 'high standard' in skill, physical fitness, and 'character'. Certainly there was a widespread belief that 'standards' had fallen, but it was not possible to deduce what they had fallen *from*.

THE INTRODUCTION OF COMMONWEALTH IMMIGRANTS TO CENTRAL BUSES

The background to the employment of coloured immigrant staff in Central Buses was the persistent staff shortage which had prevailed since 1952.[1] Although women conductors were employed from the

---

[1] See the *Report of the Committee of Inquiry to Review the Pay and Conditions of Employment of the Drivers and Conductors of the London Transport Board's Road Services* (the 'Phelps Brown' report) (London, H.M.S.O., 1964).

early days of the Second World War this was seen as a temporary expedient for the 'duration of the emergency'; ultimately, the Department would return to its pre-war situation of an all-male operating staff. Some of the women conductors were discharged in the early post-war years, but it soon became apparent that it was not possible to maintain an all-male staff at the existing wages and conditions and the women conductors who had been discharged were invited to return in 1949.

Staff shortages have of course been a feature of several of the service industries in the post-war period, particularly in those areas where a high level of employment has been maintained. In Central Buses, a major cause of this shortage has been a high wastage rate of existing staff.[1] In terms of *relative* wage rates, the busman's job is less attractive than it was before the War;[2] with a high level of employment, job security is likely to be a less salient consideration. That the task is both more difficult and less satisfying than it was in pre-war times is a tenable hypothesis.

One institutional factor of some importance to the reactions of native busmen to the employment of coloured immigrants and particularly recruitment overseas needs to be explained. Wages and conditions of service are negotiated with the Transport and General Workers' Union and apply only to London Transport's busmen. Thus the argument that in a period of staff shortage the tapping of an additional source of labour weakens the bargaining power of the employees has more *immediate* relevance than in situations where bargaining is industry-wide. Moreover, the situation is different from that of the railway departments, where wages and conditions tend to follow the pattern set by British Railways, although they are negotiated separately. I do not necessarily subscribe to this argument: it is

[1] *Report of the Committee of Inquiry . . .*, p. 13.

[2] In the period 1906–60, the relative wage rate for London bus (and tram) drivers fell from first to ninth position in a ranking of the rates for fourteen semi-skilled occupations (Registrar General's occupational class 6). In the same ranking, the rates for London bus (and tram) conductors fell from eight to fourteenth position. Part of the fall in the London busmen's relative wage position took place in the years 1906–24, but in the following ten years their rates increased more than average for the occupational class. The years 1935–55 showed the major fall in the relative position of the rates for both drivers and conductors. Over the whole period 1906–60, the difference between the driver's and conductor's rates has decreased: in 1906, the conductor's rate was 67 per cent of that of the driver; by 1935 it had risen to 72 per cent, by 1955 to 84 per cent; and by 1960 the conductor's rate was 89 per cent of that of the driver. See Guy Routh, *Occupation and Pay in Great Britain, 1906–60* (Cambridge, Cambridge University Press, 1965), pp. 92–4.

not self evident that the employment of immigrants has significantly alleviated the staff shortage; the absence of immigrant recruits would not necessarily have improved the pay and conditions of the then existing staff—more rapid technical innovation or a more drastic reduction of services are credible alternatives.[1]

It was not possible to establish precisely when the first coloured immigrant staff were recruited for Central Buses. There is no evidence that coloured staff were employed in the *Department* before 1952–3, but it is possible that some were.[2] The first written evidence dated from late in 1954 and referred to two coloured conductors recruited 'during the past year'.[3] It is not clear if the two coloured conductors referred to were immigrants: there was some suggestion that they were British-born, possibly of mixed parentage.

The first time that the employment of coloured immigrant staff in the Department became an issue was in 1954, when two other coloured conductors were recruited and sent to the Southside garage.[4] The Central Bus Committee[5] of the T.G.W.U. 'did not object in principle to these appointments' but was concerned lest there had been a change of policy by London Transport without consultation. This was after the Birmingham Corporation Transport Department had taken on what was described as a 'large group' of coloured staff. The Central Bus Committee reported that:

Some of the staff were suspicious that the [London Transport] Executive were endeavouring to recruit coloured men in large numbers in order to undermine the staff case for the wage increase. Men recruited from

---

[1] This is further discussed in Chapter 17. See also E. J. Mishan and L. Needleman, 'Immigration: Long-Run Economic Effects', *Lloyds Bank Review* (No. 87, January 1968).

[2] One source indicated that the first coloured recruit joined Central Buses in 1951. See also Chapter 7 on the employment of coloured staff in the Railway Operating Department since before the Second World War. As long ago as 1908 a Jamaican bus driver was employed by the London General Omnibus Company. See John Brown, *The Un-Melting Pot* (London, Macmillan, 1970), pp. 23–4.

[3] Minutes of a meeting between the Department of the Operating Manager (Central Road Services) and the Central Bus Committee (T.G.W.U.), 10 November 1954, Minute 131/11/54. Source: L.T.B.

[4] The names given here for the garages, depots, and stations where the detailed studies were made are fictitious.

[5] The Central Bus Committee, consisting of elected 'lay' members and appointed permanent officials, is the negotiating body for staff in Central Buses. It enjoys a somewhat privileged position in the T.G.W.U. in that it has direct access to the Union's Executive Committee, bypassing the Passenger Transport Trade Group in the Union's federal structure. See Clegg.

countries with low living standards would be more willing to accept low standards here. There had been rumours that there were already two hundred coloured men at the training centre.[1]

According to a London Transport spokesman, the rumour was ill-founded: there were no coloured men at the training centre.

He also said that:

The governing principles regarding the recruitment of operating staff were that they should be suitable in all respects for the job and that preference should be given to British nationals. During the past few months there had been a considerable influx of Jamaican immigrants and large numbers applied for jobs in London Transport, most of them as labourers. Of those who wanted operating jobs the number suitable was extremely small; a few had been engaged as stationmen. The Jamaican Welfare Officer responsible for helping them to find work in England had been told some months ago that London Transport was willing to consider Jamaicans for any job for which they were potentially suitable.[2]

It was not envisaged that many would be engaged—given the 'quality of applicants'. A figure of 'about two a week' was mentioned. London Transport agreed to notify the trade union Group Secretary of the recruitment of any further coloured staff, and the garages to which it proposed to allocate them. It further expressed its willingness to discuss with the Committee any problems arising from the employment of coloured staff.[3]

This was the beginning of the employment of coloured immigrants by the Department. The sentiments expressed by the Union's spokesman were, as I remember, common enough both at that time and since: no objection in principle to the engagement of coloured staff, concern lest their employment should in any way jeopardize the wages and conditions of existing staff. As an official trade union reaction to the recruitment of coloured immigrants, this perhaps inevitably reveals an 'immigration' perspective. How far this represented the views of the majority of busmen in service then cannot be established, but our interview data indicate that considerations of colour, and thus of 'race', were not unimportant.[4] This is one example of trade union spokesmen 'playing down' the racial views of their white membership with a view to minimizing antagonism.

[1] Minute 131/11/54.
[2] Minute 131/11/54. It is not clear from the minute how the phrase 'British nationals' was intended to be interpreted.
[3] Ibid.   [4] See below, Chapter 5.

When the two coloured conductors referred to appeared at South-side garage, the then garage representative advocated 'bringing the buses in', that is, taking strike action.[1] He was however persuaded not to do so and a delegation from the garage visited the Union's regional headquarters. The viewpoint expressed by the garage representative was similar to that of the Union's spokesman at the meeting referred to above: there was no objection on grounds of colour; there was concern to protect wages and conditions and to prevent 'exploitation'. In the event, no action was taken, apart from the meeting with management already described.

Apart from the Southside episode, there was apparently one other threat of strike action over the *introduction* of coloured staff to the garages; and the coloured workers involved were moved to another garage.[2] The general situation appears to have been that the early immigrants made little impact and were often regarded as something of a 'novelty'. According to some informants, there was less controversy over the introduction of coloured staff than there had been over the employment of women conductors.[3] Managers, supervisors, full-time and part-time Union officials were all but unanimous in assessing the early coloured staff as 'very good'. This referred both to their performance as conductors (the earliest coloured operating staff in Central Buses were all conductors) and to their personal qualities. Numerous coloured 'characters' were cited in discussions on this topic; they were commonly described as 'real gentlemen'.[4]

There is little doubt that London Transport derived some benefit from the discriminatory practices of other employers. Coloured immigrants who in other circumstances would not have sought work as bus conductors found their way into the organization. This was

[1] The 'garage representative' represents the union membership in garage discussions. Union branches are based on garages: one branch for each garage. The offices of garage representative and branch secretary are often held by the same person. The garage representative is also the conference delegate, representing the branch at meetings concerned with the whole Central Bus membership.

[2] Further controversy in 1961 arose over L.T.B.'s employment of coloured immigrants and again in 1963 over the recruitment of staff in Malta. See below.

[3] The presence of women conductors in the Department is still controversial, see Chapter 5.

[4] The phrase 'real gentlemen' was a recurring one in interviews with staff at all levels. It was used principally in relation to West Indians, but some individual Africans and Indians were also so described—in the singular. It referred in the main to a type of courteous behaviour that is perhaps slightly 'Old World' in the British context.

beneficial for the development of smooth relations between white native and coloured immigrant staff: the early coloured recruits were 'good ambassadors' for their countries and for their country-men who had yet to join London Transport. Some of those early recruits have since moved on to other occupations, but many have stayed on.

Those early ones were better equipped for the job. Most have since gone—this job was a stop-gap. [U.K. Driver.]

The suggestion in the quotation that the early recruits were 'better' than later arrivals was echoed by many. Virtually all our informants considered the early coloured recruits to be 'very good', but felt that 'standards' had since fallen. Hostility between white and coloured staff was reported by many to be minimal in the early days; but as the numbers of immigrants began to build up, there has been in-creasing evidence of hostility.

In April 1961, busmen at one South London garage passed, by a majority of thirty-seven to thirty-five, a resolution calling for re-strictions on immigration and the recruitment of immigrant busmen, but this was reversed in the following June.[1] Meanwhile, in May of that year, a London busmen's delegate conference had passed with a majority of two a resolution 'opposing the influx of immigrants into this country and their employment in London Transport'. The T.G.W.U. declared this resolution invalid as it conflicted with pre-vious national decisions. In the following month, the same body passed, by sixty-five votes to fourteen with two abstentions, a reso-lution opposing racial discrimination.[2]

The Board's policy of *recruiting* overseas again became an issue in 1963. In September of that year, the Central Bus Committee passed a resolution that staff would not work with any *more* immigrant labour until pay and conditions were improved. This resolution was sent to the Union's Executive Council, which expressed the view that the resolution could be misunderstood, and it was con-sequently withdrawn.

The Executive Council, however, supported the [Central Bus] Committee in their criticism of London Transport for their refusal to provide satisfactory pay rates and to improve the working conditions for their

[1] Patterson, *Immigrants in Industry*, pp. 96–7.
[2] Patterson, *Dark Strangers*, p. 156; and Bob Hepple, *Race, Jobs and the Law in Britain* (London, Allen Lane, 1968), p. 213.

operating staff in order to avoid the necessity for recruiting labour from areas of acute economic depression.[1]

This resolution related specifically to an attempt to recruit drivers in Malta. At the request of the Malta Government, the Board had sent a recruitment team to the island. The visit was not an unqualified success: thirteen drivers were recruited, nine of them travelled to England, but four quickly returned and only five completed their training.

In these early years, management attempted to spread the immigrants over a number of garages to prevent concentration. In practice, though, the relative numbers of coloured staff varied quite widely. From time to time, usually at the request of garage managers, there were restrictions on the recruitment of coloured busmen for some garages. Given the prevailing staff shortage, it was usually possible to place recruits at other garages. Such restrictions were occasioned by local managers' perceptions of the situation at their garages: specifically, as 'potentially dangerous' from the point of view of natives' reactions.

One final item remains to be added to this Department-wide chronicle of events concerning the early years of the employment of coloured immigrant workers. It was perhaps the most important and provided a turning-point: the long drawn out London bus strike of 1958. We have seen the importance of the fear that the introduction of 'outsiders' might jeopardize the wages and conditions of existing staff. Historically, this has been a common reaction to the arrival of any outsiders in numbers, be they from the West Indies or West Hartlepools. This is in part a fear that outsiders will weaken the market power of the indigenous workforce by relieving a staff shortage, that outsiders are accustomed to and will accept 'lower standards', that their loyalty could not be relied on in times of organized industrial conflict. All three aspects had a place in the reaction of white native staff to the recruitment of coloured staff. The last mentioned aspect of this fear was decisively removed in Central Buses by the action of the coloured staff in supporting the Union, to a man, in the 1958 bus strike.[2]

They stuck by the Union in the big strike, although no one expected them to. It was O.K. after that. [U.K. Woman Conductor.]

[1] Notes of a meeting between representatives of the L.T.B. and representatives of the T.G.W.U., 12 December 1963.

[2] The loyalty of coloured staff during strikes and overtime bans was also a positive factor in their acceptance in the Railway Operating Department; see Chapter 8.

THE CHOICE OF GARAGES FOR THE DETAILED STUDIES

In our original design we proposed to make detailed studies at two garages, preceded by a small pilot study. At the suggestion of the Central Bus Committee, we decided to make detailed studies at three garages, one in each of the three operating divisions. (The Central Division functioned only for traffic purposes at that time.) It proved convenient to conduct the pilot study at a fourth garage which subsequently became one of those in the Central Division when it acquired garage management functions.

The proportions of staff in each of the seventy-odd garages who were coloured varied widely: from zero to 41 per cent. The totals for Central Buses are shown in Table 4.1.

TABLE 4.1
*Drivers and Conductors in Central Buses, in Percentages.**

	Drivers	Conductors	Women Conductors	Total Conductors	Total
White native	91	70	87	75	83
Coloured immigrant	9	30	13	25	17
(Number)	(13,311)	(9,520)	(4,077)	(13,597)	(26,908)

* As at September 1966. Source: Central Buses, L.T.B. These figures were apparently based on a 'census count' and are liable to a small margin of error. We saw in Chapter 1 that descriptions given for sampling purposes were not always accurate.

As the proportions of staff who were coloured varied widely between the garages, we decided to select three where coloured immigrants comprised roughly 10 per cent, 20 per cent, and 30 per cent of the total staff at the garage. This selection was not atypical of the majority of garages where coloured immigrant staff were employed in any numbers.

Our management and union contacts all agreed that it was not possible to find a 'typical' garage: each, we were told, had characteristics peculiar to itself. Any differences were perhaps overstressed, but we did not want to make a study at a garage where an important atypical factor would affect the validity of the research results. We therefore excluded one or two garages where immigrants of Asian origin were over-represented in the coloured staff. Three garages were eventually selected; in this selection we consulted both management and union representatives, but the choice was ours in terms of the selection criteria outlined. The three garages are described below.

Central garage (used for the pilot study) is located in an older working-class area of inner London. Its buildings are old, as are most of the houses in the narrow streets that surround it. Central has always been a bus garage; it was not a tram or trolley depot. It has a reputation for 'left-wing militancy', and it has provided some active leaders of London's busmen. Whilst its reputation for militancy lingers, Central is now no more militant than a number of other garages, and possibly less so than some. The first coloured immigrants arrived at Central in the early days of immigrant recruitment and some of them are still at the garage. There is little doubt that the left-wing political commitment of the leaders of Central's busmen was one factor making for acceptance of the newcomers.[1]

Central had a staff of 417 drivers and conductors, and was then in the middle of the size range. Its coloured immigrant population (23 per cent of the total) again put it near the middle of those garages with any number of coloured staff. With a staff 13 per cent below its establishment, Central was again not atypical at that time.

Built as part of the South London tram conversion of the early fifties, Southside, is modern.[2] It is located in a district adjacent to an area of considerable immigrant—predominantly West Indian—settlement. Originally staffed by men transferred from both tram and bus depots, Southside had a relatively small staff establishment; it has, however, grown. A nearby bus garage, formerly a tram depot, was closed in the late fifties and the majority of its staff transferred to Southside.

Southside was regarded by management as a 'difficult' garage for a number of reasons, the most important being that it lacked a 'tradition'. It was a relatively 'young' garage and lacked a nucleus of long service Southside men. It was staffed by men—many not busmen—who possibly resented the transfer and, for some, the changeover

---

[1] Left-wing political views were not always associated with a lack of hostility towards coloured staff: we met one or two self-styled left-wingers in other departments who expressed very hostile views.

[2] For a report of a study of the South London tram conversion, see J. H. Smith, 'Social Aspects of Industrial Change', *Occupational Psychology* (Vol. 27, No. 2, April 1953).

from trams. They came from several garages and depots and were thus not one cohesive group. A further complicating factor was the transfer of staff when the nearby garage was closed: many resented the transfer and, as we found, this resentment still lingers. Before there had been time for a 'garage tradition' to be established, the coloured immigrant staff had arrived in numbers, Southside being one of the first garages to receive such staff. Southside appears to have had a relatively high turnover of chief depot inspectors.[1] It has a reputation for a high number of public complaints, a relatively high accident rate, and a lot of late running. We were not able to establish whether this part of its reputation was accurate. If it was, it may, of course, be a factor of the routes served rather than any other variable.

Some managers thought Southside 'too big': given present levels of staff turnover, it is not possible for the garage manager to know all his staff and he tends to see them only when they are involved in alleged breaches of discipline. Moreover, it is not possible for busmen to know all the other busmen; several of those interviewed shared the view that Southside was 'too big'. In its establishment, though not of staff at the time of sampling, it was smaller than Eastside, but it was never suggested by managers or busmen that Eastside was too large.

Southside was then a relatively large garage. With a staff of 662, it was 2 per cent short of establishment. As coloured immigrants comprised 31 per cent of operating staff, it was selected as representative of those garages with a higher percentage of immigrants.

Eastside is situated in East London outside the traditional 'East End', but in a predominantly working-class area. Over the past few years, a considerable number of coloured immigrants, mostly West Indians, have made their homes in the district. Eastside has always been a bus garage; it has been largely rebuilt in recent years and most of its accommodation and facilities are modern.

Generally regarded as a 'good' garage by both management and union, Eastside was said to have no other distinguishing features. In the late fifties, a nearby trolley bus depot was closed and most of its staff transferred to Eastside. This movement into the garage of a group with different traditions and practices did cause some minor problems, we were told, and there was still a tendency for ex-trolley staff to say 'if we only had ... as we did in the old days'.[2]

---

[1] Now known as garage managers.

[2] The different practices of trolley crews appeared to be that drivers did not book on and off; that 'early running' was common partly due no doubt to technical

However, these difficulties do not appear to have been on the scale of those reported at Southside.

As at the other garages studied, coloured staff had been at Eastside since the early days of immigrant recruitment. They comprised 14 per cent of the total, and the garage was selected as representative of those on the lower end of the scale in terms of immigrant population. With a staff of 653, Eastside was 7 per cent short of establishment at the time of sampling.

Westside is located in a rather cosmopolitan area of West London. Many of the houses in the surrounding streets have been converted to multi-occupation. Westside, a bus garage for many years, has been largely reconstructed and the present buildings are modern. In the early 1960s a nearby trolley bus depot was closed and most of its staff transferred to Westside. The reported problems of absorbing this minority were similar to those at Eastside.

Management saw Westside as a garage that was difficult to staff adequately. The West Division has for a number of years had the highest rate of staff shortage.[1] Within the Division, Westside has had one of the most severe staff shortages, the shortage of drivers being particularly acute. Conductors have been less scarce, and Westside had had a sizeable minority of young single male conductors, often migrants—white rather than coloured—living in shared accommodation. According to management, this presents problems of late attendance, for which Westside had a reputation. However, it was not possible to test the validity of this reputation.

Nor was it possible to establish precisely when the first coloured staff arrived at Westside; however, it appears to have been early on during the period of coloured recruitment. At the time of sampling, coloured staff comprised 20 per cent of the total. The garage was therefore selected as broadly representative of those in the middle range in terms of the coloured population. With a staff of 287, Westside was 20 per cent short of its establishment and this shortage was overwhelmingly in the driver grade. It should be noted that Westside was a small garage.

---

factors; they could not 'pass'; that they carried tea cans, a practice inherited from trammen; and that trolley conductors could 'pay in' their takings part way through a shift. (This latter practice has now been introduced at bus garages.) Generally, then, trolley practices were less constrained by formal rules.

[1] It competes for staff with the West London industrial complex and with the operators and ancillary services that have grown with the development of London (Heathrow) Airport.

5

CENTRAL BUSES, II:
BUSMEN—BLACK AND WHITE

In the interviews, we asked if white native staff had 'objected' when the first coloured immigrants arrived at the garages. One problem here was that a large number of white staff who were on the buses at that time had since left. Similarly, some of those interviewed were not employed by London Transport when the first immigrants arrived. It was not possible to date *precisely* the arrival of coloured immigrants at the garages, and some of the staff interviewed could not accurately remember when *they* had joined.[1] It was not always clear if a respondent was at the garage when the first coloured staff arrived, and some could not remember if they were or not. The passage of time had obviously played havoc with memories, particularly on matters of detail: we were enquiring into events of some thirteen years or so earlier. Given this passage of time and the turnover of staff—roughly half our native samples were in the Department at the time in question—the evidence we have is less than completely reliable, but it is consistent.

Objections to the employment of coloured staff in this context were attitudes expressed in voiced disagreement or resentment, but not *necessarily* manifested in hostile behaviour towards the newcomers. We were interested both in whether or not there had been objections, and in the reasons which had been put forward for them.

There was no doubt that white native bus staff did object to the employment of coloured immigrants. Roughly one-third of the sample who were in the Department when the early immigrants arrived, stated that 'colour' was the reason for the objections,

---

[1] Length of service was later checked with London Transport records. For those with broken service, or service in another department, the date given was that of the most recent re-engagement, or of joining the Department (20 per cent of our native sample fell into this category). See above, Chapter 3.

although, significantly, it was most difficult for the interviewee to explain when pressed. For the student of race relations it is the most complex factor to understand and explain *adequately*. The following dialogue illustrates our point:

Interviewer: Was there any objection to the employment of Commonwealth immigrants here when they first came?
Interviewee: Yes.
Interviewer: When was this?
Interviewee: 1955.
Interviewer: On what grounds?
Interviewee: Colour.
Interviewer: Why was that?
Interviewee: The men didn't want to work with black men.
Interviewer: Why not?
Interviewee: I don't know—they just didn't.

The fear that wages and conditions, including the availability of overtime, would be threatened and bargaining strength impaired was the next most frequently mentioned reason for objections to coloured staff. The overtime issue is illustrated by the following quotation.

Yes, there is objection all the time. The majority of people who work the buses do it for the overtime; therefore, they are resented as a source of labour. [U.K. Conductor.]

The same conductor explained, in answer to a later question, that 'there is no animosity'. The absence of animosity, the resentment based on the 'wages and conditions' issue, and the importance of the official trade union behaviour, all came out clearly in another quotation.

Yes, but it was never outspoken. I didn't agree with it [the employment of coloured staff], but when the trade union sanctioned it we had to accept. It was on account of employment: [London Transport] should have paid satisfactory wages. [U.K. Driver.]

There is a clear implication here that had London Transport paid 'satisfactory wages' there would have been no need to employ coloured staff: a sufficient number of white staff would have been recruited and retained. Again, attitudes had been modified by time and experience: the same driver later explained that 'before long, to talk of coloured immigrants as different will be wrong'.[1]

---

[1] He was not referring to the then anticipated Race Relations Bill.

Objections that the employment of coloured staff 'lowered the tone' or 'lowered the standards' of bus work were closely related to those based on colour alone. Both can be interpreted in terms of Little's 'colour-class' hypothesis. It is, though, perhaps too simple to explain the 'lowering of standards' kind of objection *solely* in terms of 'colour-class'. A quotation from an English driver illustrates the point:

Yes [there were objections]. You had to be an angel when I was taken on. The objection was that they could be convicts or anything. Why give coloured staff a two-year contract? You can't sack him, but you can a white man.

Several points arise from this quotation from an 'old busman' with thirty years' service. The statement, 'they could be convicts or anything', clearly refers to the suitability of immigrants for public service work; the contrast with pre-war standards of recruitment is made and the immigrants are unfavourably compared with pre-war recruits. The 'two-year contract' reference arose from a mistaken belief that the Barbados-recruited staff were engaged on this basis and were therefore treated more favourably than native staff.[1] The belief that coloured staff have been treated more leniently or more favourably than native staff was a constantly recurring theme in Central Buses.

Another mistaken belief about the Barbados-recruited staff was that London Transport had paid their fares to the U.K.[2]

When coloured immigrants first came London Transport paid for their passage. If they had used this money for bonuses to entice new English staff they would have got them. They should have gone for ex-firemen, ex-policemen, ex-forces people. [U.K. Driver.]

This quotation illustrates not only the false belief about the Barbadian recruits, but also the types of Englishman considered suitable for busmen. It tells us something about the traditional status ranking

[1] Barbados-recruited staff signed an agreement with *the Barbados Government* to stay with L.T.B. one year, but were employed by L.T.B. on a similar basis to other employees. On completion of one year's service, L.T.B. paid the Barbados Government £20, which was then passed on to the Barbadian recruit. This was seen as a bonus for staying one year, which other recruits did not receive, and was therefore the object of some resentment. The practice was later abandoned and £10 per recruit was paid by L.T.B. to the Barbados Government when the recruit arrived in the U.K. This was to assist with the cost of pre-recruitment training. See Chapter 13.

[2] The Barbados Government usually made loans to the recruits for their fares. See Chapter 13.

of the occupation. The occupations mentioned all involve some measure of discipline.

The employment of coloured immigrants was then seen by some native staff as a *cause* of the 'lowering of standards', whereas others saw it merely as a symptom. There was, for example, the busman who said that the writing of racial insults on walls *proved* that the standards of *native* staff had fallen: 'the types we had years ago would not have done that'. The importance of colour in the native reactions came out clearly, but objections were not confined to this factor alone. The other main point of interest to emerge was the set of false beliefs held, particularly about the seen advantages enjoyed by the Barbados recruits.[1]

There is here some contrast between the reported reactions of the busmen which stressed colour and those made through the Union organization which dwelled on immigration aspects. Insofar as the Union was concerned with the impact of overseas recruitment on its bargaining position, the immigration aspects were dominant. On the other hand, this did not represent the total views of its membership and there were indications that to the extent that they ignored some of the voiced objections to the recruitment of coloured immigrants, the Union tried to smooth their acceptance. As in many other situations where coloured immigrants have been recruited by industry, there was a conflict between the principles of equality and brotherhood, on the one hand, and representation of the views of the predominant white native membership, on the other. The result, perhaps inevitably, was an uneasy compromise.

Given that there were these objections to the recruitment of coloured immigrants, how were they manifested in hostile behaviour? Here we take a step forward in that we can draw on the evidence of the immigrant as well as the native samples.

HOSTILITY BETWEEN WHITE AND COLOURED STAFF
The answers to two questions throw light on this. First we asked, 'has there been any hostility in this garage towards the Commonwealth immigrants?'; and second, 'is there any hostility now?' Some who answered 'no' or 'don't know' then qualified the answer in a way which indicated that they thought there was or had been hostility.[2] Table 5.1 summarizes the answers given.

[1] The bonus paid by the Barbados Government was of course a *real* advantage.

[2] A small number of immigrants stated that they had not personally experienced hostility but had 'heard' of it from others. They then recounted the experiences of 'a friend' in a way that suggested that the 'friend' was in reality the speaker.

TABLE 5.1
Native Busmen's Hostility Towards the Commonwealth Immigrants, in Percentages.

Questions and answers	Initial Answers		Including Qualified Answers	
	Native	Immigrant	Native	Immigrant
Hostility in the past?				
Yes	39	38	57	56
No	57	53	43	44
Don't know	4	9	—	—
Hostility at present?				
Yes	36	35	50	53
No	63	55	50	47
Don't know	1	10	—	—
(Sample)	(70)	(78)	(70)	(78)

Roughly one-half of each sample indicated that there had been hostility towards the immigrants in the past and the numbers who said there was still hostility were not very different. The majority of both white and coloured who indicated that there was hostility towards the coloured busmen also expressed the view that it was, and had been, confined to the 'odd one or two'; that, in other words, *overt* hostility was not shown by the majority of the native busmen. Both groups were also in broad agreement that hostility was most likely to be confined to what was described as 'bad feeling', to immigrants being pointedly ignored or to oral insults or the writing of racial *graffiti* in lavatories and the like.[1] Open face-to-face conflict was said to be rare.

The road emerged as by far the most important source of overt conflict and of much of the bad feeling that was evident. Compared with the road, other causes of native resentment were relatively unimportant. These centred on the perceived behaviour of coloured busmen in games rooms and canteens, and on the belief that coloured staff were treated more leniently in disciplinary affairs and were

[1] This is perhaps an appropriate point to record a reported example of *graffiti* at a garage not included in the study. Written on a lavatory wall were the words 'Blacks go home', to which a day or so later was added the reply, 'you're wasting your time, man, we're here to stay'.

unduly sensitive or had a 'chip on the shoulder'. On the other hand, we shall see that the coloured busmen themselves were reluctant to discuss the hostile behaviour they had encountered, that some were almost apologetic about it, and that most clearly took care to avoid 'trouble'.

The predominant view on the extent of hostility towards the immigrants can be illustrated by quotations:

There are a few awkward ones, but we mostly get on pretty good. It's best to miss the awkward ones—the older ones, those who've put in twenty years and all that . . . the younger ones are better. [West Indian Driver.]

They don't want anything to do with you . . . [but] there is only [hostility] between a few. I talk to some and ignore others because they ignore me. Some are gentlemen. [U.K. Driver.]

It will be noted that in these quotations there was a reluctance to generalize about the other group. The ease of generalization and the importance of the behaviour of peer group members emerges in the next quotation:

As a group on either side there is no bad feeling. But you get individuals who talk about 'niggers' and the man next to him agrees—without thinking about it. [U.K. Conductor.]

These quotations illustrate the perceptions of both the immigrants and the natives of the extent of hostility. They tell us little, though, about the sources of conflict. Here the road was overwhelmingly important, and again it is useful to illustrate from the interview material:

You get the trouble on the road more than in the garage: complaints of fiddling and that. [West Indian Driver.]

If one of us is behind [on the road] he is ignored. If one of them is behind they help him out. [Pakistani Conductor.]

The next two quotations illustrate a more general lack of co-operation between crews, but here again competition and conflict were sharpened by the colour differences:

The 602 has a bad name for coloured staff—from Cairnfield[1] to Eastside. Some whites are also bad: they leave the points early, run early . . .

---

[1] The route numbers and place names given in these examples are fictitious.

Cairnfield never help out Eastside buses.[1] I help a crew the first day: if he doesn't pass me soon—next day I stay behind. The coloured staff are as bad as the whites. [U.K. Driver.]

There are only one or two rows—arising from the road. But the garage would be happy if they went—it is said behind their backs. [U.K. Driver.]

The road, then, is the most important area of conflict. We have a situation where the potential for conflict is built into the organization of work, irrespective of the origins or other characteristics of the busmen concerned. In this sense, differences of race or origin inject into the situation an additional irritant and, equally important, these differences provide for easy identification. This does not mean that there would be no conflict between white native and coloured immigrant busmen if there was no potential for conflict in the organization of work. It does mean that racial differences become salient in a situation with a conflict potential and at the same time this conflict serves to exacerbate antipathy between white and coloured. There appeared to be little doubt that there was widespread competition between crews to reduce their work-load, though how widespread I cannot say. Certainly, many busmen thought that fiddling was very common, and that is perhaps more important since it shaped their own behaviour and their attitudes. In that sense, *beliefs* about fiddling took on a life of their own.[2]

So far we have discussed conflict *between* crews. Not uncommon in the early years of immigrant employment were problems arising when white and coloured were paired. In this first example a coloured conductor was ignored by the white drivers with whom he worked:

There were two drivers at Mostyn who were so hostile they never spoke to me when I was working with them.

The wish of the vast majority of the immigrants to *avoid* trouble, often at some cost to pride and self-esteem, is another recurring theme in this study. One aspect is illustrated by the following quotation:

Only on one occasion [have I met hostility.] I had a K.B.W.[3] conductor; it was boring for me. I overheard a conversation: he didn't want to work

[1] It is common for one route to be worked by two or more garages. Our evidence suggests that a crew is less likely to help out a crew from another garage than one from its own garage. There is not necessarily much *conflict* between crews from different garages, but rather a certain rivalry.

[2] Fiddling is discussed at greater length in Chapter 4.

[3] 'Keep Britain White.'

with me, he was one of Mosley's men. I said I wouldn't work with him on rest days.[1] It was better for us to stay apart. [West Indian Driver.]

I have argued that co-operation between driver and conductor is important to smooth the work of both parties. There are two aspects of this: 'normal' co-operation when in service and co-operation in an emergency, for example, an accident. This second aspect is illustrated by an incident recalled by a West Indian, which shows too that there are sanctions to *encourage* co-operation:

I was working with a driver on the 603. He never spoke when he came to the bus and stopped in the cab at the terminus. He was a pig. I wondered what he would expect of me in an accident: we usually try to shield each other. One day he had to brake hard on a wet road and hit someone. When we got back to the garage *I didn't want to know*. [West Indian Driver and ex-Conductor.]

Other sources of irritation and conflict were far less important than the road, but by no means insignificant: for example, the games rooms. Native staff complained that the coloured staff 'monopolized' the games facilities, brought in outsiders, gambled heavily,[2] and left the rooms untidy. These complaints were most common at Southside. Insofar as we were able to observe, the games facilities were by no means monopolized by the coloured staff. On the other hand, it may well be that they used the facilities *proportionately* more: many were housed in very poor and overcrowded accommodation; they were in the younger age groups; and West Indians are very gregarious.

Another minor source of irritation centred round the canteen. Again Southside was the garage most prone to such complaints. Some white busmen objected to coloured canteen staff; some mentioned that there tended to be 'segregation' in the canteen. The canteen staff issue, which appeared to upset a small minority of white staff, can best be illustrated by the following comment:

Yes [there is hostility] among a few: they will not mix [with coloured staff] or drink tea made by the coloured girls in the canteen. They bring their own food and make their own tea. About $2\frac{1}{2}$ per cent [of white staff.] [U.K. Woman Conductor.]

On the question of 'segregation':

[1] The conductor referred to was not his regular conductor.

[2] One variation in gambling practices was that in Central Buses it was almost always with cards, in the Railway Operating Department dominoes was the preferred game. In both cases this was true of both white and coloured staff.

There tends to be segregation in the canteen: between coloured and white crews. The coloureds make no effort to overcome this: they tend to prefer to sit with their coloured friends. [U.K. Driver.]

On the other hand, some of the white native staff said that they prefer to sit with their fellow-countrymen and did so, usually with some regard for the feelings of their coloured driver or conductor. Asked if they sat at the same table as their driver or conductor when they took their tea or meal breaks, just over half of both samples said 'yes'. Most of the remainder stated that one or both members of the crew went home or out of the garage for meal breaks, but if they were both in the garage they would sit together. This was one question where we sometimes suspected that the answers given were less than completely frank. We concluded that the general practice was for crew partners to sit together for tea breaks taken on the road or short breaks in the canteen. For longer breaks it was common practice for a mixed white and coloured crew to separate.

Yes [we sit together] but there is an urge for coloureds to contact other coloureds and I would prefer to converse with whites. We don't split at first but if there is a long break it is easy: there is no tension and it doesn't seem to hurt. Splitting is the general pattern. For tea breaks on the road— a few minutes—we sit together. I have no aversion to this.

Insofar as we were able to observe behaviour in the garage canteens it confirmed this comment.

One other important source of resentment was a suspicion that the immigrants 'got away with more', that they were treated more leniently than the native staff in disciplinary matters. For *minor* offences in the *early* period of immigrant recruitment, this was probably so. For instance, small errors in conductors' cash totals: some chief depot inspectors found it difficult to discipline a recently arrived immigrant for this type of offence when he, or she, was newly acquainted with the British coinage system. This was, however, a passing phase and was confined to minor offences: there was no evidence that the newcomers were treated more leniently than the native staff for other offences.

Another point of some importance emerged from asking native busmen about hostility towards the immigrants. Some claimed that hostility came only from the coloured immigrants, or that they were unduly sensitive: 'they think everyone is against them', 'they have a terrible chip on the shoulder'. The last allegation is a common one,

4

directed particularly against West Indians; it is well known to most researchers in race relations. We found that in the interview situation immigrants were usually reluctant to talk of their unpleasant *personal* experiences in Britain. It often took considerable coaxing and probing to obtain details of an 'incident'. Nor were we satisfied that we always succeeded. Indians and Pakistanis in particular were very reluctant to discuss the hostility they had encountered and to a somewhat lesser extent the same is true of the West Indians and other immigrants. They *wanted* to be accepted and a considerable loss of self-esteem was involved both in not being accepted and in revealing this to someone else, particularly a white person. I recall an interview with a Pakistani conductor; when asked if there had been any hostility in the garage, he replied indignantly, almost crossly: *'of course not'*. Not only do the great majority of immigrants want to be accepted, but they will make considerable efforts to achieve this and particularly to avoid trouble. For example, the West Indian conductor quoted below described his relationship with his driver as 'not bad'; but, he added, they had little in common to talk about:

When I first started with him I watched him: I thought it might be difficult as he didn't want to change his conductor. I decided I had to get round him. I saw him reading the racing page so I talked to him about horses; we get on O.K. now. [West Indian Conductor.]

Numerous other examples could be cited to support this point. Moreover, most of the immigrants, particularly the West Indians, *expected* to be accepted as equals by English people: the orientation of West Indian culture is towards the 'mother country'. They were surprised as well as hurt when they were not accepted as equals. Some probably did not wish to acknowledge that there was hostility directed at them and that they were not always accepted as equals by their fellow-workers and others. Some probably rationalized the hostility they had experienced.

I hear a lot about colour prejudice, but I do not know how to recognize it. If a white man insults me, I think, 'I could insult him!' If I go to a house for accommodation and he says, 'no—I won't have coloureds', I think, 'I could do the same to him!' If I get beaten up by a gang of white men on the way home, they could just as easily beat up a white man—in my country, gangs beat up people. [West Indian Driver.]

Many West Indians were tolerant, almost to the point of being apologetic, about the hostility they had encountered. A Barbadian driver exemplified this attitude:

There is not very much outraged hostility. You have to use psychology: observe unspoken things—nasty looks. Some may not know much about other countries or other skins. There is a poor class in every place: here they don't have much knowledge of other countries, especially the West Indies. They know more about Africa. They claim we are all from Jamaica.

This understanding and toleration comes out again in the next quotation about behaviour which was obviously unpleasant.

One driver I had never got out of the cab. When we got a relief or finished—he was off. I was told he was the same to everybody. You don't know *why* he is like that. [West Indian Conductor.]

It is often argued that West Indians are acutely colour conscious, and hence are liable to attribute to colour behaviour which has other causes. There was, though, little indication of a wish to use colour as a blanket explanation for every slight or set-back. The reverse was nearer the case and, as we saw above, some were almost apologetic about the hostility they had encountered. Clearly, there was a considerable area of ambiguity over the meaning of behavioural cues, and what was attributed by our native informants to a chip on the shoulder could have arisen from a misreading of such cues. These variations in the perceptions of cues and the meaning attached to them clearly spring from cultural differences. The ambiguity and lack of *reliable* cues about natives' attitudes were also very much in evidence. Immigrants often stated that they could not be sure that a person was not hostile in his attitudes, irrespective of behaviour. In the words of one West Indian busman:

I've never witnessed any hostility, but you don't know. You may see a person and talk to him good—but you never know his feelings.

One other aspect of absorption can usefully be mentioned at this point. I have argued that London Transport as a large, bureaucratic organization, was particularly suited to the absorption of minority groups. The important point is that the application of policies and rules tends to be impersonal and thus fails to distinguish between staff on grounds of race or ethnicity. This aspect of the organization was well understood by some of the coloured staff.

Yes [there has been hostility], but with London Transport they can't do much: they have to follow the rules. [West Indian Conductor.]

The evidence indicated that white native hostility towards the coloured immigrants increased as their numbers grew. There was not, though, necessarily a uni-causal connection: the early recruits were in some ways found more acceptable than those who arrived later. I argue below that the speed of build-up of the relative numbers of immigrants is more important in conditioning the native response than are the relative numbers.[1] From the point of view of smooth absorption and of minimizing native fears and hostility, the rate of build-up of the coloured immigrant bus staff was probably 'too rapid'. I concluded, though, that hostility between white and coloured staff had decreased markedly as both groups learnt more of each other. The hard core of the native staff who still *actively* resented the presence of the coloured immigrants was a small one.

There are a few who can't accept the fact that they have to settle down and work with them. [U.K. Woman Conductor.]

The majority of white staff were at least able to coexist with their coloured fellow-workers, though colour or race injected a spark that sometimes ignited in situations of competition and potential conflict. A fitting end to this section was provided by two West Indian conductors.

You might have a rough word amongst yourselves: it is not hostility, it is human nature. We are beginning to learn more about each other.

There is bad feeling—they feel you are taking away their share. I was *very* conscious of it—but not now.

RELATIONSHIPS BETWEEN DRIVERS AND CONDUCTORS
The method of pairing and allocating crews to routes was as follows: on completion of his training, the newly recruited driver or conductor was allocated to a garage. Given the staff shortage, it was usually possible to send the recruit to the garage of his choice,[2] and he would normally have done part of his training at that garage.

On arrival, the driver or conductor was allocated to the 'spare list': that is he was available for any duty to cover staff shortages caused by absences due to sickness and the like. If the staff shortage

---

[1] See Chapter 17.

[2] The Barbados-recruited staff were an exception in this respect: they were regarded as more mobile and often used to fill severe staff shortages. If, though, they requested to be allocated to a specific garage—to enable them to lodge with friends or relations, for example—they were treated similarly to other recruits. Like other busmen they could apply for transfer to another garage. See Chapter 13.

was particularly acute, he may have gone straight into service without being placed on the spare list; otherwise the length of time on
the spare list was dictated by the speed with which vacancies on the
duty rota occurred.

Drivers and conductors may apply to change their partners or
their route,[1] and a driver and conductor may ask to be paired.
Many apply for a change of route rather than a change of partners,
but because they cannot coexist with their driver or conductor.
Such requests are dealt with in order of seniority of application.

TABLE 5.2
Crew Partners of Samples, in Percentages.

| Crew partner | Native Sample | | Immigrant Sample | |
	Male	Female	Male	Female
U.K./Irish male	58	91	31	73
U.K./Irish female	14	—	7	—
West Indian male	17	—	33	18
West Indian female	2	—	9	—
Indian/Pakistani male	3	—	7	—
Indian/Pakistani female	—	—	1	—
Other/D.K. immigrant male	3	—	1	—
On spare list	3	9	9	9
(Sample)	(59)	(11)	(67)	(11)

The table shows that roughly three-quarters of the white natives
in the samples were paired with others of similar origins. Somewhat more than half of the white drivers had white conductors;
almost all the white conductors were paired with white drivers. The
coloured staff were more evenly divided: nearly half had coloured
partners; almost as many had white partners; and several were still
on the spare list. There was some overlap within and across the
samples: in a few cases both members of a crew were interviewed.
All the white women conductors in service were paired with white
drivers, but the sample was too small for us to draw much significance from this. On the other hand, 15 per cent of the coloured

[1] In most garages there is a 'popularity ranking' of routes, though busmen's
preferences are not uniform. A route is liked or disliked for a number of reasons: its
proportions of very early or very late ('dead early' or 'dead late') duties; its length;
characteristics of the area served; the passenger load; type of vehicle used; the
nearness of the 'relief point' to the busman's home.

drivers in service had white women conductors. Three-quarters of the coloured drivers in service were paired with coloured conductors. In the garages studied there was a predominance of white conductors and this pairing did not therefore result solely from chance.[1]

As we have noted, busmen's preferences regarding their crew partner are met if possible. One-third of the white native sample were members of crews in which one or both had requested pairing, compared with one-sixth of the coloured staff. A white busman's preference sometimes reflected a wish to be paired with another white, rather than any seen merit of the individual selected. In the words of an English woman conductor:

My driver knew I was going spare [on the spare list] and was white so he put in for me.

Coloured busmen on the other hand by no means always wished to have a coloured partner. Some coloured drivers in particular preferred a white conductor: they reasoned that all-white or mixed crews were treated more leniently by point inspectors than were all-coloured crews.

Exploring the pattern of relationships between drivers and conductors, we asked: 'How do you get on together?'

TABLE 5.3
Busmen's Relationships with Crew Partner, in Percentages.

Evaluation	Native	Immigrant
Very well	63 ⎫ 77	41 ⎫ 65
Well	14 ⎰	24 ⎰
Fair	17	18
Poor	1	4
Bad	—	4
On spare list	4	9
(Sample)	(70)	(78)

[1] When the figures were broken down by garage, Westside stood out as the garage with appreciably less pairing across racial boundaries than at the other garages. Pairing practices have varied between garage managers: some preferred to pair coloured with coloured, white with white, but this practice appeared to be decreasing. Some tried to avoid placing coloured staff with a white known to be extremely hostile; a white woman conductor's preference for a white driver was sometimes met. Any combination is possible, excluding a woman driver.

In their own estimation, over-all the immigrant busmen did not get on with their partners so well as did the natives, but the difference between the two groups was small. When we looked closely at the few who evaluated the relationship as poor or bad, we found that the partner complained of by the immigrants was in most cases another immigrant, but of different origins: for example, a West Indian driver with a Pakistani conductor. In the two cases of poor relationships between partners of similar origins—specifically, one native and one West Indian—both drivers had women conductors. Whilst the numbers in these categories are very small, the data suggest that sex differences in a crew can be as important as those of race or ethnicity. The reported periods of time our samples had worked together are shown in Table 5.4.

TABLE 5.4
Time Worked with Crew Partner, in Percentages.

	Native	Immigrant
On spare list	4	9
Under 6 months	27	37
6–12 months	23	22
1–2 years	23	23
3–4 years	11	8
5 or more years	11	1
(Sample)	(70)	(78)

The table shows that over-all the immigrants had been with their partners for a somewhat shorter time than had the natives, but apart from those in the 'five or more years' group, there was very little difference between the two samples. Some busmen 'change partners' until they find one who is compatible. The longer service men are more likely to have found a compatible partner and the difference here probably reflects the different length of service patterns.

In order to compare (a) the expectations that both groups had of their crew partner's behaviour and (b) their perceptions of their own roles, we asked both groups how the driver could 'help' his conductor with his work and vice versa. The answers to these questions provide us with one index of the extent to which the immigrants had acquired the values and norms of the natives. Table 5.5 summarizes the answers to the first of these two questions.[1]

TABLE 5.5
How a Driver Can Help his Conductor, in Percentages.★

	Native	Immigrant
Give a smooth ride	49	22
Check that platform is clear before starting	26	38
Run to time	27	35
Drive slower when there are many short-riding passengers	10	9
Work as a team	9	9
Wait for passengers	9	5
Driver cannot help conductor	7	3
Other answer	21	14
(Sample)	(70)	(78)

★ More than one answer was recorded and the percentage totals may therefore exceed 100.

Table 5.5 shows that while there were some differences between the two groups, the pattern of answers followed a fairly similar drift.

Giving a 'smooth ride', that is, avoiding harsh acceleration or deceleration, violent swerving, cornering, or braking, is of some importance to the conductor. It was not clear why the immigrants were less concerned about this, but we will see that 'rough' handling of buses was one of the most frequent criticisms made of immigrant drivers.[2]

Using the nearside rear-view mirror, to check that the platform is clear of passengers when the conductor gives the starting signal from a point other than the platform, furthers the aim of safe running, but it is not sanctioned by the *Rule Book*.[3] Practices and expectations vary considerably here: some drivers will only move when

[1] As many busmen, mostly drivers, had experience of the roles of both driver and conductor, it was not useful to analyse this material separately by grade.
[2] See below, pp. 89–92.
[3] At compulsory stops the conductor should give the starting signal from the platform, to comply with the *Rule Book*.

the correct starting signal is given, others will start when a coin is tapped on the upper deck destination blind cover. The difference between the two samples in this respect suggests a greater perception of interdependence by the immigrants than by the natives.

Both groups—particularly the immigrants—emphasized the importance of the driver running to time. The greater concern of the coloured staff with this particular aspect of the driver's role may reflect their less smooth relationships with point inspectors; it may also indicate that a coloured crew is less likely to be helped out by a white crew if it is running late. More important, perhaps, it reflects their greater *consciousness* of the various time constraints of public transport work.

'Work as a team' emphasizes the over-all interdependence of driver and conductor and, equally important, the necessity for a clear understanding between them on what they expect of each other.

The meanings of the answers in the remaining coding categories are clear, and they were all given by relatively few. The 'other answer' category covered a wide range: helping the conductor count up the day's takings, passing stops when full, 'booking on' on time. Each response was given by very few, but the category is larger than for most other questions.

The ways in which our busmen thought the conductor could help the driver are summarized in Table 5.6. (See p. 84.)

We again found that immigrants put somewhat greater emphasis on the time factor. This quote from an English driver illustrates the importance of the conductor being 'quick on the bell':

Quick on the bell is the main thing—not drag the road.[1] Time is the thing. Some [conductors] can be awkward on this: they go slow and we are all in the cart as they pick up more.

Various aspects of behaviour relevant to passenger safety were thought to be an important part of the conductor's role by the next largest group in each sample. Under this heading were grouped 'correct signals, be reliable [in terms of safety], be safe'. This clearly emphasizes the expectation that the driver ought to be able to rely on his conductor in respect of passengers' safety. Of primary importance here is the conductor's role as opposed to that of the driver, which, as will be recalled, involved checking the platform

[1] The expression 'drag the road' was often used by busmen to describe slow running by a crew.

TABLE 5.6
How a Conductor Can Help his Driver, in Percentages.

	Native	Immigrant
Quick or slow with bell signals in order to run to time	50	62
Gives correct signals/be reliable/safe	57	38
Gives hand signals when bus turning/ when reversing	7	14
Work as a team	10	14
Conductor cannot help driver	10	1
Avoids trouble with passengers	7	4
Collects fares quickly to enable him to spend maximum time on platform	6	4
Other answer	3	8
(Sample)	(70)	(78)

* More than one answer was recorded and the percentage totals may therefore exceed 100.

with the rear-view mirror. The conductor signalling to following traffic to indicate the driver's intended action—turning right or left, or pulling into a point—and signalling to the driver when he is reversing the bus, stresses the interdependence of driver and conductor. This co-operation is sanctioned by the Central Buses *Rule Book*. A difference of note between the two groups was in those saying that the conductor *cannot* help the driver.

The patterns of answers to both these questions on co-operation between crew partners, reveal few differences. Taken together they suggest that the coloured busman was somewhat more conscious of the interdependence of the crew relationship, of both helping his partner and expecting help.[1] By contrast, the native busman tended to stress that each should perform his task adequately and be reliable. This conclusion is reinforced by the differences in the numbers saying that a busman cannot help his partner. The coloured busmen appeared to be less conscious of the importance of a smooth ride but more conscious of the time constraints.

[1] The evidence from the trainmen, though, pointed to the opposite conclusion. See Chapter 8.

MALE ATTITUDES TOWARDS WOMEN CONDUCTORS

Early in the pilot study it became apparent that the employment of women conductors was still controversial and that some drivers had a definite preference for a male conductor. We therefore asked the remaining drivers in the pilot study for their preferences and the reasons for them, and these questions were subsequently included in the questionnaire.

Two-thirds of the native drivers preferred a male conductor, nearly one-third had no preference, and one driver preferred his own woman conductor—his wife. Somewhat over half of the immigrant drivers expressed a preference for a man conductor, a quarter had no preference, a small number preferred a woman conductor, and another small group said they did not mind, so long as the conductor was white.[1]

The major consideration for the native drivers who preferred a man was that in an all-male crew the relationship between them was 'more equal'. They did not have to be careful about 'bad' language, two men had more 'in common' to talk about, the driver was not expected to carry his conductor's shopping bag or machine box. The immigrants also stressed this equality, but for them it was second in importance to their opinion of women conductors as 'lazy' and 'slow'. Some of the native drivers shared this opinion, but for them it rated second to equality. An English driver summed up this view of women conductors as lazy:

Women conductors are lazy—especially the younger ones. They want no work. They have praises for the driver who gives them an easy time by getting [his bus] in behind someone else.

Small numbers in both groups regarded male conductors as more able to control passengers. With a male conductor the driver was less likely to have to leave his cab to deal with a difficult passenger. A small number of drivers—mainly natives—preferred a male conductor on the grounds that a sex difference in a crew is disruptive. It is not unknown for a married driver to leave his wife in favour of his woman conductor. Some wives prefer their driver husbands to work with male conductors.

What of the immigrants who preferred a woman conductor?

---

[1] It is possible that more preferred a white conductor, since our information on this came incidentally from the question on their preferences for a male or female conductor.

Their reasoning was that a woman conductor was less likely to interfere in the driver's work.

You get less bother with them [women conductors]: they don't try to tell you how to drive and they don't want to get back to the garage to play snooker.

As we have noted, a small number of coloured drivers expressed a preference for a white conductor, regardless of sex.

I am not particularly bothered [about the sex of the conductor], but I prefer an English person: the inspectors are more lenient.

I prefer English—I am not bothered about the sex. They know how to handle passengers.

Given that the traditional pre-war norm of the Department was an all-male staff, the women conductors can be regarded as the first group of 'immigrants': a number of parallels can be drawn between white male attitudes to women and to coloured staff.[1] Whilst we asked drivers for their preferences regarding the sex of their *own* conductor, it was clear that the objections to women staff were far wider than this. With the London Transport policy of equal pay— though not all conditions—a woman conductor is better paid *relative* to prevailing rates in the wider labour market than is a man conductor.[2] From this condition emerged the first parallel between native male attitudes to women and to coloured immigrants: it was felt that their absence from the Department would improve bargaining power and earnings. The parallel was drawn by a number of busmen themselves. It can be illustrated by a native busman's reply to a question on hostility towards the immigrants:

If they weren't here we would get a better wage—it's the same with the clippies. I don't mind clippies, but . . .

The next parallel related to the disruptive effect in the relationships between crews on the road. It was widely believed that women

[1] In the United States (Los Angeles) similar attitudes towards the employment of women and Negroes have been found amongst urban transit workers. 'Some of the platform men stated simply that they would feel their " . . . jobs had been downgraded if women or Negroes were hired to perform them." ' Philip W. Jeffress, *The Negro in the Urban Transit Industry* (Philadelphia, Pa., University of Pennsylvania, 1970), p. 33, quoting the President's Committee on Fair Employment Practice, *Final Report* (Washington, D.C., Government Printing Office, 1947), p. 15.

[2] London Transport policy required women conductors to have a longer period of service to qualify for sick pay and pensions. See Chapter 6.

conductors expected an 'easy ride' and that some drivers were prepared to oblige by running early. This caused more than a little
resentment. Moreover, it was sometimes suggested that a point
inspector was likely to be more lenient towards a crew with a
woman conductor than an all-male crew. We have seen that colour
or ethnic differences have a disruptive effect on co-operation between
crews and the parallel is obvious.

EVALUATIONS OF THE QUALITIES REQUIRED BY THE 'GOOD' BUSMAN
Pursuing further the busman's perception of his role, we asked both
groups what makes a good driver or conductor, as appropriate.
Again, we were concerned to see how far the dominant values of
the native workforce have been acquired by the immigrants. The
question was open-ended, perhaps vague, and invited a wide
variety of responses. In the event, the responses fell into a clear
pattern and were easily coded into a number of categories: some
refer to personality characteristics, others to behaviour, and yet
others to skills. Between the two samples the similarities in the
patterns of response were more striking than the differences, as is
shown in Table 5.7.

TABLE 5.7
*The Qualities and Behaviour Required of the 'Good' Busman,
in Percentages.**

	Native	Immigrant
Patience/tolerance/good temper	74	68
Drives properly/does the job properly/ is safe	23	27
Helpful to passengers/knows the road	20	23
Alertness/concentration/judgement	19	18
Tidiness/smartness	1	15
Punctual attendance/runs to time	3	12
Avoids trouble with passengers	3	6
Other answer	19	15
(Sample)	(70)	(78)

* More than one answer was recorded and the percentage totals may therefore
exceed 100.

For both groups the oustanding quality was patience: under this
heading were included such answers as 'a good temperament',

'tolerant', 'patient', 'good tempered', and 'polite'. Drivers stressed that patience was required with other road users and, to a lesser extent, in relation to passengers who gave wrong or late signals. For conductors, patience was required for their dealings with passengers.[1] The comments of an English conductor illustrate this:

You need a good temperament—plenty of patience. It makes it a pleasant day—forget troubles.

Both samples rated other attributes or behaviour as far less important than patience. The next group of answers was concerned with doing the job properly. Typical replies here were 'drive properly', 'have a concern for safety', 'road sense', 'do the job properly', and 'follow the rules'. Some are specifically concerned with the driver's task whilst others are applicable to both driver and conductor. Clearly, safety figured either explicitly or implicitly in these replies. Again, there was broad agreement between the two groups.

A service orientation was revealed by those who spoke of being helpful to passengers. Conductors stressed this, and particularly the importance of knowing the road in order to tell passengers where to alight and to give them directions.

You need a good knowledge of the road. I get embarrassed if someone asks for somewhere and I don't know. [U.K. Conductor.]

The other area of broad agreement between the two samples centred round the qualities of alertness and concentration. Typical answers here were: 'keep your head', 'concentration', 'quick thinking', 'confidence', and 'judgement'. Drivers stressed these qualities more than conductors, but they were not absent from the image of the good conductor.

In relation to the next two attributes or behaviour of the good busman, there was less agreement between immigrant and native staff. A significant proportion of the immigrant sample mentioned that the good busman should be tidy or smart. Clearly, the immigrants were more conscious of appearance, but it is not obvious why this was so.[2]

---

[1] Relationships with passengers are analysed in greater detail below: see Chapter 6.

[2] After seeing many London busmen over a period of several years as a passenger, and meeting and seeing others as a researcher, I have concluded that by 'conventional' British standards the coloured busmen are no less 'well' dressed and no more 'untidy' than their white counterparts. I was then a little surprised to find that the 'appearance' of coloured staff was compared unfavourably with that of the white staff by a small number of managers—not garage managers—in Central Buses.

Time, in terms of punctual attendance for duties and running to time, was the other area where the two groups differed. This again probably reflects the patterns of relationships between coloured busmen and point inspectors, as well as the fact that one of the most important adjustments that immigrants, particularly West Indians, have to make is to accept the time values in relation to public transport work. They were therefore more conscious of time, as compared with the native staff.

In addition, the immigrants put more stress on avoiding trouble with passengers, but it was mentioned by so very few and little significance can be attached to this difference. On the other hand, it may be one more indication that coloured staff are more likely than their white counterparts to meet difficulties with passengers. Several other qualities or aspects of behaviour each received a few mentions and the pattern of responses from both samples was very similar: these included honesty, common sense, liking the job, and a good memory.

Over-all, there was broad agreement between the immigrants and the natives on the attributes and behaviour of the good busman. The immigrants were more conscious of time and of the importance of a good appearance than were the natives. With these differences, though, we can conclude that the dominant values of the native workforce have been acquired by the immigrants.

NATIVE BUSMEN'S EVALUATIONS OF IMMIGRANTS AS BUSMEN

Central to our understanding of immigrant-native relationships in London Transport is the thesis that the adequate performance by the

TABLE 5.8
Native Busmen's Assessments of Whether Commonwealth Immigrants Make 'Good' Busmen, in Percentages.

Evaluations	As drivers	As conductors
Yes, most do/some do, some don't/ same as Europeans	64	67
Some do, most don't	23	29
No, none do	6	4
Don't know	7	—
(Sample)	(70)	(70)

immigrants of their work roles has been a key factor encouraging their acceptance by the native workforce and by managers and supervisors. Adequate has been defined in terms of the expectations these groups have of public transport workers—in this case, drivers and conductors. To explore this we asked the native busmen, 'do Commonwealth immigrants make good conductors?' and 'do Commonwealth immigrants make good drivers?' The answers to these two questions are summarized in Table 5.8. (See p. 89.)

The table shows that the majority of native busmen refused to generalize about the performance of immigrants in the roles of driver and conductor, and this was in answer to a question which invited a generalized reply. The native conductors tended to be less critical of the immigrants in the role of both driver and conductor than were the native drivers, but the difference between the two grades was not large.

Whilst the majority of native busmen refused to generalize absolutely about their coloured workmates, they often qualified their answers with critical comments, summarized in Table 5.9.

TABLE 5.9
Native Busmen's Criticisms of Immigrant Busmen, in Percentages. *

Criticisms	As drivers	As conductors
Reckless/impatient	31	19
Lazy	9	30
Clannish/have chip on the shoulder	9	11
Slow	—	7
Other criticisms	7	13
No criticisms	53	33
(Sample)	(70)	(70)

* More than one answer was recorded and the percentage totals may therefore exceed 100.

The major criticism of coloured conductors was that they were lazy. Such criticisms were made proportionately more by drivers than conductors. This statement is typical of such comments:

They are no better or worse than any other conductors, but I find a number tend to be lazy.

On the other hand, some drivers praised their coloured conductors.

There are big differences between them [as conductors]. One I had had only been here [in England] a short time and he was very good: he laughed at hard work. [U.K. Driver.]

The second criticism of coloured conductors was that they were impatient, unreliable, and irresponsible. Such comments often referred specifically to their relationships with passengers and especially to the safety of passengers—being 'too quick on the bell' and the like. Such comments came mainly from drivers and women conductors.

The third criticism to be made by any number again referred to relationships with passengers and with fellow-busmen: the immigrants were alleged to have a chip on their shoulders, and were considered clannish and arrogant. This quote from an English woman conductor illustrates several of these points:

No [they do not make good conductors] . . . they are too arrogant and too slow. They have a chip on their shoulders—they think we don't like them. They treat us with contempt—but it is our country.

The same woman conductor had, however, a very different opinion of coloured drivers:

Yes, they are very good drivers. I have had coloured drivers when my own driver has been on holiday. Some are better than our own drivers—a very smooth ride.

The critics did not share her opinion on the smooth ride provided by coloured drivers. Reckless, irresponsible, and impatient were words often used to describe coloured drivers who were thought to be inconsiderate to passengers, rather than to drivers of other vehicles. The critics referred to control of the bus and alleged too rapid acceleration, harsh braking, and violent swerving.

I've had a few good [coloured drivers] and I've had others I would rather never work with again. They pull up so sharply at stops it is a wonder you don't end up sitting on the engine. [U.K. Conductor.]

They [coloured immigrants] are good drivers—but not of buses. They don't understand the job. Bus driving is different from all other driving: you have passengers to think of and the coloured immigrants don't. [U.K. Driver.]

Such criticisms came mostly from drivers and women conductors.[1]

---

[1] It will be seen above that immigrant staff put less emphasis than did native staff on the importance of a smooth ride as one way in which a driver helps his conductor in his work. See above, pp. 82–3.

Whilst most native busmen refused to generalize about the work performance of their immigrant workmates, save that generally they were no better or worse than other busmen, a number of defects were alleged. That the majority did refuse to generalize is of far more significance than these alleged shortcomings of the coloured staff. There is no evidence to suggest that the work performance of immigrant busmen generally is any better or worse than that of any other group of busmen. Such criticisms may be seen as manifestations of antipathy towards the coloured staff, as well as indicating that their visibility is an important factor.

To conclude this chapter, we have seen the importance of both race and immigration variables in the early objections to the employment of coloured immigrants, but race emerged as of paramount importance. In the day-to-day work of busmen, little *overt* conflict was reported, and most of this conflict was seen to originate from the conflict potential inherent in the organization of work: difference of race and ethnicity exacerbated rather than caused this conflict. Some parallels were drawn with conflict occasioned by the presence of women conductors.[1]

Insofar as there was increasing acceptance of coloured busmen by their white workmates, there had been some absorption. On the other hand, outside of the strictly task-determined areas of behaviour there was considerable separation, and to that extent the pluralistic model is most appropriate. Both white and coloured indicated that they saw the situation in absorption terms, but the unwillingness of a number of the former group to accept the latter groups *on an equal basis* served to maintain a pluralistic situation. This restriction of contact across the boundaries of race and culture reduced the areas of possible conflict and therefore 'eased the strains' somewhat. On the other hand, it caused resentment from both white and coloured, it was probably an unstable situation, and acculturation and acceptance were impeded.

[1] It should be added that we have no evidence that the work expectations or task performance of women conductors were different from those of their male colleagues, but the widespread *belief* that this was so had a disruptive effect. Some women conductors who do expect an 'easy ride' have sanctions available to encourage driver co-operation: they can 'favour' some drivers with their company and ostracize others.

6

CENTRAL BUSES, III:
BUSMEN, SUPERVISORS, PASSENGERS

RELATIONSHIPS WITH SUPERVISORS

One element in the relationships between operatives and supervisors is the expectations which the former have of the latter. It seemed not unlikely that the immigrants, with their different cultural backgrounds, would not share the same set of expectations as the native busmen. To compare these expectations, we asked both groups, 'what makes a good inspector?' The responses are summarized in Table 6.1.

TABLE 6.1
Busmen's Expectations of the 'Good' Inspector, in Percentages.★

	Native	Immigrant
He is patient/knows how to handle people/can earn respect	34	33
He is fair/impartial/has no favourites	20	29
He is helpful/will co-operate with crews/will give and take	23	28
He has experience/knows his job	21	19
He is not too strict	21	6
He knows his staff	7	—
He is not too lenient	4	5
Other answer	6	7
(Sample)	(70)	(78)

★ More than one answer was recorded and the percentage totals may therefore exceed 100.

A number of points emerge from this table. First, there is the broad similarity in the answers given by both samples. Second, the desired qualities are in the main social skills rather than technical

93

expertise. Third, there is a difference between the samples on the question of the importance of an inspector knowing his staff. The number of native busmen who gave this answer was small, but this difference is important and we shall return to it when considering the pattern of inspector-crew relationships. Fourth, the responses in the 'not too strict' category differ between the two samples. There is no obvious explanation for this difference, but it may be that the immigrants were less likely to object to strictness provided other expectations were met: for example, that inspectors were 'impartial', which they mentioned somewhat more than the natives.

Next we asked, 'how do you get on with your inspectors?'[1] The answers are summarized in Table 6.2.

TABLE 6.2
*Busmen's Relations with Point Inspectors, in Percentages.**

Assessments	Native	Immigrant
Very good/very well	34	10
Good/well	19	17
Not bad/not much trouble/fair	29	54
Most good, some difficult/unhelpful	9	6
Some good, some difficult	4	12
No trouble if I do my job	4	—
Not very well/poor	1	1
(Sample)	(70)	(78)

* The question, as posed, was open-ended, and the answers were subsequently coded in these categories. With this type of question a wealth of meaning can be conveyed by the inflection of the voice in answering: 'not bad' can mean 'fair' or 'very well'. When there was any doubt about the intended meaning, we checked with the interviewee on *his* meaning.

Clearly, in their own estimations, the native staff got on with point inspectors significantly better than did the immigrant busmen: over half of the answers from natives were in the 'very well' or 'well' category, whereas a comparable majority of the answers from immigrants fell in the 'not bad'/'fair' category. We have seen that

[1] It was made clear that we were interested in relations with inspectors on point duty, rather than with those on revenue duty, or with depot or garage inspectors. However, a number also commented on their relations with these other inspectors and they are discussed below, pp. 98–9.

the expectations of the two groups did not differ markedly in respect of desirable qualities or behaviour of an inspector. With these two sets of data and a considerable amount of qualitative information, it is possible to explain the social situation of the point inspector and his relationships with crews.

One vital element in the social situation of a point inspector is the information available to him concerning both the work performance and reliability of crews and the pattern of vehicular traffic on his routes. First, he supervises a large number of crews in the course of one shift—the number may run into hundreds. Second, face-to-face contact with these crews is usually of short duration. Familiarity is not, then, an important element of his relationship with most crews. Moreover, given the relatively high wastage rates of staff over the past few years,[1] the 'population' is a constantly changing one.[2]

For information on the traffic situation, the point inspector relies on his own visual observation, on telephonic communication with his route controller and fellow-inspectors, and on reports by bus crews.[3] Often this information is out of date by the time he is able to act on it. Moreover, the information on traffic is not very comprehensive: point inspectors may be two or three miles apart.

That only about one-fifth of either sample mentioned the importance of an inspector having experience or knowing his job provides another clue to his role. Whilst an inspector must know the rules and the law relevant to bus operations, he does not possess *technical* skills greater than do the busmen he supervises. To legitimate his authority, he must then rely solely on his rank—this is likely to be one of the most difficult supervisory roles to perform adequately.

The point inspector does not have enough *reliable* information to enable him to assess the work performance of crews. Thus, it follows

---

[1] High, that is, in relation to previous London Transport experience; but some provincial municipal bus undertakings have experienced wastage rates of 'platform staff' (drivers and conductors) well above those of London. See National Board for Prices and Incomes, *Pay of Municipal Busmen* (Cmnd. 3605), (London, H.M.S.O., 1968), Appendix D., Table 1.

[2] Familiarity is even less likely to be an element in the inspector-crew relationship on those routes covered by the small number of garages operating a 'common rota'—that is, where all the busmen work all the duties over a period of months or years.

[3] On some six routes, the movement of buses was recorded by Bus Electronic Scanning Indicator equipment (B.E.S.I.), but none of these routes was serviced by the garages included in our study.

that many of his actions must essentially be of an arbitrary nature. For instance, when a crew arrives late at his point, he cannot be certain that the crew has, or has not, been deliberately running late, hoping for a 'turn'. Yet a crew may be reported and penalized for late running.

Inspectors don't realize what goes on between points. Buses—obviously— get in the right order before they reach him. But one has probably done all the work.

Another aspect of the point inspector's role is important: he often has to make decisions quickly: whether to turn a bus to cover an extended headway; whether to send a bus to the garage when its crew has finished its duty or is due for a meal relief and the crew due to take over has not arrived at the point.[1] One further element of the point inspector's dilemma is that his actions are circumscribed by the rules: on the length of a crew's duty without a meal relief, on the minimum length of 'stand time' at a terminal point, and so on.

The way out of this dilemma is for him to persuade crews to 'break the rules', with their agreement. Over a period of time a point inspector will become familiar with a small number of crews. They may well be crews he had worked with when he was a driver or conductor. He will, to his own satisfaction, know that some crews are reliable. This puts into context the comments of that small number of *native* busmen who said that a good inspector is one who knows his staff.

A good inspector knows what crews he can rely on and those he cannot. If we are late they know we will make it up—some crews will get turned. [U.K. Woman Conductor.]

It is those crews whom the inspector assesses as reliable that he relies on to break the rules when he feels this is necessary for the service. For instance, at the request of an inspector, a crew will leave a terminal point early to reduce the headway in a service. Doing so may necessitate cutting short its meal relief or tea break. This is known as 'doing the inspector a favour'. The crew in turn will expect the inspector to do it a favour at some future date: either by overlooking a misdemeanour or, more likely, by a 'turn' when it is not called for by the traffic situation. Similarly, 'making up time' when asked to do so by an inspector is seen as 'doing him a favour'. The basis of the relationship between the inspectors and a

---

[1] The police tend to view buses parked on busy roads with considerable disfavour.

relatively small number of crews is then one of reciprocity: favours are rewarded. This situation is well understood by busmen, both those who have this reciprocal relationship and those who do not. Busmen who stressed fairness, impartiality, and a lack of favouritism as desirable aspects of an inspector's behaviour are more likely to be those who do not enjoy this reciprocal relationship. Two quotations illustrate the contrasting viewpoints:[1]

Sometimes if you are late in on the first bus you go out to the second bus on time: that is, take a short meal relief. A decent inspector will remember this. [U.K. Driver.]

Most [inspectors] don't give and take. If you help him out he should not forget it when you are in a tight spot. Some are spiteful. [West Indian Driver.]

That the first quotation was from a native driver and the second from an immigrant is indicative of the pattern of relationships between crews and inspectors: those busmen who enjoy the reciprocal relationship are almost always natives; some may be members of mixed crews. Cultural differences put inspectors at a disadvantage when assessing the work performance of immigrant busmen; and apparently they find it especially difficult to be sure that an immigrant is 'telling the truth'.[2] The other side of the coin is of course that immigrant busmen are likely to find it harder to persuade inspectors, and other supervisors and managers, that they *are* telling the truth. Consequently, they are less likely to be believed than are native staff.

Thus, even if we *assume* that all point inspectors are free of antipathy or prejudice towards coloured busmen, they are none the less likely to find it more difficult to assess their performance than that of native busmen.

Amongst the coloured staff a widely held and possibly predominant view was that inspectors were often partial in their dealings with crews: that they favoured the white staff. Sometimes it was suggested that it was to the advantage of a coloured busman to have a white partner: inspectors would be more lenient towards a mixed

---

[1] It should be stressed that there is no clear dichotomy between those busmen who are part of this reciprocal relationship and those who are not: some busmen have such a relationship with some inspectors and not others. Some busmen's favours are not reciprocated by inspectors.

[2] Some managers maintained that coloured immigrants are far more prone to lying than are native staff. We have no direct evidence either way on this.

crew than an all-coloured one. Some quotations illustrate the view-point of many of the coloured staff:

When I have a white conductor and I'm a bit late we get a turn quicker. [West Indian Driver.]

When they [inspectors] book you for running early or late they ask you 'why?' If you say something in your favour, they don't write it down; if it will incriminate you, they do write it down. I find that a white crew gets away with more than a coloured crew: running early, and they turn themselves. This is serious, there is a bias. [West Indian Driver.]

This driver stated that inspectors would ask him why he was late, but a common complaint of both white and coloured busmen was that some inspectors were not interested in *why* a crew was late— or early.

Some [inspectors] I cherish, others not. Some don't want to know *why* I am late. Drivers at Chiswick [Training Centre] are told not to try to make up time. [West Indian Driver.]

These quotations from coloured busmen illustrate the widely held view that *some* inspectors favoured white busmen, that coloured busmen were discriminated against. Relationships between inspectors and white busmen were, however, often far from amicable. The coloured busmen were often careful to point out that their remarks applied to *some* inspectors; white staff, too, often refused to generalize.

If you reach a point early, the first question a *good* inspector will ask is 'what time did you leave the other end?' Sometimes a bus is sent out early and it's not the crew's fault if it arrives early . . . A bad inspector will just book you without asking.[1] [U.K. Conductor.]

Whilst we were chiefly concerned with relations between crews and point inspectors, some busmen commented on relationships with inspectors on revenue duty and with garage inspectors. The small number of complaints about revenue inspectors came mostly, but not exclusively, from coloured busmen and centred round a perceived tendency for inspectors to believe a passenger rather than the conductor in any dispute between the two. Two quotations from coloured conductors illustrate this complaint:

[1] Another potential for crew-inspector conflict arises here: some drivers calculate that by running early over part of the route they will reach the terminal point on time; they anticipate traffic delays. But again they may be reported for early running.

On a 604 in the rush hour we were full from Phillimore to Kenway Street. A passenger got on at Phillimore, he [later] said he gave me a shilling and twelve pennies, but I didn't see the shilling piece and I issued a shilling ticket. The inspector checked the tickets and the passenger said he gave me two shillings in all, I said he gave me a shilling. The inspector reported it to the garage—he took the passenger's word, but he couldn't be sure.

Whatever happens—overriding—inspectors always blame the conductor, even though you have asked for fares.

Complaints about garage inspectors were mostly directed at alleged unfairness in the allocation of overtime and rest-day work. Often they were made in answer to a question on 'dislikes' of the job. Typical of these answers is the following:

Officials behind the counter—at all garages. They have favourites for rest-day jobs and that. Most of the favourites are English.[1]

PROMOTION ASPIRATIONS AND NATIVES' ATTITUDES TOWARDS THE PROMOTION OF IMMIGRANTS TO INSPECTORS

One of our indices of immigrant absorption is the extent to which their *occupational* distribution mirrors that of the native workforce. Important factors influencing the occupational distribution of immigrants *within* an organization are their own aspirations and abilities, the attitudes and behaviour of the native workforce, and the extent to which management perceive immigrants to be suitable for some occupational roles and act accordingly. To discover these aspirations and to compare them with those of the native workforce, we asked a number of questions: first, 'do you want to be promoted to another job?' The answers to this question, together with the grades aspired to by those who wished to be promoted, are summarized in Table 6.3. (See p. 100.)

Clearly, the immigrant busmen were far less likely than the natives to state definitely that they did not wish to be promoted. A number of factors are relevant here and go some way towards explaining the different patterns of aspirations.

---

[1] Overtime and rest day work allocation was governed by an agreement which aimed to keep driving hours and rest periods within the requirements of the road traffic acts. Requests for rest-day work and rest days worked were recorded towards ensuring a fair distribution. Some union branches appointed a committee member to monitor rest day work and overtime allocation. Whether 'fairness' was achieved I do not know. The allocation of overtime at the end of a shift was more flexible and hence more susceptible to 'favouritism'.

Universitas

BIBLIOTHECA

traviensis

TABLE 6.3
*Busmen's Promotion Aspirations, in Percentages.**

	Native	Immigrant
None	75	34
To next grade (driver)	3	22
To Inspector	12	13
To B.O.C. (rail) or other clerical	—	4
Other	3	10
Don't know	5	15
No answer	2	—
(Sample)	(59)	(67)

* This table relates to male staff only: there is no direct promotional avenue for women conductors and their answers would therefore distort these findings.

First, there was a considerable difference in the age distribution of the two samples. The immigrants were overwhelmingly in the under-40 age group; over half of the natives were over 40. The relevance of age is shown by the age distribution of those native busmen who wished to become inspectors: all but one were under 40. Second, relatively more coloured than native conductors wished to become drivers. Again, the different age patterns of the samples is relevant: it seems probable that younger conductors would be more likely to desire upgrading to driver. Secondly, there was a difference in their length of service patterns and those native conductors with longer service had had more time to be upgraded if they wished. In the Department as a whole and in the garages visited, there was an imbalance between the numbers of coloured drivers and conductors; therefore there was a 'pent-up demand' for upgrading by the coloured conductors.

Thirdly, many natives are drivers because they like driving. This may appear to be merely a truism, but it is not unimportant. This, of course, is also true of many immigrant drivers; but, as I have argued earlier, their job opportunities elsewhere are more restricted and but for this, many would not have become busmen.[1]

The difference in the numbers aspiring to clerical or other posts may reflect again their restricted labour market. Finally, there was a difference in the 'don't know' category: this may reflect the re-

[1] See Chapter 3.

luctance of some coloured staff to admit to a white interviewer
their perception of discrimination in promotion within London
Transport.

By far the most important avenue of promotion open to busmen
is via the grade of inspector.[1] It was clear that inspectors' tasks were
seen as unattractive by many native busmen: 'standing on a street
corner all day long' was not an attractive prospect for them, and the
possibility of having to discipline former workmates was not
viewed with favour. Some who would like to be promoted do not
apply because promotion is via the inspector grade.

These are some of the differences between the two samples which
explain in part at least their different patterns of aspirations. It is
unlikely that this is the complete explanation, and we return to this
when considering comparable data from the two other departments.[2] There is no evidence to indicate how realistic—in the sense
of being attainable—the aspirations of either sample were.

With a ratio of one inspector to nineteen drivers and male conductors, there were perhaps fewer opportunities for promotion than
in some industries, but certainly more than in others.[3] On the other
hand, the skills of a bus inspector are largely specific to the industry
and it is likely that there is little movement out of the grade apart
from promotion, retirement, or death.[4]

Next we asked both samples if they had applied for promotion
in the past. Table 6.4 shows the responses to this question. (See
p. 102.)

It will be seen that the pattern of answers of the two groups was
almost identical. The wishes of a number of immigrants for promotion had not, then, been reflected in their actions. We then asked
both groups if they intended to apply or reapply for promotion in
the future; those who expressed an intention to apply or reapply

[1] It is possible for drivers and conductors to become garage assistants (who carry
out clerical work in the garages), but the number of staff in this grade is small: 116
in August 1967, of whom nine (8 per cent) were coloured. (Source: L.T.B. Staff
Administration Office.) It is further possible for garage assistants to be promoted to
garage inspectors, but the major source of recruitment to that grade is from that of
inspector.

[2] Chapter 17.

[3] In their study of the manufacturing industry in Luton, John Goldthorpe and his
colleagues found operative-foremen ratios that ranged from 1:20 at the lowest in
one company to not lower than 1:120 in another. See Goldthorpe, et al., p. 130.

[4] In the twenty-one months beginning 1 January 1967, a total of 168 drivers or
conductors became inspectors. (Source: L.T.B. Staff Administration Office.)

TABLE 6.4
Busmen's Applications for Promotion, in Percentages.

	Native	Immigrant
None made	71	73
Unsuccessful or failed training	17	19
Awaiting results or training	5	7
No answer	7	—
(Sample)	(59)	(67)

were asked if they thought they would be promoted and 'why'? or 'why not?' as appropriate. Table 6.5 summarizes the answers to these questions. Apart from those immigrants who indicated that they thought there was a bar to the promotion of coloured busmen to the grade of inspector, the reasons given for being optimistic or pessimistic were often both vague and diverse and therefore have not been shown.

TABLE 6.5
Busmen's Promotion Intentions and Perceived Prospects, in Percentages.*

	Native	Immigrant
Will not apply/reapply	76	34
Will apply/reapply—optimistic	2	18
Will apply/reapply—pessimistic	—	3
Will apply/reapply—don't know	5	9
Don't know if will apply/reapply	10	34
Bar on promotion of coloured staff	—	24
No answer	7	—
(Sample)	(59)	(67)

* The 24 per cent of coloured staff who indicated that they thought there was a bar on promotion of coloured staff constituted a double code and the percentage total therefore exceeds 100.

The figures for those saying that they did not intend to apply or reapply for promotion are of course very similar to those who had said they did not wish to be promoted.

The relatively large number of coloured staff in the 'don't know' category was in part, at least, related to the perceived bar on the promotion of coloured busmen: some required evidence that an application would not be a complete waste of time. That only a quarter of the coloured sample indicated that they thought there was a deliberate policy of not promoting coloured busmen to inspector probably understates the number who held this view. First, it seems likely that a number who said they did not wish to be promoted were of this opinion: we did not ask respondents if they believed there was such a bar on promotion. Second, as with some other questions on discrimination and hostility, there was often a reluctance to discuss the subject with a white interviewer. Third, had there been visible evidence that coloured staff were promoted to the grade of inspector, it is possible that more would have expressed a wish for such promotion. All but one of those who said they wanted to become inspectors also said that they thought there was a deliberate policy preventing such promotion. Only two stated an intention to apply or reapply and neither was optimistic.

It is probably no overstatement to say that the predominant view amongst the coloured busmen, particularly the West Indians, was that London Transport had a deliberate policy of not promoting them to the inspector grade. This belief was the source of one of their major discontents. A quotation from the interview material illustrates this discontent:

If London Transport doesn't want to promote coloureds to inspector level then they should be honest enough to say so. As it is, they just find a polite excuse which everyone knows is a polite excuse, because those who have applied have been well educated and perfectly capable of doing the job.

At the time of our study there were no West Indian inspectors in the Department. There was one Anglo-Indian and there had been another of Asian origin, again possibly of mixed parentage. A few of the native staff regarded these inspectors as 'Commonwealth immigrants'; they came to our notice in answers to a question on such inspectors. How they were viewed by passengers and most busmen, I do not know; but I know of no suggestion that they were not accepted by both. The first West Indian inspector was appointed in May 1968.[1] He might be regarded by passengers and by both

[1] *Guardian* (14 May 1968). In April 1968, busmen at Holloway Garage had voted against a one-day strike in support of a West Indian conductor whose application for promotion to inspector had been rejected. The proposed strike was supported by the West Indian Standing Conference. *Guardian* (10 April 1968), and *The Times* (10 April 1968). By February 1969, there were three coloured inspectors and by April 1970 the number had risen to eleven.

white and coloured busmen as the first 'coloured' inspector. (The Anglo-Indian appeared to be regarded as more 'Anglo' than Indian; some who mentioned the Asian pointed to his origins and the fact that he was *not* West Indian.)

The promotion of coloured immigrants to posts putting them in a superordinate-subordinate relationship with white natives has, from the available evidence, been rare in British industry. This, together with the fact that there were large numbers of coloured busmen, led us to ascertain the attitudes of white native busmen towards the possibility of a coloured inspector. On this specific topic the attitudes revealed have relatively little value for predicting behaviour, but they give an indication of likely objections and, more important, they are illuminating on the wider significance of colour in Britain. Table 6.6 summarizes the answers to our questions on objections to a Commonwealth immigrant inspector and the reasons given for these objections.

TABLE 6.6
Native Busmen's Attitudes Towards a Commonwealth Immigrant Inspector, in Percentages.

i	No objection	4
ii	No objection if he had the experience/ability	9
iii	No objection personally, but others might/would object	21
iv	No objection: there should be coloured inspectors	9
v	Objections: because of lack of experience/ability	4
vi	Objections: would be wrong/would not get respect/ because of colour	36
vii	Objections: coloured inspectors might misuse authority	9
	Don't know	9
	(Sample)	(70)

The 'no objection' category is self-explanatory, and it will be seen that very few expressed this view. The next group made an important qualification. Acceptance of a coloured inspector would depend on how well he was fitted for the role and how he behaved in it.

Personally, *as long as he did his job correctly*, I would have no objection.

This quotation leads us to the next group: those who stated that they as individuals would have no objection, but others would or might object. Typical of their comments was the following:

Yes, it would cause resentment. Some would say 'I'm not taking orders from a black B!', but I'd have no objection.

It will be seen that one-fifth answered in terms of no personal objection to the notion of coloured inspectors. More positive were those who stated that there 'should be' coloured inspectors. Their reasoning was of two kinds: that the coloured staff were being denied promotion and that coloured inspectors would be more effective in supervising coloured busmen. None suggested that coloured inspectors should *only* supervise coloured busmen and it is legitimate to group these answers together.

I would like to see it—it's unfair at the moment. There are some good chaps that could do the job.

It would be a good idea because some of the inspectors won't choke some of them off, as the first cry is 'race prejudice'. They could talk in the same language.

Some suggested that the coloured staff lacked either the experience or ability thought necessary for an inspector.

Yes [there would be objections]. They wouldn't be accepted yet: many of our lads have much more experience [but] it will come eventually.

By far the largest single group thought there would be objections to the promotion of coloured immigrants to the inspector grade and that objections would be related to colour. The reasoning and emotions behind these answers are clearly complex, but the attitude can be stated simply: it would be wrong or, less often, degrading for a white man to take instructions from a coloured man. Probing for reasons why it would be wrong seldom produced a response other than 'I don't know why, but it would be wrong'. This kind of attitude is apparently widespread and also deep-seated, both in the London Transport situation and in the wider society, and it is useful to illustrate it at some length.

Yes [there would be objections because of] colour: we would object to being told what to do by a coloured man. The [London Transport] Board realizes this and turns them down when they apply.

The majority of crews have accepted them here [as drivers and conductors], but they wouldn't accept them as senior.

There may be [objections] but I don't see what good it would do—it would be prejudice. But I wouldn't like [having coloured inspectors]: I would feel it would be a slight to me.

A fear that coloured inspectors might 'misuse' their authority and favour coloured staff was expressed by some.

Coloureds stick together like flies. They'd be out to catch the locals and look after their own.

The attitudes revealed by these quotations are a compound of antipathies, prejudices, and fears. Within some of the quotations there are contradictions; views were often far from clear-cut.

Over-all, the attitudes expressed were extremely diverse: there were those who thought there ought to be coloured inspectors on the grounds of equal treatment, and those who were extremely hostile to that possibility. Many, probably most, had at some time thought about the question of coloured inspectors, and there was an awareness of the possibility that some would be appointed. Coloured busmen who were, to some extent at least, accepted as equals would be unacceptable to some in a superordinate role. Whilst the question was an indirect one—asking 'would there be any objection'—most busmen answered in a way that revealed their own attitudes. Somewhat under one-half indicated a lack of objections (codes i–iv, 43 per cent) and one-half indicated definite objections (codes v–vii, 49 per cent).

Some staff had deep-rooted objections to taking instructions from a coloured inspector, but there was also evidence of the feeling that an all-white inspectorate would not and could not continue indefinitely. I concluded that *initially* the first coloured inspectors would probably meet more difficulties from staff than would their white colleagues. For this reason, they would need to be 'better' than the average white inspector: they would have to *earn* their acceptance by white busmen. One consequence of the seen absence of coloured inspectors and the fairly universal assumption that this was not accidental was that it served to legitimate and reinforce the views of those white busmen who were hostile towards their appointment: it appeared to them that their views had the stamp of official approval.

So far the question of why there were no coloured inspectors at that time has remained unanswered. One possible reason could have been that coloured staff had not the necessary experience in terms of service. To eliminate length of service as the crucial variable we obtained data on the years of joining and of promotion of the inspectorate and calculated the time between joining and promotion. The results of this analysis are shown in Table 6.7.

TABLE 6.7

*Time Between Entering Service and Entering Grade of
Central Bus Inspectors, in Percentages.**

Years	
0–4	24
5–9	35
10–14	22
15–19	15
20 and over	5
(Number)	(1,210)

* As at 1 January 1967. Source: L.T.B. Staff Administration Office. As the data gave the *years* of entering service and grade, there is the possibility of some errors, but it is likely that these cancel each other out.

We were not able to obtain data on the length of service of coloured busmen only. Although our sample is very small in relation to the total number of coloured busmen, the length of service pattern is not likely to be wildly atypical. One-third of the coloured drivers and male conductors in our sample had over five years' service, and it is likely that there were many in the Department with this same length of service. A quarter of the inspectorate had been promoted after less than five years' service. It cannot be completely established that length of service was not the key variable, but the evidence points to this conclusion. On the other hand, it was argued by some London Transport managers that even with equal service, white native and coloured immigrants did not start from an equal position in their promotion chances. The coloured immigrant, by virtue of his relative 'strangeness' to the whole society, would need to spend some considerable time in Britain before he was sufficiently acculturated, and therefore might be expected to have longer service before promotion than his native counterpart.

We were not able to obtain data on the previous grade of the existing inspectorate, but the prevailing management view was that a driver was more likely to be promoted to inspector than was a conductor, though the latter was not excluded. These conclusions were confirmed by data on the 168 busmen who became inspectors in the twenty-one months beginning 1 January 1967: 133 (79 per cent) were ex-drivers and 35 (21 per cent) were ex-conductors.[1] The

[1] L.T.B. Staff Administration Office.

coloured staff were concentrated in the conductor grade, and their chances of promotion were correspondingly reduced. This was not however a sufficient explanation for the absence of coloured inspectors.

After long discussions with management at most levels in the Department, I concluded that the absence of coloured inspectors at that time was not fortuitous. Apprehension over the appointment of coloured inspectors appeared to be threefold: it was feared that coloured inspectors would not be accepted (1) by the public, (2) by white native staff, and (3) by coloured busmen of different origins. Fear of negative public response was certainly paramount, and could not be lightly dismissed. Coloured busmen have to contend with proportionately far more 'trouble' from passengers than do white native staff.[1] An inspector on point duty *by himself* is isolated; he cannot always easily obtain assistance. Moreover, he often has to go to the assistance of crews who have difficult and at times violent passengers. In addition, inspectors carry out revenue duties: observations indicate that the inspector on this type of duty is not the most popular figure with passengers. In short, the physical safety of a coloured inspector could not be guaranteed. Nor, it should be added, can that of any inspector; but a coloured inspector would be considerably more vulnerable.

This situation was in marked contrast to that in the Railway Operating Department where a small number of coloured staff had reached the inspector grade. They were employed on London Transport premises, they were not alone, and they were more easily able to summon assistance when confronted by difficult passengers. It ought to be added that the bus inspector's role *vis-à-vis* subordinate staff is a far more difficult one to perform adequately than is that of the railway inspector.

On the one hand, there were the frustrated aspirations of those West Indian busmen who wished to become inspectors; on the other, the very real fears that the first West Indian inspectors would be exposed and vulnerable. These two considerations were not reconcilable. It may be that on balance London Transport was over-cautious. The absence of coloured bus inspectors served to legitimate the views of hostile white busmen and possibly a wider public. Much bitterness was caused among the coloured busmen by the lack of seen promotional opportunity. Such bitterness was hardly con-

[1] See below, pp. 109–15.

ducive to harmonious relationships and may have been reflected in the wastage and work motivation of coloured staff.

The change in management practice regarding the promotion of coloured busmen to the inspectorate was probably occasioned by the then-impending Race Relations Act 1968, ministerial interest in the question, and, possibly, a preliminary draft paper of the findings of this section on native busmen's attitudes.

RELATIONS WITH PASSENGERS

Continuous face-to-face contact with passengers is of course a feature of the conductor's role. The driver is largely insulated from direct passenger contact, but passenger behaviour can nevertheless impinge on his work. This area of passenger contact is then an important one for all busmen. For coloured staff, acceptance or non-acceptance by passengers could obviously make a considerable difference to the satisfactions or dissatisfactions of work. We therefore asked both samples about the 'passenger difficulties' they experienced; we further asked the native sample if they had witnessed any instances of immigrant staff experiencing difficulties with passengers. Table 6.8 summarizes the answers to the first of these two questions.[1] (See p. 110.)

It will be seen that apart from insults and violence, the pattern of responses from both samples was very similar. Two important qualifications need to be made. First, the figures reflect those aspects of passenger behaviour which the respondents find troublesome or annoying, rather than the extent of such behaviour. For example, fare overriding and giving late or wrong signals are both widespread and are met by most conductors and drivers. Second, the figures tell us nothing about the *frequency* with which these difficulties occur. I concluded that the coloured staff meet proportionately more difficulties than do the white staff, though this does not apply to every type of difficulty listed.[2]

Overriding, that is travelling beyond the fare stage paid for, is

[1] The question addressed specifically to native busmen produced very little detailed or comprehensive material. A quarter (24 per cent) of the sample reported that they had seen or heard immigrant staff being insulted by passengers; 13 per cent reported that they had seen violent incidents. Most of this material was, however, very fragmentary: the witnesses did not know *in detail* what had happened; in assault cases they had often arrived on the scene after the event. In sum, this question added little to our knowledge.

[2] An investigation of 123 items, mainly complaints, from London Transport's 'public correspondence' files revealed nothing of significance for this study.

TABLE 6.8
*Busmen's Difficulties with Passengers, in Percentages.**

	Native	Immigrant
Fare overriding/fare evasion/ticket offences	46	45
Insults	14	46
Attempts to board or alight at 'wrong' time or place/late or wrong signals	27	33
Complaints over service, etc.	29	29
Drunks/louts or rowdies	21	24
Violence (physical assaults)	4	9
Other	7	8
None	11	8
(Sample)	(70)	(78)

* More than one answer was recorded and the percentage totals may therefore exceed 100.

thought to be widespread. The conductor is of course responsible for the collection of the correct fare and failure to do so can lead to disciplinary action. Passengers' tickets are checked by inspectors and, as we saw above, some conductors thought that inspectors tended to believe the passenger rather than the conductor when there was a difference between the two over the fare asked for or the amount tendered. In short, conductors find overriding troublesome. New conductors and coloured conductors are more likely to experience overriding.

The main difficulty is overriding ... You tell some passengers they are overriding and they tell you that you don't know your job. Some swear— 'you coloured bastard'—and some try to fight. [Pakistani Conductor.]

Many, probably most, of the coloured conductors have learnt the areas of possible conflict with passengers and behave accordingly. The avoidance of conflict is, though, often accomplished at the cost of some loss of face and self-esteem. Possibly white and coloured conductors see overriding and fare evasions in different terms: to the former it is an attempt to defraud L.T.B.; to the latter it is an attempt to take advantage of *him* and is a personal affront. One possible area of conflict is the correct fare.

At times you meet an awkward passenger, but you can do something—
you may have to give way. Some [passengers] argue over the fare:
don't argue—just show him the fare chart. [West Indian Conductor.]

Some conductors—coloured and white—said that coloured
passengers, particularly West Indian women, attempted to override
more than white passengers. It is perhaps significant that the coloured
conductors who suggested this were mostly Indian or Pakistani, but
more than one West Indian conductor said that they had been told
by West Indian passengers to 'stop thinking and acting like a white
man' when they had asked for the correct fare.

Arguments arise between conductor and passenger over the
amount tendered, and many conductors keep the coin or coins tendered in one hand until the fare transaction is completed, in order to
meet this kind of argument.

Both white and coloured busmen are the butt of insults from passengers, but the latter experience far more insulting behaviour, often
of a racial character.

You get insults left, right and centre. I'm not bothered now—'bastard'
is just a national name. [West Indian Conductor.]

When I was at home [Jamaica] I never thought the English were any
different: I had not expected any problem over colour. I tried to help one
old woman off with her shopping—'take your black hands off me'.
[West Indian Woman Conductor.]

Apart from verbal insults, other passenger behaviour can be
perceived, and intended, as insulting.

I slowed down when I saw a passenger running and waited for him.
When he got off he came to the cab to thank the driver. When he saw *me*
he turned the other way. [West Indian Driver.]

Passenger insults are nothing new for London busmen.

I have often to put up with insolence from vulgar fellows, who think it
fun to chaff a cad, as they call it. There's no help for it. Our masters won't
listen to complaints: if we are not satisfied we can go.

Apart from the archaic language, the quotation could be from a
present-day conductor, but it is from an interview recorded by
Mayhew in the middle of the nineteenth century.[1]

Passengers attempting to board or alight at a 'wrong' time or
place, or giving late or wrong signals appear to afflict white and

[1] Peter Quennell (ed.), *Mayhew's London* (London, Spring Books, undated), p. 568.

coloured busmen alike—both find them equally irritating. Drivers find the starting and stopping bell ringing 'behind my ear', exasperating, particularly when it is over-used.

Complaints over the frequency of and delays in the service, the behaviour of the driver and of other crews, fare increases—all are met by the conductor. Apart from his limited ability to ensure that the bus runs 'to time', he is powerless in respect of these complaints.

People moan about the service when it is not your fault. [U.K. Conductor.]

Much depends on the conductor's skill in handling complaints, possibly by ignoring them. It seems unlikely that coloured busmen receive appreciably more complaints, but they are more vulnerable if a complaint leads to a potentially violent argument. Their skill in avoiding conflict with passengers in this kind of situation is then of considerable importance. Many, probably most, have learnt this skill.

Some passengers get offended—maybe it is their fault or your fault. They may be rude, but you cannot retaliate: if you say nothing you end it there and then. I don't know how some conductors manage to get hit. Some passengers do things for kicks—especially youngsters. A lot of passengers say things for a joke. [West Indian Conductor.]

This conductor was perhaps over-optimistic in supposing that violence could be *completely* avoided by social skills; otherwise his point is valid. It does, though, bring out clearly that trouble is often avoided at the cost of some loss of face and, for some, of self-esteem.

In most situations of passenger complaints the conductor has no sanctions at his disposal, but this is not always so. One such incident is described in the following quotation.

A woman passenger boarded the bus—at a crossing, not a stop—with a dog. She alighted at the next request stop after a journey of about a minute. I asked for her fare and she said 'if you don't come upstairs for it, next time you won't get it'. Next day she attempted to board the bus at the same crossing, with a dog. I said 'sorry, no dogs'. [U.K. Woman Conductor.]

The conductor is the major butt of passenger's criticisms, but the driver is not completely immune. Again, many of the coloured staff have learnt to deal with these situations.

A lot call you names, especially if you have to go past a stop to pull in. They call you names, but I laugh at them—it saves a 'punch-up'. [West Indian Driver.]

Coloured staff do suffer one particular handicap: the reluctance of passengers to believe them when they give information on the route and destination of the bus, where to alight, and so on. Many prefer to ask other passengers, sometimes having already asked the conductor. This kind of behaviour was perhaps more frequently met by station staff on the railways,[1] but many coloured conductors found it both irritating and insulting.

Conductors and all service workers in face-to-face contact with the public are required to use certain social skills when dealing with 'drunks', 'louts' or 'rowdies', as they were commonly known. On Friday and Saturday evenings particularly, drunks are encountered by conductors and, clearly, many believed that 'discretion is the better part of valour' when dealing with these passengers.

I give drunks a ticket out of my own money rather than have trouble. [U.K. Woman Conductor.]

I was slung off my bus by a drunk passenger who was annoyed because I queried the age of a 'half-fare'. My [English] driver intervened and was turned on by the drunk who said 'are you another nigger lover?' This driver hadn't been particularly friendly up 'til then. [West Indian Conductor.]

This was perhaps one occasion when a difficult passenger cemented relations between white and coloured. More often such incidents appear to have the opposite effect: some white busmen resent having to intervene in a dispute between a coloured busman and passengers, and some conductors are reluctant to seek their driver's assistance.

Problems arising from groups of what were described as 'louts' or 'rowdies'—usually in their teens or twenties—constantly recur in the interview material. Again, the necessity for discretion on the conductor's part is emphasized.

It is not always policy to interfere: you get four or five louts on the bus and you know what to expect if you interfere. [U.K. Conductor.]

We get a lot of trouble: they don't want to pay and some want to override. I took eight boys to court: when I asked for fares they sent me around to each other and opened the emergency window. I went for the police and they ran and the police caught four and they gave away the other four. The case went to the Juvenile Court: they were fined and bound over. [West Indian Conductor.]

[1] See Chapter 9.

In such situations violence is either overtly or covertly threatened. The evidence points to the conclusion that whilst all conductors meet this problem, it is met proportionately more by coloured staff.

In some situations though the conductor will meet violence or the threat of violence, no matter how skilful he is. Two such situations from our interview material illustrate the risk of assault that conductors face.

The bus stopped at a stop and a man, a woman, and three children went upstairs. I gave the starting signal. The man grabbed me and said 'you black bastard' and went to hit me. I gave the emergency stop signal and went for the police and the London Transport inspector. The inspector and the police put [the passenger] off and the bus was curtailed. Statements were taken—and from the passengers—and two summonses were issued by London Transport: for assault and swearing on a public vehicle. [West Indian Conductor.]

. . . there was a couple at a bus stop, the other passengers all got on, but they were kissing and I thought they didn't want to get on so I gave the bell. They ran, and I gave the emergency stop and they got on. The woman took off her shoe and gave it to the man to hit me and she called me all the bastards and they refused to pay the fare—two elevens . . . They did not hit me but I was very hurt: she called me all the dirty things and said 'go back to the jungle'. That was the worst [experience]— I've had nothing as bad . . . A passenger—a woman—wrote to London Transport and she said how calm and polite I was. The C.D.I. called me in and read the letter and shook me by the hand. [West Indian Conductor.]

These two incidents illustrate the vulnerability of the conductor: in the first case he was able to summon assistance from an inspector, in the second none was available. In any event an inspector or police officer may be some distance away and not easily contacted. In almost all the instances of violence reported to us other passengers appear to have played a passive role, apart from acting as witnesses. Assistance to a conductor in difficulties is sometimes provided by his driver, but he is physically isolated in his cab and will often not be aware of what is happening 'on the back'.

The conclusion that coloured busmen are more likely than white busmen to be physically assaulted was reinforced by data collected and analysed by London Transport's legal staff. In 1968, roundly 60 per cent of reported assaults were on coloured staff. Most of these were assaults on Central Bus conductors. As only about one-third of Central Bus conductors were coloured and they experienced about three-fifths of the assaults, the coloured conductor was roughly three times as likely as his white colleague to be assaulted. The trend of assaults on public transport staff in London is rising. In 1966, 727 cases were reported. By 1969, the figure had risen to 1,120.[1]

The majority of busmen, particularly conductors, experience difficulties with passengers, but it is not an exaggeration to say that coloured busmen are still not fully accepted by large numbers of passengers, in spite of the fact that many have been in service for several years. Many, probably most, of the coloured busmen have learnt the areas of possible conflict with passengers and attempt to avoid such situations, often at some cost to themselves. Such evasive action is by no means always successful: these busmen still experience behaviour which they find painful—often mentally, less often physically.

LIKES AND DISLIKES OF LONDON BUSMEN

One other area where we compared the attitudes of white native and coloured immigrant busmen was that of the features of their employment which they liked and disliked. This is of interest mainly as one further indication of the extent to which the two groups shared the same set of attitudes. A number of the conditions of employment in the service sector are very different from those in manufacturing industry, and given the relative lack of knowledge about service industries in Britain, the attitudes revealed are of interest in their own right. The two questions asked here were 'what do you like . . .' and 'what don't you like about working for London Transport?' Table 6.9 summarizes the answers to the first of these questions. (See p. 116.)

The pattern of responses was broadly similar for both samples. By far the most important was the job or task itself, and there were a number of aspects to this. Many drivers liked driving as such; some specifically preferred bus to lorry driving. Some readers might perhaps expect that drivers would find travelling the same road all and every day boring, but this was not so; they mentioned the variety of the job, and its ever-changing scene. Both drivers and conductors valued the 'open-air life'. They found the job clean and interesting. Conductors, and some drivers, mentioned the pleasures and interest of meeting people and this was especially stressed by the immigrants, somewhat surprisingly in view of the difficult passengers they in particular encountered.

[1] London Transport Section, British Transport Police.

TABLE 6.9
*Features of Their Employment which Busmen Liked, in Percentages.**

	Native	Immigrant
The job/open-air work/clean work/ interesting/meeting people	70	63
Freedom from close supervision	40	38
Hours: shift work/freedom to change shifts/days off mid-week	33	22
Pay is reasonable/good	29	21
Job security	24	23
L.T.B. good or fair employers/welfare, sports, social, and canteen facilities	16	15
Free travel/free uniform	7	12
Nothing	6	5
(Sample)	(70)	(78)

* More than one answer was recorded and the percentage totals may therefore exceed 100.

Freedom from close supervision, the second most frequently mentioned feature, involves two separate but related aspects. First, the question of *what* to do. Apart from those on the spare list or on rest day and overtime work, 'receiving instructions' is largely a matter of reading a duty rota, rather than face-to-face direction.[1] Second, there is not constant supervision on *how* to do the work.

[I like] the freedom of the job: there is no one looking over your shoulder. [U.K. Driver.]

No one tells you what to do: you read it and you know what to do. [West Indian Conductor.]

Both white and coloured busmen valued this feature of their job. In some respects freedom from supervision is more important for the coloured staff: it largely eliminates one potential source of discrimination. Many indicated that they were aware of this, particularly those with experience of factory or building work.

Next, the hours of work of public transport. Some preferred shift work to 'a normal eight-to-five' day. The freedom to change a

---

[1] Another exception is, of course, instructions from point inspectors on the road. This, as we have seen, causes some problems.

duty with another driver or conductor was appreciated. Working shifts was seen as advantageous in that it was possible to visit a business or agency which was only open for normal hours. Some liked rest days at mid-week, when amenities and facilities are less crowded than at week-ends. Other said that the hours were short and that they seemed to spend more time at home than people working normal hours.[1] Time off in daylight was valued by some, especially for those interested in gardening and household repairs. In short, this is another aspect of the freedom which many associated with bus work.

It's not routine hours. I like late turns: it gives me more free time. Days off in the week are very useful. [U.K. Conductor.]

You get time to follow hobbies. You can swop turns to suit—it's the flexibility. I often jump on a bus on a day off and go to a museum or something. [West Indian Driver.]

The other side of the coin is that various aspects of the hours were the most disliked feature of bus work. The advantages of the hours were mentioned somewhat less by the coloured than by the white busmen. This may be related to the fact that they are in the younger age groups. On the other hand, the coloured sample mentioned hours as a dislike only slightly more frequently.

Some busmen described the level of pay as reasonable or good. These replies came disproportionately more frequently from the women conductors, and some specifically mentioned that the pay was reasonable or good *for a woman*. To that extent, the inclusion of women in the sample distorts the findings. Small numbers of men in both samples made the important qualification that the pay was reasonable or good, *provided* a rest day or some overtime was worked. We do not know in detail what criteria are used for evaluating pay levels, but some said that the pay was good compared with what they could earn elsewhere, and others that it was reasonable for the work done.

The money is good *for a woman* or a single man—but not for a married man. [U.K. Woman Conductor.]

The money is good compared with what I could get elsewhere. [U.K Driver.]

The basic pay is good in comparison with building. [West Indian Driver.]

[1] This is probably related in part to the fact that most busmen live close to their garages or relief points.

Job security was the feature receiving the next highest number of mentions. Important here was the perceived freedom from fear of redundancy[1] and from arbitrary dismissal. Both aspects were mentioned, though many simply spoke of security or stated, 'it's a secure job'.

Even the C.D.I. can't sack you—you've got a chance. [West Indian Driver.]

It's secure—you don't have to think of being laid off. [U.K. Conductor.]

Both aspects of job security are important for both groups. Freedom from *arbitrary* dismissal is, it is argued, especially important for the coloured staff.

Other aspects of their employment were mentioned by a few in either group. Those who said London Transport were good or fair employers spoke in general terms, though some amenities were also mentioned.

London Transport are good people to work for. [U.K. Driver.]

The facilities for entertainment . . . and some factories have no facilities for eating. [West Indian Conductor.]

Small minorities in both groups found nothing to like in their employment.

Nothing particularly—but what other job is there? [West Indian Conductor.]

I don't like it: I always had a desire to get satisfaction from work, but there is no satisfaction on this job. If you did it 100 per cent you'd get no thanks. You never see the guv'nors . . . During the War I only went to the shelter once—we got no thanks from the Board. If you saw an inspector on his point you were lucky—but all the inspectors received thirty pounds each for keeping the buses running. Bus driving? It is not driving: it is keeping out of trouble. [U.K. 'long service' Driver.]

The first of these two quotations reflects some of the bitterness felt by the coloured staff about job discrimination. The second, in perhaps an extreme form, reflects the fairly widespread dissatisfaction felt by both white and coloured busmen. I return to this topic below.[2] It now remains to discuss the workers' dislikes of their employment, which are summarized in Table 6.10.

[1] With the increasing use of one-man operated buses, many conductors may now feel less secure in this respect.

[2] See pp. 120–2.

TABLE 6.10

*Features of their Employment which Busmen Disliked, in Percentages.**

	Native	Immigrant
Shift work/early turns/late turns	34	37
Difficult passengers	13	12
Bad supervision/impersonal management	11	12
Pay/sick pay	10	9
Other answer	16	12
Nothing	27	28
(Sample)	(70)	(78)

* More than one answer was recorded and the percentage totals may therefore exceed 100.

The pattern of dislikes for both samples was very similar. The most frequently mentioned feature was the hours of work. Late turns and week-end duties were particularly disliked, less because of the work task than because of the interference with domestic and social life. Wives, too, often resented their husbands working these unusual hours. Changing hours of work, combined with driving, were believed by some drivers to cause upset stomachs.[1]

Shift work—late turns and week-end work especially—was seen by both white and coloured staff as a major disadvantage of the job. On the other hand, shift work had some compensations, and it was often specific duties which were disliked rather than shift work as such. Nevertheless, it appeared that on balance the disadvantages of shift work were seen by many to outweigh the advantages.[2]

Complaints about supervision and management were sometimes

[1] I am advised that there is no evidence that diseases of the stomach and duodenum are found significantly more amongst busmen than amongst the population at large. For a summary of the earlier studies on the health of busmen, see Clegg, pp. 130–2. See also Richard Doll and Francis Avery-Jones, *Occupational Factors in the Aetiology of Gastric and Duodenal Ulcers with an Estimate of their Incidence in the General Population* (London, H.M.S.O., 1951); and Andrew Raffle, 'The Occupational Physician as Community Physician', in *Proceedings of the Royal Society of Medicine* (Vol. 63, No. 7, July 1970), pp. 731–9.

[2] To some extent, of course, busmen are self-selected, and those in the working population who dislike shift work very much will be under-represented in the bus staff. This is, though, less true of the immigrants, given their restricted job opportunities elsewhere.

general, sometimes specific. Coloured busmen, as we have seen, accused supervisors of favouritism. Other complaints by coloured busmen reflected their difficulties in adapting to and accepting the formal procedures of a large bureaucratic organization. White busmen, too, complained of the 'bureaucracy' or of 'too many officials', but mostly in these general terms. Coloured staff gave instances of specific conflicts with management which they found hurtful, and of rules which they found difficult to accept.

I had a row—I couldn't attend work because of domestic difficulties and I phoned in to tell the C.D.I. I [later] had to see him: I had to report failure to attend work. I was asked what were the domestic difficulties, but that is private ... I am not accustomed to this. Nothing has happened yet, but it will go on my record. I refused to sign the book,[1] but this is not like me: I am not carefree and I need the money.

If you don't come to work they don't pay you—but you still have to say 'why'.

Both these quotations illustrate the difficulty which many immigrants have in accepting the rules and requirements of a large, public service organization.

The only other dislikes mentioned by any number concerned pay and sick pay.

The money is poor—about fourteen pounds *clear*. [West Indian Driver.]

The sick pay scheme is awful: you get nothing for five years; for five to ten years' service you only get it for six weeks a year and you only get two-thirds wages less National Insurance.[2] [U.K. Woman Conductor.]

Roughly similar proportions of both groups reported that there was nothing they disliked about London Transport employment.

SOME OBSERVATIONS ON BUS WORK

The theme for this section might well have been provided by the driver who said, 'Bus driving? It is not driving, it is keeping out of trouble.' Others made comments with a similar meaning, though with perhaps less bitterness. I concluded that motivation to do a

---

[1] That is, accept a 'caution'. See Appendix 2 on disciplinary procedures.

[2] Male staff qualified for sick pay after one year's continuous service, but women did so only after five years. The period of payment ranged from seven weeks a year for those with under ten years' continuous service to eighteen weeks a year for those with over twenty years' continuous service. From May 1970, women qualified for sick pay after three years' continuous service and from May 1971, after one year. The amounts of sick pay and period of entitlement have also been increased.

good job or do the job properly was not high amongst many bus-men, white and coloured. There was little doubt that the most im-portant factor contributing to this situation was the inability of management and supervision effectively to monitor and assess the performance of individual crews. The system of supervision, as we saw above, was extremely arbitrary in operation: crews were 'booked' when they felt they were doing their level best to do the job properly. Crews that were seen to be fiddling were seen to 'get away with it'. Given this situation, it is hardly surprising that the incentive to do the job properly was low. Clearly, many felt that there was little or no incentive.

Some [drivers] try to catch the one in front; it makes it easier for both [driver and conductor]. I'm not lazy, but the one behind is trying to catch you—it's a vicious circle. [U.K. Conductor.]

Busmen who in other circumstances would wish to do the job properly found they were caught up in the system and fiddled with the fiddlers.[1] Management and supervision were not seen to be effectively attempting to correct the abuses which were perceived by busmen; therefore, why should they (individual busmen) bother? That, in essence, was the outlook of many, both white and coloured.

The discontent arising from this situation was reflected far more in apathy and resigned acceptance than in militance. The Union was viewed by many as ineffective and 'too close' to management,[2] which, in turn, was seen as distant and impersonal. These were further contributory factors in the situation.

One further thread would appear to be the decline in demand for bus transport and, associated with this, a perceived decline in the status of busmen. Comments in this vein came mainly from older, long-service native busmen, who, of course, no longer constitute the majority.

I realize it is a dying industry. Years ago the buses would be full on a fine Sunday; they only run 25 per cent of the buses on a Sunday now. [Ex-L.G.O.C. Conductor.]

The perceived decline in busmen's status was related in part to this decrease in demand, and in part to a seen lowering of the standards of staff, which, as we have seen, was by no means always associated with the recruitment of coloured staff.

[1] It is likely that the incentive to fiddle was reduced by the introduction in Septem-ber 1970 of a bonus based on individual crew receipts.

[2] See Chapter 15.

Comments on a lowering of standards and such like postulate a 'golden age' which probably only partly accorded with reality. Perhaps there was something of a golden age for London busmen: from the twenties to the Second World War. This was a period of growth in the demand and expansion of services, a period when busmen were better paid relative to many other occupations and when traffic flowed far more freely than it does now. And it is this last factor which is the key.

It may well be that bus transport has passed its nadir. There appears now to be a growing realization that the rapid movement of large numbers of people in urban areas can only be accomplished by a comprehensive public transport system, that the provision of more road and parking space for private motorists is self-defeating. Obviously, this has implications for busmen. Of more immediate relevance is the technical change which is taking place. The adoption of one-man operation is increasing earnings levels; the introduction of two-way radio communication will probably increase the effective utilization of vehicles and, equally important, reduce conflict between drivers and supervisors. The individual crew bonus might well deter fiddling. The future for busmen may be less bleak than the recent past.

7

THE RAILWAY OPERATING DEPARTMENT, I:
RAILWAYS AND RAILWAYMEN

THE STRUCTURE OF THE DEPARTMENT

The Railway Operating Department, as its title indicates, operates London Transport's railway system. Its four tube and two sub-surface[1] lines are grouped into four operating divisions. Diagram 7.1 shows the typical structure of a division.

A few words of explanation are called for. The diagram suggests a chain of command which does not exist: for example, for operational reasons a crew may receive instructions from any station-master or inspector, or from a traffic controller. Divisional inspectors are usually allocated to a section of the line and are responsible for it in the sense that they deal with abnormal occurrences, rather than routine operations.

Similarly, division suggests a separation of organization which may be misleading: many stations are located on lines which are the responsibility of different divisions and the stationmaster may therefore have to act on instructions from a division other than his own. For routine administrative matters, then, the divisional structure exists. Operations cross divisional boundaries.

Stationmaster is a grade rather than an office: a large busy station, or a station with a trainmen's depot, may have a senior stationmaster and two or three stationmasters. At the other end of the scale, one stationmaster may be responsible for two or three small stations.

Trainmen—motormen and guards, that is—are attached to depots. A depot is usually located at a station and is essentially a booking-on point, with office, canteen, and mess room accommodation. Some depots have a railway club with games rooms and bar facilities near by.[2] Most depots have stabling for trains, though this

---

[1] The study was carried out before the completion of the Victoria Line, which was added to one of the existing divisions; the Circle Line operates as part of the Metropolitan Line.

[2] See Chapter 16 on sports and social facilities.

DIAGRAM 7.1.

Organization of a Railway Operating Division

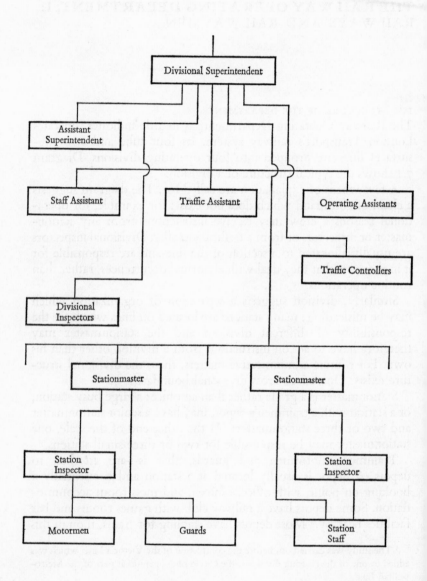

is possibly located some walking distance away. At the time of our study, there were thirty-one trainmen's depots, varying in size from less than a dozen crews to more than one hundred and fifty. The fleet consisted of over 4,000 cars, coupled as roundly 500 trains.

The station staff with which we were mostly concerned in this study were stationmen, stationwomen, male and female ticket collectors, and station foremen. 'Station foreman' is perhaps a misleading designation: the most appropriate parallel in many other industries in terms of responsibilities and duties is that of charge-hand.

Staff establishment in stations varies from about a dozen to over eighty, including 'cover' staff, depending on traffic, the numbers of platforms, entrances, and exits. Cover staff are of two types, rest day and relief, and exist for most grades. Owing to the fact that staff normally work a five-day week and the rail system operates for seven days a week, staff are employed specifically to 'cover' the other two days—that is, rest days. Rest day cover staff then may work one or two days at one station, the next day or two at another, and so on. Usually they are based at a larger station. Relief staff function on a somewhat similar basis, except that they cover absences due to annual leave and sickness.

SOME KEY VALUES AND TRADITIONS OF THE DEPARTMENT, THE TECHNICAL AND SOCIAL ORGANIZATION OF WORK

First, the two key values: time and safety. London's underground system is complex, its constituent lines are closely interrelated in that traffic on two or more services runs over the same track, and it works to a tight time schedule with a small headway—some platforms are served by up to thirty-six trains an hour. 'The second hand of his watch', as Cottrell dramatically puts it, 'becomes a sword of Damocles to the railroader.'[1] Services operate up to twenty hours each day, seven days a week. The importance of regular attendance for work at the prescribed times, and acceptance of the unusual and irregular hours of work, together with a motivation to assist the service to run to time is thus underlined. Moreover, time is more important in train than bus operations: the loss involved in a cancelled bus journey in terms of passenger capacity is but a small fraction of that of a cancelled train journey. A bus running late can,

[1] W. Fred Cottrell, *The Railroader* (Stanford, California, Stanford University Press; and London, Oxford University Press, 1940), p. 69.

of course, be passed by other buses, a procedure hardly possible on the railways.

The importance of safety scarcely needs to be underlined: railway rolling-stock is potentially dangerous equipment, particularly when operated on lines electrified at a voltage that can be fatal. The restricted access of underground operation re-emphasizes the importance of safety.

The organizational responses to the needs of rapid passenger movement with safety have been two-fold: there exist technical safeguards to ensure a high safety factor; and a comprehensive set of rules which specify how rolling-stock and other equipment are to be used. Railway work is first and foremost work to rules.

We can now turn to the implications of these various constraints so far as the workforce is concerned, and here it is useful to note the ideal workforce, as postulated by managers and supervisors—one that many believe existed in the golden age prior to the Second World War. Some operatives, too, shared this view of the ideal railwayman.

In our discussions with staff at several levels many mourned the passing of the 'old railwayman'—a species often said to be all but extinct. The old railwayman can usefully be regarded as an ideal type to which actual railwaymen more or less approximated.[1] First, he accepted the various time values: regular, prompt attendance, the unusual hours, the importance of running to time. He was, for example, prepared to leave Stockwell at 02.30 and cycle several miles to Golders Green to take the first train out. Second, he accepted the quasi-militaristic discipline of the organization, typified by prompt, unquestioning response to instructions.[2] Third, he was smart in appearance and bearing.[3] Fourth, he was alert and remained calm in conditions conducive to stress. Fifth, he had a dedication to all that is railways: knowledge of the rules and equipment; knowledge of and enthusiasm for the *beauty* of the Westinghouse braking system. Railway work, in other words, was of the nature of

---

[1] It ought to be emphasized that the old railwayman need not be chronologically old: we met a small number of operating staff—including some immigrants—who appeared to approximate this ideal type fairly closely and were far from old in years.

[2] In many situations, of course, particularly emergencies with an element of danger, such obedience is functional from the points of view of safety and the operation of services.

[3] It was no accident that preference was given to ex-regular servicemen recruits prior to the Second World War. They were accustomed to discipline and smartness.

a vocation. He possibly lived near other railwaymen and associated with them in his off-duty hours.[1] In short, railways filled most of his waking hours. Sixth, a railwayman joined the industry for the remainder of his working life, and he was a railway *man*.

The actual railwaymen probably resembled this ideal type more closely in some respects than in others. Some who had cycled from Stockwell at 02.30 to work at Golders Green many years ago claimed they 'thought nothing of it'—whether this was so at that time may be another matter.[2] Those railwaymen who told us that employees of the Metropolitan Railway Company were sent home 'in the old days' for arriving for duty wearing *brown* shoes, did not appear very enthusiastic for the revival of such practices. In some respects, the old railwayman is probably a myth: he did not exist in any numbers to the specification of the ideal type.[3] In terms of knowledge of rules and equipment—and enthusiasm for this equipment—the ideal type probably approximated more closely to reality. Here it is useful to introduce another strand in the tradition: that of experience.

The skills of railway operation are mostly specific to the industry: on London Transport's system some skills are specific to the organization. Whilst training is provided in these skills,[4] experience in one grade has been thought an essential prerequisite for promotion to the next. Seniority has been and remains the major mechanism of role allocation. The channels of recruitment and promotion are shown in Diagram 7.2.

Prior to the Second World War, many staff were recruited for the summer months only to cover the period of staff holidays and were discharged in the autumn.[5] A man might work two or three summers before being given a full-time appointment. The major grade of recruitment was that of porter. This designation was later changed to stationman. Given that promotion was and is by seniority, he might spend several years in one grade before being promoted to the next. Thus a man might have been a railwayman for twelve or

---

[1] This association with other railwaymen was partly caused by the unusual hours: when the railwayman was off duty others were working, and vice versa.

[2] Many railwaymen today travel some distance to work in the early hours.

[3] A recently published study of mid-nineteenth century railwaymen has shown too that staff turnover rates were often relatively high. See P. W. Kingsford, *Victorian Railwaymen* (London, Cass, 1970), especially Chapter 3 and pp. 146–7.

[4] See Chapter 14.

[5] This practice was abandoned in 1938: Clegg, p. 153.

DIAGRAM 7.2.   *Channels of Recruitment and Promotion*[1]

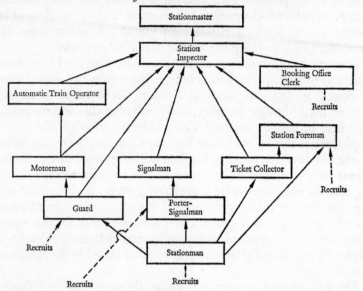

[1] The diagram is an over-simplification to the extent that for some of the grades shown there were *classes* within the grade. The grades open to women were station-woman, ticket collector, and booking-office clerk.

fifteen years before he became a motorman.[1] 'Long' experience was thought necessary and it was assumed that this slow progression through the grades would provide it: by the time a man became a motorman he would know a great deal about trains and railways. Part of this experience he would have acquired by working for several years as a guard. One of the 'traditions' of the Department was that a crew invariably sat together for its tea and meal breaks— in fact the crew was together for the whole shift apart from running time. During much of this time they 'talked railways' and the guard learnt a great deal. How far this tradition is based on fact and how far on myth we do not know, the myth element is, though, probably quite large. It is nevertheless important when we come to consider reactions to the build-up of the immigrant sector of the labour force. The importance of experience was a value shared by some in our samples, as well as by managers and supervisors.

[1] A small number of the older men in our native sample had reached the grade of gateman after several years' service by the time that grade was abolished on the lines of the Underground Group in 1930. They then spent some years as porters before their promotion to guards. Gatemen opened and closed the doors—'gates'—on tube trains before the universal adoption of guard-controlled, air-operated doors. See Jackson and Croome.

The relevance of experience becomes more apparent when we consider the tasks of motormen and guards.[1] Driving a modern underground train—that is, starting it, controlling it, and stopping it—does not require a high degree of *manual* skill. The motorman's skills and abilities are tested when he is confronted by anything un-usual: failure of mechanical, pneumatic, or electrical equipment on the train or track;[2] accidents involving passengers or staff. To meet these situations, the motorman must have a knowledge of the train equipment and the sequence of procedures to be followed in order to locate and isolate a fault; he must also have a detailed knowledge of the railway *Rule Book*.[3] He must also remain calm in conditions conducive to stress: a train fault on a service working to a close headway has to be remedied quickly to prevent a major dislocation of services; railway accidents involving personal injury to passengers or staff can be extremely distressing.

Emergencies do not occur every day, and a motorman or guard may work for years without meeting one. Yet he must learn *and retain* a knowledge of the appropriate rules and procedures. All in all, hardly ideal circumstances for the retention of this knowledge. The relevance of experience is now apparent: given the comparative infrequency with which emergencies are met by most railwaymen, a man may, at present-day promotion rates, progress through the grades of stationman and guard to motorman without seeing or meeting an emergency situation. The important point here is that his experience of an emergency while he was a guard is likely to be useful when he meets one as a motorman. Whether this is objectively so is less important than the fact that it is part of the value system shared by many in the organization, management and operatives alike. Its relevance becomes more obvious when we analyse reac-tions to the recruitment and promotion of coloured immigrant railwaymen. Opportunities for co-operation and conflict between

[1] The exception to the motorman/guard crew arrangement is on those lines where there is automatic train operation (a short section of the Central Line, experimentally, and on the Victoria Line). In these circumstances the train operator monitors rather than controls the movement of the train, performs the guard's door opening and closing functions, and is available should any defect or emergency arise.

[2] Train crews are expected to be able to correct some train faults to enable a train to be moved either to complete its journey or to be taken out of service.

[3] This 230-page document details the procedures to be followed in all matters connected with rail operation and safety on the track. A knowledge and understand-ing of the appropriate rule is especially important in any emergency situation. This *Rules for Observance by Employees* is afterwards referred to as *Rule Book* or *Rules*.

crews are largely absent in the rail situation under normal operating conditions. It is of course important that preceding trains run to time, from the point of view of a crew finishing its journey on time, but it is far easier for railwaymen than busmen to run to time. In an emergency situation, there is some scope for crews to co-operate: for example, a train can 'push out' a defective train. But emergencies do not happen every day.

We now look at the everyday situation of rail crews. On beginning duty a crew may take a train from the depot stabling or take over a train already in service. The former entails train preparation: a sequence of checks that train equipment is correctly positioned and functioning satisfactorily. The duty may be worked on several trains: when a meal break is taken and the train remains in service another crew will take over; the first crew will take over another train, possibly originating from another depot. It may work one or more further trains during the day, its duties may end at another depot or station. In this case the crew will return to the home depot as passengers[1]—or 'on the cushions' in railway slang.[2] A crew perform duties on this pattern for one week and a different pattern, with different hours, the next week, until it has covered all the rostered duties. This is in marked contrast to Central Buses, where a crew normally work one or at most two routes, on vehicles from its own garage. Further contrasts may be drawn between bus and railway work. We have seen the scope for co-operation and conflict both between members of a crew, and between crews, which is inherent in bus operation. We have also seen how other traffic affects bus operation. Rail traffic is under the complete control of the Department, apart from that on British Rail track, and consequently performance is more accurately predictable.

When we examine the possibilities of co-operation and conflict

[1] Whilst most duties are for a period of eight hours, 'wheel-turning' time averages about five hours. The difference is accounted for by the difficulty of scheduling services to exactly fit shifts, and by 'booking on time', 'walking time' (to and from stabling and depot), meal breaks, the time taken to change ends of the train at a terminus, and so on.

[2] Railway slang provides illustrations of traditions in the anachronic terms used. On London Transport railways a signal is commonly referred to as a 'stick', despite the fact that semaphore signals have, with few exceptions, not been used for years. (Possibly the term 'stick' had its *origins* in the days of 'token' working.) See Harvey Sheppard, *Dictionary of Railway Slang* (Somerset, Dillington House College for Adult Education, 1965), the Glossary in Cotterell, and Frank McKenna, *A Glossary of Railwaymen's Talk* (Oxford, Ruskin College History Workshop, 1970).

between motorman and guard, we find a very different situation from that of the bus driver and conductor. Running to time is again important; but given the signal control system, there is far less opportunity to depart from the time-table. Nor is there the incentive: whether the train is full or near-empty makes little difference to the work of the motorman or guard. In any case, neither has much control over the passenger load carried.

In *normal* service conditions, then, provided each carries out his task adequately—that is, largely as prescribed by the rules, but without the unusual zeal displayed during periods of working to rule—there is not much possibility of co-operation or conflict. Of greatest importance is ensuring that the train runs to time: on the guard's part, being quick to close the doors and give the bell signal; on the motorman's part, responding quickly to signals and driving to time.

Any defect or emergency provides more opportunities for co-operation and, in the absence of such co-operation, a potential for conflict. The most common defect experienced is 'sticking' car doors, that is, doors that do not close, a fault most commonly experienced in cold weather. Time is saved if the guard, who is responsible for the doors, checks those of the rear half of the train, whilst the motorman does likewise with the front half.[1]

Likewise with any more serious defect or emergency: both can co-operate to ensure the safety of passengers and resumption of services. In an emergency it is vital that each tells the other what he is doing. Whilst the motorman has no authority to instruct his guard he will normally have had more experience of train operation and will be able to advise the guard in some emergency situations.[2] Ways in which train crews co-operate in practice are discussed more fully below.[3] We can now examine briefly the situation of station staff.

The functions of ticket collectors are largely explained by the grade's designation, though some also carry out platform and cleaning duties. The position of station foreman in the supervisory hierarchy has been explained briefly above; his role is further discussed below.[4]

---

[1] Neither guard nor motorman is subordinate to the other: each has his specific duties and responsibilities. Broadly the division between the two is that all matters concerned with the traction, control, and braking are the province of the motorman, whilst the doors, windows, seating, and passenger comfort and safety in the cars are the guard's responsibility.

[2] The reverse is also sometimes true: some guards with long service can probably help short-service motormen with advice.

[3] Chapter 8, pp. 150–3.　　[4] Chapter 9, pp. 173–4.

The major tasks of stationmen and stationwomen are of two types: platform duties and cleaning duties. Platform duties are to ensure that passengers leave and enter the cars quickly; to advise the guard when he may safely close the doors, in other words, 'give the guard the "right" '; and to answer passengers' queries. In peak traffic periods, three or four stationmen[1] may be on one platform, sometimes supervised by a station foreman, inspector, or station-master. Speed and safety are the two key factors in this work: twenty to thirty seconds is regarded as a reasonable maximum time for a train stop at a platform and often these times are shorter.[2] The need for safety is self-evident. It is important, then, that platform staff work in unison to the extent that they advise passengers to stand clear of the doors at the same time. They can assist the guard— and the service, to maintain time—by closing any sticking doors and by quickly giving him the right when it is safe to do so.

Most cleaning work in stations is done by stationmen.[3] It consists of sweeping platforms, washing walls and passageways, and cleaning windows, lavatories, waiting-rooms, messrooms, and the like. Such work is usually done during off-peak traffic hours. Most of this cleaning work is 'rostered', that is, the days and duties on which, for example, the station escalators should be dusted are shown on the work roster prepared by the stationmaster. Thus, by consulting the roster, a stationman can learn which cleaning duties he should carry out on any given day. A potential source of conflict here among stationmen involves the allegation of one stationman that the last person to carry out a specific cleaning task failed to do it properly, thus making his own task more difficult.

There appears to be far more of a common culture which is shared by the whole Railway Operating Department than exists in Central Buses. We were far less conscious of differences between locations in the railway department, and there appeared to be less self-identification with one location. One important variable here is that railwaymen move from one location to another, particularly on promotion, far more than busmen. Train crews, as we have noted, often work trains from other depots, and take their meal breaks and finish their running duties away from the home depot. Rail staff,

---

[1] For 'stationman' also read 'stationwoman', unless otherwise stated.

[2] Longer waits often result from delayed starting signals, particularly when a service is working to a close headway.

[3] At some busy stations some of this cleaning work is done by cleaners at night; Permanent Way staff clean the track in the station.

too, are far less likely than busmen to live near their place of work.

A partial exception to this general rule of a common culture and tradition, and lack of identification, is the Metropolitan Railway. Here railwaymen, including some scarcely born in the days of the Metropolitan Railway Company, are still apt to say proudly, 'I'm a Met man.' A consciousness of company differences has to some extent been preserved by the continuation of pre-1933 working practices and by protected promotion rights.[1] Many 'Met' men still claim that the Met is the 'premier line'.

THE INTRODUCTION OF COMMONWEALTH IMMIGRANTS TO THE DEPARTMENT

Commonwealth immigrants may be seen as the most recent of a number of groups of non-traditional workers recruited for the Department. Women were employed during the First World War: as station staff from 1915, as gate operators on the tube trains from 1917.[2] There were apparently still a small number of these 1915–18 recruits with the Department in 1939. The Second World War led to women again being recruited in considerable numbers and they appear to be regarded now as a permanent part of the workforce. Certainly, their presence causes little or no controversy. Apart from the traditions aspect, this lack of controversy over the employment of women is in no way surprising: the social and technical organization of work is such that their presence does not cause or increase conflict.[3] They are in any case restricted to the station grades: management proposals that women should be employed as guards have been successfully resisted by the unions.[4]

In the years immediately after the Second World War, a number of Poles and other Eastern Europeans joined the Department. They appear to have made little impact: it seems likely that their command of English was sufficient to enable them to perform their tasks without creating a safety hazard. A number are still with the Depart-

---

[1] Some pre-1933 employees were given preference over other candidates in the undertaking for promotion vacancies on their own line.

[2] One station had an all-female staff. See Jackson and Croome, p. 159.

[3] For a discussion of the controversy surrounding the employment of women in Central Buses, see Chapter 5. Some railway managers and supervisors still find difficulty in disciplining women: they say they are unable to cope with tears.

[4] Given the eventual spread of automatic train operation and the replacement of the motorman-guard crew by a train operator, the employment of women guards is likely to remain a dead issue—unless it is accepted that they may qualify as motormen and train operators.

ment and most, we were told, have become naturalized British subjects.

Dating the arrival of the first coloured *immigrant* staff has proved as difficult as in Central Buses. For many years, certainly before the Second World War, a small number of coloured staff had been employed. In the words of one manager, 'it was just accepted that one in a thousand or so of our staff was coloured'. It seems likely that these men were U.K.-born. Any appreciable increase in the number of coloured staff in the Department does not appear to have taken place before 1953–4, and even then the rate of recruitment was probably fairly slow.[1] The rapid build-up of the numbers of coloured staff appears to have occurred from the mid-fifties onwards.

Reactions of the native staff to these early immigrant recruits appear to have been very similar to those described above in Central Buses,[2] and for that reason are given here in less detail. The general opinion of managers, supervisors, and railwaymen was that the early recruits were very good and that the quality of later arrivals had deteriorated. That the quality of recruits generally, white and coloured, had fallen in the post-war period was a viewpoint commonly expressed by managers and supervisors. Moreover, this view appeared to be far more widespread than in Central Buses. It seems likely that one important variable was the length of service of the informants: most of the railway managers and supervisors were with the Department in the inter-war period; a number in Central Buses had joined after the War.

Given the small numbers of coloured staff in the early days of recruitment, they had to fit in: there was little or no opportunity for the development of separate immigrant groups, which was to cause concern later. As in Central Buses, a number of coloured 'characters' were cited; some of these are still with the Department, others have left.

The first coloured immigrant recruits were employed as stationmen. The prevailing view amongst native trainmen at that time, as reported to us, was that the coloured staff would 'never get off the

---

[1] Referring to opposition to the employment of coloured workers by N.U.R. branches, Bagwell states: 'by September 1950 . . . many more coloured men were being employed, especially on London Transport . . .' See Philip S. Bagwell, *The Railwaymen* (London, Allen & Unwin, 1963), p. 618. It is most unlikely that these men were employed in the Operating Department; it is possible, but again unlikely, that they were in the Permanent Way Department. See Chapter 10.

[2] Chapter 4.

platform', that is, they would not qualify for, or be promoted, to guards. Later, when this prophecy proved false, the attitude changed to 'they will never get off the back'; in other words, they would not become motormen. This also proved false.

We did not find any instances of *organized* opposition to the employment of coloured staff. Some motormen, we were told, refused to take out coloured trainees, but we were not able to obtain definite confirmation of this. When the first coloured station foreman was appointed, the white staff at the station sent in a round robin to the management stating that they would not work under him. The matter was referred to the Sectional Council representative[1] who met the staff concerned and nothing more was heard of this opposition.[2]

It appears that resentment from local staff increased as the numbers of immigrants in the Department increased: when, in other words, there was a sufficient number for separate immigrant groups to develop in the stations and depots. This separation appears to have caused resentment. Moreover, it challenged the tradition of the motorman and guard spending the shift together. Perhaps equally important, some coloured guards were reluctant to make tea in the messrooms for themselves and their white motormen: they preferred a 'Coke', but again this upset a tradition. A number of instances of West Indians cooking a well-known proprietary brand of cat food in messroom frying pans were reported to us. In most cases, however, it turned out that our informants had heard of, rather than seen, the behaviour complained of.

Management views and practices were influenced by a number of factors. In the early years, it was found that coloured staff were not, in numbers, 'getting off the platform'; later, it was found that they were not 'getting off the back'. A number of managers emphasized that the Department is a pyramid: that it relies largely on internal promotion to fill supervisory and management posts.

Whilst efforts were made to spread coloured recruits throughout the system at their initial allocation, the ability of staff to transfer locations at their own request when vacancies arose often acted in opposition to the dispersal policy, and some concentrations of coloured staff did occur. Management views, but not, apparently, actions, were powerfully influenced by a report of a well-known

[1] On Sectional Councils, see Chapter 15.
[2] On native staff attitudes to coloured station foreman, see Chapter 9, pp. 173-4.

firm of management consultants on the organization of the Department in the early sixties; the report recommended, *inter alia*, that coloured staff should not exceed 10 per cent in any one grade.[1] It seems likely that in some grades the 10 per cent point had been passed when the report was written. At the time of our fieldwork, 'selective' recruitment was being used to keep the coloured proportion of staff roughly at the level it had reached, or at most to allow a much slower increase than in the past.

At the beginning of our study, coloured staff comprised some 22 per cent of the wages grades in the Department, up to and including the supervisory grades. The proportions in the different grades varied considerably; those coloured staff in the grades we are mostly concerned with are shown in Table 7.1.

TABLE 7.1
Coloured Immigrant Staff in Selected Railway Operating Grades.*

Grades	Immigrant staff as % of total in grade	Total staff in grade
Guards	50	1,691
Stationmen (including messroom attendants, etc.)	40	605
Stationwomen	38	474
Station foremen	28	501
Women ticket collectors	27	528
Motormen	13	1,669
Ticket collectors	10	652
Total of these grades	30	6,120
Total of Department	22	9,110

* As at September 1965. This list is not exhaustive: it includes only those numerically important grades with which we were concerned in the study. The discrepancy between the two totals is largely accounted for by the omission of the figures for booking-office clerks and the supervisory grades, in both of which coloured immigrants were under-represented. Source: Staff Administration Office, L.T.B.

[1] The report is useful as a further confirmation of the widespread opposition to recruitment of coloured railwaymen in large numbers. Most staff criticisms appear to relate to work performance, safety hazards, and, from motormen, the fear 'that the idea of a motorman/guard "team" has gone'. Source: L.T.B.

Taking the figure for the whole Department as the average, it will be seen that coloured staff were over-represented in a number of grades, including guard and station foreman, and under-represented in the last of the two grades listed, motorman and ticket collector. Some reasons for these differences will become apparent in this and following chapters.

THE STATIONS AND DEPOTS CHOSEN FOR THE DETAILED STUDIES

A pilot study was made at Midway station, which also had a trainmen's depot. The depot, with between fifty and sixty crews, was very much in the middle of the size range in terms of numbers employed. The coloured staff—comprising 52 per cent of the total—were over-represented. Midway's trainmen crewed trains on sub-surface services.

Station staff, including cover and relief grades, numbered about sixty. This makes it large in these terms, but a smaller station might well have produced sampling problems. Coloured staff comprised 51 per cent of the total in the grades with which we were concerned. Again they were somewhat over-represented. A total of twenty-four train and station staff were interviewed in the pilot study.

Following the pilot study, detailed studies were made at two trainmen's depots and six stations. Two important considerations influencing the choice of depots were that the staff should be sufficiently numerous and balanced for sampling purposes, and that an interview room should be available.[1] Both depots were larger than average in terms of staff numbers.

Southway depot, with over one hundred crews, had a coloured population of 41 per cent. Southway is located on the Blue Line, a tube line, and has been a train depot for many years. A small number of the older native staff had been there since it was opened. Apart from its size, Southway was not thought by our management informants to have any particular distinguishing features. The Blue Line is regarded as difficult for two reasons: its layout makes it a complex line to operate and these complexities become formidable when services are interrupted by train or track failure or accident;[2]

[1] One depot initially selected had to be abandoned for lack of a suitable interview room.

[2] The aims in these circumstances are to resume services as quickly as possible, *and* to arrange for crews to be travelling in the right direction at the right time for meal breaks and duty changes to be made roughly as scheduled. Lost mileage is, in effect, written off and the service is reformed: for example, a set of cars scheduled to leave a station at 10.00 becomes the train scheduled to leave at 11.00. The problem is to ensure that the appropriate crew is on the right train.

it has a reputation for a large number of minor errors by trainmen, for example, misreading of time cards and the like. Some managers associate these errors with the fact that Blue Line work is predominantly tunnel work.

Northway depot had more than 150 crews working two lines: the Grey and Red Lines. The former is a sub-surface line, the latter a tube line. Forty per cent of the staff was coloured. The only feature of note about Northway, apart from its size, is that it is a very old established depot, with a history stretching back many years.

The six stations selected differed from each other in a number of respects. They ranged in size, from one employing a dozen to one employing over fifty.[1] In traffic, too, they varied considerably: one was at a main line terminus, two were busy West End inter-change stations, two others were important inter-change stations. All were located in the inner London area, as there was no interviewing accommodation at most stations.[2]

The composition of the interview samples is shown in Table 7.2.

TABLE 7.2
*Interview Samples in Railway Operating**

Grades	Native	Immigrant
Motormen	26	30
Guards	27	30
Station foremen	3	3
Stationmen, ticket collectors	15	20
Stationwomen, women ticket collectors	12	13
	—	—
Total	83	96
	—	
		179

* The figures shown represent those interviewed; information on refusals is given in Chapter 1.

[1] These figures are the numbers in those wages grades included in our study.

[2] We wished to avoid having our interviewees travel any distance for two reasons: the loss of time involved (there was a considerable staff shortage at the time) and the fear that the journey might act as a further disincentive to prospective interviewees. The refusal rate at those stations where we could not interview on the spot was higher than at other stations. In this type of study, the familiarity of the interviewers, in the sense of being seen and known at the location, is probably an important factor influencing refusal rates.

8

THE RAILWAY OPERATING DEPARTMENT, II:
RAILWAYMEN—BLACK AND WHITE

EARLY WHITE NATIVE OBJECTIONS TO THE EMPLOYMENT OF COLOURED
STAFF

It proved impossible to date accurately the arrival of the first
coloured immigrants at most of the depots and stations, and in only
one case, a depot, was it possible to establish when the first arrived.
It appears that at both Northway and Southway depots there was a
lapse of at least several months between the arrival of the first
coloured guard and later arrivals. It is probable that coloured staff
were employed at the stations before they reached the depots.

The problem of uncovering the attitudes and behaviour of some
twelve to fourteen years previously proved to be more difficult
than in Central Buses, and that was difficult enough.[1] The passage
of time and the turnover of staff made it impossible to glean much
detailed information on the reactions of staff at individual stations.
At the depots, the difficulties were not quite so great, as there had
been a greater continuity of staff and a number of the native trainmen were at these depots when the first coloured staff arrived.

Roughly one-third of our native sample reported that white
native staff had objected when the first coloured staff arrived;
another third reported that there had been no objections. The remaining third had joined the Department after the arrival of the
first coloured immigrants.

The most common reason put forward for the objections was
colour, and, as with the busmen, probing failed to reveal the rationale
behind this answer.[2]

The next most frequently mentioned reason was the fear of cheap
labour: wages and conditions would be threatened, not so much
absolutely, but it would be more difficult to get them improved.

[1] See above, Chapter 5.
[2] See above, Chapter 5, on this question, where the various objections to coloured
staff are spelled out in more detail.

Related to this was a fear that coloured staff would be unreliable in times of organized industrial conflict.

There were mixed feelings. We feared that London Transport were looking for cheap labour, but then we got to know them as individuals. When there is any trouble with London Transport [i.e. strike or work to rule] they are with us. [U.K. Motorman.]

The fears of cheap labour and blacklegging by coloured staff were, as I have shown, important also in Central Buses. In both departments the fact is that coloured staff have never blacklegged, and this has been an important factor encouraging their acceptance by white staff. Any blacklegs have been white. The few railwaymen who were still *very* hostile to coloured staff could explain away their behaviour by saying that 'they knew what would have happened to them if they didn't support us', but this explanation was not put forward by the majority.

Other objections, reported by small minorities, were that coloured staff would 'lower the standards'; that they 'got away with more'; that there was suspicion of 'something new'; that the coloured staff initially were not competent to do the job. This last objection was of some importance for trainmen.

The motormen had to 'mother' them and they [the motormen] resented this. I had to know the job [when I became a guard], but they [London Transport] were short of staff and hoped they would learn on the job. [U.K. Motorman.]

As has been shown, both the channel and the speed of promotion to the motorman grade have changed over the past few years. Guard is now a recruit grade, and the period of time a man has to spend as a guard before he can become a motorman is much shorter than it was (assuming he passes the training course, that is). Whereas a pre-war recruit might have been a railwayman for twelve or fifteen years before he became a motorman, recent recruits have joined as guards and have become motormen in two or three years. Comparing our two samples of trainmen, 60 per cent of the native staff had five or more years' service in the Department before promotion to their present grade, as opposed to only 30 per cent of the immigrant sample. Moreover, 26 per cent of the native trainmen sample had ten or more years' service before promotion to their present grade, compared with only 2 per cent of the immigrant sample. The variable here is, of course, the date of joining the Department. The important point is that an old railwayman with many years' service could identify the early coloured guards; he *knew* they did not have long service. He was less likely to know the length of service of white guards who had joined at the same time. Thus objections to the current speed of promotion and to coloured immigrants became intertwined.[1]

Some trainmen who objected to the employment of coloured staff appear to have taken comfort in the belief that they would never get off the platform:

Yes [there were objections]. It was said they would never get beyond porter—but times have changed. [U.K. Motorman.]

Others who said there had not been objections to the early immigrants specifically mentioned that the very first coloured guards at both Northway and Southway depots had arrived some time before the more rapid influx:

No [there were no objections]. The first one came two years before the others—everyone liked him. [U.K. Motorman.]

That the very first coloured guards were popular with at least some of the native staff was an important factor encouraging the acceptance of later arrivals. One at least of these early pioneers acted as a sponsor for later arrivals in that he gave them advice, helped them with housing problems, and so on. Older than the majority of the coloured staff, he was seen by some as something of a father figure.

HOSTILITY BETWEEN WHITE AND COLOURED STAFF
To explore this problem, we asked both samples, 'has there been any hostility in this depot/station towards the Commonwealth immigrants?', and 'is there any hostility now?' Some who gave a 'no' or 'don't know' answer to one or both of these questions then went on to qualify the answer in such a way as to indicate that they thought there had been or still was *some* hostility. Both sets of answers are shown in Table 8.1. (See p. 142.)

It will be seen that the native sample answered both questions consistently: similar numbers reported hostility in the past and at present, both in the initial answers and when the qualifications are taken into account. The immigrants were more likely to report

---

[1] It may be that promotion was too fast in the sense that many railwaymen had not gained 'sufficient' experience by the time they reached the motorman grade. A number of managers and supervisors certainly thought so, as did some railwaymen.

TABLE 8.1.

Hostility Towards the Commonwealth Immigrants in Railway Operating, in Percentages.

| | Initial Answers | | Including Qualified Answers | |
	Native	Immigrant	Native	Immigrant
Hostility in the past				
Yes	27	40	48	55
No	71	56	52	45
Don't Know	1	4	—	—
Hostility at present				
Yes	27	27	48	46
No	71	69	52	54
Don't Know	1	4	—	—
(Sample)	(83)	(96)	(83)	(96)

hostility in the past than at present. Roughly half of each sample indicated that they thought there had been, and still was, some hostility towards immigrants; a small minority of the natives insisted that the hostility came only from the immigrants.

I have shown that there is far less potential for conflict built into the technical and social organization of railway work than in bus operations. An exception to this is to be found with station staff. On the other hand, the traditions of railways, railway work, and railwaymen emerged as powerful obstacles to the acceptance and absorption of newcomers who in most senses of the word were strangers. Most hostile behaviour reported by trainmen sprang more from attitudes than from conflict about work. These attitudes appear to be powerfully influenced by the traditions of the Department. The most frequent *specific* cause of conflict between white and coloured trainmen related to behaviour in messrooms. No instances of physical violence between staff were reported by the staff interviewed, though a few cases were brought to our notice by managers.

On the extent of hostility, almost all the coloured staff who said there was hostility also said it was confined to a few, though this emphasis was less marked amongst station staff than trainmen. The white staff, too, mentioned that hostility was largely confined to 'the odd one or two', but emphasized this point far less than did the coloured staff. They were more likely than the coloured staff to say that hostility was seldom open, rather it was confined to 'bad feelings'. These differences suggest that the white staff thought that hostile *attitudes* were more widespread than did the coloured staff, but the latter were more aware of the extent of hostile *behaviour* than were the former. I concluded that hostile behaviour by native trainmen was confined to a relatively small number. Amongst station staff it was more prominent, in that with the smaller numbers of staff employed and their closer physical proximity for more of the working day, any hostile behaviour was more noticeable and would be brought to the attention of other staff more quickly.

The immigrants' perceptions of the extent of hostile behaviour on the part of the white trainmen can be illustrated from the interview data:

Yes [there is hostility]. Anywhere there are one or two who will be difficult—you just ignore them. There are a few here. [West Indian Motorman.]

The coloured trainmen agreed that hostile behaviour was confined to a few of their white counterparts and that it had diminished over the years. From their point of view the situation had improved.

They used to ignore you and be rude. They wouldn't take tea from you or offer it. It was mainly the older men who have now left. There was jealousy when the coloureds first started becoming motormen. They [the older motormen] wouldn't take coloured trainees. [West Indian Motorman.]

This brings us to a point of contention between white and coloured staff, and a common focus of complaints from white trainmen: tea-making and messroom behaviour generally. One tradition of the Department has been that in messrooms the guard makes the tea for himself and his motorman, although sometimes the reverse occurs. Given that West Indians, initially at least, are far less addicted to tea than are the English, there has been some reluctance to make tea; they did not see why they should make it when they did not drink it. The English motormen resented this:

It irks them to make tea when they don't drink tea; they sit at the tables and ignore the whites. But this is natural—to feel at home! [U.K. Motorman.]

'Sitting at the table and ignoring the whites' refers to the wide-spread practice amongst mixed crews of 'splitting' in a canteen or messroom. This lack of conformity caused some resentment, though it was not universal or always deeply felt:

In the majority of cases in canteens the motorman and guard split up if one is coloured and the other is white. The coloureds don't want to be unfriendly, but there is an indefinable something. [U.K. Guard.]

The other major area of complaint over messrooms concerned dominoes, the game favoured by railwaymen, both white and coloured. The West Indians in particular brought more outward enthusiasm and gusto to the game than is customary amongst English railwaymen, and this caused some annoyance:

The older ones get upset at the way the coloureds slam the dominoes down on the tables. [U.K. Guard.]

Midway was an exception in the Railway Operating Department in that card games were preferred.[1]

There are two card schools down below [in the messroom]: one white, one coloured. If someone goes to the 'wrong one' someone will say – jokingly – 'there is a colour bar'. [U.K. Motorman.]

This comment provides one more indication of the extent to which the pluralistic as opposed to the absorption model is appropriate. It is likely that the behaviour described is explicable in terms of what anthropologists call 'joking relationships'.[2]

As with the busmen, the outward manifestations of hostility were largely confined to *graffiti* and snubbing.

Yes [hostility] is there. You can tell by the writing on the walls opposite the motorman's compartment at the 'seven-car stop'.[3] It must be by drivers. Some of our boys retaliate, but I don't stoop so low . . . it will

[1] Card games were also preferred by busmen. See Chapter 5.

[2] That is, in situations with a possibility of divergences of interest and therefore of conflict, but where structural factors require the avoidance of conflict, the joking relationship serves to emphazise the separateness of groups but at the same time 'any serious hostility is prevented by the playful antagonism of teasing . . . ' The joking relationship 'expresses and emphasizes both detachment (as belonging to separated groups) and attachment'. A. R. Radcliffe-Brown, *Structure and Function in Primitive Society* (London, Cohen and West, 1952), pp. 92, 110. For a discussion of joking modes of behaviour with less emphasis on structural factors see Barry A. Turner, *Exploring the Industrial Subculture* (London, Macmillan, 1971), pp. 42–6.

[3] At some stations on tube lines the platforms are shorter than a seven-car train; when stationary, the motorman's compartment is thus inside the tunnel mouth.

be better when they [white railwaymen] can take us for granted. [West Indian Motorman.]

Graffiti with racial overtones are commonly found on the walls of platforms and public passages in many stations, particularly in Central London, as well as in railway cars. It seems likely that the writers are passengers rather than staff: the latter have to remove it.

In sum, overt hostility was confined to a small proportion of the white native trainmen, and to *graffiti*. Such hostility was, however, seldom complete.

[There is hostility] from individual people, but even so we talk and change duties.[1] There is a more friendly atmosphere now than there used to be. [West Indian Motorman.]

This statement from an English guard provides a fitting conclusion to this discussion:

Both sides are tolerant to each other, but there is no question of deep friendship—it's not exactly Darby and Joan.

Turning to the station staff, both samples were less likely than were the trainmen to say that hostility was seldom open. The coloured station staff, too, were less likely to say that hostility was confined to a few. There are, of course, a number of differences between the social situations of train and station staff. The latter spend far more of their working day in close proximity to each other; apart from cover staff, they spend the whole day at one location and often take their meal breaks in the messroom. Numbers are usually smaller and an individual can make more impact. It is comparatively less easy for them to avoid a person known to be hostile.

Conflict over the use of messrooms was in evidence at both Abbey Street and Bell Street stations. Some of the native staff said they took their meal breaks away from the station to avoid using the messroom.

They are arrogant. We hardly use the messroom—it is filthy. They shout and scream—if you try to reason with them they call you a white basket. [U.K. Woman Ticket Collector.]

---

[1] A mutual change of duties is a very common practice amongst trainmen, possibly more so than amongst busmen. Stories are told of enterprising individuals who sell duties—sometimes ending up with the same duty, but a pound or two in pocket. Such stories are, in part at least, probably based on fact.

This statement, it should be added, came from a person who admitted to being prejudiced and who expressed a wish to emigrate to get away from 'them'.

Allegations that standards of performance had fallen and that coloured staff were treated more leniently were made by some.

[Hostility] is all over the job [London Transport]. The job is going down and the old hands are losing interest. They [coloured staff] get away with murder—years ago you'd be out. [U.K. 'Old Railwayman' Ticket Collector.]

In the Railway Operating Department, we found no evidence of coloured staff being treated more leniently in any respect. Amongst most managers and supervisors there appeared to be a *rigid* insistence that they be treated equally.[1] On the other hand, some of the coloured railwaymen thought that supervisors lacked impartiality.[2]

RELATIONSHIPS BETWEEN MOTORMEN AND GUARDS, AND THEIR RELATIONSHIPS WITH PLATFORM STAFF

The method of allocating newly qualified trainmen was as follows. On completing their training, guards nominated the depots they would like to work from in terms of first preference, second preference, and so on. In this allocation, seniority of service was all-important: if two or more nominated the same depot and there was only one vacancy, the most senior man was successful. Thus a guard who was an ex-stationman had an advantage over a direct-recruit guard. If there were more newly qualified guards than vacancies, those who could not be immediately allocated became station-guards: that is, they performed, nominally at least, the duties of a stationman, but covered as guards when the regular guards were required for other purposes, for instance, training as motormen. When vacancies arose, they were allocated to them.

The system for allocating newly qualified motormen was broadly similar. If there were not a sufficient number of vacancies for motormen, those who could not be immediately allocated became guard-motormen: that is, they performed guards' duties, covering as motormen when regular motormen were absent due to training or long-term sickness. Again, they were allocated to vacancies on the basis of seniority of service.

[1] This rigidity may be dysfunctional for the organization. See Chapter 14 on railway training.

[2] This is discussed further in Chapter 9.

Whilst there is a parallel here with spare staff in Central Buses, there is an important difference: spare duties were included in trainmen's duty rotas and absences due to lateness or short-term sickness were covered by those on spare duties. Up to 15 per cent of trainmen's duties were spare duties.[1] The rules governing the use of spare staff, station-guards and guard-motormen provided that absences due to lateness and short-term sickness were covered by spare trainmen; absences due to training or long-term sickness were covered by station-guards or guard-motormen. Should a motorman be required, a guard-motorman would cover the duty and his duty would in turn be covered by a station-guard. Seniority dictated which guard-motorman would be allocated to the cover duty. In short, spare staff covered unpredictable absences; station-guards and guard-motormen covered predictable commitments.[2]

A motorman-guard crew is permanent in the sense that once both are allocated to work together they continue to do so. An exception to this general rule was found on some of the sub-surface services included in our study: here trainmen were rostered to work with a different partner every week, a practice apparently inherited from one of the pre-1933 railway companies. Moreover, mutual changes of duties are common and a trainman is far less likely than a busman to work with his regular rostered partner. The pairing of the trainmen in our samples is shown in Table 8.2.

TABLE 8.2.
Crew Partner of Trainmen Samples, in Percentages.

| Crew partner | Samples | |
	Native	Immigrant
U.K. or Irish	38	30
West Indian	26	40
Asian	—	3
Other/Don't know	8	2
Not regularly paired*	28	25
(Sample)	(53)	(60)

* Including a small number of guard-shunters and motormen-shunters who work in the depots.

[1] See Select Committee on Nationalised Industries, *Report: London Transport* (London, H.M.S.O., 1965), Vol. 2, pp. 111–12.
[2] There have apparently been changes here since the field work.

A coloured trainman was more likely to have a coloured than a white partner, and *vice versa*, but the difference in this respect was not very great. If those motormen who did not have a regular guard are excluded 75 per cent of coloured and 56 per cent of native motormen had coloured guards. (Of the total number of guards at the three depots, 59 per cent were coloured.) There was then some tendency for the pairing of two coloureds and of two whites, but the bias in this direction was not very great.

As with the busmen, we asked our trainmen samples 'how do you get on together?—that is, with the partner. The answers are summarized in Table 8.3.

TABLE 8.3.
Trainmen's Relationship with Crew Partner, in Percentages.

	Native	Immigrant
Very well	36	38
Well	8	22
Fair	23	13
Poor	6	—
Not regularly paired	28	25
(Sample)	(53)	(60)

The pattern of the two samples is fairly similar, but a higher proportion of the native sample evaluated the relationship with their partners as only fair or poor than did the immigrant trainmen.[1] When the fair and poor answers were related to the origins of the partner, however, no significant difference was found: racial or ethnic differences did not figure as variables in the evaluation of crew relationships.

Table 8.4 shows that there was little difference in the length of time the trainmen in the samples had worked with their partners. (See p. 149.)

Clearly, there was a considerable amount of partner-changing amongst the trainmen: over one-third of both samples had worked with their partners for less than one year. Related to this are trainmen's preferences for permanent partners or for changing weekly. Table 8.5 shows these preferences. (See p. 149.)

[1] With the busmen, this pattern was reversed. See Chapter 5.

TABLE 8.4.
Time Worked with Crew Partner: Trainmen (in Percentages).

	Native	Immigrant
Not regularly paired	28	25
Under six months	23	32
6–12 months	11	8
1–2 years	25	27
3–4 years	9	5
5 or more years	4	3
(Sample)	(53)	(60)

TABLE 8.5.
Trainmen's Preferences for Partner, in Percentages.

	Native	Immigrant
Prefer permanent motorman or guard	53	58
Prefer to change motorman or guard	21	8
No preference	8	23
No answer*	19	10
(Sample)	(53)	(60)

* This category is composed of those interviewed in the pilot study, who were not asked the preference question, and of the shunters, for whom the question was not applicable.

Roughly similar proportions of both samples showed a preference for a permanent motorman or guard. Amongst the natives, proportionately more expressed a positive preference for changing partners; the immigrants were more likely than the natives to be indifferent. Few in either sample who did not change expressed a wish to do so. When the preferences of those who did change were examined, the majority of the natives in this group preferred to change, but the immigrants split equally, with a small remainder having no preference.

Advocates of a permanent partnership usually pointed to the seen advantages of knowing the motorman or guard and consequently being better able to work as a team. Immigrant staff found some of the natives' behaviour ambiguous, and with a regular partner much of this ambiguity and uncertainty was removed.

You know the man you have to work with. Some [motormen] can be awkward, so I prefer a permanent one. [West Indian Guard.]

Arguments against a permanent partnership were more diverse:

If you have a regular guard who isn't popular with the other men, then it is difficult to get anyone to change turns with you. [U.K. Motorman.]

You don't get stuck with someone you don't like this way. [West Indian Motorman.]

Those who expressed no preference often pointed out that as many trainmen change duties, the permanency is more apparent than real.

One element of the motorman-guard relationship is the set of mutual expectations. To explore these expectations, and to see how far the immigrants had accepted the predominant values of the native trainmen regarding the performance of their roles, we asked both groups how a motorman could help his guard with his work and *vice versa*. Table 8.6 summarizes the responses to the first of these questions.

TABLE 8.6.
How a Motorman Can Help his Guard, in Percentages.★

	Native	Immigrant
Gives him advice	43	37
Checks half the train when 'trouble'/ assist with defect	23	25
Co-operates/works as a team	25	13
Quick response to signals/ runs to time	13	17
Stops at the car stop	9	12
Knows his own job/does his own job	9	8
Attends to 'own end' when turning train	4	8
Assists with train preparation	—	8
Passes on information/tells him of intended action	6	3
Other	6	4
Cannot help him	6	5
(Sample)	(53)	(60)

★ More than one answer was recorded and the percentage totals may therefore exceed 100.

With the exception of the 'co-operate' and 'assist with train preparation' categories, the pattern of responses of both samples is broadly similar. At this point, it might perhaps be useful to explain more fully the coding categories used for the answers.

'Giving advice' stems largely from the fact that motormen are all ex-guards, and are likely to have longer experience of railway work than their guards. Thus they are often able to advise a guard on the action he should take.

It has been noted that the train defect most commonly experienced is sticking passenger doors. Obviously time is saved if the guard checks one half of the train and the motorman the other. The same kind of co-operation works well in situations where a passenger operates the emergency stop device. In any emergency situation there is scope for co-operation between motorman and guard, and a defect is normally rectified more quickly through this co-operation. To meet most train defects there is a definite sequence of checks and operations to be performed, some by the guard, some by the motorman. Given that guard and motorman are at opposite ends of a train, the importance of one telling the other of the action he is taking to remedy a defect will be apparent. 'Passing on information' refers to the fact that station staff may tell a motorman or guard of delays in the service ahead, and so on. If one passes this information to the other, they both know if they need to take any unusual action.

'Stopping at the car stop' is especially important at those stations where a train is longer than the platform. If the position of the train does not match that of the platform, the guard may have to 'cut out' (that is, leave closed) passenger doors at one end of the train, possibly causing some delay whilst passengers use alternative doors.

At a terminus, motorman and guard 'change ends' of the train. There is a sequence of operations to be performed, for example, changing the destination indicators, releasing the air pressure, before the train is ready to proceed in the opposite direction. Time is saved if both partners attend to their own ends of the train before they change.

Thus far the discussion has dealt exclusively with those aspects of the guard's relations with his motorman on which there was a large measure of agreement between native and immigrant trainmen. Where they differed was on the emphasis they gave to helping with train preparation and more so to co-operation and working as a team.

When we pressed trainmen on their meaning of 'co-operation' we seldom received a reply more specific than 'you've got to work as a team'. It appeared that most aspects of a motorman and guard helping each other are grouped under this umbrella term; including a crew checking (vetting) each other's work, particularly when dealing with a train defect. It is not obvious why the immigrant train staff stressed this less than did the native: it may be that their notion of co-operation was more specific, for example in train preparation, though relatively few mentioned this. On the other hand it may be that they attach less importance to working as a team, which emphasizes a general, overall interdependence.

Whilst a motorman can help his guard, the guard can also help his motorman. The answers to our question on this aspect of the crew relationship are shown in Table 8.7.

TABLE 8.7.

*How a Guard Can Help his Motorman, in Percentages.**

	Native	Immigrant
Checks half the train when 'trouble'/ assists with defect	36	40
Quick or slow on doors and bell to run to time	28	13
Knows his own job/does his own job	25	22
Co-operates/works as a team	21	13
Attends to 'own end' when turning train	8	7
Assists with train preparation	6	8
Passes on information/tells him of intended action	4	7
Books on in time to prepare train	6	5
Other	6	5
Cannot help him	4	5
(Sample)	(53)	(60)

* More than one answer was recorded and the percentage totals may therefore exceed 100.

With the exception of the emphasis on two aspects of behaviour, there was again a wide measure of agreement between the two samples. That the immigrants mentioned the importance of the guard being quick or slow on the doors and bell to facilitate running to time less frequently than did the natives, provides something of a puzzle. In the bus situation, the comparable action by the conductor was stressed more by the immigrants than the natives.[1]

[1] See above, Chapter 5.

Of the other notable difference of emphasis between the immigrant and native trainmen—namely, over 'co-operation'—there is little to add to the previous discussion of this point in relation to the motorman helping his guard. A close examination of the answers, however, suggested a slight difference of emphasis between the native and immigrant trainmen in their perception of the motorman-guard relationship. The native trainmen, particularly when talking about 'work as a team', stress the *equality* of the relationship which accords with the rule that neither is subordinate to the other. There was some tendency for the immigrants to indicate that they saw the motorman-guard relationship as a superordinate-subordinate one—put at its crudest, one in which the guard should do what the motorman *tells him*. Possibly this superordinate-subordinate definition reflected the reality of the early days of immigrant guards when apparently many motormen complained that they had to 'carry' them. The difference in emphasis between the two samples was not large, but possibly it is explicable in terms of this passing phase of an all-native motormen workforce which saw the early immigrant guards as subordinate.

Finally in this section I turn to relationships between train crews and platform staff. In order to see how far the trainmen's expectations of the platform staff accorded with the latter's perception of platform duties and, more important, to compare the expectations and perceptions of native and immigrant railwaymen, we asked, 'how can the platform staff help the train crews in their work?' Table 8.8 summarizes the answers given. (See p. 154.)

It is useful here to explain the coding categories used. With a service working to a close headway, speed in the loading and unloading of passengers is called for if the service is to run to schedule and the headway maintained. Ensuring that all passengers who wish to alight are able to do so before others board the train, helps minimize the train's stopping time, as does checking that all who wish to, have boarded before signalling to the guard to close the car doors. Related to this is checking car doors that are stuck owing to passengers holding them open or to an equipment defect. On busy platforms in peak hours there are usually several station staff on duty and time is saved if one pushes the offending door shut.

On curved platforms it is not possible for a guard to see that it is safe to close the car doors without leaving his compartment; on a busy platform it may be impossible or near impossible to ensure that it is safe to do so. Those who emphasized the importance of

TABLE 8.8.
*How Platform Staff Can Help Trainmen, in Percentages.**

	Native Respondents		Immigrant Respondents	
	Trainmen	Station staff	Trainmen	Station staff
Make sure passengers are all on and off before signalling guard/help with difficult passengers/check doors if trouble	28	57	42	69
Give proper signals/be visible	11	27	17	53
Present, especially on curved platforms and in rush hours	42	10	30	6
Pass on messages to and from trainmen	15	23	28	3
'Do their job'	9	3	—	7
Cannot do much	—	—	2	11
Implied criticism of platform staff	43	—	35	—
Don't know	2	—	2	—
No answer†	—	13	—	6
(Sample)	(53)	(30)	(60)	(36)

* More than one answer was recorded and the percentage totals may therefore exceed 100.

† This category is comprised of those in Ticket Collector Class I, for whom the question was not applicable.

station staff being visible and giving the correct signal were thinking in terms of this situation. Related to this, but less precisely stated, were the answers of those who said that platform staff should be *on the platform*. Such answers came mostly from trainmen and were often accompanied by criticisms of platform staff and especially of their failure to be present on the platform.

'Passing on messages' is a two-way process: a train crew may, for example, require a fitter to correct a fault, or a relief motorman or guard to take over because of illness or physical relief. It may be necessary for trainmen to be informed of delays ahead, or of a 're-formation' of the service.[1]

[1] See above, Chapter 7.

The table indicates that platform staff, both immigrant and native, were more specific in the ways in which they thought they could assist trainmen than were the trainmen themselves. The tendency for the immigrant trainmen to be more specific than their native counterparts may be related to their more recent experience of platform work.

The difference between the two samples of station staff in their mention of 'passing messages' possibly reflects the recency of being called upon to perform this task, rather than any difference in their perception of it.

Trainmen were often critical of platform staff: of their absence, particularly from busy or curved platforms, or when the trainmen require a message to be passed on; and of the passing of inaccurate messages. The following comments illustrate these criticisms.

In peak traffic they should always be there. Often they are not and passengers try to get in and they can't and the train can't get away. [West Indian Motorman.]

They are very short of staff, and they can't do much 'til they are fully staffed. Stations that are fully staffed are O.K. The only difficulty is when you put out a message for a physical relief and they send a fitter. [U.K. Motorman.]

EVALUATIONS OF THE QUALITIES REQUIRED BY THE 'GOOD'
RAILWAYMAN

I have outlined above the attributes of the 'old railwayman' as he was presented to us by numerous informants; it is useful to regard him as an ideal type. To establish the image of the good railwayman as held by both immigrants and natives and to compare the perceptions of both groups to see how far the dominant values have been acquired by the immigrants, we asked, 'what makes a good . . . motorman? guard? stationman?' and so on, as appropriate. Table 8.9 summarizes the replies given. (See p. 156.)

The table shows a striking pattern of agreement between the immigrant and native staff in their image of the good railwayman. There are some differences of emphasis between the two groups, but these are relatively small. There are of course differences between the train and station staff, and these serve to underline the similarities of the occupational groupings. The meaning of most of the coding categories used is self-evident, but they can be usefully filled out and illustrated from the interview material.

TABLE 8.9
*The Qualities and Behaviour of the 'Good' Railwayman, in Percentages.**

| | Native Respondents | | Immigrant Respondents | |
	Trainmen	Station staff	Trainmen	Station staff
Tolerant/patient/good tempered/polite	21	57	17	50
Drives properly/observes speed restrictions/has a concern for safety/does the job properly/follows the rules	40	37	57	31
Likes the job/interested/eager to learn	30	3	22	14
Experience/knows the job	19	10	28	8
Keeps his head/concentration/confidence/judgement/quick thinking/alertness	17	20	25	19
Helpful to passengers/avoids trouble with passengers/knows how to deal with difficult passengers	9	23	10	25
Punctual and regular attendance/runs to time	15	7	22	11
Tidy/smart	6	7	5	6
Other answers	6	10	2	6
Don't know	2	—	—	6
(Sample)	(53)	(30)	(60)	(36)

* More than one answer was recorded and the percentage totals may therefore exceed 100.

First, the trainmen. Of paramount importance here is that the good motorman or guard does his job properly in all respects, with an underlying emphasis on safety. Driving properly, observing speed restrictions,[1] following the rules—all are concerned with safety.

[1] Speed restrictions exist for safety reasons where the track curvature follows a tight radius—particularly on some sections of the older tube lines which closely follow the street alignments—across complex line junctions and, temporarily, when track is undergoing repair work.

London Transport would say [a good motorman is] 'reliable'. I would agree, plus observing speed restrictions and doing the job as it is taught. [West Indian Motorman.]

Liking the job, being interested in it and eager to learn about it, were also stressed.

If he is interested—he must be interested or it is no good him getting on the back of the train: it is dangerous to him and to others. [West Indian Guard.]

Related very much to both doing the job properly and to being interested in it is the quality referred to as knowing the job. Knowing the rules and train equipment were both stressed, as, to a lesser extent, was experience. One U.K. motorman mentioned 'years of practice'.

The importance of alertness and concentration in railway operations scarcely needs to be stressed; likewise avoiding panic in an emergency:

A chap on his toes [is a good motorman]. Observant . . . reaction is the most important thing. [U.K. Motorman.]

A person who is calm and steady, can cope with an emergency and doesn't panic. [West Indian Motorman.]

These qualities are of course very much related to tolerance and patience, those qualities mentioned more by the station staff who thought them important in their dealings with passengers.

A more positive orientation to passenger comfort was displayed by some who spoke of being helpful to passengers:

If passengers treat you nice, treat them nice. Be helpful with information, and help them if they are sick. [West Indian Guard.]

Finally, in relation to the trainmen, there are the various aspects of time: booking on on time, running to time, regular attendance for work.

[A good guard has] a sense of responsibility over time—and everything else. [U.K. Guard.]

The answers of the station staff fell into the same categories as did those of the trainmen, but there were differences of emphasis. Station staff are more constantly in a face-to-face situation with passengers and their answers reflected this interaction. Both native and immigrant station staff stressed the importance of being patient, tolerant, and good-tempered with passengers. Ticket collectors particularly emphasized this:[1]

Cheerful ... have a good temperament, use your discretion—this is necessary for all jobs dealing with the public. [U.K. Ticket Collector.]

An ability to cope with difficult passengers was stressed by some:

[A good ticket collector] knows how to handle passengers—especially when they are nasty. [West Indian Ticket Collector.]

Some of the answers illustrated or hinted at a theme that was emphasized by both immigrant and native staff: namely, that the passenger is always right, that station staff must be tolerant, polite, helpful, even when, or perhaps especially when, passengers are awkward or difficult.

When stationmen or stationwomen spoke of doing the job properly they were seldom very specific, though there was often an emphasis on doing what they were told to do:

Do your work as you should. If you are told by the stationmaster, get on with it. [West Indian Stationman.]

Ticket collectors' answers under this heading were more specific: they spoke of making sure that passengers had tickets, and the correct tickets at that, and of 'clipping' the tickets.

When speaking of quick thinking, alertness, keeping your head, stationmen and stationwomen had in mind any emergency situation in which this might be necessary.

The other categories of answer given by the station staff either had a similar emphasis to those already discussed in relation to the trainmen, or their meaning is self-evident and needs no further expansion or explanation.

The good railwayman, as he is perceived by both immigrants and natives, can now be compared with the ideal type 'old railwayman'. The essential qualities of this ideal type, it will be remembered, were briefly: acceptance of the various 'time' values, (in practice, regular and punctual attendance at unusual hours, and recognition of the importance of running to time). Prompt and unquestioning obedience of instructions; acceptance of a quasi-militaristic discipline; a smart appearance; alertness and calm; dedication to all that is railways.

[1] It will be seen below that ticket collectors meet considerable difficulty with passengers, particularly over attempts at fare evasion, and often feel vulnerable. See Chapter 9.

First, the various time values. Looking at the components of time there is no reason to suppose that the importance of running to time was not accepted by either immigrant or native trainmen. There is, in any case, far less incentive or opportunity for trainmen than for busmen to depart from the time schedules. It is the necessity for regular and punctual attendance that some of the immigrants did not appear to fully accept. Some complained that they were expected to explain absences, arguing that as they were not paid for the time lost, why should they have to explain?[1]

Both samples fail to measure up to the ideal type on the question of acceptance of unusual hours. Substantial numbers of both native and immigrant railwaymen dislike shift work, and it is likely that discontent over this is one of the most important reasons why some cease to be railwaymen. Possibly it is the most important single factor in staff wastage. The acceptance by actual 'old railwaymen' of these unusual hours is probably, in part at least, a myth: given the lack of alternative employment opportunities, they had little choice but to *conform* to the pattern of hours required.

The need for prompt, unquestioning obedience to instructions was stressed by the station staff only. The immigrant station staff appeared to rate obedience to instructions at least as highly as did the natives when describing the good railwayman, and here there appeared to be little or no difference between the two groups. Trainmen are largely free from constant face-to-face supervision—and this is one aspect of the job which they liked, particularly the immigrant trainmen[2]—which perhaps explains their omission of obedience among the traits of the good railwayman.

Smartness in appearance and bearing was another quality of the ideal type. Few in either sample mentioned being tidy or smart as important for the good railwayman. There is less insistence now by management and supervision on rigid conformity in dress and appearance than there was, apparently, in the past. By conventional English standards, the immigrants appeared no less smart or tidy than did the native railwaymen. It seems likely that current norms of dress and appearance are some way removed from those postulated in the ideal, the 'old railwayman'.

The 'old railwayman' was always alert and remained 'calm' in any emergency. Both natives and immigrants accepted these as

[1] See below, Chapter 9. No comparative data on absences were available.
[2] See Chapter 9.

attributes of the good railwayman, although immigrants marginally more so. One of the alleged deficiencies of immigrant railway-men was a tendency to panic in conditions of stress. There were some managers and supervisors who *thought* this might be so, but little evidence was offered.

The ideal type had a sense of dedication to railway work, which was seen as a vocation, rather than a mere job. Both groups stressed the importance of doing the job properly but somewhat more immigrants did so. The ability to do the job properly implies a knowledge of *what* to do. Vital here is a knowledge of the rules: some managers told us that *understanding*, as distinct from knowledge, of the rules was low amongst both immigrant and native railway-men, but I am not competent to comment on this.[1]

The 'old railwayman' had an interest in and liking for railway work. Both our samples mentioned this quality, the native trainmen somewhat more so than the immigrants. If the difference between the two samples here is significant, it may reflect job discrimination elsewhere: it will be seen that proportionately more immigrant than native trainmen said there was nothing they liked about their jobs; they were, in other words, 'reluctant railwaymen'.[2]

A further index of 'interest' in the job is participation in the voluntary training courses for railwaymen at the Training Centre. Proportionately more of the immigrant than the native trainmen had attended these classes.[3] Possibly they have an instrumental approach here, intending to improve their promotion prospects rather than their proficiency in their present grades. If this is the correct explanation it indicates a motivation fully in accord with the traditions of the Department.

Finally, there is the 'good' railwayman's relationships with passengers. Whilst elements of the ideal type 'old railwayman' are ultimately concerned with the safety and comfort of passengers, and the *Rules* emphasize this, there is, in the railway tradition, such a concern with *railway* techniques of operation and so on that an outsider might be forgiven for assuming that passengers do not count for much. It is almost as though the operation of a railway provides its own *raison d'être*. The mystique of railway operations, and its esoteric language, serve to buttress and legitimize this some-what closed social system—the passenger is very much an outsider.

---

[1] The Department's policy is to test trainmen annually on their knowledge of the *Rule Book*. In practice, the interval between rule book tests is much longer.

[2] See Chapter 9 below.   [3] See Chapter 14.

One reason why passengers do not loom large in the railway tradition is that the 'old railwayman' is concerned with the movement of rolling stock: as a trainman, possibly as a signalman or a supervisor. He is less likely to be thought of as a ticket collector or stationman, who are relatively low in the internal status hierarchy.

The image of the 'good' railwayman as presented by the immigrants was very similar to that drawn by the native railwaymen. In some respects this image differs significantly from the ideal type 'old railwayman'. The unusual hours of railway work in particular are only grudgingly accepted by many. The 'vocational' aspect of railway work, too, is diminishing in importance. As more than one native told us 'this "old railwayman" business is going out—it's more like any other job now'. Experience is a less salient value and is becoming less relevant—but it is still *one* of the key values and far from irrelevant. Present-day levels of staff wastage, too, serve to undermine the vocational aspect of railway work; for many it is no longer a 'job for life'.

The demise of the 'old railwayman' is by no means complete. We met a number of railwaymen, immigrant as well as native, who appeared to conform fairly closely to the ideal type. Perhaps, too, the immigrants will provide a new generation of old railwaymen, different in some respects from the ideal type. Many have joined at a relatively young age. The skills of railway work are largely non-transferable. Many coloured railwaymen, particularly those in the grade of motorman and above, are likely to find earnings levels available elsewhere unattractive. In spite of the 1968 Race Relations Act covert job discrimination is likely to remain an enduring feature of many sectors of industry. For many years to come the coloured working population is likely to be over-represented in public transport.

NATIVE RAILWAYMEN'S EVALUATIONS OF IMMIGRANTS AS RAILWAYMEN

I have argued that the 'adequate' performance by the coloured immigrants of their occupational roles has been a key factor in their acceptance by their fellow-workers, and by managers, supervisors, and passengers. 'Adequate' I have defined in terms of the expectations these groups have of railwaymen in their occupational roles. To explore native railwaymen's assessments of coloured railwaymen's abilities and performance we asked them 'do Commonwealth immigrants make good [own grade]?' Further, we asked the native trainmen: 'do Commonwealth immigrants make good [crew partner's grade]?' The answers to these two questions are summarized in Table 8.10.

TABLE 8.10.
Native Railwaymen's Assessments of Commonwealth Immigrants as 'Good' Railwaymen, in Percentages.

	As motormen	As guards	As station staff
Yes, most are/some are, some aren't/ same as Europeans	64	60	57
Some are, most are not	21	36	33
No, none are	—	4	3
Don't know	9	—	7
No answer	6	—	—
(Sample)	(53)	(53)	(30)

The table shows that between one-half and two-thirds of the native railwaymen regarded their immigrant fellow-workers as being on the whole no better or worse than native railwaymen: between roughly a quarter and a third said the majority did not make good railwaymen and very few said that no immigrants were good railwaymen.[1]

A number of the natives, including some who rated immigrants as no better or worse than other railwaymen, then went on to make specific criticisms.[2] These criticisms are shown in Table 8.11.

The most frequent criticism of the coloured staff involved their alleged recklessness or irresponsibility:

Definitely not [they do not make good guards]. They have no interest in the job—it's just a means to an end. They have no sense of reponsibility. Their work is slipshod: they pick up [a train] at the wrong place, they have no train journal[3]—they say they haven't had time to get one. They will not 'see' the train out of the station—they sit down and read a book. [U.K. Guard.]

[1] The pattern of answers from the native busmen to the same question was very similar. See Chapter 5.

[2] Native station foremen's comments on their immigrant colleagues are discussed in detail in the section devoted to immigrant station foremen in Chapter 9.

[3] A log in which arrival and departure times, delays, and the reasons for them are recorded by the guard.

TABLE 8.11.
*Native Railwaymen's Criticisms of Immigrant Railwaymen, in Percentages.**

	As motormen	As guards	As station staff
Reckless/irresponsible/excitable	28	45	33
Lazy/slow	2	6	17
Difficult to understand	4	8	7
Only interested in money	4	8	3
Clannish/chip on the shoulder	4	6	3
Get away with more	—	—	3
No answer	6	—	—
No criticisms	54	34	43
(Sample)	(53)	(53)	(30)

* More than one answer was recorded and the percentage totals may therefore exceed 100.

The complaint that immigrant guards read books or newspapers on the train was a fairly common one. Observation suggests that this practice is at least as popular with native guards as it is with the immigrants.

Some native trainmen said that whilst the immigrants did the job all right in *normal* service conditions, they thought that they were liable to panic in an emergency, or at least feared that they might.

They haven't a sense of responsibility. I don't know how they would react in an emergency, but they do the [motorman's] job all right. [U.K. Motorman.]

Only a few [make good motormen], really. In an emergency a lot are liable to get over-excited. [But]

The majority [of immigrants] who are motormen are as good as anyone else—they [London Transport] are selective.

This brings us to a point of some importance in relation to the different assessments often made of immigrant motormen and immigrant guards. A common view was that whilst relatively few immigrants were capable of being good motormen, those who became motormen *must* be good *because* they had passed the training course and the test.

Those [immigrants] that get through do [make good motormen]: they must have passed at the school. [U.K. Motorman.]

Some immigrant motormen were evidently held in high esteem by their native workmates, both as motormen and as individuals, as, of course, were some of the immigrant guards; but the immigrant motormen were criticized less frequently than were the guards.

They are very good [motormen], the ones that I have worked with. They are more 'with it' as motormen than they are as guards. [U.K. Guard.][1]

Sometimes, too, there was a suggestion that nowadays almost anyone could become a guard, particularly with direct recruitment to the grade, and the 'poor quality' of some of the immigrant guards was but part of a more general decline of staff standards:

They've not the conscientiousness. Some—50 per cent—are O.K., but the others couldn't care less. This is not particularly the coloureds, but all new London Transport staff. [U.K. Motorman.]

Problems of communication arising from differences of accent were mentioned by relatively few of the native trainmen. These differences can, however, lead to some difficulty in an industry that relies heavily on the telephone and where for safety reasons there should be no misunderstanding. The motorman-guard telephone appears to be not a very effective instrument even when there are no accent differences. Such differences can aggravate the problems of communicating clearly.

The other criticisms made by the native trainmen were mentioned by relatively few and their meaning is self-evident.

Turning to the station staff, there was a fairly similar pattern of answers, though slowness or laziness was mentioned relatively more.

Complaints of the excitability of immigrants came mostly from ticket collectors, and referred specifically to immigrant ticket collectors' behaviour with passengers. The native ticket collectors complained that their immigrant colleagues did not use tact and became excited when dealing with passengers who were possibly

[1] That attitudes on race and colour were still very fluid and not hardened to a consistent set, can be illustrated by the fact that this same guard then went on to talk of 'selling our [white] brothers in Rhodesia down the river' and 'England is my country and I'm not having anyone telling me what to do in my own country'.

attempting to evade payment of the correct fare. Further, when there was a disagreement between a passenger and an immigrant ticket collector, the latter was not able to handle the situation effectively, but would call for assistance from his native colleagues, which they resented.

If they have any bother [with passengers] they will not deal with it, but they call you over and get you involved. It's their attitude to the public: they don't use any tact—it might be a genuine mistake. [U.K. Ticket Collector.]

Immigrant staff experience proportionately more difficulties with passengers than do their native workmates. They often feel vulnerable and are reluctant to use their authority with passengers when this might have unpleasant and possibly violent consequences.[1] Some of the native staff had observed this reluctance, and some were aware of the reasons for it:

If you take over a train from a coloured guard there will be people smoking [in a 'no smoking' car]. They are shy to use their authority as they will get insulted. But when you tell the passengers not to smoke, they say 'the other bloke didn't mind, why should you?' [U.K. Guard.]

The allegations of laziness from station staff related mostly to cleaning work:

Mr. Brown [a manager] said that in six months they would make good railwaymen, but only one out of ten is any good. They don't like sweeping or cleaning toilets—that's the only thing we've got against them. They say how good it is in the West Indies: go down to the beach and no rent to pay. I say, 'if it is so good, why come here?', and they say, 'we were told how good it is here, but the rents are high and the work is hard. We can't go back: we don't have the fare.' A lot would go back if they had the fare.[2] [U.K. Stationwoman.]

I have given in some detail the criticisms made of the immigrant railwaymen by their native workmates. It ought to be stressed that the majority of the natives regarded their coloured colleagues as no better or worse than other railwaymen, and some immigrant motormen in particular were singled out for praise. The vast majority of the native railwaymen refused to generalize about the

[1] See below, Chapter 9.
[2] The reported intentions of our immigrant samples on their length of stay in Britain are discussed in Chapter 16.

immigrants in answer to a question which invited generalization. The evidence supports the thesis that the performance of their occupational roles by the immigrants has been a key factor in their acceptance by the native railwaymen. The refusal to generalize is, from the point of view of those committed to the peaceful absorption of immigrants, one of the most encouraging findings to emerge.

Again in the reported objections to the employment of coloured immigrants there was a combination of racial and immigration factors. Colour was of paramount importance, but this was complicated by a wider decline in the stardards of railway work and of railwaymen perceived by some: from their perspective the employment and promotion of coloured workers was but symptomatic of this more general change. Particularly relevant here were the changes in the channels of recruitment and the increase in the speed of promotion which had occurred. Experience was a prerequisite of the old railwayman. It legitimated a claim to prestige; but if the job could be done by coloured men with relatively little experience, what was left? Supervisors in particular stressed the importance of experience: many had been railwaymen all or most of their working lives, the salience of experience in the value system served to legitimize their own positions.

Experience was becoming less important though, both to task performance and in the value system. Modern rolling stock is easier to operate and more reliable than that which it has replaced, though it is more complex technically. Present-day training methods too are probably more effective than those used in the past, and there appears to be a greater appreciation that skills can be *taught,* rather than merely picked up. These factors all tend to reduce the value attached to experience.

Apart from station staff, the organization of work was relatively conflict-free, and this contrasted very much with the bus situation. For both the station and trainmen's situations the pluralistic model appeared to be the most appropriate: mixed crews splitting in messrooms and canteens, little mixing of white and coloured station staff in messrooms.

Finally, I argued that a number of factors together make it likely that the immigrants will constitute or form part of a new generation of old railwaymen. It will differ from the ideal type, but in so far as this ideal type reflected the behaviour and attitudes of actual railwaymen it was more appropriate to an era that has largely passed.

9

THE RAILWAY OPERATING DEPARTMENT, III: RAILWAYMEN, SUPERVISORS, PASSENGERS

RAILWAYMEN'S RELATIONSHIPS WITH SUPERVISORS

To compare the expectations that immigrant and native railwaymen had of their first-line supervisors, we asked both groups 'what makes a good inspector?'[1] The answers to this question are summarized in Table 9.1.

TABLE 9.1
Railwaymen's Expectations of the 'Good' Inspector, in Percentages.★

	Native Respondents			Immigrant Respondents		
	Train-men	Station staff	Total	Train-men	Station staff	Total
He is patient/knows how to handle people/can earn respect/has the right approach/gets to know his staff	53	33	46	48	53	50
He has experience/knows his job/is an ex-trainman	36	33	35	13	31	20
He is helpful/will co-operate with crews or staff/will give and take	9	27	16	38	11	28
He is fair/impartial/has no favourites	21	17	19	12	17	14
He is not too strict	4	3	4	12	—	7
He is not too lenient	8	3	6	3	3	3
He lets staff get on with the job	—	13	5	—	6	2
Other answer	—	7	2	5	18	6
No answer	2	—	1	—	—	—
(Samples)	(53)	(30)	(83)	(60)	(36)	(96)

★ More than one answer was recorded and the percentage totals may therefore exceed 100.

[1] At those locations where the lowest supervisory grade was that of stationmaster the wording of the question was changed to 'stationmaster'.

The desired attributes of the good supervisor, as seen by both native and immigrant railwaymen, were predominantly social skills, rather than technical expertise, though experience, knowledge of the job, and being an ex-trainman were thought to be important, particularly by the native railwaymen. Patience was thought to be especially important when services were disrupted and things went wrong. Both immigrant and native railwaymen rated these attributes highly. The differences between the two samples of station staff possibly assumes some significance when relationships between staff and supervisors are discussed.[1]

Turning to the value accorded knowledge of the job and experience, a difference of some importance appears between the immigrant and the native trainmen: the latter rated these characteristics far more highly. Experience referred specifically to experience *as a trainman*. This was seen as desirable on two counts. First, the supervisor would understand the motorman's job and his difficulties. Second, by virtue of his experience, he would handle crews better. His experience as a motorman appeared to increase the legitimacy of his authority.

A few trainmen drew a distinction between experience in the platform grades and as a trainman, but mostly ex-trainmen were judged in relation to ex-booking office clerks. The ex-trainman was preferred, and there was some resentment that ex-booking-office clerks appeared to be favoured or have an advantage in promotion.

Knowledge of the job was thought to be particularly important when services were disrupted.

The immigrant trainmen in particular stressed that a supervisor should co-operate with the crews and be prepared to give and take in the sense that the supervisor should overlook minor misdemeanours—often concerned with time, and especially late booking on—in return for favours.

Someone who gives you a chance now and again—will disregard a late booking on *as long as* you are in time to pick up the train [West Indian Motorman].

There appeared to be definite limits to the amount of give and take expected, as is indicated by this quotation. Some explicitly mentioned that there were disadvantages to being too lenient.

The station staff, too, expected some reciprocity between themselves and the supervisor:

[1] See below, pp. 171-3.

Sometimes things have to be done that are not on the roster. I will do it if asked right—he grants you a favour and you will for him. [West Indian Ticket Collector.]

Supervisors were expected to be fair and impartial.

He keeps as open a mind as possible before hearing both sides of the story. [U.K. Guard.]

The good supervisor should not be too strict about matters similar to those over which he was expected to give and take; but here there is not the reciprocity implied in give and take. It may be, though, that the expectations suggested by both groups of answers were broadly similar.

Only the station staff stressed that the supervisor should let his staff get on with the job. The expectation here was that the supervisor should not continually check on the activities of staff.

These were the expectations that the railwaymen had of their supervisors. How far, in their opinion, did the supervisors measure up to these expectations; how did they get on with them? The answers to these questions are shown in Table 9.2.

TABLE 9.2
Railwaymen's Evaluations of Their Relations with Supervisors, in Percentages.

	Native Respondents			Immigrant Respondents		
	Train-men	Station staff	Total	Train-men	Station staff	Total
Very good/very well	36	50	41	17	17	17
Good/well	11	20	14	17	8	14
Not much trouble/fair/not bad	51	27	42	43	53	47
Not very well/poor	2	—	1	—	3	1
Most are good, but some are difficult or unhelpful	—	—	—	12	6	9
Some are good but some are difficult or unhelpful	—	3	1	12	14	12
(Sample)	(53)	(30)	(83)	(60)	(36)	(96)

Clearly, in their own estimation, the native railwaymen had better relations with their supervisors than did the immigrants. At the same time, for three-quarters of the immigrants these relations were at least not bad and most of the others drew distinctions between those supervisors who were good and those who were difficult or unhelpful.

The role of the supervisor in relation to his subordinate staff can now be described. Let us consider first the supervisor at a trainmen's depot. In normal service conditions, the supervisor does not impinge greatly on the working life of a trainman. Apart from when he is on spare duty, is thought to have broken a rule, or been involved in any incident, such contact is largely confined to booking on and off or arranging duty changes. Duty allocation is impersonal, and rostered for months in advance.

Important too, is that a trainman's shifts do not necessarily coincide with those of the supervisors, and there is a considerable turnover of supervisory staff at depots and stations.[1] Familiarity is then often not an important element in the relations between trainmen and supervisors, though some stationmasters and inspectors had been at their depots for some time, either because they were near the top of the promotion hierarchy or preferred not to be promoted higher or away from their depot or station. These supervisors were on familiar terms with the trainmen.

When anything goes wrong with the service, the skills and personality of the supervisor are more important. This puts into context the emphasis of the trainmen on social skills and knowledge of the job.

I have shown that the immigrant trainman in particular expected the supervisor to give and take. Trainmen's expectations here appeared to relate largely to the supervisor overlooking minor offences, particularly late booking on. Another was the supervisor allowing trainmen to go home early.[2] A further element in this reciprocity related to gambling in messrooms. From time to time management attempted to stop gambling on the Board's premises, but

[1] Seniority is the major criterion for allocating supervisory staff. Stations and depots are graded in terms of the number and grades of supervisors, depending largely on traffic flow at stations, and numbers of trainmen's duties at depots. In this hierarchy the office of *senior* stationmaster at a large busy depot or station is high, and often when a man attains this office he is near retirement. On retirement he will be replaced by the next most senior man who has nominated for that post. (A 'suitability' clause is seldom invoked.) Consequently, the retirement of a senior stationmaster is followed by many supervisors moving up one place.

[2] A trainmen's 'unwritten law' was that men on spare duties be allowed to go home about an hour before the end of the shift, when the remaining time was too short to be useful. Similarly, some running duties end before the shift ends and again men go early. Both were largely accepted by supervisors.

this was resisted by some supervisors: they reasoned that if they were lenient with crews they could more readily ask for their help in an emergency. These supervisors clearly understood the *reciprocal obligations* inherent in leniency.

Helping out a supervisor appeared to be usually in the form of accepting a duty other than that rostered—especially at short notice —or accepting a journey which finished after the rostered time. Rest-day work, too, possibly comes under this heading, though as there was usually no lack of volunteers for such work it was a less important form of helping out.

I have shown that the major differences between the native and immigrant trainmen in their expectations of the good supervisor related to the greater importance that the former attached to experience, particularly as trainman, and the greater emphasis of the immigrant trainman on the supervisor being helpful and prepared to give and take. Much of the give and take expected of the supervisor related to time, especially late booking on.

The time and attendance values have not been accepted and internalized by the immigrants to the same extent as by the native workforce. The supervisors, particularly the senior supervisors, are by and large 'old railwaymen' *par excellence*.[1] Those in the senior posts had often been recruited during or immediately following the First World War. They had been promoted slowly through the grades, and attained senior posts fairly late in their working lives. They had been subject to the quasi-militaristic discipline of the organization at a time when it was far more rigorous. It is perhaps not surprising that they were not always sympathetic towards different attitudes and behaviour in respect of late attendance or absences from duties.

The differences between the conceptions of immigrant trainmen and supervisors of what could legitimately be regarded as give and take, do much to explain the reported difference between the immigrant and native trainmen's relations with their supervisors.

Turning to the station staff, their situation differs from that of the trainmen in a number of ways. Both supervisors and staff are on the premises all the time and consequently there is more interaction. The numbers of both staff and supervisors are usually smaller than at a depot. Consequently, there is a greater familiarity between supervisors and staff than exists at depots, though the situation is

---

[1] Cottrell (p. 34) makes a similar point: 'The railway supervisor is *par excellence* a railroad man. Railroaders insist that only those who are "bred in the bone" and have "coupling grease on their elbows" ever know anything about railroading.'

7

complicated by cover and relief supervisors. Some station staff, too, are in the cover and relief categories.

The duties of station staff are rostered, but the work roster does not cover every task, particularly cleaning tasks. As with the trainmen, there is considerable reciprocity between supervisors and staff. On the part of the staff, this involves doing tasks that are not rostered and accepting duty changes; on the part of the supervisors, it means overlooking minor misdemeanours and allowing staff to leave early. This latter element of reciprocity is of some importance: it is a common practice for station supervisors to allow staff, particularly stationmen and women, to leave work half an hour or an hour before the end of their shift, when this does not coincide with peak hour traffic. It is a means whereby the supervisors ensure that duties, particularly cleaning duties, are carried out to their satisfaction. It is a negative sanction in that it can legitimately be withdrawn at any time.

The immigrant station staff emphasized somewhat more than their native workmates that a good supervisor should know how to handle staff and have the right approach. Comparing the reported relations of the two groups of station staff, the immigrants clearly did not get on with their supervisors as well as the natives. Comments made by the immigrants indicated that they thought that supervisors did not always have the right approach, and that tasks were not allocated impartially.

Those immigrants who criticized the behaviour of supervisors often declared emphatically that they were not generalizing; rather, they were complaining of *some* supervisors.

The station supervisors' attitudes towards the immigrants and their assessments of them varied widely, but the two criticisms most commonly made were that the immigrants resented discipline and cleaning work.

Some evidence of this resentment of station cleaning duties was provided by the Barbados-recruited station staff, who complained that they had been misled on the work content of a stationman's duties.[1] For some supervisors, the change in cleaning practices between pre-war times and the present appeared to have achieved almost symbolic importance and was seen by them as symptomatic of the 'decline' of London Transport standards—and staff. In the pre-war years, tiled passage-ways and the like were scrubbed by hand. In present-day practice, the cleaner uses a mop and bucket.

[1] See Chapter 13. Also see pp. 192–3.

Some supervisors alleged that the change came about as the result of the immigrants' refusal to scrub by hand, but there was no other evidence to support this contention.

That the immigrant station staff emphasized that a supervisor should possess social skills to handle people and have the right approach, that they appeared to get on with their supervisors less well than did their native colleagues, and that they were alleged to resent discipline, are all, perhaps, mutually explanatory. Comments made by some supervisors indicated that their perception of their role was still partly in terms of the quasi-militaristic approach which was discussed earlier. Clearly, this was very much out of accord with the emphasis of the immigrant station staff on social skills: in their view, a good supervisor should *ask* rather than *tell* a man what to do; he 'doesn't have to give you an *order*—he suggests it to you and you jump to it'. This difference, together with the partiality of some supervisors, as perceived by the immigrants, does much to explain the differing assessments of relationships with supervisors by native and immigration station staff. It was likely, too, that the antipathies and prejudices of some supervisors influenced their behaviour towards the immigrant staff.

THE RELATIONSHIPS OF STATION STAFF WITH IMMIGRANT STATION FOREMEN

At the time of our railway interviewing, coloured immigrants were found in positions of authority over native subordinates in only one grade: station foreman.[1] The reader will remember that the designation of this grade is somewhat misleading: charge-hand would be an appropriate parallel in many other industries. The reader will also remember that compared with the Department as a whole, coloured immigrants were slightly over-represented in the station foreman grade.[2] We questioned our native samples on their experience with coloured immigrant superordinates in the grade of station foreman. The majority of our native station staff sample had at some time worked at stations where there had been coloured immigrant station foremen. Sometimes the foremen had been relief or cover staff; sometimes the interviewee had been in one or the other of these categories.

Whilst there were indications of resentment when coloured

[1] Before the field work was completed, coloured immigrants were beginning to enter the inspector grade. See p. 178.
[2] See Chapter 7.

immigrants first entered the station foreman grade, we only found one instance of organized opposition by native station staff.[1] A commonly held view amongst the native staff was that the extra pay which went with promotion to the grade was not a sufficient reward for the extra responsibilities involved. If, therefore, native staff were unwilling to become station foremen, and coloured men could do the job, then 'good luck to them'. This, in essence, was the most common view.

The comments of station staff with experience of working for coloured immigrant station foremen split fairly evenly between those which indicated approval of specific station foremen and those that were mixed or neutral. Very few were at all hostile, and some that were could rationalize the authority relationship in a manner least hurtful to their self-esteem.

He [the station foreman] doesn't order us about. *As far as I'm concerned it is the Stationmaster talking to me through him.*[2] [U.K. Ticket Collector.]

That 'he doesn't order us about' provides a clue to the relationship between coloured station foremen and native staff. Whilst coloured station foremen appeared to be accepted by most native station staff, a condition of this acceptance by some was that they did not fully exercise the authority vested in their grade. Station staff often told us that the station foreman did not interfere—and he was praised for this. A criticism commonly made of coloured station foremen both by supervisors and by their native colleagues was that they were reluctant to use their authority.

The acceptance by native station staff of immigrant station foremen provides a very limited test of the wider question of the acceptability of coloured supervisors. The station foreman has little authority, and the coloured foremen have been reluctant to use it. The role of a coloured foreman in relation to white native subordinates is a difficult one: disgruntled staff can often go over his head to a friendly inspector or stationmaster.

PROMOTION ASPIRATIONS AND NATIVES' ATTITUDES TOWARDS THE PROMOTION OF IMMIGRANTS TO SUPERVISORY POSTS
We set out to compare the promotion aspirations and expectations of immigrant and native railwaymen by asking a number of questions, among them: 'Do you want to be promoted to another

[1] See Chapter 7.   [2] My italics.

TABLE 9.3
Railwaymen's Promotion Aspirations, in Percentages.★

	Native	Immigrant
None	68	18
To next grade	17	36
To B.O.C./other clerical	—	5
To inspector grade	4	19
To T.T.I.	6	1
Other	1	14
Don't know	4	6
(Sample)	(71)	(83)

★ These answers are from the male samples only, as there was no direct channel of promotion for women above the grade of Ticket Collector I. The trainmen and station staff samples have been combined as their patterns of answers were almost identical.

job?' and 'What sort of job?' Table 9.3 summarizes the responses.[1]

First a word on the coding categories used. 'Next grade' refers to the next non-supervisory grade in the promotion structure: for example, promotion from guard to motorman, or from stationman to either guard or station foreman.[2] 'B.O.C.' is of course booking office clerk; 'T.T.I.' is travelling ticket inspector, a grade principally concerned with detecting fraudulent travel. Answers in the 'other' category were very diverse; some referred to occupations outside the Department.

Clearly, the immigrants were far more likely to indicate a wish to be promoted than were the natives.[3] There were two important differences between the samples: firstly, the immigrants were mostly in the under-45 age groups, whereas two-thirds of the natives were

[1] A question was also asked on the reasons for wanting promotion, but the answers were diverse and often vague and have not been coded. Some who did not wish to be promoted gave their reasons: age and the prospect of having to move to another depot were strong disincentives for the native motormen, the latter was particularly prevalent at Southway.

[2] The channels of promotion up to the supervisory grades are shown in Chapter 7.

[3] A not very dissimilar pattern of answers came from the busmen, though the proportion of immigrants not indicating a wish to be promoted was somewhat higher. See Chapter 6.

over 45;[1] secondly, the immigrants had generally achieved their present grades more quickly than had the natives.[2] Yet these differences do not completely explain the different patterns of promotion aspirations, and I return to this topic again when discussing the evidence from all three departments.[3]

Next we asked 'have you applied for promotion?' Table 9.4 summarizes the answers to this question, indicating the results of any applications made.

TABLE 9.4
Railwaymen's Applications for Promotion, in Percentages.

	Native	Immigrant
None	85	59
Unsuccessful/failed training	10	12
Awaiting result of application/training	3	19
Awaiting transfer*	3	10
(Sample)	(71)	(83)

* This category is comprised of those who had successfully completed training for another grade and were waiting for a vacancy: For example, 'guard-motorman'.

The greater propensity of the immigrants to report that they wished to be promoted was to some extent reflected in their actions. Some railwaymen, both native and immigrant, who wished to be promoted had not applied because they were aware they had not the necessary seniority.

Finally in relation to this topic, we asked, 'do you intend to apply for promotion (again)?' and 'do you think you will be promoted?', together with a question on the reasons for the interviewee's optimism or pessimism. The answers to the first two questions are sum-

[1] Ninety-two per cent of the male immigrants in our samples of trainmen and station staff were under 45; 62 per cent of the native males were over 45. See Chapter 3.
[2] This is, of course, related to the fact that *all* the immigrants joined the Department during a period of staff shortage, when promotion has been much more rapid than it was before the Second World War. See Chapter 3.
[3] See Chapter 17.

marized in Table 9.5. The answers to the last were diverse and often vague; apart from those from the coloured railwaymen which alleged discrimination, these responses have not been coded.

TABLE 9.5
Railwaymen's Promotion Intentions and Perceived Prospects, in Percentages.

	Native	Immigrant
Will not apply/reapply*	72	27
Will apply/reapply: optimistic	15	37
Will apply/reapply: pessimistic	—	1
Will apply/reapply: don't know	7	19
Don't know if will apply/reapply	7	16
Possibly a bar on the promotion of coloured staff†	—	11
(Sample)	(71)	(83)

* Including those who had earlier said they did not wish to be promoted.

† This was a 'double code' and the percentage total for the immigrant railwaymen therefore exceeds 100.

It will be seen that apart from those who inferred that coloured railwaymen were at a disadvantage in their promotion prospects compared with their white colleagues, there was considerable optimism amongst the coloured staff. This was, though, almost matched by those who either did not speculate on their own chances or were uncertain whether they would apply or reapply for promotion.

The feeling that coloured staff were being discriminated against in promotion was neither so widespread or deep-seated as it was amongst coloured busmen.[1] In Central Buses there was a widespread *conviction* that this was so. Amongst coloured railwaymen, very few were convinced that promotion practices were discriminatory; the predominant feeling—as expressed by those who mentioned the topic, that is—was that it *might* be so. As with the busmen, the number who mentioned discrimination was possibly smaller than those who perceived it: we did not ask a *direct* question on this; there was sometimes some reluctance to discuss any discrimination with a white interviewer.

Several interviewees thought that it was more difficult to achieve

[1] See Chapter 6.

internal promotion or transfer than to apply for another post in the recruit grades, for example, station foreman or booking office clerk; but this view was not widespread. Some were of the opinion that discrimination was practised by supervisors; others indicated that they thought it originated from a higher level. The predominant view was, though, suspicion of discrimination, rather than a firm conviction. It may be that some were not fully aware of the overriding importance of seniority, but amongst some of the coloured immigrants with most service there was a keen awareness that within a short time they would have the necessary seniority.

I don't know [if I will be promoted]. I should be, but I don't know about colour of skin. A lot are waiting to see if a black man is going to get it. There is one coloured man who is x years senior to me.

At the time of our interviewing, there were no coloured immigrants in the inspector or stationmaster grades, though there was one West Indian traffic regulator. However, in late 1966 and early 1967 the first coloured immigrants entered the inspector grade. All had eleven or twelve years' service before promotion.[1] A completely comparable analysis of the total inspectorate giving length of service before promotion to the inspector *grade* was not available: the available data showed the dates of commencing service and of entering the present *class*. The length of service before promotion of those inspectors who had changed classes within the grade could not, therefore, be established. However, an analysis of data on length of service before promotion of inspectors in the lowest class (class three) showed that only one had been promoted with less than fifteen years' service.[2] Somewhat over half of those in the station inspector grade, class three, had entered the class with sixteen or seventeen years' service; the remainder varied widely.

Whilst these data are not completely conclusive, they do strongly indicate that coloured immigrants were entering the inspector grade when they had the necessary seniority. It ought to be emphasized that seniority, though necessary, is not sufficient qualification for promotion to the inspector grade: a training course followed by a test must be successfully completed. The test methods used are far from objective; opportunities for discrimination are not absent, but I have no evidence that it has occurred. Once this training course

[1] L.T.B. Staff Administration Office, May 1967.
[2] These figures refer to the inspectorate as at 1 May 1966. L.T.B. Staff Administration Office.

and test have been taken the only obstacles between coloured immigrants and the stationmaster grade are seniority and suitability—and the suitability clause is seldom invoked.

A point of some importance to emerge from this analysis concerns the use of seniority as a mechanism for role allocation. It does not guarantee that members of minority groups are not discriminated against in promotion, but it makes such discrimination far more difficult and less likely to occur: it provides an objective criterion which can be easily measured, and it is an impersonal mechanism.

For similar reasons to those given in relation to the busmen, it appeared useful to discover the attitudes of native railwaymen to the possibility of a coloured superordinate. The data on this question are revealing, too, of some basic and deep-seated attitudes of white natives towards coloured immigrants. All the native railwaymen in the samples were therefore asked, 'would there be any objection if a Commonwealth immigrant was appointed inspector?'[1] If the answer was 'yes', a follow-up 'why?' was asked. The answers to these two questions are summarized in Table 9.6. The patterns of answers from trainmen and station staff were very similar and they have been combined.

TABLE 9.6
*Native Railwaymen's Attitudes Towards an Immigrant Supervisor, in Percentages.**

i	No objection	16
ii	No objection if he had the experience/ ability/seniority	11
iii	No objection personally, others would/ might object	19
iv	No objection, we should have some	1
v	Objections: lack of experience/ ability/ seniority	11
vi	Objections: would be wrong/would not get respect/because of colour	28
vii	Objections: might misuse authority	8
viii	Objections: there are still white men available	2
	Don't know	5
	(Sample)	(83)

* More than one answer was recorded and the percentage total may therefore exceed 100.

[1] At those locations where the lowest supervisory grade was stationmaster, the grade in question was changed to stationmaster.

The coding categories used were similar to those used for comparable data from the busmen and the platelayers,[1] with the single exception that seniority is only applicable to the Railway Operating situation. There is a close parallel between the busmen and railwaymen in the over-all patterns, and the reasoning of many of the answers is very similar.

The meaning of the 'no objection' category is clear.

The second group of answers indicated a lack of objections to a coloured supervisor, *provided* he was seen to have the necessary experience, ability, or seniority.

It would depend on their length of service and qualifications [but] I don't see why there should be objections. [U.K. Guard.]

The meaning of the third group of answers is clear, but again it can be illustrated from the interview material:

There might be objections from the men and the management [but] I wouldn't mind. [U.K. Motorman.]

Next of importance were those answers which argued that the coloured staff did not have the experience, ability, or the seniority necessary for the role of inspector.

[There would be objections because of] experience—lack of it. [U.K. Motorman.]

The largest single group of answers suggested that it would be *wrong* for a white man to take orders from a coloured man; that the coloured inspector would not be treated with respect by his white subordinates. The reasoning behind these objections is clearly both deep-seated and complex: in essence, they rest on the premise that the coloured man is inferior to the white. Objections on this score were numerically most important from the busmen also, and again it is useful to quote from them at length. In both departments women were over-represented amongst those who gave the answers in this category—nearly 50 per cent of the female samples in both departments—but given the relative smallness of the female samples, I can only speculate as to whether this is significant.[2]

I wouldn't like it—I just don't think it is right. It is the sort of thing I've been born with. [U.K. Woman Ticket Collector.]

A white person wouldn't take orders from them—he would regard

<hr>

[1] See Chapters 6 and 11.   [2] See below Chapter 17

them as lower class. Half of them are still savages you must remember. [U.K. Stationwoman.]

It would cause trouble. It would be the limit. White people don't mind working with coloureds, but taking orders would be very different. It is a topic which is spoken about a lot. It will come—according to trade union policy. [U.K. Station Foreman.]

The attitudes revealed by these answers are largely explicable in terms of the colour-class hypothesis.

Related to the thought that whites have always ruled blacks was the fear that with a reversal of roles coloured supervisors would discriminate against white staff, that they would misuse their authority:

I've seen it in India: with a bit of authority they try to keep you down. [U.K. Ticket Collector.]

Some were aware that it was possible, indeed likely, that coloured railwaymen would become supervisors. Grouping together those answers which indicate a lack of hostility towards the possibility of coloured supervisors (codes i to iv), nearly half fall in this category. Another half indicate an expectation of hostility, and often this was strongly expressed. The over-all pattern from the busmen was broadly similar.[1]

Comparing the rail and bus supervisory roles, the latter is a far more difficult one to perform adequately; adequately, that is, in terms of meeting the expectations of others. Thus whilst the attitudes expressed in the two departments were broadly similar, a coloured inspector might be expected to meet less hostile *behaviour* from subordinates in the rail situation than would his counterpart supervising busmen. There is less potential for conflict built into the railway situation. Moreover, in dealing with difficult passengers the railway inspector is far less vulnerable than is his equivalent on the buses: he is on railway premises and more easily able to summon assistance if required. For these reasons, therefore, a coloured inspector would be likely both to be more acceptable and to meet fewer difficulties in the rail than in the bus situation. That coloured supervisors achieved their grades through seniority would tend to increase their acceptance. The possibility of acceptance by native railwaymen was probably increasing as coloured railwaymen came to be more widely accepted as part of the permanent work force— yet this acceptance was far from complete.

[1] See above Chapter 6.

RELATIONS WITH PASSENGERS

The difficulties reported by motormen, particularly the immigrant motormen, included *some* experienced as guards. Some distortion is then introduced as the immigrant motormen's experience of the guard's role was more recent than that of the native motormen, and it is likely that this recency resulted in a higher recall and, therefore, reporting of difficulties. On the other hand, the incidents which the immigrant motormen reported had occurred in recent years, and to have excluded them would have been a greater distortion. In any case, the analysis does not completely rest on the statistics.

TABLE 9.7
*Railwaymen's Difficulties with Passengers, in Percentages.**

	Native railwaymen			Immigrant railwaymen		
	Guards	Station staff	Total (inc. M/M)	Guards	Station staff	Total (inc. M/M)
Passengers attempting to board or leave car through guard's door	56	—	—	72	—	—
Insults	17	48	25	31	69	47
Drunks/'louts'	39	37	40	52	61	55
Complaints over service/ 'unnecessary' questions	44	33	40	31	58	43
Ticket offences/attempts at fare evasion	—	48	—	—	31	—
Hold car doors open/all attempt to board one car/ take time to select a particular car	28	—	—	38	—	—
Physical violence	5	—	1	10	6	12
None	11	—	10	—	3	4
(Sample)	(18)	(27)	(68)	(29)	(36)	(95)

* The inconsistencies between the sample figures shown here and those given earlier are due to the fact that this question was not asked of the native samples in the pilot study, or of the shunters in the main study. More than one answer was recorded and the percentage totals may therefore exceed 100.

The data have been coded in discrete categories, but they are often related. For example, a passenger attempting to board a train through the guard's door may be physically violent or abusive, as may a drunken passenger or one attempting fraudulent travel.

On tube and most sub-surface rolling stock the guard is located in the last car of the train, and occupies the gangway between the two leading doors of that car. The remaining car space is occupied by passengers, a narrow metal bar separates the guard from them. On the exterior of the car there is nothing to indicate that the 'guard's door' *is* the guard's door. When the direction of the train is reversed the guard's gangway becomes passenger accommodation, the guard's door is available for their use. Passengers often attempt to enter or leave the car through the guard's door when all the doors are open. This happens most frequently when the car is crowded. A guard may move to allow a passenger through or, more likely, he will advise the passenger to use the other doors. When the guard closes the passenger doors he leaves his own door open and is expected to keep it open until the train has travelled the length of two cars or so. This is done for safety reasons: if a passenger's clothing is caught in the closed doors the guard may be able to stop the train before the passenger is dragged to the tunnel headwall. When the guard has closed the passenger doors he signals to the motorman by means of an electric bell that it is safe to proceed. A few seconds may elapse between this signal and the motorman starting the train.[1] During this time a passenger may attempt to leave the rear car through the guard's door or, more commonly, one will attempt to board through this door. The guard should not leave his door as this is potentially dangerous. A passenger wishes to enter and may attempt forcibly to do so. Half of the native and three-quarters of the immigrant guards mentioned this area of conflict with passengers. Some had been physically assaulted.

That's the trouble: [a passenger tried to get through my door] I got bitten and lost my glasses. The stationmaster called the police and said that he [the passenger] bit me. But the passenger gave a wrong address and that was the end of that. Another man came through my door and was abusive. The booking clerk went on the train and the man was traced and he was found guilty on three charges and fined. [West Indian Guard.]

You give the [starting] signal to the driver and they try to get in … Passengers who try to be awkward come through the guard's door, and you get tourists who don't know any better—you have to make exceptions. [West Indian Motorman—ex-Guard.]

---

[1] Guards *usually* keep the car doors open until the starting signal shows the 'proceed' (green) aspect. A 'repeater' signal visible to the guard is positioned near the rear of the train.

Not all the guards mentioned passengers attempting to board or alight through their door, but it is highly probable that most experience it. The more frequent mention of this area of conflict by the immigrant guards reflects their greater likelihood of suffering adverse consequences: they are more likely than their native colleagues to be assaulted or abused by passengers attempting this means of entry or exit, and to be *deliberately* singled out for physical assault. Guards often felt that they needed 'more protection', especially in the form of a separate compartment.[1]

'Insults' or 'rudeness' from passengers are most likely to arise out of conflicts between passengers and staff, for example passengers attempting fraudulent travel or trying to push through the guard's door. Often though they were completely unprovoked. Again the coloured immigrant railwaymen were more likely to suffer, and insults often had a specifically racial content.

They can be rude ... One poked an umbrella at me as he got to the platform when the train was leaving and called me a black bastard. This doesn't worry me—but it would annoy some. [West Indian Guard.]

Whilst many railwaymen experience insults and abuse from passengers, all the evidence indicates that the coloured railwaymen suffer substantially more in this way. Be it unprovoked abuse or insults arising from some other conflict, colour and race quickly come to the fore.

One context in which such insults are likely to arise is when staff meet with drunken passengers. Whilst the coloured staff are no more likely to *meet* drunken passengers than are their native colleagues, such contact is more likely to be unpleasant for them and this is reflected in their answers on this topic. Drunks are most commonly encountered at week-ends, particularly on Friday and Saturday evenings. Drunks are not only abusive, they are sometimes violent. Most staff have learnt to be cautious in dealing with them: to call a supervisor or a policeman if they fear trouble. With the aim of avoiding trouble—and possibly of assisting the passenger —station staff often 'help' drunks to board the train, where, of course, they are liable to be troublesome to the crew, particularly the guard. Crews, in turn, have their own means of meeting the

[1] On some older sub-surface rolling stock the guard is located in the rear motor-man's compartment, but this arrangement is not possible on tube lines where the train is longer than some station platforms. (Our guard samples worked stock where the guard is located in a passenger car.)

problem: by not 'disturbing' a drunk until the train reaches the terminus or, less frequently, leaving him on the train until it reaches the depot. Either way the drunken passenger may arrive very late at night at a place several miles from his intended destination. Moreover, at a terminus or depot station there is a greater likelihood that a supervisor will be available to deal with the problem than at many smaller stations.

You get a lot of drunks—I leave them on the platform if possible. [West Indian Motorman.]

As a guard, I wouldn't take drunks—the platform staff are fond of putting them on the trains. [U.K. Motorman.]

A recurring criticism in the interviews held that staff were not sufficiently backed up by London Transport and were thus vulnerable.

One station, which had acquired a reputation as a drug addicts' meeting place, posed another kind of problem.

We get trouble from drug addicts—they are vicious and keep us scared. There is no co-operation from the coppers: one [addict] was giving a girl a shot in her backside—and she was standing talking to a copper. The left luggage lockers are mostly used by foreigners—French—they peddle the drugs there ... It encourages a lot of beatniks and layabouts—they are always there. They peddle the drugs on the [emergency] spiral stairs: We don't like going up there alone, you get queers and everything and no-one can hear you if you shout. [West Indian Stationman.]

The description 'louts' was applied to those, usually in their teens or twenties, whose behaviour was seen as deliberately provocative, threatening, and disruptive of the services. Physical violence was covertly or overtly threatened. Coloured staff were more likely to meet trouble from louts, as much of their behaviour was overtly racial, but white native staff were not immune.

Some hold back the doors for no reason and jeer. Some walk through [the cars] when the train is running or pull the 'emergency' [stop] for no reason. You can't touch them, you call a stationmaster. Sometimes children hold back the doors, but you tell them and they let go. [West Indian Guard.]

I've only had a couple of real problems. Usually it's young chaps: they throw down a chocolate paper when you've just swept up. [U.K. Stationman.]

People go out of their way to embarrass me: one spat at me, another kicked my guard. [West Indian Motorman.]

A further and apparently increasing source of violent, disruptive and damaging behaviour, has been crowds attending football matches. Violence and damage from this source were not very much in evidence at the time of our fieldwork, but there have since been a number of reports of assaults against staff, damage to rolling-stock and disruption of services. Again it is possible that the coloured railwaymen were most adversely affected.

Complaints over service, particularly when it is disrupted, appear to be commonly experienced by both coloured and white railwaymen. A number of staff complained, too, of what they termed unnecessary questions from passengers. Questions are, in the view of many railwaymen, unnecessary when they are too detailed, when a passenger asks the final destination of a train, rather than if it calls at 'his' station, or when the passenger queries the answers given. It was evident that a number of railwaymen preferred to avoid face-to-face contact with passengers so far as possible, and this inclination was most marked amongst the native trainmen. The railwaymen's views of passengers in general indicated that they were not always held in high esteem.

[Passengers complain] when you have to empty a train because of a defect. Most passengers are stupid. [U.K. Guard.]

If a train is running late they think it is your fault. [West Indian Guard.]

The evidence indicated that coloured staff were no more likely to experience complaints than were their white colleagues. Given the marked reluctance of many British people to interact in any way with coloured staff, this conclusion is in no way surprising. Coloured railwaymen do, however, endure another form of behaviour which they find hurtful and insulting: there is a widespread refusal on the part of passengers to believe them when they give directions. The answers given are queried, or checked with a *white* railwayman or passenger. Native railwaymen, too, have their answers questioned, but this is far less common. The reluctance of passengers to believe coloured staff, is illustrated from the interview material:

They don't believe you when you give them directions. Two old people wanted to go to Liverpool Street. I told them to catch the next train— a city train to Liverpool Street. They then asked a passenger, who denied that it went to Liverpool Street. They got off and they were rude and they missed the train. [West Indian Stationman.]

The preference of many passengers to ask a white rather than a coloured railwayman for information or directions had been observed by the native staff.

Passengers are ruder to coloureds; also they ignore them if they are with an English member of staff. If there is a coloured foreman standing on the platform with an English stationman and a passenger comes and asks questions, he *always* addresses himself to the English stationman, ignoring the coloured foreman, even though he is higher in rank. [U.K. Stationman.]

Fare evasion is very common on London's Underground. Most of the ticket collectors interviewed mentioned fraudulent travel as a difficulty they meet, and it seems highly likely that most, if not all, experience it. The coloured ticket collectors are, though, doubly handicapped: it is probable that fare-evading passengers are more likely to attempt to pay less than the correct fare if the collector is coloured. In the event of conflict, the coloured collector is more likely to be insulted or assaulted. A number of them clearly felt exposed and vulnerable. They thought they did not receive enough backing from London Transport in conflicts with passengers over the collection of correct fares and tickets. Some had decided that at times it was politic not to insist on the correct fare. Their authority was clearly not accepted by many passengers, and some coloured collectors called in their white colleagues to assist them in a dispute. This was often resented by the native collectors.

A few white ticket collectors claimed that coloured passengers were particularly prone to attempt fraudulent travel. Some of the coloured ticket collectors reported difficulties with coloured passengers from countries other than their own; at times they were accused of 'thinking they were white'.

Coloureds can't count above fourpence [they never offer more than fourpence for an excess fare]. White people are not so bad. [U.K. Woman Ticket Collector.]

One African turned ugly when I queried his ticket, and he accused me of 'thinking I was white and acting like it'. [West Indian Ticket Collector.]

The white staff acknowledged that their coloured colleagues did not discriminate in favour of coloured passengers.

They [the coloured staff] deal with their own all the same: they don't give any favours. [U.K. Ticket Collector.]

Passengers holding doors open for others, or attempting to

'crowd' into one car, or wanting to travel in one particular car are an irritant for guards because their actions delay the train's departure. Time is important, especially during the rush hour.

Physical violence was reported by far more of the coloured than the native railwaymen:

One thumped me—he was holding the doors open—and called me a black bastard. He was fined five pounds for disorderly behaviour. [West Indian Guard.]

Drunks: I have been assaulted twice. I had checked them for using bad language in front of women. [West Indian Motorman.]

Public transport workers are vulnerable in several respects. Public service workers in Britain appear to be considered fair game for criticism; that they are *public* servants is emphasized. A standard of service, and often servility, is demanded of the public sector which would not be asked of private industry. The quality of Underground services has in some respects been reduced over the past few years: headways have been increased, the times of last trains have been brought forward.[1] This reduction in the quality of service probably means that the operating staff are more likely to receive vocal criticism: they are immediately available to the disgruntled passenger.

Public transport workers are vulnerable, too, in that they work at hours of the day and night when drunks and other potentially violent people travel. They often work in situations where they are isolated; assistance is not always easily available.

The coloured railwayman is then doubly handicapped: he is a public transport worker and he is coloured. He is more vulnerable *because* he is coloured. In conflicts, colour becomes a salient consideration, in the eyes of many passengers. He is more likely to be insulted, assaulted, and to have his word questioned than is his white colleague. The authority of coloured railwaymen is clearly not accepted by many; that of coloured ticket collectors in particular is challenged. Many of the coloured railwaymen felt exposed and vulnerable, especially when they were isolated from their colleagues. They thought it prudent not to exert their full authority in conflict situations, not to push passengers too far. They felt, too, that they received insufficient support from London Transport in conflict with passengers. That they experienced proportionately more

---

[1] There have, of course, also been improvements in the quality of service provided.

trouble from passengers was widely recognized by their white colleagues, though some blamed them for this.

LIKES AND DISLIKES OF LONDON'S UNDERGROUND RAILWAYMEN
As with the busmen, and for similar reasons,[1] we asked our samples of railwaymen both what they 'liked' and what they 'disliked' about their employment with London Transport. The answers to the first of these two questions are summarized in Table 9.8.

TABLE 9.8
*Features of Their Employment which Railwaymen liked, in Percentages.**

	Native railwaymen			Immigrant railwaymen		
	Train-men	Station staff	Total	Train-men	Station staff	Total
The job/interesting work/ meeting people	58	60	59	27	28	27
Freedom from close super-vision	21	20	20	48	22	39
Job security	38	23	33	32	33	32
Hours: shift work/freedom to change shifts/days off mid-week	17	27	20	22	14	19
Free travel/free uniform	8	13	10	10	22	15
Reasonable pay	13	20	16	13	6	10
Nothing	6	7	6	10	14	11
L.T.B. good or fair em-ployers/welfare sports, social, and canteen facilities	8	7	7	10	11	10
No answer	—	—	—	2	—	1
(Sample)	(53)	(30)	(83)	(60)	(36)	(96)

* More than one answer was recorded and the percentage totals may therefore exceed 100.

The natives showed a greater positive orientation to various aspects of the job than did the immigrants who stressed more the freedom from close supervision. Otherwise the pattern of answers was very similar, though there were some differences of emphasis.

When both natives and immigrants spoke of the job they were

[1] See Chapter 6.

seldom very explicit, beyond saying that it was interesting, that they enjoyed meeting people, liked trains, or found the work not hard.

[It is] a cushy job—you don't want to work too hard as you get older. [U.K. Stationman.]

It's not a hard job and I enjoy the work. [West Indian Station Foreman.]

Considerably more natives than immigrants mentioned various aspects of the work task, and this probably reflects the lower extent of self-selection amongst the latter: but for job discrimination elsewhere they would not have become railwaymen.[1] Possibly, too, it reflects the fact that coloured railwaymen meet more difficulties with passengers than do their white colleagues. These conclusions are supported by the fact that somewhat more immigrants than natives found nothing to like about employment with L.T.B. On the other hand, slightly more immigrants than natives found nothing to dislike about their employment.[2] There is though no contradiction: the absence of dislikes is compatible with a lower positive attachment to the work task. Moreover, other aspects of employment were viewed as more favourable, particularly the freedom from close supervision.

This freedom from personal supervision is important for all operating railwaymen; it is greatest for the trainmen and valued most by the immigrants: one possible source of friction and discrimination is very much reduced.

You are your own guv'nor—no one interferes as long as you do the job properly. [U.K. Motorman.]

There were two main aspects of job security: the perceived freedom from redundancy and from arbitrary dismissal. Some spelled out one or the other of these two, others spoke of their job being secure, steady, permanent, safe, or regular. It is possible, too, that some had in mind the absence of short-time working when they spoke in these terms. Whilst both aspects of job security are important for both groups of railwaymen, the freedom from arbitrary dismissal is especially important for the immigrants: the fear of discriminatory dismissal at the behest of a supervisor, for example, is removed. This does not mean that all the coloured immigrants were convinced that there were no discriminatory dismissals, or that the

---

[1] Self-selection was, of course, a less salient factor for those native railwaymen who joined L.T.B. before the Second World War, when jobs were scarce. See Chapter 3.

[2] See below, p. 192.

opportunity for them is completely absent. It does, though, mean that they are far less likely to occur.[1]

They give you a fair chance . . . if anything goes wrong. If they haul you up for something, they let you explain before deciding to sack you or not . . . You have a fair chance—you can lose a job in industry fairly easy. [West Indian Stationman.]

It's a steady job if you behave yourself—London Transport are good people to work for. [U.K. Motorman.]

The next group of answers were all concerned with the hours worked: shift work as such, the ability to change turns and have rest days mid-week. Some like shift work because it allows them to be at home more in the daytime—and in the hours of daylight. Freedom to change turns is valued: some trainmen arrange their changes so that they seldom work the 'dead early' or 'dead late' turns, and there is a flexibility of hours of work which is absent in many other occupations. Rest days at mid-week are appreciated because entertainment and recreational facilities are less crowded than at week-ends, and shops and offices are open. Some obviously prefer the hours of work of public transport to those of manufacturing industry. On the other hand, these hours of work are also the source of widespread discontent.

The meaning of the 'free travel' and 'free uniform' category is clear and need not be added to, save to say that some who mentioned free travel also pointed out that 'it is really part of your wages'. Those who said that 'pay is reasonable' said precisely that. As with the Central Bus staff, such answers came disproportionately more from the women, particularly those in the native samples.

Turning to the last group of answers on features of London Transport employment that were liked, some spoke in very general terms; others mentioned specific facilities:

[I like] trains, and London Transport looks after its staff better than British Railways. [U.K. Guard.]

They look after you when you're ill—the welfare is good. [U.K. Guard.]

Some found nothing specific to like about their employment, but seldom expressed a strong dislike:

It's just a job—[I like] nothing in particular. [U.K. Guard with a lifetime's service.]

[1] Disciplinary procedures are described in Appendix 2.

The patterns of answers on aspects of employment which were 'liked' were, then, with one important exception, very similar for both the immigrant and native railwaymen. The answers from the busmen followed a broadly similar pattern.[1] What features of their jobs did railwaymen dislike? The answers to our question on dislikes are summarized in Table 9.9.

TABLE 9.9
*Features of Their Employment which Railwaymen Disliked, in Percentages.**

| | Native Railwaymen | | | Immigrant Railwaymen | | |
	Train-men	Station staff	Total	Train-men	Station staff	Total
Nothing	30	33	31	33	44	37
Shift work/early turns/late turns/week-end work	40	40	40	40	25	34
Cleaning work	—	10	—	—	17	—
Bad supervision/impersonal management	6	7	6	10	17	12
Poor pay/pension/other fringe benefits	8	—	5	12	6	9
Boring work/tunnel work	9	3	7	5	—	3
Short or long duty before meal break	6	—	—	4	—	—
Difficult passengers	—	3	1	2	6	3
Other answer	8	7	7	8	—	5
No answer	4	—	2	1	—	1
(Sample)	(53)	(30)	(83)	(60)	(36)	(96)

* More than one answer was recorded and the percentage totals may therefore exceed 100.

It will be seen that roughly one-third of each group found nothing specific in their employment to dislike—a slightly higher proportion than was found among the busmen.

Clearly, the major dislike is concerned with hours of work: over half of those who had a specific discontent mentioned some aspect of the hours they worked. Some merely spoke of shift work or the hours, others objected to working at week-ends, to starting very early and finishing very late. The arrangement of rest days was

[1] See above, Chapter 6.

criticized;[1] and the disruption of social and domestic life was a source of much discontent, and probably the most important aspect of most criticisms of the hours of work in public transport. An additional handicap for public transport workers is that they often have to travel to and from home at hours of the night when public transport is not available. Staff buses and trains are provided, but several found them inadequate or inconvenient.

Other dislikes were mentioned far less frequently. Some were mentioned by very few and little significance can be attached to any differences between the native and immigrant samples. Some answers were coded separately to avoid an over-large 'other answer' category.

Some of the station staff disliked cleaning work, but fewer of the immigrants mentioned this than might have been expected, in view of the comments of some supervisors.[2] Some of the Barbadian direct recruits complained that they had been misled about the cleaning work content of a stationman's duties.[3]

There was some difference of emphasis between the immigrant and native railwaymen in their complaints about management and supervision. The latter tended to stress that management was too remote or that there were too many managers; the immigrants complained of the formal requirements of management and supervision, of rules which they found difficult to accept. Again the difficulty that some immigrants experience in adapting to the requirements of a large, bureaucratic public service organization is emphasized.[3]

[I don't like] having to explain absence when I take a day off. I don't expect to get paid for it, but I don't see why I should say what I've been doing. [West Indian Guard.]

Most of the native railwaymen's complaints about management and supervision were less specific:

It's very impersonal. London Transport has no idea of labour relations: it's not interested in people as people, but just as numbers to drive trains. [U.K. Motorman.]

I've never seen the Operating Manager, he should come down to the depot and make himself known. This applies to many at fifty-five Broadway [L.T.B. headquarters]. The Divisional Superintendent also— I've never even seen him. [U.K. Guard.]

[1] Sunday work is compulsory overtime. Most operative railwaymen work one Sunday in two, but a Sunday off does not necessarily accompany a Saturday or Monday rest day.
[2] See above, pp. 172–3.   [3] See Chapter 13.

These grievances—some from railwaymen with thirty and forty years' service—were obviously deeply felt. Some of the immigrants, too, complained in these general terms:

There are too many bosses: a stationmaster and a D.I. [Divisional Inspector] and another D.I. [West Indian Station Foreman.]

London Transport are not very good employers: they don't investigate complaints. [West Indian Guard.]

A miscellaneous group of answers all criticized some feature of the conditions of service: pay, pensions, holidays, canteen facilities, and so on.

The short holidays and the time of year you have to take them. [U.K. Motorman.]

The catering service on London Transport could be improved: they could cater more for the migrants. At present it is 'chips with everything'. [West Indian Motorman.]

The uniforms are horrible. [West Indian Guard.]

The boredom of work, and particularly tunnel work, was mentioned by a few:

It does get boring—you don't see much daylight. [West Indian Guard.]

Trainmen's meal breaks—meal reliefs—are taken not less than two and a half hours and not more than five hours after the beginning of the shift. Some found that the time before the meal relief was either too short or too long.

Some turns are too long before a break is given. [West Indian Guard.]

Dislikes recorded in the other answer category varied widely:

Suicides: I've had five. It can happen *any* time. [U.K. Motorman.]

They employ far too many coloureds: they are breathing down your back. [U.K. Guard.]

We have seen that with one important difference, the features of their employment which native and immigrant railwaymen like are very similar. The freedom from close supervision is especially valued by the immigrants: the potential for discriminatory treatment at this level is far less than is found in many other occupations, and there is little doubt that this is one key factor contributing to the absorption of the immigrants in the organization. Important, too, is job security, particularly the freedom from arbitrary dismissal.

Again the evidence points to the advantages for the absorption of immigrants inherent in the large bureaucratic organization, with its formal and, consequently, impersonal procedures.

On the other hand, some of the West Indians find it difficult to accept some requirements of the large public service organization, particularly the need for regular attendance at prescribed times and having to explain absences for which they are not paid. In part, this is a resentment against having to give *any* explanation, but, more important, it is against its formal nature: a written memorandum.

There was though no evidence that the immigrants were more prone to lateness or absences; there were differences in their attitudes towards them, and both were said—by some managers and supervisors—to be offences in which immigrants were over-represented. On the other hand, some coloured immigrants indicated that they thought that some supervisors were partial in their relationships with white and coloured subordinates, and it appeared unlikely that their fears were groundless.

The major discontent, though, for natives and immigrants alike, arises from the hours of work. This factor, more than any other, must account for much of the staff wastage.

The dislikes of the railwaymen and the busmen followed a somewhat similar pattern, with some obvious differences explicable in terms of the technical and social organization of work, particularly the greater incidence of face-to-face contact with passengers for the busmen. Whilst there was this broad similarity between the staff in the two departments, there was not, in the railway situation, the widespread lack of motivation to do a good job, so prevalent amongst the busmen.

IO

THE PERMANENT WAY DEPARTMENT, I:
THE PLATELAYERS' WORLD

INTRODUCTION

Permanent Way is that branch of civil engineering concerned with track construction and maintenance: it is involved with the ballast or concrete bed, sleepers, running and conductor rails, points, cross-overs, track drainage, maintenance of embankments, fences, and so on.

The essential differences between various types of track are as follows. Open track is the conventional type of railway: steel running and conductor rails affixed to creosote-impregnated pine sleepers, laid on and in a bed of crushed limestone chippings—the ballast. The track of sub-surface railway, constructed by the 'cut and cover' method, is similar to open track. In London's tube railways an Australian hardwood is used for sleepers to minimize fire risk. These sleepers are laid on and in a concrete bed: the clearance between a tube car and the tunnel is small; with a conventional ballast bed it is possible that track movement would cause a car to collide with the tunnel 'walls'. Hence the need for a rigid, concrete track bed.

THE STRUCTURE OF THE DEPARTMENT

Diagram 10.1 shows the structure of the Department.[1]

The main focus of our attention will be the group and gang level, but some explanation of other parts of the diagram is called for.

The gardening section was concerned mostly with the provision and maintenance of trees, shrubs, and grasses which are used to help stabilize embankments and cuttings.

[1] It should be emphasized that the structure shown, the size of the Department, the description of work tasks and so on, relate to the situation prevailing at the time of the fieldwork. At that time mechanized maintenance of open track was at an experimental stage, but it was subsequently fully adopted. This brought about considerable changes in work tasks, organizational structure and some reductions in the workforce. These changes were made some time after the fieldwork and are therefore beyond the scope of this study.

AGRAM 10.1.

ructure of the Permanent Way Department[1]

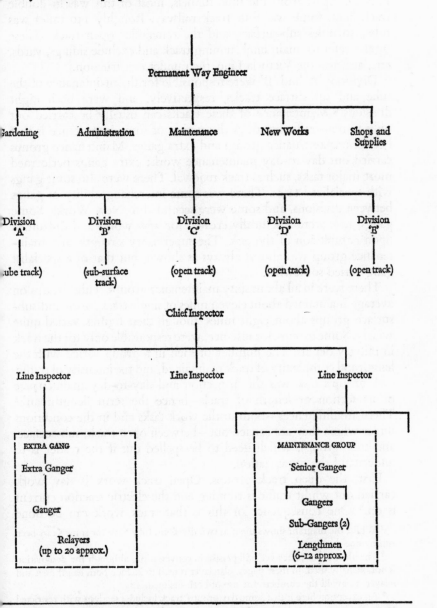

---

[1] A number of miscellaneous staff - hand-signalmen, ballast train guards, and so on - are not shown on the diagram.

The Department maintained about 500 miles of single track railway. Apart from the tube tunnels, most of this was in double track lines, some was four track railway. Roughly 130 miles was tube, 50 miles sub-surface, and the remainder open track. These figures refer to 'main line' running track and exclude sidings, yards, etc., and also the Victoria Line, then under construction.

Divisions 'A' and 'B' were responsible for the maintenance of the tube and sub-surface tracks, respectively, and were both night divisions.[1] Maintenance of these tracks can usually be carried out only in non-traffic hours. A distinction of some importance is that between maintenance groups and extra gangs. Maintenance groups carried out day-to-day maintenance work; extra gangs performed more major tasks, such as track renewal. There were also some gangs with specialized tasks. There was some interchangeability of gangs between divisions, and some were seconded to New Works. Some gangs, too, were specifically created for new works and disbanded upon completion of the task. The supervisory strength of a maintenance group was almost always as shown, but that of a specialist gang varied somewhat.

There were in all about sixty maintenance groups. Tube groups on average maintained about eleven miles of single track, open and sub-surface groups about eight miles, though these figures varied quite widely. Some groups, for instance, were responsible only for the track in railway depots. The number of men in a group varied with the length and complexity of track maintained, and the intensity of traffic.

A group's task was the inspection and day-to-day maintenance of its section or length of track—hence the term 'lengthman'.[2] There are differences—both in the work tasks and in the conditions under which they are carried out—between open track, sub-surface, and tube groups, which need to be spelled out if the reader is to understand the organization.

First, the open track groups. Open track work is day work carried out whilst traffic is running and the electric traction current is on.[3] One consequence of this is that track work can be done

[1] Whilst the diagram shows them as two divisions, they have for some years been run by one Assistant.

[2] The older term 'platelayer' still persists in conversation, although the designation is not officially used. In these pages, platelayer is used to include both lengthmen and relayer, to avoid the cumbersome use of both designations.

[3] An exception here is that some day groups' track includes sections with restricted access, for instance, on bridges. Maintenance of such sections is done at night on an overtime basis.

during most of the working shift, apart from during the peak traffic hours. Another is the threat of danger that is ever-present: from trains, from 'live' conductor rails.

Maintenance of ballasted tracks requires a wide variety of work tasks. Inspection of most track is carried out daily. For this purpose the track is 'walked', usually by the senior ganger or one of his gangers or sub-gangers. Practices vary between groups: some senior gangers prefer to do a lot of inspection walking themselves, as the ultimate responsibility for the safety of the track is theirs or, as they put it, they 'carry the can'. The practice of daily inspection by a senior ganger, ganger, or sub-ganger, incidentally, accounts for the apparently top-heavy group structure: that is, the large number of supervisors relative to that of lengthmen. Permanent Way day group staff normally work a Monday to Friday five-day week; Saturday and Sunday track inspections are carried out on overtime. It might be useful to add that in terms of duties and responsibilities, a rough parallel to the grades of senior ganger, ganger, and sub-ganger in some other industries would be foremen, charge-hand, and leading hand, respectively.

Whilst the allocation of time between tasks varies according to track conditions and its layout, up to about 50 per cent of a day group's time was spent on what is colloquially known as 'fettling', otherwise 'lifting and packing' the track: that is, raising the track and packing beneath the sleepers—with small limestone chippings—to maintain the track's stability, the correct 'top' (an even surface *along* the rails), and the appropriate 'cross level' or 'cant' (*across* the running rails).[1] It is appropriate to add that the term *permanent* way is misleading when applied to a ballasted track, particularly one laid on a soft, wet, clay sub-soil formation: *continual* maintenance is required to keep the track to an acceptable standard. On the other hand—and this applies to all track maintenance—the higher the standard at which a track is maintained, the less work is required to keep it at that standard, as less wear and tear results. Good track maintenance has, then, a cumulative effect. Most day groups had a fettling gang comprised of about half its members.[2]

---

[1] Most readers will not want me to take them far into the esoteric technicalities of track construction and maintenance and I will only do so when this is necessary to understand some feature of direct relevance.

[2] The work tasks described in this paragraph were subsequently mechanized: track-mounted 'tampers' lift the track and consolidate the ballast beneath and between the sleepers.

Apart from fettling, a group carries out a number of other tasks: among them are the maintenance of conductor rails at the correct level and gauge, replacement of broken insulators, attention to fishplates, rail keys, and other 'fastenings'.[1] Other tasks are the maintenance of points, rail oilers, and de-icing equipment. Yet others included the maintenance of the correct gauge of running rails, the general cleanliness and tidiness of the track and surrounding areas, embankments, and cuttings. This list of tasks is not exhaustive, but includes most activities. The important points are that day group lengthmen perform many tasks; some are physically arduous, some require skills. Moreover, track work is carried out for most of the working shift, in conditions of constant potential danger.

Turning to the night groups—tube and sub-surface—the first contrast with the day men is the period of time when track work may be carried out: on most lines the last train runs at about 00·30–01.00, the first at about 05.00–05.30. Effective 'possession' time of the track is then about four hours, and this is often reduced by the operation of ballast trains—that is, trains carrying equipment and materials, usually for permanent way maintenance.[2] A consequence of this restricted possession time is that all track tasks, for groups and for gangs, have to be carried out during this relatively short period. Whilst, then, the night staff book on at 23.30 and off at 07.00, there is often little they can do during traffic hours, apart from travelling to and from the night's work site, maintaining tools and equipment, cleaning the cabin, and so on. Night staff work Tuesday to Saturday nights: the times of the first trains on Sunday mornings are up to two hours later than on week-days and possession time is correspondingly longer; major operations requiring track possession during normal traffic hours are carried out on Sundays, when there is less passenger traffic. Saturday night work was not popular with lengthmen and relayers.[3]

The work tasks of groups engaged on the maintenance of sub-surface tracks are essentially similar to those of open track groups. Track movement is less of a problem than it is on open lines: most

[1] Fishplates are metal plates used to join lengths of rail; keys are the wood or metal wedges which secure rails in their chairs. Chairs are the sockets in which running rails sit and are secured to sleepers by coachscrews inserted through wood or fibre bushes (shaped washers).

[2] Electric or battery-powered locomotives were used to haul these trains on tube and open tracks; steam engines were used on some open tracks, but they have since been replaced by diesel engines.

[3] See below, Chapter 11.

are roofed over and this ensures a drier track; the edges or shoulders of the ballast bed are usually supported by the tunnel walls.

For the tube groups, there is an important difference in that they maintain concreted track. Whilst there is little problem of track movement, the absence of a shock-absorptive ballast bed makes necessary more attention to fastenings: fishplates, chair screws and bushes, and so on. The conditions under which these groups work are also different: working space for some tasks is very restricted; tube tunnels are dust-laden and warm. This heat was seen to have advantages: some of the West Indians preferred a warm, dry, if dirty tube tunnel to a cold and possibly wet open track, especially in winter.

These, then, are the tasks and work environments of maintenance groups. Major operations are carried out by the extra gangs. The largest of these tasks is track relaying—that is, the renewal of rails or sleepers[1]—hence the designation 'relayer'. Extra gangs carry out new track installation work, and there are also a few with specialist tasks: drainage, current rail renewal, fencing, and so on.[2] Most extra gang work is night work.

Some of the consequences of the different tasks performed by groups and gangs will become apparent as we proceed. It is sufficient at this point to say, first, that gangs are usually larger than groups. Second, group tasks are often performed by two or three men; gang tasks often require all or most of the gang: dragging, lifting or throwing rails or sleepers, concreting tube tracks, and such like.

Each group and gang has a 'cabin'. Those of open track groups and gangs are what the designation suggests: a brick-built or wooden hut. The cabins of tube groups and gangs are more likely to be found in disused passenger tunnels, lift-shafts, and the like; those of sub-surface men may be found in all manner of accommodation. The facilities of most cabins are very similar: tables and chairs for meals, equipment for cooking, water heating, and washing, lockers for clothing, and for open section groups, equipment for drying clothes.

At the time of our study, the Department employed roundly 1,750 in the wage grades—that is, up to and including senior gangers. Nearly half of this number were in maintenance groups, about

[1] In the tubes sleeper renewal is more commonly termed track reconditioning. As a consequence of the need to break up—'open out'—the concrete bed, it is a very dusty occupation.

[2] There is also an all-female gang, known as the 'fluffers', which cleans the track in tube tunnels. (Tube tunnels become coated with 'fluff'—a mixture of clothing fibres, human hair, brake lining, and other dust which becomes matted together and is removed by hand, using scrapers and so on. It is removed to prevent a fire hazard.)

one-fifth in extra gangs, and the remainder in a wide variety of occupations: workshops and gardening staff, crane drivers, hand signalmen, lorry drivers, ballast train guards, emergency squad men, and so on.

THE TRADITIONS AND VALUES OF PERMANENT WAY[1]

There is an old saying still heard from Permanent Way men that a good platelayer is 'strong in the arm and weak in the head'. Much of the work is indeed physically arduous. Some platelayers with wide experience of construction and civil engineering work considered that opening out a track, that is, loosening and removing the tightly packed ballast between the sleepers, was one of the hardest jobs they had met. Other tasks appeared equally demanding of physical effort. A co-ordination of effort is also required. On some tasks, twenty or more men must, in effect, work as one: for example, when lifting and throwing a sixty-foot length of running rail. Moreover, Permanent Way tasks often have to be completed within a definite time scale, and this applies to any task which requires track possession. On the other hand, arduous physical effort must often be sustained for a considerable period of time. Much of the work is dirty and open track work often has to be carried out in uncomfortable weather conditions. Finally, there is an element of danger: from traffic, from live conductor rails, and from the handling of heavy objects—rails, sleepers, and so on. This threat of danger is probably a cohesive influence in that platelayers have to rely very much on each other for their safety.

We have already discussed the 'old railwayman' in relation to railway operations and found it useful to regard him as an ideal type.[2] In Permanent Way, too, we met a similar set of beliefs: sometimes the designation 'old railwayman' was used, but more often it was the 'old platelayer' and this is the term we will use to distinguish him from his operating counterpart. Again it will be useful to regard the 'old platelayer' as an ideal type.

There were two differences in the sets of beliefs concerning the 'old railwayman' and the 'old platelayer': first, the qualities and behaviour of the former were spelled out in greater and more precise detail than were those of the latter; second, whilst the 'old railway-

[1] I am not suggesting that there is a unitary system of values, shared by managers, supervisors, and platelayers. In this section, I am concerned mostly—but not exclusively—with the values of management and supervision.

[2] See Chapter 7.

man' was often thought to be largely a figure of the past, the 'old platelayer' was still seen to be present in some numbers, though again he belonged to a dying species and if not chronologically old, he was definitely ageing. 'I don't know what we'll do when the old platelayers are gone' appeared to be a fairly common management sentiment.

The 'old platelayer', as he was presented to us by management and engineering staff, was capable of hard and sustained physical effort. Next, he was prepared to make this effort without continual supervision—reliability in this respect was thought important. He was reliable, too, in terms of attendance and time, though there was not the same emphasis on prompt attendance that we met amongst the operating staff.[1] Fourth, the 'old platelayer' had a sense of urgency about the performance of his tasks, and responded to commands quickly and without question. Finally, he could be relied upon to be concerned with safety: his own, that of his workmates, and that of traffic.

A traditional source of recruitment for permanent-way work has been agriculture, and in the past there were some similarities in the skills required in the two occupations. Both required hard physical effort, often with hand tools. 'For more than a century it had been the policy of the railways to augment their labour supply by offering a shilling or two more than the farmers paid their labourers.'[2] Agriculture is, though, less relevant to a railway system concentrated predominantly in an urban area, and the building industry is thought now to be one major source of recruits for L.T.B. Permanent Way, particularly in the winter months.

The emphasis in the image of the 'old platelayer', as he was presented to us, was very much then on *physical* capacity, plus a willingness to exert this capacity both with little supervision and with promptness when instructed. It was not completely clear what was thought to motivate him. Certainly there was no suggestion that he should in any sense be dedicated to railways, quite unlike the expectation of the 'old railwayman'. The predominant view amongst managers appeared to be that in the past the fear of unemployment had provided the necessary spur, and that no substitute incentive had been found in the post-war years.

[1] This difference is explicable in terms of the consequences of late attendance: lateness of a few minutes would have less serious consequences in Permanent Way than in the operating department.

[2] Bagwell, p. 616.

8

There is in this concept of the 'old platelayer' probably some over-emphasis of physical capacity at the expense of mental ability. Permanent Way has relied on internal promotion to fill supervisory posts up to the grade of chief inspector, posts which require not only physical ability. Until recent years, most supervisors were each responsible for very few men, but the size of work groups has increased and is increasing. The emphasis on physical ability under-estimates, too, the skills of permanent-way work—although mostly manual, these skills are not exclusively so. Techniques are changing; the hard physical manual element is being taken out of permanent-way work and replaced by machine. The extent to which this has happened so far should not be exaggerated, but these changes do have implications for the workforce.

The stress on experience which we found amongst the operating railwaymen was again in evidence, though to a lesser extent. Whilst some skills acquired in other industries are not without their value in permanent way, many of the techniques are specific to railway work. Whereas experience is formally acknowledged to be important in railway operating, in that promotion is on a seniority basis, this is not so in Permanent Way: promotion is on merit, with seniority used only when two or more candidates for one vacancy are seen to have equal merit. Nevertheless, we will see when we come to pro-motion that the importance of experience is tacitly acknowledged. Supervisors with long experience told us that they were still learn-ing, though this is possibly as much a reflection of changing tech-niques as of the complexity of the permanent-way world.

Perhaps at this point it is useful to stress the importance of judge-ment, as it relates to experience. We were repeatedly told that in permanent-way work there are few *precise* indications that, for example, a section of track is in good or bad condition. There are numerous factors to consider, few are amenable to precise measure-ment, and the over-all assessment must be a matter of judgement. Comparisons were often made with signals work, in which, we were told, it is possible to test whether or not a piece of equipment is functioning correctly. Such precision is, we were assured, seldom possible in permanent-way work. It ought to be added, though, that more precise measurement has been attained and *standards* of both quantity and *quality* are used for the incentive bonus scheme.[1] Experience was then seen as a prerequisite for the judgement neces-sary, for example, for supervisory posts.

[1] See Chapter 11.

In relation to the movement of traffic and passengers, two values appeared to be of paramount importance. The first was that it should always be possible for the first train to go through on time. The restoration of the track in time for the first train clearly provides a target and when track possession is for a relatively short period, as it usually is, it is a fairly immediate target. The other key value in relation to passenger traffic is that of safety. Its importance is self-evident, but it appeared to be constantly in the minds of Permanent Way men, particularly supervisors. The safety of staff, too, was stressed.

Whilst a department employing some 1,750 men scattered over many miles of track at numerous locations can hardly be considered small, in social terms I was conscious of being in a 'small' organization. Most Permanent Way men at senior or extra ganger levels or above appeared to know most of the others at these levels, as well as many in the lower grades. There was, too, far less formality in behaviour than was obvious in Railway Operating—'sir' was a form of address seldom heard in Permanent Way, in marked contrast to Railway Operating. In short, there appeared to be a more friendly rapport between most managers and supervisors than was evident in the operating department. This appeared to extend, too, to the relationships between supervisors and platelayers, though in some instances *commands* were issued in a pronounced military style and obeyed 'at the double'.[1]

At the maintenance group level there appeared to be many characteristics of a small organization, or, to put it another way, many features of the large organization were not very much in evidence. The cabin was an important focal point: for booking on, meals, tea breaks, and just 'sitting about' when nothing else could be done. This last point of course applied far more to night than to day groups. Horizons, too, were limited: the group maintained the same local stretch of track; the effective boss was the senior ganger and there appeared to be little direct interaction between lengthmen and anyone above inspector. A group was a *local* group. The analysis of this paragraph applies far less to an extra gang. First, it is usually larger in numbers. Second, whilst it has a 'base' cabin, its work sites may be anywhere in the system.

In some respects Permanent Way appeared to be more isolated from the outside world than did Railway Operating. The latter

[1] Supervisory styles and relationships between platelayers and supervisors are discussed in Chapter 11.

department of course caters directly for the demands of passengers, and many staff are in constant face-to-face contact with passengers. This isolation applies most of all to night staff: an important social division in Permanent Way is that between the day and the night men. In spite of the fact that night work requires track possession and that possession time is comparatively short, I was seldom conscious of a greater sense of urgency at night, though presumably this varies according to the task and the time available. A perceptive West Indian relayer summed up the distinctive features of the night work culture: 'The mood of night work—it is a way of living, it is the same in all the gangs—they [night men] *move more quietly.*'[1]

It would perhaps be inaccurate to describe the prevailing attitudes amongst L.T.B. Permanent Way managers and supervisors as conservative: the organization has been responsible for technical innovation and was the first in Western Europe to develop continuous welded running rails.[2] Yet the prevailing attitude is undoubtedly one of caution: the worth and reliability of change has to be demonstrated and proven beyond doubt before it is accepted. This attitude of cautious scepticism was very much in evidence at the time of our fieldwork in relation to the then-impending widespread adoption of machine 'tamping'.

In the status hierarchy of the L.T.B., Permanent Way staff thought they occupied a low position, though they did not necessarily accept the low position to which they thought others had allotted them. Busmen and railway operating men, I was told, were at the same level, but different; both looked down on Permanent Way men. A sentiment more commonly met was an envy of the Signals Department. Signals, I was told, could more easily succeed in persuading senior management of the necessity for expenditure than could Permanent Way. This was often explained in terms of the greater complexity of signalling equipment: the layman could not understand it and was therefore in the hands of the expert. By contrast, Permanent Way requirements could more easily be understood and assessed. This more favourable treatment of Signals was, though, seen to extend intonon-technical are as, for example, messroom accommodation. Permanent Way men saw their department as very much a poor relation to Signals.

In sum, we see an organization with a strongly and widely held

[1] My italics.   [2] *London Transport Magazine* (Vol. 23, No. 4, July 1969).

belief that thirty years ago it had a workforce composed largely of 'old platelayers', and that this element is now a small and diminishing one. I do not know how far this image of the past ideal workforce accorded with reality and how much is myth, but the myth element is probably quite large. The prevailing belief amongst managers was that the quality of recruits was lower than it was in pre-war times. On the other hand, it was thought that standards of track maintenance are higher now than they were thirty years ago, but credit for this was given to the incentive bonus scheme, almost as though it could be divorced from the men who maintain the track.[1] We see an organization numerically quite large, but in social terms small and informal, and somewhat isolated from the non-railway world. Caution is the prevailing attitude to change, and there is a widespread belief in the Department's high standards of track construction and maintenance.[2] Change may be seen as threatening these high standards, but must not be allowed to impair them. The Department was proud of its reliability: the first train usually *does* go through on time. Finally, and perhaps of greatest immediate relevance, the *performance* of the individual platelayer is important: certainly to his workmates, as well as to supervisors and other superordinates. It matters to them that the individual platelayer pulls his weight and that he has a concern for safety—theirs as much as his own.

THE INTRODUCTION OF COMMONWEALTH IMMIGRANTS TO PERMANENT WAY

Irish immigrants have been employed in Permanent Way for many years, certainly since before the Second World War. In terms of the proportion of the whole L.T.B. workforce that is Irish, they are over-represented in Permanent Way.

In the immediate post-war years a number of Eastern Europeans from Poland, the Baltic states, and other countries were recruited, some at the resettlement camps, and a number are still with the Department. Most, we were told, are now British subjects. The only problem of note reported to us concerning these Eastern Europeans was that of language, but it was of less importance that they should be able to speak good English than that they could understand it. Good spoken English became important later, when they applied

[1] See Chapter 11.
[2] It was widely believed that L.T.B. standards of track maintenance were higher than those of British Rail.

for promotion.[1] Initially they were placed on the outer edges of the system, where traffic is lightest, but now they appear to be scattered widely. It seems likely that some accepted occupational down-grading when they joined L.T.B., but some have since been promoted. Eastern Europeans were found as senior gangers; at least one was an inspector; and others had various specialist posts. The evidence indicates that as a group they have been largely absorbed in the organization. They have obviously made some adaptation and appear to be largely or fully accepted.

It was not possible to date the arrival of the first coloured immigrants with any precision. Some, variously described as West Indians, West Africans, or specifically Nigerians, were employed on the Western extension of the Central Line, a part of the 1935–40 New Works programme delayed by the War. This was in the period 1947–8, and it seems likely that some were ex-servicemen. They were employed on the New Works staff on a temporary basis and appear to have left or been discharged when the Western extension was completed. Although memories of this period were very hazy, these workers do appear to have made little impact on the Department. By about 1950 all expansion of the system had ceased, the New Works staff was disbanded, and recruitment slowed or halted.

There appears to have been a period from the late 1940s to about 1954 when there were no coloured immigrants in Permanent Way. Written and statistical information confirmed their presence in 1955. The earliest date of recruitment to the Department of those who had subsequently been promoted to sub-ganger or ganger was 1955, though it is of course possible that others had joined earlier. Again in 1955, a West Indian asked what his position would be with regard to promotion should he be accepted on the permanent staff. (New recruits serve a three-month probationary period before their appointments are confirmed.) The context of this request for information was the existence of an agreement between management and union that *non-British* staff were not eligible for promotion.[2] The question was referred to the Sectional Council,[3] and 'it was agreed that British Subjects of the Commonwealth should follow the normal line of regular appointment and promotion'.[4] The De-

---

[1] Non-English speaking gangs with bilingual go-betweens were apparently employed for some engineering work, but not in the Permanent Way Department.
[2] Such agreements relating to *foreign* workers were quite common; see Hepple.
[3] For Sectional Councils, see Chapter 15.
[4] Minute S.Cl. 8/934, 21 December 1955. Source: L.T.B.

partment then circularized all Eastern European staff, telling them of the necessity to become British subjects if they wished to be promoted and how this status could be attained.[1]

Initially, the coloured immigrants were dispersed on the basis of not more than one or two to each group or section,[2] and four or five to each extra gang.

As reported to us some years later, the reactions of the existing workforce were mixed. As most of the complaints which reached management were made through the supervisors, it is not clear how far they originated from the platelayers or reflected the attitudes of the supervisors themselves. It seems highly likely, though, that the latter was more frequently the case. This interpretation was given added weight by the comments of some platelayers that previous supervisors had been 'anti-coloured'. The supervisors, too, were more likely than most to be 'old platelayers', and possibly to want their staff to be the same.

The objections to the newcomers which reached the ears of management concerned smells, hygiene, personal habits, laziness, cooking smells, and a reluctance or inability to understand instructions. The reaction of management was that the coloured immigrants had been recruited by the Board on the same conditions as anyone else; they were therefore part of the permanent workforce and were to be treated no differently from other employees. Any short-comings or misdemeanours on the part of the immigrants could be dealt with through the normal machinery. This did not necessarily reconcile the supervisors to the new situation, but it probably made it clear to them that *they* had to deal with any problems—they could not be evaded or pushed up to management.

[1] Some readers might interpret this action as being aimed against the coloured immigrants. On the other hand, it would have been discriminatory to have left the Eastern Europeans in ignorance, if they were in ignorance, of the steps they had to take if they wished to be promoted. They had been in the Department for some years, and were unlikely to return to their native lands. The agreement was of course discriminatory and deliberately so. For evidence on a similar agreement in British Rail and of an attempt to apply it in a redundancy situation to the detriment of the Eastern Europeans, see Patterson, *Immigrants in Industry*, p. 217. One effect of this in the British Rail situation was an upsurge in applications for naturalization.

[2] There is a conflict of evidence here: sections, each composed of about five men, were responsible for track maintenance and were merged into groups (three sections to each group) following the 1953 incentive bonus scheme agreement. It is not clear how long the process of amalgamation lasted or whether it was largely completed before the coloured immigrants had joined in numbers. (One or two sections still existed at the time of the fieldwork.)

Whilst the evidence on these early days is patchy, it does strongly suggest that there was less adverse reaction from the Permanent Way native workforce than from those in either Central Buses or Railway Operating. There were no threats of strike action, such as was met in Central Buses.[1] This apparently less hostile reaction is explicable partly in terms of the colour-class hypothesis, in that there was perhaps seen to be less disparity of status and it was not therefore seen to be threatened; and partly by the fact that there had been earlier experience of coloured immigrants in the Department—it was not an innovation.

On the other hand, we did not hear any reports of outstanding 'characters' in these early days, such as those we were told about in Central Buses and Railway Operating; and no one reported that the early immigrants had been very good. Any outstanding individuals are probably less likely to be noticed in permanent-way work, and it is probable, too, that any immigrants thought by the recruitment staff to be in any sense outstanding would be sent to either of the two operating departments, rather than to Permanent Way.[2] In the words of one manager, the early immigrants 'merely fitted in'.

The restriction on the numbers of immigrants in any one group or gang appears to have lasted three or four years, after which time it was overlooked. This appeared to be less the result of a conscious decision at a high level within the Department: there was, rather a gradual recognition that this restriction on numbers was no longer necessary or appropriate, particularly in view of the lack of suitable native recruits. Attempts were, however, still made to spread the immigrants widely, and to prevent any group or gang becoming *overwhelmingly* composed of immigrants, but at the time of our fieldwork the immigrant proportion of groups and gangs varied considerably. There have, though, been attempts to keep down the total number of immigrants in the Department. At times when few recruits have been required, native applicants have been favoured. In the words of one manager, 'it would be fair to say that we discriminate this far.' This was done 'in fairness to the supervisors: they prefer to deal with their own people'.[3]

[1] See Chapter 4.

[2] For recruitment and selection procedures, see Chapter 12. There is, of course, some self-selection of occupation.

[3] A senior ganger in one all-white group mentioned that 'they will not send me any coloured immigrants'. Apparently the previous senior ganger, responsible for one of the busiest sections of four-track railway, had refused to accept responsibility for the safety of any coloured immigrants and his wishes had been complied with.

One exception to the dispersal policy was the formation of an all-immigrant gang. It is not clear how far there was a *deliberate* intention to have an all-coloured gang, but in so far as it was not prevented, it was at least a *conscious* decision. This gang reconditioned a section of tube line. All its members, apart from the supervisors, were new to permanent-way work. The verdict of the manager concerned, some years later, was that there would have been the same 'comedy' with *any* group of new recruits 'straight from the labour exchange'. The work was done, but at a cost of far more detailed supervision than is usual. Lack of experience, rather than ethnic origins, was seen as the major handicap. When the task for which the gang had been formed was completed, it was disbanded.

At the beginning of our study, coloured staff comprised 18 per cent of the wages grades in Permanent Way.[1] This figure had increased only slightly in the previous three years, which suggests that there was a fairly rapid build-up of coloured staff in the late 1950s and early 1960s. The coloured immigrants were thought to be mostly from the Caribbean. All those interviewed were West Indian.

THE FIELD WORK

Whilst we were able to ascertain the total number of coloured immigrants in the Department, it was less easy to find out where they were located. We therefore selected at random a number of groups and gangs and obtained detailed information on the ethnic origins of their members. This showed that there were wide variations: some groups had no coloured members, in others the number varied up to a maximum of five out of seven lengthmen.[2] All the extra gangs in our preliminary sample had some coloured relayers. Their numbers ranged from three out of a total of thirteen in one gang to twelve out of seventeen in another. In these extra gangs the coloured staff were over-represented and it seems likely that this was balanced by some under-representation in other areas, notably on the fringes of the system and amongst workshop staff. We selected matched samples of immigrant and native platelayers from eight of these groups and three of the gangs. Five of the eight groups

---

[1] Source: L.T.B. Staff Administration Office. This percentage may have changed slightly by the time of the fieldwork as there was some increase in the number of New Works staff for laying track for the Victoria Line.

[2] The number of coloured lengthmen as a percentage of the total in this preliminary sample almost exactly matched the percentage of the whole Department that was coloured.

were night groups: the immigrants were found to be concentrated mostly in the inner London area in tube or sub-surface groups which are, of course, night groups. Similarly, two of the three gangs were night gangs. In the groups and gangs selected, coloured plate-layers comprised on average about one-third of the total. The inter-views in the first day and night groups and in the first gang were regarded as a pilot study.

The samples selected totalled fifty platelayers and represented between one in two and one in three in these groups and gangs. However, there were a number of complications[1] and we eventually interviewed forty-two, divided equally between white natives and coloured immigrants.[2]

The interviews were held in the cabins during the day or night, as appropriate. For the night interviews, I usually arrived by the last train and left by the first. As there was more than enough time for the interviews, I was able to spend a considerable time on observation and informal discussion.

Additionally, we spent some considerable time on non-participant observation. This was very fruitful in that it gave an insight into Permanent Way tasks, methods, and behaviour. It is unlikely that this observation made any impact on behaviour: on some sites both Permanent Way and contractors' staff were working and the obser-ver could easily have been thought by each of these two groups to belong to the other. Night staff in particular are accustomed to visitors viewing operations.

[1] There was only one direct refusal, two others failed to attend for interview and were regarded as refusals. Ten others could not be interviewed for various reasons: some had been transferred to other groups or gangs; some were on annual or sick leave; some had resigned. In almost all these cases we did not know of these absences until we arrived for the interviews, so it was not possible to select substitutes imme-diately. To have subsequently interviewed those originally selected or their replace-ments would have been very time-consuming, and we therefore decided to substi-tute a further sample from another group. Five of the six so selected were available and agreed to be interviewed; the sixth had resigned. The relatively low refusal rate was probably at least partly due to the fact that most interviews were held during working hours: the prospect of missing part of a shift provided some inducement. (The interviews of the two who failed to attend were scheduled for the end of their shift.)

[2] Two of the lengthmen selected for interview—one immigrant and one native—had been promoted to sub-gangers by the time they were interviewed. One of the natives selected for interview turned out to be a visitor from the 'white Common-wealth' on a working holiday. Otherwise, there was nothing to distinguish him from the natives interviewed and, consequently, he has been regarded as part of the native sample.

Apart from one group, there was nothing to suggest that the groups or gangs selected for the interviews were in any way atypical of those that had some coloured members. They were drawn from four of the five divisions: none of the groups in our preliminary sample from this fifth division had any coloured immigrant members. This appeared to be largely due to the fact that the division maintained tracks some distance from the central area and the main centres of immigrant settlement. Possibly, too, it reflected a personal preference. One group, 'X group', was regarded as atypical in that it had had problems arising from a change of senior ganger; this situation is discussed in the section on relations with supervisors.[1]

[1] Chapter 11, pp. 221–6.

THE PERMANENT WAY DEPARTMENT, II:
PLATELAYERS—BLACK AND WHITE

INITIAL WHITE OBJECTIONS TO THE EMPLOYMENT OF COLOURED
IMMIGRANTS AND HOSTILITY BETWEEN WHITE AND COLOURED STAFF
Between one-third and one-half of our native sample had been with
the Department when the 'first' coloured immigrants were recruited
in the early to mid-fifties.[1] Most reported that there had been no
objection to the employment of coloured immigrants at that time.
Previous experience of coloured workers, coupled with the initial
slow rate of intake, was seen by some to be responsible for the lack
of objections from the existing staff.

No, they came in ones and twos and there was no opposition. If they had
all come together, there would have been opposition, but they came
gradually and fitted in. [U.K. Relayer.]

The small number who reported objections were not at all
specific on the reasons for them:

The men didn't like the idea—this was the last gang to have them.
[U.K. Relayer.]

You hear a lot about [objections to coloured workers], but there was not
here [sic]. But you always get it. [U.K. Lengthman.]

The evidence, coupled with that gathered from managers and
supervisors, indicated that there was some initial resentment from
the native staff to the employment of coloured immigrants in their
midst, but that it was far less widespread or intense than in the two
operating departments.

Turning to the manifestations of resentment in the form of hostile
behaviour towards the newcomers, roughly three-quarters of both
the native and immigrant samples reported that there had been none

---

[1] Those employed in the New Works staff in the late forties were largely isolated
from the rest of the Department and, in any case, it was too long ago for us to be
able to gather much information on them.

in the past, and very few thought there was any at the time of the study. Both groups agreed that hostility had been, and remained confined to a minority of native workers, and that it was seldom openly displayed.

The few coloured platelayers who said there was hostility were as likely to say that it was from supervisors as much as from their fellow-platelayers. The two complaints made against supervisors were discrimination in the distribution of work tasks and of overtime opportunities. On the other hand, the senior ganger in one group was thought by some of the natives to favour the immigrants in the distribution of work tasks. Some saw this as legitimate *because* the immigrants had longer service in the group, but others objected.

Relations between platelayers and supervisors are discussed in the section devoted to that topic.[1] In one group a previous senior ganger was said to have been 'very anti-coloured', but our native informant was reluctant to expand on this: the senior ganger had retired and he —the platelayer—preferred to 'leave it buried'.

In one of the gangs there appeared to be a somewhat curious situation of a New Zealander (not interviewed) who was thought by the English and Irish to be 'odd' and was rejected by them, to the extent that he became—and was regarded as—part of the 'coloured group' within the gang:

It's kind of clannish [this gang]. Everything tends to segregate, but it doesn't worry me. The Irish are different: they are always laughing, I like them. The New Zealander—he's one of those out of another century. The English can't understand him; I do, in a way. They don't see eye to eye with him, so he is stuck with us. . . . I wouldn't call it hostility, but you always find that gentle type of withdrawal. The thick-skinned wouldn't see it, but you see it in so many ways. The hardest jobs fall to us—and the New Zealander. [West Indian Relayer.]

This quotation sums up quite a lot of what we found in Permanent Way: the tendency 'to segregate' and the 'gentle type of withdrawal' rather than overtly hostile behaviour. The distinction between the English and the Irish is revealing too: in so far as West Indians distinguished between the Irish and the English, the former were favourably compared with the latter, sometimes with the explanation 'they're immigrants too'. On the other hand, it was not obvious that the Irish we interviewed were more favourably inclined towards the West Indians than were the English.

<hr>

[1] See below, pp. 221–6.

Resentment of the coloured staff sprang from diverse causes, or was rationalized and explained in varied ways. Apart from the allegations that the West Indians 'get away with more' or are lazy, and both these criticisms came from minorities, there was one complaint that they 'got the jobs' whilst other candidates were rejected. One Irish platelayer had a cousin who wanted to join the Permanent Way staff, but as he could neither read nor write he could not complete the application forms. The platelayer reasoned that it was not necessary to read or write to *be* a platelayer—and was plainly resentful about this situation, adding that 'these coloured blokes can read and write and they get all the jobs'. He claimed, though, and appeared, to 'get along O.K.' with the West Indians he worked with.

The immigrants' uncertainty about the *attitudes* of the natives which we met in the other departments was again in evidence: however friendly the natives may *appear* to be, the coloured immigrant could not be *sure* of their basic attitudes. This uncertainty was reflected in the caution of some of the immigrants in their dealings with their white workmates, with an awareness of the pitfalls and a willingness to back down in a situation of potential conflict.

Some are nice; some are upset very quickly. I don't want trouble, so I draw back if I see trouble. [West Indian Lengthman.]

The dominant theme of this section is, then, that we found a situation comparatively free from overt conflict between white natives and coloured immigrants, compared with the other two departments, that is. The main source of discontent of the coloured platelayers was the perceived unequal distribution of work tasks and opportunities for overtime. Hostile attitudes too appeared to be neither so widespread or intense as we found elsewhere, though they were far from absent. The situation between white and coloured can best be summed up by the following quotation:

At meals we [West Indians] go by ourselves. We talk across the space and laugh, but we are never really one of them [the natives]. But when we work, we work as a team—it is beautiful. It is nice to know you have dependable workmates. If a man asks for a hand, the nearest one gives a hand. [West Indian Relayer.]

Some confirmation of the two main points of this statement was provided by observations. In the cabins each platelayer has his own 'place' at a mess table. In most cabins the tables are small, each with three or four chairs. During my visits to the cabins, the West Indian platelayers present usually sat at different tables from the natives. This was the predominant but not universal pattern. Certainly, there was plenty of talking and joking 'across the space'. The predominant pattern was conversation and joking of a very obscene variety, but it is, of course, possible that this was to some extent stimulated by my presence. On one occasion a West Indian lengthman joked to his white workmates about his 'Kit-E-Kat sandwiches'; on another a native platelayer jokingly menaced a West Indian with a knife. Again it is possible that my presence was an important variable: they all knew *why* I was there. On 'joking', see Chapter 8.

Observation served to confirm, too, the comment that 'when we work, we work as a team'. On one major operation viewed much of the work was manual: dragging lengths of running and conductor rail, lifting and throwing sleepers, and so on. It was not obvious that the West Indians in the gang behaved, or were treated, any differently from the others, save perhaps that they shouted with greater gusto when throwing sleepers. For example, sections of rail were dragged manually with the aid of tongs, two men to each pair of tongs. Pairing appeared to be indiscriminate: the only distinction was that the relayer who acted as team leader was a native. The work tasks on this operation were mostly ones that required all the gang to work together, so it tells us nothing about the alleged discriminatory allocation of work tasks, which would apply to those tasks requiring smaller groups of men.

EVALUATIONS OF THE QUALITIES REQUIRED BY THE 'GOOD' PLATELAYER
I have shown that Permanent Way engineers and managers had their image of the 'old platelayer' and I have regarded him as an ideal type. To discover the image of the good platelayer, as he was perceived by both immigrants and natives, and to enable us to compare these perceptions to see how far the values of the numerically dominant native workforce had been acquired by the newcomers, we asked, 'what makes a good lengthman?' or 'relayer?' as appropriate. The answers to this question are summarized in Table 11.1. (See p. 218.)

The samples used are, of course, small and caution must be exercised in drawing conclusions from any differences found. Some answers, too, were given by very few, but the coding categories used emerged from the answers and could not be compressed. The table shows a fairly similar pattern of responses from both samples,

TABLE 11.1

*The Qualities of the 'Good' Platelayer, in Percentages.**

	Native	Immigrant
Interest in the job/learns the job/likes the job	53	76
Does what he is told/ does it properly/ works hard	53	33
Alertness/careful/safety conscious	10	25
A good ganger: one who will teach you	10	14
Works with others/co-operates	10	14
Physical fitness/strength	14	5
Experience	10	10
Regular attendance/timekeeping	5	10
Common sense	10	—
Don't know	10	—
(Sample)	(21)	(21)

* More than one answer was recorded and the percentage totals may therefore exceed 100.

with some difference of emphasis between the two.

Interest in the job, the necessity to learn it and like it were stressed by both groups and somewhat more by the immigrants. The emphasis was very much on interest.

In the next category, the emphasis was on the platelayer doing what he is told, doing it properly, and working hard.

Other answers were given by relatively few platelayers. The immigrants stressed alertness and safety somewhat more than the natives. Those who spoke of the importance of having a good ganger saw him as a prerequisite for adequately learning the job. An ability to work with others was stressed by some. Physical fitness, strength, experience, and common sense were all mentioned. The emphasis on regular attendance and timekeeping which we found elsewhere was again in evidence, though few mentioned it.

The similarities in the two sets of answers are more striking than the differences, yet the total pattern suggests that the native platelayers accorded more closely to the ideal type 'old platelayer' than did the immigrants. The greater emphasis of the natives on doing 'what you are told', and on hard work and strength contrasts with the immigrants' view of interest and learning the job as 'the main thing'. If this difference is significant, it is explicable, in part at least, in terms of the different length of service patterns of the two samples.[1] Those answers which stressed that the good platelayer should do what he is told and have the ability to work hard came disproportionately more from those natives with over fifteen years' service. None of the immigrants had this length of experience. Possibly, too, the immigrants bring a somewhat different set of expectations to the work situation: over half of them had been tradesmen before emigrating; possibly they were more likely to expect a job to be interesting.[2]

The differences between the two groups in their image of the good platelayer are, though, small compared with their common difference from the ideal type, the 'old platelayer'. The emphasis there, it will be remembered, was very much on physical ability and obeying instructions. No one suggested that he should *like* the work or be interested in it.

NATIVE PLATELAYERS' EVALUATIONS OF IMMIGRANTS AS PLATELAYERS
One of my most important hypotheses is that the adequate performance of their occupational roles by the coloured immigrants has been a major factor encouraging their acceptance by workmates, supervisors, and managers. The answers to our question, 'do Commonwealth immigrants make good [own grade]?', are summarized in Table 11.2.

TABLE 11.2.
Native Platelayers' Assessments of Commonwealth Immigrants as 'Good' Platelayers, in Percentages.

Yes, most are/ some are, some are not/same as Europeans	71
Some are, most are not	14
No, none are	10
Don't know	5
(Sample)	(21)

Roughly three-quarters of the native platelayers regarded the immigrants as being on the whole no better or worse platelayers than are others.[3] Nearly one-half then went on to make criticisms

[1] See Chapter 3.   [2] It is possible that some natives were also ex-tradesmen.
[3] A broadly similar pattern was found amongst the operating railwaymen and the busmen. See Chapters 5 and 8.

of immigrant platelayers. By far the most frequent criticisms were that immigrants are lazy, slow, or only interested in money. Such criticisms were made by one-third of the natives interviewed, and the emphasis was very much on the alleged laziness.

They like it easy; they don't like hard work. I've only worked with these two here: they are O.K., but they have to be kept up to it. [U.K. Lengthman.]

At the least chance they have their heads down [asleep]. [U.K. Relayer.]

Other criticisms, that the coloured immigrants were clannish or had a chip on the shoulder or got away with more, were made by single individuals only. Whilst, then, a number of the natives were critical of immigrant platelayers, most refused to generalize and criticisms were seldom complete.

Important here is that the immigrants were mostly in the younger, more physically fit age groups: all those interviewed were under 50 and over half under 40; by contrast, half the natives interviewed were over 50. In most groups and gangs it appeared that the older members were to some extent carried by their workmates and given the lighter tasks. Some acted as 'cooks' or 'tea boys'. It seemed likely that *some* of these older men had what can almost be described as a fatherly relationship with some of the coloured platelayers, and appeared to be very popular with the West Indians. I recall one incident when one of these older platelayers—who in the interview had described the immigrants in the group as 'all good boys'—went out at the beginning of traffic to fetch the morning newspapers for the group, and was very much feted on his return.

The predominant viewpoint of management on the abilities and working capacities of coloured immigrants was that it was difficult to generalize. Having said this, though, many thought that they needed closer supervision, that their pace of work was slower, and that they 'tend to wilt sooner than the locals' on a shift that goes past the normal finishing hour. Generally, though, the emphasis was that there was not *much* difference between the immigrants and the locals in terms of their working abilities and capacities. It was almost unanimously agreed that the quality of staff was far below the standards of twenty or thirty years previously, when the 'old platelayer' was thought to be a commonplace and numerically dominant figure.

The evidence of this section tends, then, to support the hypothesis that the coloured immigrants' performance of their occupational roles has been an important factor encouraging their acceptance.

RELATIONSHIPS WITH SUPERVISORS

In order to compare the expectations that immigrant and native platelayers had of their supervisors, we asked both groups 'what makes a good senior ganger?'[1] The answers given are summarized in Table 11.3.

TABLE 11.3.
*Platelayers' Expectations of the 'Good' Senior Ganger, in Percentages.**

	Native	Immigrant
He has experience/knows his job	33	67
He is patient/can handle people/earns respect	43	43
He is fair/impartial/has no colour prejudice	19	43
He is able to control men	29	5
He will co-operate with the men/will give and take/will let men get on with the job	19	24
Don't know	5	—
(Sample)	(21)	(21)

* More than one answer was recorded and the percentage totals may therefore exceed 100.

The table shows a fairly similar pattern between the two groups, with one or two possibly significant differences. Those who said that a senior ganger should have experience or know his job—the emphasis being very much on this latter quality—seldom said much more on this aspect. They had in mind the essentially *technical* skills of the senior ganger, rather than social skills, of which they spoke separately.

He knows his job thoroughly. [U.K. Relayer.]

A lot of experience: everything is a burden on the ganger; he takes the blame. [West Indian Relayer.]

The ability to handle people referred specifically to social skills:

He commands respect from the men. [U.K. Relayer.]

[1] In extra gangs, the appropriate designation was extra ganger. For purposes of simplicity, senior ganger is used here for both designations.

He's courteous—he has to be able to get co-operation. He's genuine—
he doesn't shout off at the men and doesn't put on a show because he's
boss. [West Indian Relayer.]

Impartiality, fairness, and a lack of colour prejudice related to
every aspect of the interaction between the senior ganger and his
subordinates, but with a pronounced emphasis that tasks, and to a
lesser extent the opportunity for overtime, should be allocated
impartially. The good senior ganger is one:

. . . who divides the work equally among his men. [West Indian Relayer.]

There was a clear difference of emphasis between the ability to
control men and the ability to handle men. The latter implied
persuasion, but control had connotations of discipline.

He gives you a job and sees you do it. [U.K. Relayer.]

He's got to be able to control men. [U.K. Lengthman.]

The final group of answers all related to the *amount* of work
that the senior ganger expected from his men and the extent to which
he directly supervised them while they were doing it. There was a
norm of what constituted a day's—or night's—work, and a good
senior ganger did not expect his men to exceed it.

He'll give you a certain amount to do and you do it, and then he'll give
you a break. Some want more done. [U.K. Lengthman].

He will more or less muck in—and a bit of give and take. [U.K. Lengthman.]

The reciprocity implied in give and take was that on the one hand,
the men would do a fair day's work; and on the other, that the senior
ganger would not continually supervise them while they were
doing it, nor would he expect them to do more when it was
completed—at the very least, he would 'give them a break'. It
was recognized, though, that he would *check* their work: 'he is
responsible.'

Comparing the two sets of answers, the immigrants put more
stress on experience, knowledge of the job, and impartiality; the
natives emphasized the ability to control men. It is not obvious why
the immigrants should have given this greater emphasis to knowledge
and experience or, to put it another way, why the natives mentioned it far less. It can be argued that knowledge and experience
are prerequisites for a good senior ganger. Possibly the native platelayers saw it this way: the senior ganger would not have been

promoted if he did not know his job. Whilst a number of criticisms were made of senior gangers, none were alleged to lack technical expertise. Impartiality was mentioned relatively more by the immigrants and this is explicable in terms of, and consistent with, the belief of some that certain senior gangers lacked impartiality.

The greater emphasis of the natives on the ability to control men is consistent with their more frequent mention of the good platelayer doing what he is told, and working hard—it is the other side of the coin, as it were. The ability to control men was mentioned mostly by those natives with over twenty years' service, and again it points to the conclusion that these long service workers accorded closest to the ideal type, the 'old platelayer'. More recent recruits, both white and coloured, stressed more the human relations skills of *handling* men.

Turning to the platelayers' evaluations of their relationships with their supervisors, we asked 'how do you get on with your senior ganger?' The answers to this question are summarized in Table 11.4.

TABLE 11.4.
How Platelayers Got on with Senior Gangers, in Percentages.

	Native	Immigrant
Very well	33	19
Well	14	33
Not much trouble/fair/not bad	33	38
Not very well/poorly	19	10
(Sample)	(21)	(21)

No clear over-all difference between the samples is revealed by these figures. The considerations which led to the evaluation of relationships with supervisors as very good, on the one hand, or poor, on the other, were clearly related to the behaviour of individual supervisors. All the immigrants and half of the natives who told us that they did not get on very well with their senior ganger were members of one group. This group—'X group'—was thought both by management and union representatives to be atypical. Some in other groups who evaluated the relationship as not bad then went on to complain of the unequal distribution of work tasks or overtime opportunities.

Those who said that they got on very well, or well, with their senior gangers seldom elaborated on this, but some mentioned various aspects of the supervisor's behaviour in approving terms.

You couldn't ask for a better bloke. [U.K. Lengthman.]

Well: the best ganger I have worked with. He shows no preference for any of the men when delegating work. [West Indian Relayer.]

Most of those who evaluated their relations with their senior gangers as fair or not too bad were equally vague, though sometimes further comments were added:

We have arguments, same as everywhere else, but then it is forgotten. [U.K. Lengthman.]

We have rows sometimes, but he tries to keep it to the lowest and he soon forgets. [West Indian Lengthman.]

The pressures from subordinates that the senior gangers are subject to, can be illustrated by this comment:

He's not a bad old bloke. He's a very nice ganger, but sometimes some of the gang twist him to do other things. [West Indian Relayer.]

Complaints of the behaviour of senior gangers came mostly from three groups. In one group they were made by the West Indians and had to do with the distribution of work tasks and overtime. In the second group they came both from West Indian and native lengthmen and were almost completely confined to overtime opportunities. In the third, 'X group', most of those interviewed complained of the manner of the senior ganger and the way he addressed the men, and of the way he 'drove' them. The line inspectors responsible for two of these groups also came in for some criticism. First the issues of overtime and task allocation:

The ganger will hold a grudge. If you complain it goes through the right channels and the inspector doesn't want to know. Complaints are about overtime ... the white lengthmen get overtime every Sunday. We complain to the inspector but he says he doesn't know. Overtime should be shared ... The ganger is hard. When there is a hard job to do we West Indians get it. Sometimes we get thirty chairs to [rebush]—the other fellows only get twenty. [West Indian Lengthman.]

The overtime is not fair: the West Indians don't get it; the English and the Irish do. [West Indian Lengthman.]

I don't get on with him [the senior ganger]. He has cliques. The gangers and sub-gangers get overtime every second week; the lengthmen don't get it unless they are flagmen. I am a flagman, but I only get one Sunday in six.[1] [U.K. Lengthman.]

This perceived lack of partiality in the distribution of tasks and overtime had clearly engendered some considerable bitterness in these two groups. Overtime was seen as important not only for its immediate effect on earnings, but also for its effect on the bonus payments received. At this point it is necessary to explain briefly the bonus system.

Each maintenance group is allocated X thousand man-hours for its work. This includes some overtime: for week-end track inspections and, for day groups, tasks that can only be carried out when there is no traffic operating. The number of hours allotted varies with the length, type, and complexity of track maintained, the intensity of traffic, and a number of other factors. The difference between the *allowed* hours and *actual* hours is calculated every eighteen weeks and is known as the primary saving. This is then multiplied by a quality multiplier to determine the amount to be paid to the group. The quality multiplier is derived from an assessment of the *standards* of track maintenance. Some objective—and some less objective—measures of quality are used. The distribution of the bonus *between* the members of the group is, however, determined partly by grade—gangers, for example, receive more than lengthmen—and partly by the attendance hours of the individual. Thus the lengthman who works a lot of overtime could receive a larger bonus than his workmates who work little or none.[2] This was clearly in the minds of some who complained about the distribution of overtime: it was said in one group that it was deliberately made very uneven partly to make a large primary saving and to favour some in the distribution of the bonus.

The bonus scheme for extra gangs was broadly similar to that used for maintenance groups. Both were based on 'historical' times and some methods study, but there had not been the minute breakdown of tasks usually characteristic of *work* study.[3]

---

[1] A flagman is a Permanent Way man trained to carry out hand signal duties in order to protect traffic and men working on or near the track.

[2] Not all overtime qualified for bonus payments; such payment depended on the category of work carried out.

[3] This over-simplified description of the bonus scheme is drawn from *Codes of Practice for Incentive Bonus Scheme, Permanent Way Conciliation Staff* (London, Department of the Chief Civil Engineer, L.T.B., 1966).

To return to our main subject matter, the situation in 'X group' was clearly a complex and, for those concerned, a very unhappy one. It is not my intention to attempt a full analysis, and in any case it is of interest only in so far as it illustrates problems that have a wider significance. We have seen the expectations that platelayers have of their senior gangers: they should be able to handle men, be fair, and be prepared to give and take. We have also seen the importance which some platelayers attach to the senior ganger instructing his men and teaching them skills. In the opinion of most of the 'X group' lengthmen interviewed, their senior ganger was lacking in these behavioural characteristics.

The major criticisms were that the senior ganger had 'no manners'; that he spoke to the men in a 'nasty way, with plenty of effing and blinding'; that he did not give them a 'breather' when they had finished a task but *immediately* put them on another; that he was unreasonable over punctual attendance—if a man arrived five minutes late he would tell him to stay in the cabin and book on half an hour late, although the group had not left the cabin. Other criticisms were that the senior ganger did not have the patience to show any-one how to do a job: if they did something incorrectly, he would angrily rebuke them, without showing how the job should be done. Largely as a consequence of his behaviour, the group allegedly lacked unity and was cliquey.

He would be O.K. if he were not so piggish. He's a hard worker and he knows the job. But he drives hard . . . Our senior ganger knows his job, he couldn't know it better, but he has a bad manner, a bit rough. I've never had trouble [with him] but I've seen others—he shouldn't talk like that. [U.K. Lengthman.]

He's heartbreaking . . . sometimes you get the salt and they [the natives] get the sugar, but you can't help it. This group is not friendly . . . The atmosphere is heavy. [West Indian Lengthman.]

These grievances were obviously deeply felt. The importance that platelayers attach to the behaviour of a senior ganger is illustrated by the fact that in one year seventeen men were transferred to 'X group' and eighteen transferred out.[1]

---

[1] I have no evidence to indicate that the perceived short-comings of the senior ganger were the *only* reasons why men left 'X group', but those I interviewed certainly thought that this was so.

PROMOTION ASPIRATIONS AND NATIVES' ATTITUDES TOWARDS THE
PROMOTION OF IMMIGRANTS TO SUPERVISORY POSTS

We asked a number of questions on the promotion aspirations and
expectations of the platelayers. First, their aspirations are summarized
in Table 11.5.

TABLE 11.5.
Platelayers' Promotion Aspirations, in Percentages.

	Native	Immigrant
None	43	14
To sub-ganger grade	33	33
To other grades	10	43
Don't know	14	10
(Sample)	(21)	(21)

The greater propensity of the immigrants to say that they wished
to be promoted, already seen in the two operating departments, is
repeated here, though the difference between the two samples is
less marked.[1] The miscellaneous 'other' category was made up partly
of immigrants who had previously been tradesmen and wished to
return to their trades in L.T.B.; the remaining respondents were
usually vague about the occupations they aspired to—one or two
wanted to learn something which would be useful if they returned
to the Caribbean.

Few in either sample had applied for promotion, but most who
had said they wished to be promoted also stated an intention to
apply. There was no significant difference between the natives and
the immigrants in their optimism about their chances of being
promoted: of those who stated an intention to apply, both samples
split fairly evenly between expressing optimism and uncertainty
about their prospects. Very few of the coloured platelayers indicated
that they thought colour *would* adversely affect their prospects,
though a number suspected that it might. Over-all the attitudes
expressed were similar to those we found amongst the operating
railwaymen.[2] Certainly, they were less pessimistic than the busmen[3]

---

[1] See Chapters 6 and 9, for comparable data from the operating departments.
[2] See above, Chapter 9.   [3] See above, Chapter 6.

on this score, and with some reason. At the time of our fieldwork, there were a number of coloured gangers and sub-gangers, but no coloured senior or extra gangers,[1] and this appeared to be widely known. Some of these workers were with the groups and gangs included in our study. A fairly widespread view amongst the coloured platelayers was that if there was a vacancy, any applicant who could do the job would get it, no matter where he came from.

Yes [I think I will be promoted]. I don't give no trouble, I don't like arguments so I should get a good report. [West Indian Lengthman.]

The key role of the local supervisor in giving a 'good report', hinted at in this last quotation, was widely recognized. Several of the coloured platelayers drew a distinction between supervisors and managers, in favour of the latter. The image of London Transport's managers amongst the coloured platelayers was mostly a very favourable one: they were thought to be both fair and courteous:

The people—apart from the workers—are very nice. They speak to you so nice, you feel happy—it goes for every London Transport top guy. It's different on the job: they try to knock the piss out of you. [West Indian Relayer.]

Promotion in Permanent Way is on merit. Vacancies are advertised internally and applicants recommended by their supervisors are interviewed by a promotion board which includes a trade union representative. Candidates are asked a number of set questions and awarded points for each answer given. They are also assessed for personality. If two or more candidates are thought to have equal merit as assessed by these criteria then seniority counts as a deciding factor.

The completed years of service before promotion to their present grades for the senior gangers, gangers, and sub-gangers are shown in Table 11.6.

Few senior gangers had attained their present grade with less than ten years' service. Indeed, the majority had served between eleven and thirty years before they became senior gangers. In the case of the gangers, nearly half had served less than eleven years before they became gangers, but more than half had over eleven years' service before they reached this grade. Most of the sub-gangers had been promoted with less than eleven years' service and given that few coloured immigrants were likely to have had more than eleven years'

---

[1] One or two coloured extra gangers have since been appointed.

TABLE 11.6.
Years of Service Before Promotion to Present Grade for Supervisors, in Percentages.★

Years	Senior gangers	Gangers	Sub-gangers
0–10	14	44	70
11–20	42	41	25
21–30	36	13	5
31–41	8	2	—
(Number)	(64)	(157)	(174)

★ These figures show the strength as at 1 May 1966. They exclude a few who were *recruited* to their present grades and had presumably transferred from British Rail. They also exclude a small number of extra gangers and extra sub-gangers. Source: Staff Administration Office, L.T.B.

service when these data were collected, this is the most relevant group.

We set out to compare coloured gangers and sub-gangers with all others in these grades in terms of the length of service before attaining the present grades; and to do this, we obtained separate data.[1] These showed that there were five coloured gangers and seventeen coloured sub-gangers. Coloured sub-gangers then comprised 10 per cent of the total in this grade. Given that coloured staff made up 18 per cent of the total in the Department, they were somewhat under-represented in the sub-ganger grade, but not strikingly so. Turning to their length of service before promotion, and confining it to those (70 per cent of the total) who had been promoted with less than eleven years' service, half had less than five years' service before promotion. Seven (41 per cent) of the seventeen coloured sub-gangers had less than five years' service before they were promoted. This reinforces the conclusion that the coloured staff were achieving this grade more or less on a par with the natives, though it tells us nothing about the rates of rejection of coloured and native applicants, nor of their relative merits, the criteria of which are in part subjective.

[1] These figures are as at 20 June 1967, but it is unlikely that the difference in dates between the collection of the two sets of data significantly affect the results of the comparisons made. Source: Permanent Way Department, L.T.B.

Turning to the gangers, none of the coloured gangers had reached this grade with less than six years' service; 13 per cent of the total in the grade had done so. Coloured staff were under-represented in the grade, but as it was not possible to obtain data showing the length of service patterns of white and coloured staff separately it is not clear how significant this is.

I concluded that Permanent Way management had been cautious in its attitudes and behaviour in relation to the promotion of coloured immigrants to these minor supervisory roles. It was somewhat apprehensive initially about their acceptance by white platelayers, but this appeared to have lessened. It may well be that the first coloured immigrants promoted had to be seen to be better than their native counterparts. As elsewhere, cultural differences probably make assessment more difficult and possibly the coloured applicant had to *prove* that he was suitable more thoroughly than did a native candidate.[1] At the stage when coloured immigrants are first entering supervisory grades, their acceptance by native superordinates and subordinates is probably enhanced if they are seen to be somewhat better than average. Certainly, the coloured gangers and sub-gangers in the groups I visited appeared to be fully accepted by *most* of the native platelayers met. It is not clear, though, how far they fulfilled their *supervisory* roles: the reader will remember that in the Railway Operating Department a condition of acceptance of coloured station foremen by some station staff was that they did not exert the authority vested in their grade.[2] The same kind of relationship may have existed between coloured gangers or sub-gangers and their white subordinates, and there were indications that this was possibly so. We did not consistently ask a direct question on attitudes towards immigrant gangers and sub-gangers, or on experiences of working for them. In retrospect we should have done so, but we were not aware that there were coloured gangers until we arrived at the interview locations, nor did we know where the coloured sub-gangers were located. The following comment, in answer to a direct question, is illustrative of the kind of relationship which may well exist between coloured gangers or sub-gangers and white platelayers—a relationship which is very similar to that found between coloured station foremen and white subordinates:

[1] There was, though, no consistent pattern when the years of service before promotion of the coloured sub-gangers were plotted against their *dates* of promotion.
[2] See above, Chapter 9.

[There is] no trouble in having a coloured sub-[ganger]—*he is easy going.*[1] [U.K. Lengthman.]

On the other hand, some native senior gangers appear to be susceptible to pressure from their subordinates, and much obviously depends on the personality of the supervisor, white or coloured.

There were, as we have seen, no coloured senior or extra gangers at the time of our fieldwork. As they were the senior local supervisors, acceptance of coloured men in these grades by native platelayers provides a key to their acceptance in supervisory roles with considerable authority content. It appeared useful, therefore, to inquire into the likely reactions of native platelayers to a coloured senior ganger, so we asked 'would there be any objection if a Commonwealth immigrant was appointed as senior ganger?'[2] Table 11.7 summarizes the answers given.

TABLE 11.7.
*Native Platelayers' Attitudes Towards a Commonwealth Immigrant Senior Ganger, in Percentages.**

i	No objection	29
ii	No objection if he had the experience/ability	19
iii	No objection personally, but others would/might object	10
iv	No objection: should be coloured senior gangers	—
v	Objections: lack of experience/ability	5
vi	Objections: would be wrong/would not get respect/ because of colour	29
vii	Objections: coloured senior gangers might misuse authority	10
viii	Objections: still white men available	5
	(Sample)	(21)

* More than one answer was recorded and the percentage total may therefore exceed 100.

The coding categories were similar to those used for the comparable questions asked of the busmen and operating railwaymen, and the over-all pattern of responses was very similar, particularly between the two railway departments. For these reasons, it is not necessary to elaborate so fully as has been done for the other two departments, but again it is illustrative to quote from the interview material.

[1] My italics.   [2] In extra gangs, the term 'extra ganger' was used.

Some who thought that there would be no objections to coloured immigrant senior gangers pointed out that there were already immigrant gangers and sub-gangers, or that there were Polish senior gangers, and all were accepted. On the other hand, as we discovered, some drew a distinction between the acceptance of coloured and Polish senior gangers.

Others qualified their views on the acceptance of an immigrant senior ganger: he must have the experience or ability, or be fair. Some said that although they personally would not object, they thought others would. Of those who foresaw objections from the native platelayers, the largest group numerically related these objections to colour. A similar emphasis was found amongst both the busmen and the operating railwaymen, and again it is useful to illustrate from the interview material:

There would be murder. Smith [a coloured sub-ganger] is a good bloke, but the blokes resent it—it is inside. [U.K. Lengthman.]

I wouldn't like to work under one. I think most of the men would disapprove. I wouldn't like to see black men over white—it would be wrong. [U.K. Lengthman.]

Few expressed the fear that coloured senior gangers would be partial in their relations with subordinates.

The emphasis was very much on the notion that it would be wrong for a white man to take orders from a coloured man. Again no explanation of this deeply held belief was offered by those who subscribed to it. I return to this topic when comparing the evidence from all three departments.[1]

Over-all the pattern of answers indicated a less hostile reaction to the possibility of coloured supervisors than existed in the two operating departments, though the Permanent Way sample was small and any conclusions based on it must be treated with caution. One difference between the three departments was that coloured staff had been appointed to grades in Permanent Way seen to be nearer to what we regarded as the 'key' supervisory roles. This suggests that experience of coloured supervisors is not unimportant. This conclusion is reinforced when the Permanent Way data are broken down between groups and gangs.

None of the extra gangs had coloured gangers or sub-gangers; some of the groups did. Of the fifteen white native *lengthmen* interviewed, eleven gave answers coded in categories i-iii, that is,

[1] See below, Chapter 17.

those indicating no objections to coloured senior gangers, albeit some with qualifications. Of the six *relayers* interviewed, five gave answers in codes v-viii, all indicating objections. Moreover, of the eight lengthmen in groups with coloured gangers or sub-gangers, seven gave answers in codes i-iii and only one in the v-viii grouping. Those lengthmen from groups without coloured gangers or sub-gangers split almost evenly between codes i-iii and v-viii. This is not conclusive evidence, but it does strongly suggest that experience of coloured men in these minor supervisory roles is related to a perception of a less hostile reaction to them in the key supervisory role.

Further complicating variables are the differences between groups and gangs. Gangs usually have more men than groups and the pattern of work tasks is somewhat different. It may be that the relayers regarded the role of the extra ganger as a more difficult one to perform adequately as compared with the lengthmen's assessments of the senior ganger's role.

Before concluding this section, it might be useful to mention briefly management attitudes towards the possibility of coloured staff being promoted to the senior ganger grade. The predominant view was that few if any of the coloured staff had the potential to become senior gangers. Generally, it was feared that finding the next generation of senior gangers would be a problem. Many of the existing sub-gangers and gangers were thought to lack 'that bit extra' necessary for a senior ganger, and there was, in any case, thought to be a shortage of suitable applicants for the sub-ganger grade. Coloured staff were mostly thought to lack 'that bit extra, call it initiative' thought necessary for senior gangers. A minority held the view that some of the coloured immigrants had the necessary potential and within this minority a view was expressed that those with ability would move out of the industry to other occupations. This could, of course, have become a self-fulfilling prophecy. Some managers, too, were apprehensive about the reactions of the native workforce—as well as those of the senior supervisors, the inspectors.

LIKES AND DISLIKES OF UNDERGROUND PLATELAYERS

We asked two questions designed to provide data for a comparison of the features of their employment that were liked and disliked by immigrant and native platelayers. Table 11.8 summarizes the answers to the first of these two questions.

TABLE 11.8.

*Features of Their Employment which Platelayers Liked, in Percentages.**

	Native	Immigrant
The job/open-air work/interesting work	67	24
Job security	53	62
L.T.B. good/fair employers	10	43
Pay reasonable/good	24	5
Pay reasonable/good with overtime work	19	—
Do not 'get pushed around'	5	19
Free travel	5	10
Night work/day work	5	10
Nothing	10	5
(Sample)	(21)	(21)

* More than one answer was recorded and the percentage totals may therefore exceed 100.

With three exceptions, the two samples show a broad measure of agreement about the features of their employment which they liked. The first of these differences was the natives' more frequent mention of the job as something they liked. Those who spoke of the job seldom elaborated: some—in day groups—mentioned open-air work; some found railway work interesting.

[I like] the job—I'm sorry I didn't come here fifteen years ago. [U.K. Lengthman.]

I would go crackers indoors. [U.K. Lengthman.]

I like working on the railway—I was always interested in it, ever since I was small. [West Indian Relayer.]

A similar difference between immigrant and native railwaymen in their references to various aspects of the job was found amongst those in the Railway Operating Department.[1] It was suggested there that this reflected a lower extent of self-selection of employment amongst the immigrants as compared with the natives. This possibly applies also to the Permanent Way situation, particularly as some of the immigrants had been employed as tradesmen and wished to return to their trades.

[1] See above, Chapter 9.

A range of answers all referred to some aspect of job security. Some merely said it was a steady or regular job; others, that they were not likely to be laid off or that they could be sure of their pay every week. Some natives contrasted this situation with the building industry, of which they had experience.

The formal aspect of job security—'they don't call you up and sack you'—was mentioned somewhat more by the immigrants, and this freedom from arbitrary dismissal was especially important for them. The threat of one kind of discriminatory treatment was seen by them to be largely absent. The union was seen to be important, too, both in this context and in relation to other possible problems.[1]

Those who said that London Transport are good or fair employers were seldom very explicit, but again some referred to various aspects of the formal procedures, and other comments on management reflected the favourable image which has been discussed earlier.[2]

I like the co-operation they try to give you: if you have a grievance they look into it and try to assist you. [West Indian Lengthman.]

London Transport are O.K. as employers. [West Indian Lengthman.]

It [London Transport] is fair to you. [West Indian Lengthman.]

The more frequent mention of this topic by the immigrants supports the hypothesis that the existence of *formal* procedures, in relation to promotion, discipline, and so on, which are more likely to be found in the large organization, is conducive to the smooth absorption of immigrants. Such procedures do not guarantee that there will be no discrimination, but they make it less likely to occur.

The third difference between the two samples was in the relative emphasis they gave to pay. It is not entirely clear why there was this difference, but possibly in part it reflected the perceived discrimination in the allocation of overtime opportunities and the higher extent of self-selection amongst the natives, which appeared likely. For some natives, the pay was reasonable or good: provided overtime was worked.

Those who mentioned that they did not 'get pushed around' appeared to have had in mind relationships with their supervisors. They, the platelayers, did not get 'much interference', but could 'get on with their jobs', and some contrasted this with experience elsewhere.

The other answers to this question were given by very few, and

---

[1] See below, Chapter 15.   [2] See above, p. 228.

their meaning is clear. Features of their employment which the platelayers disliked are summarized in Table 11.9.

TABLE 11.9.
*Features of Their Employment which Platelayers Disliked, in Percentages.**

	Native	Immigrant
Nothing	67	57
Week-end work	15	10
Bad supervision	—	15
Dirt and dust	5	10
The work	5	5
Other answers	10	5
No answer	—	5
(Sample)	(21)	(21)

* More than one answer was recorded and the percentage totals may therefore exceed 100.

A majority of both samples found nothing to dislike about their employment, and the relative numbers giving this answer were higher than in the operating departments.[1]

Week-end work, and particularly Saturday night work, was strongly disliked by some.

Those who spoke of bad supervision were in 'X group' and one of the groups where tasks were thought to be allocated in a discriminatory way, and these complaints need not be repeated here.[2]

Tube men complained of dirt and dust:

The one thing wrong with the job is the dust and dirt—no matter how much water you put down [when opening out concreted track] the dust still rises. Otherwise the job is fine. [West Indian Relayer.]

Conditions could be better: the dust—you can't have a shower. [U.K Lengthman.]

Apart, then, from the few immigrants who were very resentful of the behaviour of their supervisors, the pattern of 'dislikes' of both native and immigrant platelayers was very similar.

Finally in this section, we asked the platelayers for their preferences for day or night work. Not surprisingly, most preferred the shift

[1] See Chapters 6 and 9.   [2] See above, pp. 223–6.

they did work, though a few were indifferent. The reasons given for preferring days or nights were many and varied. Amongst the more frequently mentioned reasons given by both samples for preferring day work were those relating to domestic life: they liked to be at home at night with their families. 'Health', and a preference for 'open air work' were valued too by the natives. Financial reasons —the higher rate paid and the greater opportunities for overtime which were thought to exist—were the most important reasons for the native platelayers who preferred night work. Amongst the immigrants on nights the most frequently mentioned advantage was that they were able to look after their children during the day-time, whilst their wives were working. They thought too that it was warmer and more protected from the weather in the tubes at night than on an open track in the day, and it was safer with no traffic or live rails to worry about.

To conclude, whilst there was resentment from the white native platelayers at the initial employment of coloured immigrants, it was neither as widespread or intense as in the two operating departments. Again compared with the two operating departments, Permanent Way was comparatively free from open conflict. In the previous Chapter it was suggested that the less hostile reaction towards the coloured immigrants was explicable in terms of the 'colour-class' hypothesis—that there was seen to be less disparity of status between the existing workforce and the newcomers than in the two operating departments. This conclusion is reinforced by the interview data.

In terms of some indices—promotion attainments, some attitudes —there had clearly been some absorption, but elements of pluralism were also present. Particularly relevant here was the tendency for white and coloured platelayers to separate in the cabins—but with plenty of 'joking across the space'. This pluralism was though combined with 'working as a team' in task performance: the two situations were compatible.

12

RECRUITMENT IN ENGLAND

Since the early 1950s, London Transport has suffered from a shortage of staff in the operating grades. In an attempt to combat this problem it began recruiting in Northern Ireland in 1950, Eire in 1952–3, Barbados in 1956, and more recently in Jamaica and Trinidad. It has also attempted to recruit staff from other parts of England and from Malta, but with little success. At the time of the fieldwork, London Transport was still visiting Eire about nine or ten times a year, although it is not now as fruitful a source of recruits as it once was.

Apart from these attempts to recruit in other parts of the British Isles, the bulk of recruiting is, of course, carried out in London. The recruiting system is centralized and, for wages grades staff, based at Griffith House in Marylebone. There were three other small recruitment centres, each with an interviewer and two with facilities for medical examinations. Griffith House deals with the majority of applicants. Several advantages are claimed for a centralized system: it secures a common standard of acceptance, it makes the best use of available labour, it ensures that the less well-paid jobs have a share of recruits.

In the mid-sixties London Transport had about 60,000 applicants a year for employment in the wages grades, and of these between eleven and thirteen thousand were accepted. Some recruits drop out between the time they accept employment and the date on which they are due to start, perhaps because of family objections to weekend or shift work, or a better offer from elsewhere. There is some seasonal variation in the number of applicants. The peak periods for applicants are after holidays—in January, after Easter, and so on—but these are apparently becoming less pronounced. A bad winter brings in applicants who normally work in the construction industry; a prolonged strike in any of the large firms situated in and around London also increases the number of applicants, though these are not necessarily acceptable as they are often thought to be seeking stop-gap jobs. Conversely, any industrial dispute on the buses or the Underground keeps potential recruits away.

THE RECRUITMENT PROCESS

The basic procedure is the same for all applicants, and the staff aim to pass the applicant through all the stages in two hours. The selection procedure is as follows. The applicant fills in an application form and then completes a short test, followed by a brief interview. A number of applicants thought to be obviously unsuitable are rejected at this point. The remainder are given a second test, a further interview, and a medical examination.

Different tests are used for the various grades. For potential bus conductors, booking-office clerks, and canteen assistants, the tests have an arithmetical bias, as work in all these grades involves handling money. Applicants for nearly every grade are given some form of English test which varies from spelling to writing a short essay. Guards and station foremen, who are expected to be able to write reports on incidents which occur whilst they are on duty, are given a picture series to put into words. Every test is timed. These tests vary in their objectivity: generally, the first stage tests are more objective than those used in the second stage in that they use questions which can be answered correctly or incorrectly. Assessment of, for example, an essay describing a picture-series must be subjective.

The interviewers were all ex-operating staff who have received some training in personnel selection; all were white. Taking the number of applicants into consideration, the selection process is a rapid one. In the two hours, an applicant takes two tests, has two interviews and a medical examination. In such circumstances the interviewer's impressions of the applicant, particularly at the initial interview, count a great deal. The interviewer uses some criteria which must be subjective.

The medical examination is an important part of the selection process. The eyesight standards are particularly stringent for bus and rail operating staff and colour vision is particularly important for them. There is a height restriction for conductors, who must be able to stand upright on the upper deck of a bus. A good over-all physical condition is necessary for tasks which involve standing for many hours or driving large vehicles in London.

ANALYSIS OF THE 'TYPICAL WEEK'

In order to build up a picture of applicants for employment with

London Transport and to establish by what criteria candidates were accepted or rejected, we decided to look at all applications received at Griffith House during one typical week, chosen to avoid the known seasonal peaks and troughs. The week's analysis was preceded by a small pilot study during which a list of the reasons given for rejection was drawn up. London Transport does not normally record the country of origin of applicants, so during the typical week this information was recorded specifically for our use.

Table 12.1 shows the number of applicants and their countries of origin.

TABLE 12.1.
Number of Applicants by Countries of Origin.

Countries	Applicants	% total
United Kingdom	284	45
Eire	80	13
Jamaica	58	9
India	43	7
West Africa	43	7
West Indies (unspecified)	24	4
Pakistan	22	4
Other West Indies	12	2
Barbados	10	2
East Africa	9	1
Malta and Cyprus	7	1
Ceylon	6	1
Australia and New Zealand	5	1
Other*	18	3
Origin unknown	4	1
All	625	100

* Comprised: 4 Anglo-Indians, 4 Mauritians, 3 Indians from East Africa, 3 South Africans, 1 Armenian, 1 Chinese, 1 Iraqi, and 1 Lebanese.

The United Kingdom and the Irish Republic between them provided 58 per cent of the applicants, the U.K. group being by far the larger.[1] The West Indians together provided 17 per cent, a

[1] In 1968, 40 per cent of applicants for employment in the weekly paid wages grades were coloured. Select Committee on Race Relations and Immigration, *The Problems of Coloured School-Leavers*, Vol. IV (London, H.M.S.O., 1969), Appendix 29, Memorandum by London Transport Board.

TABLE 12.2.
Number of Applicants Rejected at First and Second Stages of the Recruitment process, by Countries of Origin.

Countries of origin	Total applicants	First-stage rejections No.	First-stage rejections As % of applicants in own group	Survived first stage No.	Second-stage rejections No.	Second-stage rejections As % of applicants in own group	Second-stage rejections As % of own group who survived first stage	Accepted No.	Accepted As % of applicants in own group
United Kingdom	284	95	33	189	73	26	39	116	41
Eire	80	30	37	50	20	25	40	30	37
Jamaica	58	32	55	26	15	26	58	11	19
India	43	34	79	9	4	9	44	5	12
West Africa	43	35	81	8	4	9	50	4	9
West Indies (unspecified)	24	15	62	9	4	17	44	5	21
Pakistan	22	16	73	6	1	5	17	5	23
Other West Indies	12	8	67	4	2	17	50	2	17
Barbados	10	7	70	3	—	—	—	3	30
East Africa	9	6	67	3	2	22	67	1	11
Malta and Cyprus	7	5	71	2	1	14	50	1	14
Ceylon	6	1	17	5	4	67	80	1	17
Australia and New Zealand	5	4	80	1	—	—	—	1	20
Other*	18	10	56	8	3	17	37	5	27
Origin unknown	4	3	75	1	—	—	—	1	25
All	625	301	48	324	133	21	41	191	30
All West Indies	104	62	60	42	21	20	50	21	20
Other 'coloured immigrants'†	148	107	72	41	19	13	46	22	15

* As per Table 12.1.
† From: India, West Africa, Pakistan, East Africa, Malta and Cyprus, Ceylon and the 'other' category.

TABLE 12.3.

*Reasons for First-stage Rejections, by Countries of Origin.**

Reasons	U.K.	Eire	Jamaica	India	West Africa	West Indies (unspecified)	Pakistan	Other West Indies	Barbados	East Africa	Malta and Cyprus	Ceylon	Australia and New Zealand	Other†	Origin unknown
Wanted part-time only	2							1						1	
Wanted clerical only				2			1							1	
No suitable vacancy	4		6	2	8	1	1	2		2				2	
Previous L.T. employment							1			1	1				
Conviction	1														
Entry permit					3										
Inexperienced driving		1	1		1				1						
Didn't want job	2														
Medical defect	4				1										
Objected to shifts	3	1	1		6					1	1				
Declined alternative employment				1											
Stop-gap job	5	1			1	1	1							1	
Unstable employment	18	11	4	2	5	3	1	1			1		4	1	
Intelligence	3	1	2	1	2	3	2				1				
Appearance	21	6	8	20	7	2	2	1		2	3	1		2	
Speech	1	1	5	17	13	7	8				3	1		3	
Test score	20	14	14	6	3	6	4	2		2	3			3	2
Didn't wait	16	9	1			6	4	2						1	1
No reason given	7	2	1	1		1		1							
Violent and abusive	1	1	1												
Apprenticeship	1														
Unfinished apprenticeship	1														
Enquiry only	2														
Other direct recruitment schemes									6						
Currently on strike						1	1								
Total rejected (301)	95	30	32	34	35	15	16	8	7	6	5	1	4	10	3

higher percentage than the Irish and significantly more than any other immigrant group.

Table 12.2. shows, again by countries of origin, the numbers of applicants rejected at stages one and two of the selection process. (See p. 241.)

The list of reasons given for the rejection of applicants was drawn up at the pilot study stage. Some of the categories, as can be seen from Table 12.3., are self-explanatory; others will be explained briefly here. (See p. 242.)

London Transport staff are likely to be in close contact with the travelling public. The organization will not, therefore, engage any applicant who has been convicted of robbery with violence, assault of any kind, or any similar offence, and, for driving posts, those with convictions for dangerous driving. Potential drivers must also be up to Public Service Vehicle (P.S.V.) standards. Similarly, it will not employ an immigrant who cannot produce his passport and the necessary entry permit. Nor will it consider an applicant who is abusive to the interviewer—as sometimes happens.

Training is given for many posts, and the recruiting interviewers do not engage applicants who in their opinion would not remain long enough to justify the cost of training. We were told that applicants looking for stop-gap jobs are often Australians or New Zealanders on a 'working tour' of Britain and Europe, West Africans studying in this country who are seeking vacation work, people from the construction industry (particularly in the winter) and from firms involved in labour disputes. The same argument is behind the rejection on the grounds of instability of previous employment. Applicants are asked to name their six previous employers or their employers during the last five years, should they have had fewer than six. I do not know whether X number of jobs in five years is sufficient to justify the label of 'unstable employment', but this is left to the discretion of the interviewer. Obviously the reasons for leaving each job must be taken into consideration as well. References are taken up for the previous two years' employment.

Appearance and speech are two of the most subjective criteria which the interviewer uses. Appearance was often, but not always, a secondary reason for rejection. The principle behind the use of appearance as a criterion is that these men and women are the 'front line representatives' of the organization, thus its public image depends to a great extent on them. However, most of these staff are uniformed, and their ability to carry out duties does not really depend on their private taste in clothes or the length of their hair.

So far as speech is concerned, there is the safety element on the railways: unclear speech can be a hazard as much of the railways' communication system depends on the telephone. It was usually immigrant applicants whose spoken English was judged to be inadequate. This is probably a greater handicap for the newly arrived immigrant than for those who have been here some years. It also militates more against Indians, Pakistanis, and Africans than against the West Indians.

The categories 'didn't wait', 'enquiry only' and 'didn't want job' ought not, strictly speaking, to be classified as rejection categories. The first category covers applicants who either did not realize how long the recruitment process takes and had given themselves insufficient time, or those who changed their minds after the initial stages. The second category speaks for itself. Those assessed as not wanting a job had presumably been sent by employment exchanges. If an applicant is thought to be unsuitable for the kind of work for which he has applied, the interviewer may offer alternative employment. If this is declined, then the applicant is rejected. If there is no suitable vacancy, then again the applicant is turned down.

Apprenticeship requirements are sometimes reasons for turning down applicants. Depending on the craft and the length of apprenticeship, applicants must be under certain age limits. If they are not, or if they have abandoned an apprenticeship before qualifying, then they are not considered for posts which require an apprenticeship.

London Transport is not the only large organization to have set up schemes for recruiting staff in the West Indies.[1] When direct recruits were taken on they signed an agreement that they would work for their new employer in Britain for a minimum of one year. An applicant who had come to Britain under a direct recruitment scheme within the previous year would be rejected.

This explains most of the categories: Table 12.3 shows the number of times each reason for rejection was given, by country of origin. Explanations of rejection figures will be dealt with by country of origin.

The greatest stumbling blocks for the native applicants would appear to be the test, their appearance, and instability of previous employment. Of the twenty rejected because of their test scores,

[1] See Chapter 13.

seventeen, whose ages ranged from 19 to 41, were given no other reason for rejection.

Twenty-one native applicants were rejected on the grounds of their appearance. For ten of these no other reason was given. For the others, additional reasons were unstable employment records for five and 'no suitable vacancies' or 'declined alternative employment' for most of the rest. Of these twenty-one 'appearance' rejects, seventeen were aged 22 or under (seven of the ten for whom no other reason was given). This suggests that dress and hairstyles may have been regarded as unacceptable. Of the older 'appearance' rejects, whose ages ranged from 33 to 56, only one was given any other reason ('no suitable vacancy') for rejection.

An 'unstable employment' record was the next most frequently given reason. In nine cases there was an additional reason which varied from several instances of unsuitable appearance to the applicant who 'didn't like coloured people' and had been dismissed from his previous job for fighting one. Of the remaining nine, six were in their early twenties or younger.

For native-born applicants there remained only one other category of rejection which occurred with any significant frequency: 'did not wait'. The ages of the sixteen who chose not to wait ranged from 18 to three in their fifties. That this was largely confined to native-born applicants probably reflects the different labour markets for native and immigrant workers which have been discussed earlier.[1] The immigrant applicant, knowing that his prospects were more limited, was prepared to wait longer.

In seven cases, no reason for rejection was given except for one applicant whom the interviewer considered to be 'not a good risk'.

The Irish applicants had roughly the same difficulties as the native-born ones at this stage. Over one-third of them were rejected because of unstable employment records—eleven out of a total of thirty—and one other was described as a poor risk. Appearance was also mentioned for three as a further reason for rejection, but for the remaining eight no other reason at all was given. Most of these were under 30 years of age. The Irish had a reputation with London Transport for being unreliable employees, and as such, they were not very popular.

Almost a third of the Irish rejects at this stage failed the test they were given, and for most of them it was the sole reason for rejection.

[1] See above, Chapter 3.

The percentage of coloured immigrants rejected at stage one is higher in every case (where the numbers are of any significance) than it is for native and Irish applicants.

The Jamaicans fared better than many, but even so, 55 per cent of Jamaican applicants were rejected at stage one in the recruitment process. The greatest stumbling-block was the test, which gave them more difficulty than it did any other group of coloured immigrants. Fourteen of the total of thirty-two rejects failed on test score—44 per cent of the rejects at this stage. Appearance and speech were the next most frequent reasons for rejection; four of the five rejected on grounds of speech were also rejected because of their appearance. The other category worth mentioning is 'no suitable vacancy': of the six Jamaicans rejected on this criterion, only one had another reason for rejection, appearance, and at 52 years of age, he was considerably older than the majority of immigrant applicants.

'No suitable vacancy' says very little about the person rejected. Yet, in an organization the size of London Transport, with the variety of jobs it has to offer, it is as complete a rejection as any.

Few of the immigrants were rejected because of unstable employment records. One possible explanation for this is that some had not been in Britain long enough to acquire unstable employment records, but most had probably been here since the Commonwealth Immigrants Act of 1962. A more likely explanation is that the immigrant knows that his employment prospects are more limited than those of his native counterpart. He is less likely, therefore, to change jobs frequently.[1]

A high proportion of Indian applicants—nearly 80 per cent of the total—were rejected at stage one of the recruitment process. The Indians' greatest handicaps would seem to be speech and appearance. As far as speech is concerned, the Indians (and Pakistanis) were at a disadvantage compared with the Caribbean immigrants. First, the 'wave' of Indian immigrants to Britain is more recent than the West Indian, and the Indians have had less time to become acculturated. Second, English is not their mother tongue, and some may have learnt English after arrival here. Of those seventeen Indians whose speech was not considered good enough, eleven also failed on appearance. Of the remainder who failed on appearance, only two also failed on some more objective criterion such as test score. Apart from conjecturing that some of the Indian rejects may have

[1] This stability was revealed, too, by the interview samples. See Chapter 3.

been Sikhs,[1] the only other clue to the criteria used by the interviewers in regard to appearance of Indians is that several times the word 'cringing' appeared on the interviewers' slips.

The West Africans appeared to have little difficulty with the test; only three of the thirty-five rejects failed it. Speech was the predominant reason for their rejection, and in this respect they suffer from the same disadvantage as the Indians in that English is not their first language. A number of the West African rejects were thought to be seeking stop-gap jobs; others objected to shift work. The West Africans were the only group to have any rejects in the 'entry permit' category. Like the Jamaicans, the West Africans had quite a few rejects in the 'no suitable vacancy' category. Only two of these eight rejects had another reason for rejection.

The origins of a number of West Indians were not specified, so these were put in a separate group. Those who failed at this stage did so for much the same reasons as those in other groups, with the exception of two who were turned down because the company they were currently working for was on strike, and a third who had broken his recruitment agreement to stay with another company.

The Pakistani rejects were similar to the Indians, except on the question of appearance. Only two out of sixteen (12 per cent) Pakistanis failed on appearance, compared with twenty of the thirty-four Indians in our sample (59 per cent). Why this should be so was not clear from the data. Again, one Pakistani was rejected because of a strike at his employers.

The numbers for the other groups are so small that nothing can be said with any assurance about most of them, with two exceptions. Most of the Barbadians rejected at this stage—six out of seven— were turned down because they had broken agreements to stay

[1] After suspending the first Sikh to report for duty wearing a turban in place of his uniform cap, London Transport later allowed black turbans to be worn by uniformed staff. It thus largely avoided the controversy over the employment of turbaned and bearded Sikhs by some public transport undertakings. See the *Guardian* (31 August 1964 and 1 September 1964). *The Times* (17 June 1968) reported that the first Sikh for London Transport buses to be *recruited with* beard and turban had been engaged, and there were later manifestations of resentment at the relaxation of the uniform rules by native busmen at one garage. Their protest —soon abandoned—took the form of wearing unusual headgear. See *The Times* (2 July 1968). The rule that operating staff should wear their uniform caps is, in any case, far from rigidly adhered to. For a descriptive account of 'turban conflicts' in Manchester and Wolverhampton, see David Beetham, *Transport and Turbans* (London, Oxford University Press, for Institute of Race Relations, 1970).

with other employers. All the Australians and New Zealanders turned down at this stage were thought to be seeking short-term, stop-gap work.

Having passed the first hurdles successfully, applicants are given a further test and interview. The test is one which bears more relevance to the type of work for which they have applied. The interview is more searching, the application form, which should give not only details of previous jobs held, but also any conviction an applicant may have, is used as a basis for the interview. At this stage comes the medical examination. A small number of applicants failed at the first stage because of medical defects: these were probably either visible defects or those of which the applicant was aware.

The categories used in stage two are basically the same as those in stage one, but a few are different, as can be seen in Table 12.4. (See p. 249.)

Occasionally an applicant is offered a job but does not accept it. Strictly speaking this is not a 'rejection' but as it does not fit the criteria for acceptance, we have included all cases of this sort under rejection. One or two were rejected because they had no fixed address, which was taken as a sign of instability.

Table 12.4 shows those rejected at the second stage of the selection process, together with the reasons for rejection. In many groups the numbers were too small to be of much significance.

Some 37 per cent—27 out of the 73—of the native rejects at this stage failed the more specialized test they were given. For six of them this was the only reason for rejection. Ten of the remainder were offered alternative employment, but refused it: several had wanted only clerical work, and were not prepared to take anything else.

Twenty-two per cent of the native applicants (16 out of 73) who were rejected at stage two failed their medical examination. Five of these sixteen applicants were also rejected because they failed the test, had unstable previous employment, or objected to shift work. The ages of the medical rejects varied from 18 to 54, the highest number being in their twenties. In contrast to this relatively large proportion of native rejects, only two of a total of forty immigrant rejects failed their medical examinations.

Unstable employment records were mentioned for fifteen native rejects. Eight of them were also rejected for another reason; for six, nearly all in their twenties, no other reason was given. Taking into consideration the number rejected at stage one on the grounds of unstable employment records, how did these six get through to

Reasons	U.K.	Eire	Jamaica	India	West Africa	West Indies (unspecified)	Pakistan	Other West Indies	East Africa	Malta and Cyprus	Ceylon	Others
Part-time only	1											
Clerical only	6											
No suitable vacancy	1				1							
Previous L.T. employment	1											
Conviction	8											
Entry permit			1			2						
Inexperienced driving	2		3			1						
Didn't want job	16	1	3			1		1				
Medical defect	5		1		1					1		
Objection to shift work												
Declined alternative employment	13	5	1		1	1	1	1	1			
Stop-gap job	3	2		3	1							
Unstable employment	15	6	2	2	1							
Intelligence	3	2	3		1	1			1			
Appearance	5	1	1		2						1	1
Speech				2							1	1
Test score	27	8	3	2	1	1	1		3		3	3
Didn't wait	10	4	1								1	1
No fixed abode	1	1					1					
Job offered, not accepted		1										
Calling back later	1											
Failed driving test			2									
Insufficient information								1	1			
Total rejected (133)	73	20	15	4	4	4	4	2	2	1	4	3

* More than one reason for rejection was often given and the total number of reasons therefore exceeds the number of applicants rejected.

† As per Table 12.1.

stage two? There could be several explanations. The reception, testing, and interviewing of applicants is a continuous process. Some fill in their application forms prior to the first interview, and so will be turned down at stage one. Others might be interviewed first, in which case such factors as convictions or the number of previous jobs would not be considered until stage two. Another possibility is that the six rejected for no other reason than unstable employment represent differences in the criteria used by different interviewers. Given that the interviewing is a continuous process, the chances are that an applicant will not see the same interviewer at both stages. Possibly, too, discrepancies are revealed in a longer interview.

Intelligence, or rather a perceived lack of it, was given as a reason for rejection of nine applicants. This was a subjective assessment on the part of the interviewer.

Forty per cent of the Irish rejects at stage two failed the test, and half of these were offered an alternative vacancy, although all refused. If an applicant fails only on the specialized test, he is usually offered an alternative post. The reason for the large proportion of refusals of alternative employment is probably that the alternative post offered is lower paid with less attractive prospects.

Of the six Irishmen turned down because of their previous employment record, three were also rejected for another reason.

In contrast to the native-born applicants only one Irishman was rejected on medical grounds.

For all other groups, with the exception of the Jamaicans, the numbers were too small to be of any significance. The largest rejection category for the Jamaicans at stage two was inexperienced driving or failure on driving test. Applicants with very little driving experience were usually turned down at the interviews: the others were sent for a driving test.

It will be noted that rejection on medical grounds was largely confined to the native-born and Irish applicants, and most of these rejects were young men. A London Transport medical officer told us that the physical condition of the immigrant applicants was probably higher than that of the native-born. We were also told that the standards of cleanliness and hygiene of immigrants were often appreciably higher. Some medical defects do not debar applicants altogether: for instance, an applicant may be perfectly suitable as a conductor, but because of an eyesight defect would not be able to become a driver. He may then be offered a job as a conductor on the understanding that he could not become a driver.

No distinction has been made in the rejection tables between men and women applicants. There were twelve native and Irish female rejects at stage one and twenty immigrants, of whom twelve were Jamaican. At stage two there were again twelve native and Irish women rejected and five immigrants. There was nothing of significance in the reasons for their rejection. Immigrant women as a group were not popular with London Transport. They form a very small proportion of the bus operating staff—far smaller than their native counterparts. They were, from all appearances, considered a poor risk as far as their potential length of service is concerned, because they were in the child-bearing, family-rearing age groups.

These, then, were the rejects. We found a greater percentage of immigrants than natives; many rejected on more objective criteria, failure on the tests and on medical grounds, but also a large number rejected on very subjective criteria, on the basis of a very rapid assessment by an interviewer. We do not know how far any of the selection criteria are appropriate, particularly since most of the recruits will be trained for their future jobs.

Table 12.5 shows, by countries of origin, those applicants who were selected for employment. (See p. 252.)

The percentage of native-born and Irish recruits was higher than that for any immigrant group (41 per cent and 37 per cent, respectively) and together they comprised 77 per cent of the total applicants selected. Of the remaining groups, West Indians and Pakistanis, broadly speaking, stood a better chance of selection than Indians or Africans; but bearing in mind the small numbers involved and that these figures are from one week only, no long-term conclusions can be drawn.

They were recruited for a wide range of jobs, from booking-office clerks and craftsmen to labourers and cleaners. The age range was considerable: from a garage trainee aged 16 to a body-maker who was 57 years of age. Within these broad limits, the weighting was towards the lower age groups: 418 of the total 625 applicants were 30 years of age or less. Table 12.6 shows the age distribution of all applicants and of those recruited. (See p. 253.)

It will be seen that the largest group of applicants from the United Kingdom came from the youngest age group, 15–20 years. In spite of this, they produced the lowest percentage of the native-born recruits. The number of applicants diminished with successive age groups, but the percentage of recruits varied, reaching its

TABLE 12.5.
Number of Applicants Selected for Employment, by Countries of Origin.

Countries of origin	Total applicants	Accepted	% of own group accepted	% of total accepted
United Kingdom	284	116	41	61
Eire	80	30	37	16
Jamaica	58	11	19	6
India	43	5	12	3
West Africa	43	4	9	2
West Indies (unspecified)	24	5	21	3
Pakistan	22	5	23	3
Other West Indies	12	2	17	1
Barbados	10	3	30	2
East Africa	9	1	11	1
Malta and Cyprus	7	1	14	1
Ceylon	6	1	17	1
Australia and New Zealand	5	1	20	1
Other*	18	5	27	3
Origin unknown	4	1	25	1
All	625	191	30	100

* As per table 12.1.

peak with the 41–45 years age group. The Irish present a similar picture in terms of age, but they did considerably better in recruitment terms as far as the youngest age group is concerned, and had less success with the late twenties and the 31–40 years age group.

There were few immigrant applicants in the upper age groups. In addition, there were not many applicants in the youngest age groups, although this has probably changed as greater numbers of second generation children leave school. None of the immigrant teenagers appearing during our typical week was accepted for employment. The peak age for West Indian applicants was slightly lower than for the other immigrant groups, the difference being between early twenties as opposed to late twenties. This latter group was the most successful in terms of percentage of applicants recruited of all the immigrant groups.

To sum up: nearly 80 per cent of all the recruits were either from the United Kingdom or Ireland, who between them provided

Countries of origin	15–20	21–25	26–30	31–35	36–40	41–45	46–50	51–55	Over 55	Age not given	All ages
United Kingdom											
Total applicants	88	69	34	20	22	20	14	12	4	1	284
Number accepted	22	30	18	9	11	12	8	5	1	—	116
Percentage accepted	25%	43%	53%	45%	50%	60%	57%	42%	25%	—	41%
Eire											
Total applicants	21	27	8	7	7	3	3	2	2	—	80
Number accepted	8	11	2	2	2	2	—	2	1	—	30
Percentage accepted	38%	41%	25%	29%	29%	67%	—	100%	50%	—	37%
West Indies											
Total applicants	11	33	24	21	6	5	2	1	—	1	104
Number accepted	—	5	9	4	2	—	1	—	—	—	21
Percentage accepted	—	15%	37%	19%	33%	—	50%	—	—	—	20%
India and Pakistan											
Total applicants	3	15	22	14	6	3	1	—	1	—	65
Number accepted	—	2	5	2	1	—	—	—	—	—	10
Percentage accepted	—	13%	23%	14%	17%	—	—	—	—	—	15%
Africa											
Total applicants	2	17	20	9	3	1	—	—	—	—	52
Number accepted	—	2	3	—	—	—	—	—	—	—	5
Percentage accepted	—	12%	15%	—	—	—	—	—	—	—	10%
Other											
Total applicants	6	10	8	9	3	—	2	2	—	—	40
Number accepted	—	2	3	3	1	—	—	—	—	—	9
Percentage accepted	—	20%	37%	33%	33%	—	—	—	—	—	22%
All											
Total applicants	131	171	116	80	47	32	22	17	7	2	625
Number accepted	30	52	40	20	17	14	9	7	2	—	191
Percentage accepted	23%	30%	34%	25%	36%	44%	41%	41%	29%	—	30%

58 per cent of all the applicants. There were more West Indian applicants than Irish; the West Indians were the largest coloured immigrant group, providing 17 per cent of the recruits. The Indians, Pakistanis, and Africans did less well, but the difference between the relative numbers who were accepted—of West Indians on the one hand and all other coloured immigrants on the other—was not very large. Many applicants were rejected after a very quick assessment by an interviewer based on the criteria which have been given in detail above. I do not know how suitable the selection criteria were for potential bus conductors, Underground guards, Permanent Way workers, and so on.

CONCLUSIONS

The recruitment process was a speedy one, using a number of standardized procedures. That it was a rapid process probably reduced the coloured immigrants' chances of acceptance. The recruitment staff thought that the assessment of the potentialities of coloured immigrants was more difficult than that of U.K.-born natives, and given the cultural differences we would expect this to be so. Relatively more of the coloured immigrants were rejected at the first than the second stage. The second stage was a slower and more deliberate procedure, which suggests that they did better with more careful selection. The tests were designed with the assistance of an organization with considerable experience of personnel selection, but they were apparently intended for use with native-born applicants.

Considerable emphasis was put on *tests* in recruitment, and to that extent the process was a rational one; but there was a large area of subjectivity. Alongside the rationality of selection there coexisted a folklore amongst the recruitment staff: they could 'smell' a good potential busman or railwayman. That they were all ex-operating staff, all white, was probably important in that—intentionally or not—they favoured applicants who were seen to conform closest to the image of the traditional London Transport employee.

There was nothing in the data collected during the 'typical week' to indicate deliberate discrimination against coloured applicants, but in some respects the cards were stacked against them. The recruitment organization was a service department; its practices in terms of the numbers recruited, and their standards, were determined by the departments for which staff were required. From time to time some departments have requested that the recruitment of coloured immigrants be reduced, as I have shown in the appropriate chapters.[1] There has therefore been some conflict between the economic rationality of the labour market—in so far as it exists—and the perceived consequences of racial and ethnic differences.

[1] I am told that the usual practice was to switch potential recruits from one department to another, rather than reject them completely.

13

RECRUITMENT IN BARBADOS

Recruitment in Barbados dates from the mid-fifties. London Transport recruitment was one of a number of fairly similar schemes set up with the active support of the Barbados Government. The background to this official sponsorship of emigration was the growing unemployment in the island and the pressure of population increase: assisted emigration was seen as one speedily effective means to help alleviate the problem. Prior to 1955, a mere handful of student nurses and hospital auxiliaries had left the island under official sponsorship. In eleven years, 1955–65, over 21,000 sponsored migrants left Barbados: slightly over half of these went to the U.S.A., a little under half to the United Kingdom, and the rest to Canada, other Caribbean countries; a very small number migrated to other locations.

In 1955, the Barbados Government sent a minister and a senior official to London to survey employment prospects. This team contacted ministries and a number of large employers, including London Transport. In the latter part of the same year, the Barbados Migrants' Liaison Service was established in London with the purpose of further exploring employment opportunities, liaising with employers and voluntary organizations, finding accommodation for and generally assisting migrants.

As a result of the 1955 discussions, in 1956 London Transport sent a recruitment official and a medical officer to Barbados; seventy

---

[1] This chapter was written when London Transport was still recruiting in Barbados and it had, therefore, some topical interest. With the intended conversion of the bus fleet to one-man operation and the eventual disappearance of the conductor grade, it was decided to cease recruiting conductors overseas in the summer of 1970. Similarly, with an 'improved staff position' in Railway Operating, recruitment in the Caribbean was suspended from October 1970. Any topical appeal the chapter had then is now lost. However, given that almost all Commonwealth immigration to Britain was unplanned and unorganized, I have thought it useful to include a detailed account of one of the major exceptions.

stationmen, fifty conductors, and twenty women conductors were recruited.[1] Arrangements were made for further selection and recruitment to be done by the Barbados Labour Department, and for medical examinations and tests to be made by local doctors. The London Transport scheme thus accorded with and possibly anticipated the report by G. E. Cumper, which recommended, *inter alia*:

That a high proportion of, and if possible all, emigrants to the United Kingdom be interviewed by qualified personnel, preferably trained for this work, before leaving the island, and be provided with as full printed information as possible on the district and occupation they intend to journey to, and the means of getting there and establishing themselves.[2]

From the migrant's point of view, probably the most important feature of the sponsorship scheme was the provision of an interest-free loan by the Barbados Government to cover the cost of his fare from the island to the place of employment. London Transport recruits were loaned up to a maximum of $W.I.400 (£83. 6s. 8d.). The loan was secured by an agreement between the recruit and two persons who would remain on the island after his departure and who acted as guarantors for the repayment of the loan. They were usually relatives of the recruit, and one had to own real estate. The loan was repaid by monthly instalments over a period of two years. Some repaid the loan in less than the stipulated period, a few defaulted, but it was never necessary to prosecute to secure repayment. Of the $W.I.400, $W.I.360 was to cover the cost of the fare to the U.K. It was estimated that over 90 per cent of London Transport recruits were assisted with loans.

The recruitment process began with registration for employment. The normal age limits were 20 to 35 years, though the upper limit could be extended if the applicant had relatives in the U.K.; a re-engagement could be over the age limit. Applicants were then called for a preliminary test. This was to eliminate those thought to be not suited for employment with London Transport, but all without any obvious disqualification could take the test. The test consisted of 'simple arithmetic'. The failure rate averaged 40 per cent.

The test procedures for bus conductors and railwaymen differed

[1] No more women conductors were recruited in Barbados: I was told their wastage was high. Generally, London Transport's image of coloured women workers was an unfavourable one; see Chapter 12.

[2] G. E. Cumper, *Report on Employment in Barbados* (Bridgetown, Barbados Government Printing Office, undated), p. 36.

somewhat. The conductors sat the standard London Transport recruits' test paper after their Barbados training; the railwaymen took the guards' test before the pre-recruitment training, as this test paper was basically an intelligence test and results would be largely unaffected by pre-recruitment training. The guards' test paper was similar to the one used for direct recruit guards in the U.K.

Candidates who passed the preliminary test were given a talk on conditions in the U.K. They were warned that they would *initially* regret the change, but would change their minds after a month or so in England. The differences between England and Barbados were emphasized: the weather dictates that living conditions were far more confined—far more time had to be spent indoors. Similarly, warm clothing and substantial shoes were required for the English climate; dark clothing was advised to conform to the U.K. pattern and to avoid being 'objects of curiosity'.[1] They were told that accommodation would be booked for them in London, and it was necessary to conform to the 'rules of the house' set by the landlady: they must measure up to her standards. The necessity for income tax documents was explained. People in England, they are told, are more reserved than Barbadians, but not unfriendly. An *Information Booklet for Intending Emigrants to Britain* was issued to each candidate. This booklet aimed to set out the facts on conditions of life in Britain; it was not specifically aimed at London Transport recruits.[2]

Candidates were then required to attend a course of evening classes. This part of the scheme was inaugurated in 1959: London Transport was dissatisfied with the standard of recruits, and the Barbados authorities were disturbed by the large numbers failing the training courses in London. In the heyday of the recruitment programme—prior to the restrictions of August 1965—these classes were held at several centres in the island, but later they were held at only one centre. Recruits for bus and railway work were expected to attend twelve two-hour classes, usually spread over a four- or six-week period, depending on the urgency of London Transport's requirements. Recruits for the grade of catering assistant attended eight two-hour classes, usually spread over a four-week period. (Because of London Transport's staff shortage, recruits were occasionally sent to London before the completion of the pre-recruitment course.)

[1] This information dates from 1966.   [2] See below, p. 270.

The classes were provided by the Ministry of Education and staffed by teachers, mostly head teachers, and officials of the Ministry. The emphasis of the classes varied depending on whether they were for potential conductors or railwaymen, and the catering assistants' course again differed somewhat.

The major emphasis was on spoken and written English: the ability to speak clearly and deliberately, and to write simple reports clearly and legibly. Reading with understanding printed forms and instructions was also covered. For spoken English, recruits used tape recorders. In 1966, a tape recording of typical London Transport sounds of the 'min'er doors' variety was supplied to help familiarize recruits with these sounds. There was considerable emphasis on calculating *quickly* in £.s.d. for both potential conductors and catering assistants.[1] Catering assistants were also given some training in food preparation; and the importance of hygiene was emphasized.

There was some preparation for life in the big city. The *Information Booklet for Intending Emigrants to Britain* was used in this part of the course, and London Transport provided a film, *This Mighty Heart*. This film, which replaced a very old one used until 1964, was essentially a public relations exercise prepared by the British Transport Commission film unit for British audiences.

One of the major problems met by the teaching staff was that many of the trainees had read and written very little since they left school. Moreover, their arithmetical ability had often suffered with the passing of the years. Hence it was necessary to begin with first principles. The levels of ability often varied quite widely which presented the problem of keeping the interest of the more able trainees: classes were, on occasions, split to meet this problem. A further problem—accentuated by the restrictions on entry to the U.K.—was that it was sometimes difficult to have a homogeneous group (e.g., all conductors) for training.

The problem of keeping the interest of the trainees was reflected in the attendance figures. Some of the teachers reported a downward trend in attendance towards the end of the course. An examination of average attendance figures for several series of classes held in the period February to June 1966 showed they varied from 41 per cent for one series to 84 per cent for another. Most were in the 70 to 80 per cent range.

All the class teachers had been to the U.K., either for training courses or on Government business. The recency of these visits

---

[1] Barbados has used a decimal currency system since 1948.

varied quite widely: one as long ago as 1949–50, one as recent as 1965.[1] Most were in the U.K. in the late fifties or early sixties. That their U.K. experience was often dated was a problem they recognized.

At the completion of the course all trainees were assessed by their class teacher. Assessments were made for English and mathematics; there was also a general assessment. These assessments varied from 'highly recommended' to 'recommended for further training' or 'not recommended'. Recruits had to complete the standard London Transport recruits' test papers—apart from recruit railwaymen, that is, who had written the test paper before the training course. These papers were marked in Barbados by the Labour Department staff and sent to London with the recruits' other documents. The failure rate for these tests was very low. Following the test, candidates were interviewed by a senior member of the Labour Department staff. The rejection rate at the interview stage was low: of the twenty-one candidates due to be interviewed on one 'typical' day, five failed to appear, four were deferred for further training, and one was rejected.

The candidate next completed his employment application form (including the names of two referees—references were taken up in Barbados) and applied for his U.K. entry voucher. He also attended a health centre for a chest X-ray and blood test: general medical examinations were made by a local general practitioner. All medical tests were to London Transport standards. A list of candidates was sent to the police to check that none had been convicted of serious offences: wounding, stealing, or a sexual offence normally excluded a candidate. Similarly, a check was made with the mental hospital to ensure that the candidate did not have a history of mental illness. Having been an in-patient—other than for observational purposes—was normally a disqualification.

One reported side effect of the various recruitment schemes run by the Barbados authorities was a greater concern for health and hygiene: potential emigrants had to pass the medical tests and examinations and were thought to take more care. Moreover, diseases could be detected in the early stages and treated, and contacts as well could be traced and checked. Barbados was said to be 'so healthy' that the authorities found it difficult to promote an adequate concern for health and hygiene.

Recruits flew to the U.K. by scheduled flights. In the early days of

[1] Like most information in this chapter, this dates from 1966.

Barbados recruitment they travelled by sea; more recently travel was by charter flight, but since the restrictions on U.K. entry of August 1965, the numbers travelling did not warrant a charter flight. On arrival in London recruits were met by a representative of the Barbados Migrants' Liaison Service and taken to their lodgings. They then began their London Transport training.

From the beginning of the scheme the Barbados Migrants' Liaison Service was responsible for finding accommodation for newly arrived recruits. London Transport tended to place the direct recruits at those locations where the staff shortage was most acute, and this flexibility was *the* most important advantage of the scheme for London Transport. Such areas were, though, often some distance from the major West Indian settlements in London and possibly in predominantly middle-class commuter districts. Finding suitable accommodation accessible to the place of work was a problem for the Liaison Service. Not only had the accommodation to be easily accessible to the place of work, but those providing it had to be prepared for the unusual and changing hours of duty inevitably associated with public transport.

Forty-six Barbadian direct recruits appeared in the interview samples.[1] Of these forty-six, forty-two had stayed in lodgings found for them by the Liaison Service; the other four had stayed with relatives or friends already in the U.K. In the questionnaire used for the railway pilot studies, no provision had been made for any questions specifically concerned with accommodation found by the Liaison Service, but it became apparent in the first interviews with Barbadian recruits that this was the focus of some discontent. Care was taken to include such questions in the remaining interviews in the railway pilot studies and they were subsequently included in the questionnaires.[2]

Eleven (26 per cent) reported that the accommodation found for them had been satisfactory, the remaining thirty-one reported that it had not. Overcrowding was the focus of most criticism, and often this was linked to a dislike of having to share a room at all. Overcrowding was often seen in the context of the rent charged for the accommodation, and both were related to the facilities and services provided: furniture and particularly storage space for clothes; meals, especially early morning tea and breakfast.

[1] They appeared accidentally, as it were, as the immigrants' countries of origin were not known before the interviews.
[2] See Appendix 1.

There were eight of us in a room—[paying] four pounds [a week] each. No morning tea, only four chairs in the room and nowhere to put our clothes. [Barbadian Ticket Collector.]

This quotation is typical of the comments of the more outspoken critics. Others thought that inadequate or unsatisfactory accommodation was better than none at all, and that it did initially suffice whilst they were able to search for something better.

Similarly, some of those who rated the accommodation as satisfactory qualified this by saying it would not be acceptable now.

Generally, immigrants face a difficult problem in finding adequate housing accommodation.[1] Expectations are not realized, hopes are not fulfilled. One of the advantages claimed by some London Transport managers for the Barbados scheme was that initially at least the migrant was shielded from the rigours of the London housing market, and this aided his adaptation to his new role. This argument is not without some force: the Barbadian recruit did at least have *somewhere* to sleep, he did not spend his first nights in London walking the streets with nowhere to go. On the other hand, many found the accommodation provided almost unbearable and were soon looking for something better. It is possible that the Barbadians' expectations here were higher than those of other migrant groups. The marked distaste for sharing a room supports this hypothesis to some extent, as does the urban bias of their previous occupations. A further factor, of course, was that the accommodation had been found by a Barbados Government organization: the stamp of official approval suggested a certain minimum standard.

It may be that the views expressed by some of the Barbados recruits on the accommodation provided reflected their wider discontents with the recruitment scheme and their subsequent employment experience. As in their answers on the pre-recruitment training,[2] the railwaymen tended to be more critical than did busmen: five of the fourteen busmen found the accommodation satisfactory; the corresponding figure for the railwaymen (including the three Permanent Way men) was six out of twenty-eight. With such small numbers it is not, however, possible to attach much significance to this difference.[3]

The restrictions on entry to the U.K. considerably reduced the flow of direct recruits from Barbados, particularly after publication

[1] See Chapter 16   [2] See below, pp. 265–8.

[3] The sample of Barbados recruits was, of course, relatively small, but we have no reason to suppose that it was unrepresentative.

of the White Paper of August 1965.[1] In the ten years 1956–65, London Transport recruited nearly four thousand employees in Barbados, an average of nearly four hundred a year. In 1966, the figure fell to one hundred and thirty-eight, and in the three years 1967–9, a total of less than two hundred were recruited. One feature of these restrictions was a delay between the application for a voucher and its arrival in Barbados. At the time of my visit in 1966, this delay was nine months, but it later became as long as eighteen months. This delay had several consequences. The waiting time caused many recruits to lose interest, and in 1966, over 50 per cent of the vouchers applied for had to be returned as the applicants no longer wished to travel. This applied both to London Transport recruits and to others who had been recruited for work in the U.K. A further consequence of the restrictions was that the Barbados authorities had to provide refresher classes for London Transport recruits when a long delay had occurred between the classes and departure to the U.K. Moreover, it was necessary for recruits to have further medical examinations at the expense of the Barbados Government.

In 1966, London Transport took steps to begin recruiting in Jamaica and Trinidad on the Barbados pattern, and in the years 1968 to mid-1970, somewhat over two hundred recruits came from these islands, mostly from Trinidad.

The Barbados Government was clearly disturbed by the restrictive measures of August 1965. It had put a lot of effort—and money —into the sponsorship schemes and the pre-emigration training in order to prepare the recruits for life in Britain. It then found itself treated no better than countries that had done none of these things, indeed Malta was given more favourable treatment in the allocation of entry vouchers. The Barbados authorities were particularly disturbed that a voucher not used was 'lost' in the sense that it was not replaced for another applicant.

SOME COMMENTS ON THE LONDON TRANSPORT SCHEME

Any assessment of the scheme must draw on a number of sources: objective data on the performance of direct recruit workers compared with other immigrants; opinions of London Transport's managers and supervisors; opinions of the Barbados recruits themselves; my own observations in England and Barbados.

Very little objective information exists. I do not, for example,

[1] *Immigration from the Commonwealth* (Cmnd. 2739) (London, H.M.S.O., 1965).

know whether Barbadian drivers are in any sense 'better' bus drivers than other West Indian drivers. No information was available to us on the present grades of Barbados direct recruits, so I cannot compare their speed and paths of promotion with those of other migrants. Information was, however, available on wastage through resignations: of the roughly 2,800 conductors recruited in Barbados in the years 1956–66, 30 per cent had left and the remainder were still in the Board's service at the end of 1966. Figures for Barbados-recruited rail staff show a wastage of 24 per cent over the same period. A detailed analysis of wastage by resignations for 1965 showed a wastage rate—expressed as a percentage of the average number in the grade during the year—of 6 per cent for the Barbadian conductors in Central Buses, compared with 21 per cent for conductors other than Barbadians in the Department. Figures for station staff, guards, and station foremen for the same year show a wastage rate of 3 per cent for the Barbados-recruited staff and 26 per cent for other staff in these grades.

A useful and revealing comparison would involve the wastage rates of Barbados-recruited staff and other migrant staff in similar grades, but figures on this were not available. It is possible, however, to compare the wastage of Barbados-recruited conductors during the years 1956–66 with that of *all* conductors in the years 1955–64. During that time the *net* intake to the grade (i.e., excluding transfers from the grade of driver) was 44,300; the outgoing figure for the grade (*including* transfers to the grade of driver) was 48,100. The numbers of conductors in service fell from 17,900 to 14,100 in the ten-year period. The total wastage rate, including conductors in service at the beginning of 1955 and expressed as a percentage of the 1955 figure, was 191 per cent. The comparison is a crude one, but it does show that the Barbadian-recruited staff were a relatively stable section of the workforce. This conclusion is reinforced by the 1965 wastage figures.

Conflicting views on the success of the Barbados scheme were expressed by London Transport managers met in the course of the study. (Supervisors were seldom able to distinguish the Barbados recruits from other West Indians, and it is open to doubt whether managers were as able as they believed themselves to be in identifying the Barbadian recruits.) The prevailing management view was that the Barbados recruits had been a 'better type'. Often this 'better type' thesis was qualified: the early Barbadian recruits were better, but later ones were no better or worse than other migrants.

The Barbados recruits were variously described as being more intelligent, more polite, or better spoken than other West Indians. Some managers pointed out that the Barbadian recruits 'did not have to worry' about finding accommodation and hence had a 'greater sense of security'. Selection in Barbados was said by some managers to be more rigorous than London recruitment, though again this view was qualified: the best recruits were those selected in Barbados *by London Transport staff*. (*Very* few were so selected.)

One advantage claimed by some London Transport managers for direct recruitment was that it avoided 'contamination' by other employment. The Barbados recruit, it was argued, had not experienced the stresses and frustrations of other employment in England. He was then less disenchanted with England and for this reason was a better employee.

The 'Barbadians are best' thesis was strongly challenged by a few managers who described it as a 'London Transport myth.' Not only were the Barbados recruits no better than other West Indians, we were told, but the newly arrived recruit had a particular disadvantage: he had no knowledge of London. Moreover, the recruit for railway work had a further handicap: he came from an island without railways and may not have seen a railway before his arrival in England. (Barbados has had no railway since the mid-thirties.) Yet, it was pointed out, he had to play a part in running a railway after a few weeks' training. By contrast, the London-recruited migrant would have some knowledge of London and some familiarity with railways.

What of the Barbados-recruited workers themselves: what were their opinions on the merits and short-comings of the recruitment scheme? The occupational distribution of the forty-six interviewed is shown in Table 13.1. (See p. 266.)

Thirty-two of the forty-six had attended the pre-recruitment training course and expressed opinions on it. (Two others had attended but were not asked the relevant questions, owing either to pressure of time in the interview or a lapse on the interviewer's part.) Those who had attended the training course were asked if the classes had been useful and if they could be improved.[1]

Of the thirty-two who had attended and expressed opinions, twenty-four (75 per cent) found them useful and eight (25 per cent) found them not useful. Opinions differed between the departments:

---

[1] See Appendix 1 for the phrasing of the questions.

TABLE 13.1.
Occupations of the Barbadian Direct Recruits.

Occupation	No.
Driver	5
Conductor	9
Motorman	8
Guard	10
Station staff	11
Lengthman or relayer	3
Total	46

criticisms were more widespread and intense in the Railway Operating and Permanent Way departments than in Central Buses. Only one of the eleven busmen found that the classes were not useful, whereas seven of the twenty-one railwaymen were of this opinion. The remaining fourteen found them useful. Usefulness was defined both in terms of training specific to the job and the organization, and, to a lesser extent, in a wider sense of providing some understanding of life in England.

Yes [the classes were useful], especially with the money. They help you know the type of people you would be working with: their habits and cultural aspects . . . fast moving . . . *and punctuality*. [Barbadian Driver.]

Yes, on speaking English, and they try to give you a better outlook on discipline. [Barbadian Driver.]

These quotations from busmen illustrate the job orientation of the majority of the answers, an orientation which is again evident in the criticisms made, although when, for example, a complaint was made that English behaviour does not always measure up to the Barbadians' expectations, it may apply to people met both on and off the job.[1] Critics complained, often bitterly, that a false picture had been painted both of the jobs for which they were recruited and of England and the English.

They [the classes] were useful, especially for someone having left school for years; they tell you about English £. s. d. and tell you what the job

---

[1] As our enquiry was job-centred, a strong job orientation was to be expected.

is like. But the *real* facts about stationmen—sweeping, cleaning lavatories
—these are not fully explained. They say the job is better than it is. They
say the Englishman is quiet, well mannered. This is wrong: they give a
wrong impression of what the English are like. [Barbadian Stationman.]

The complaint that cleaning duties were not explained was echoed
by others:

They should tell you *really* what you have to do: the duties of a stationman
They never tell you about cleaning work—it was embarrassing at first,
but you get accustomed to it. If I'd known I would never have come,
but they can only tell us at home the information they receive from here.
[Barbadian Stationman.]

Another complaint of the railwaymen was that the classes were
largely directed towards skills likely to be useful to busmen, to the
exclusion of any railway content.

No [the classes were not useful.] They were more suitable for the buses
than for trains—there was nothing about trains at all. [Barbadian Guard.]

Suggestions for improvements in the content of the training
course were, predictably, aimed at removing these seen deficiencies.
Again the railwaymen differed in their opinions from the busmen:
sixteen of the twenty-one rail staff said the classes could be improved,
compared with only three of the eleven busmen. The station staff
were most positive in their view that the course could be improved:
seven of the eight who had attended the course and gave opinions
were of this view. It is not without significance that this was the
group whose level of occupational achievement was lowest: five
of the eight had failed the guards' training course in London; at
least three of these had been recruited as guards; and one of the eight
had been recruited as a station foreman, but had failed the training
course. Suggested improvements were concerned both with the
job content and life in England, especially that information on these
aspects should be up to date.

We sometimes detected a slight reluctance to criticize the pre-
recruitment training, possibly *because* it was a Barbadian course.
Critics often pointed out that the instructors could only pass on the
information they received from London, and many of the criticisms
were directed more against London Transport than the Barbados
authorities. Possibly, too, the criticisms represented a deeper dis-
enchantment with life in England: those whose occupational and
income achievement levels were lowest were most forthright both

10

in their criticisms of the course and suggestions to remedy the defects. On the other hand, the criticisms do have a rational basis: information on the British currency system, for example, is clearly useful for all migrants from a country using a decimal currency, but it has more use *occupationally* for conductors than for most railwaymen.[1]

There were no objective criteria available on which it was possible to compare the performance of Barbadian direct recruits with that of other *migrant* workers. The comparison of wastage rates does, however, strongly suggest that the Barbadians were a relatively stable group in the workforce. This was one advantage for London Transport of the Barbados recruitment scheme. The other—most important—advantage was a ready source of recruits that could be placed at those locations where the staff shortage was most acute.

The views of the managers on the 'superiority' of the Barbados direct recruits are not to be lightly dismissed. Barbados is almost universally regarded as the most 'English' of the Caribbean islands and territories. From its initial settlement in 1627 until independence in 1966, it was always British—never occupied by another colonial power. The orientation of Barbadians is towards Britain and when Barbadians speak of the Mother Country it is very meaningful to them. This explains to some extent the *hurt*, anger, and surprise that *Malta* was given preferential treatment over Barbados in the allocation of U.K. entry vouchers. It also explains much of the Barbadian's bitter disappointment when the British do not live up to his expectations. A value system which is oriented towards the Mother Country is not, of course, confined to Barbados; it is found in varying degrees in most of the West Indian populations, but the Barbadian version is its most pronounced form.[2]

It can be hypothesized, then, that in so far as the Barbadian had internalized this value system, he was likely to be both more adaptable and more acceptable in his London Transport role than most other West Indians, and certainly more than Asian migrants—with the possible exception of the relatively small number of Anglo-Indians. On the other hand, native British staff below first line management did not often distinguish Barbadians from other West Indians, lumping them all together as 'West Indians' or 'Jamaicans'.

[1] This was, of course, before decimalization in Britain.
[2] Mention should perhaps be made at this point of the Barbados educational system. With a literacy rate of 97 per cent, Barbados compares favourably with other Commonwealth countries from which migrants have come in any numbers.

Motivation, too, is important, and the fact that the direct recruit has to repay his passage loan provides some incentive to conform to the norms associated with his role in London Transport.

The strangeness of London and for many railway recruits, the strangeness of railways, were the major handicaps suffered by the direct recruits, as compared with London-recruited immigrants. Rural Irish recruited in Ireland shared this handicap to a lesser degree, but for them other aspects of strangeness were less salient.

Next the pre-recruitment course. It had three basic and related aims, all of which were part of a re-socialization or acculturation process. First, it was intended to teach and improve *skills*: for example, written and spoken English, rapid and accurate use of British coinage. Second, it aimed to inculcate *London Transport* values: reliability, prompt obedience to instructions, punctuality, regular attendance, smartness, politeness, and so on. Third, the course attempted to *inform*, and by so doing again to influence, behaviour. There were two aspects of this information process: information on the migrant's occupational role in London; information on England and on living in England.

I have no evidence that the teaching of skills was other than effective. Recruits found this aspect of the course useful, with the reservation that skills likely to assist task performance were largely bus oriented. It was not, though, intended that specific *job* skills should be taught, but in teaching British coinage, for example, the instructors illustrated by reference to fare changes and so on. Managers who argued the 'Barbadians are best' thesis often supported this by reference to these skills, for example, spoken English; critics never mentioned this aspect to support their case. The *very* few West Indians whom we found slightly difficult to understand in interviews were seldom, if ever, Barbadian direct recruits. On this score, then, the training course fulfilled its intended function.

Next the inculcation of London Transport values. Again this aspect of the training course was mentioned by direct recruits: punctuality, 'they try to give you a better outlook on discipline'. Clearly, this was important as the salient values of London Transport—punctuality, promptness, and so on—are not always uppermost in Barbados.

It was on the question of information that the recruits were most critical of the Barbados training. This criticism had three aspects: a lack of information on the job to be done in London; a misleading impression of England and the English; and related to this, the presentation of out-of-date information. The lecturers themselves were often aware that their knowledge of Britain was dated. The *Information Booklet for Intending Emigrants to Britain* contained much useful information. Its basic messages were that life was not easy for the Barbadian in Britain, and that conformity was necessary to gain acceptance. It was, though, very dated: the price and wage levels given were for 1953.

What is open to question is the description drawn of the English as being reserved but not unfriendly. This accords with the Barbadian's traditional image of Britain as the Mother Country. Many Barbadians—and of course other migrants, particularly West Indians—were both *surprised* and hurt when they encountered hostility in Britain. This raises a very difficult question: how far should it be emphasized that the West Indian in Britain will encounter hostile behaviour *because* he is West Indian, *because* he is black? This could be over-emphasized and would thus be equally misleading and damaging, in that behaviour that was not hostile would be perceived as such.[1]

Criticisms of the lack of adequate information about the work content of jobs figured prominently in the comments of the Barbados-recruited staff. One major source of information on London Transport was the film *This Mighty Heart*. This was essentially a public relations presentation, showing how London Transport fitted into the life of the capital. There was probably more footage on London than on London Transport itself, and very little on behind-the-scenes activity. As an aid to accurate information on the organization, it was misleading and to that extent damaging: the Thames glinting in the moonlight—in colour—is far removed from the problems of dealing with drunks at Piccadilly Circus on a Saturday night and going home to one or two rooms in Stoke Newington.

Doubtless a training and information programme which *accurately* portrayed life in a North-West European metropolitan centre to inhabitants of a small Caribbean island would need to be both comprehensive and skilfully prepared and presented. The two situations are *so different*.

---

[1] As is shown in Chapter 16, the Barbadians'—and other West Indians'—expectations of Britain were very outdated, indeed almost Victorian. It is also shown in the same chapter that the feedback of information from earlier migrants to their countries of origin was less than adequate for a full and accurate picture of life in Britain.

14

TRAINING

London Transport provides training for all recruits to the grades with which we were concerned in this study. When staff are promoted or upgraded, it is again usually necessary for them to complete successfully a training course and test.[1] Clearly, the relative success of the coloured immigrant groups in these training courses could be an important variable affecting their occupational distribution within the organization. Moreover, our early discussions with L.T.B. officials indicated that it was widely believed that the failure rates of coloured immigrants were significantly higher than those of native-born Britons, though later there proved to be less comparative data available than we had hoped. Such figures as were available, however, confirmed these general impressions.

For these reasons, it appeared vital to include training in the study. Did the training of coloured immigrants present particular problems? Did immigrant trainees experience difficulties which were not shared by native-born trainees? If the answers to these questions were 'yes', what were these problems?

In our attempt to find some answers, we spent some time observing training sessions, interviewed training staff, obtained some data on success and failure rates for some training courses, and asked questions of our interview samples on their training experiences and difficulties.

I make no claim to any expertise on training *techniques*, but I can present and comment on the evidence which we were able to gather. A useful framework is to see training (a) as intended to teach technical skills, and (b) as a process of acculturation aimed at influencing behaviour and, possibly to a lesser extent, attitudes. I will examine the evidence from each department separately.

---

[1] The only relevant exception to this rule is the Permanent Way Department. See Chapter 11.

CENTRAL BUSES

Training of Central Bus staff was carried out at the Training Centre at Chiswick.[1] I will be concerned in this section with the training of drivers and conductors, by far the largest task of the Centre. Recruit bus drivers were required to have had previous driving experience. The Centre also trained for driving duties conductors who were in the Board's service. These conductors may have had driving experience, but this was not a required qualification.[2] Additionally, some garage staff, such as fitters and cleaners, were also taught driving. Existing bus drivers were 'type' trained for new or unfamiliar vehicles, for example single-deck or front-loading buses.

Direct entry drivers, that is those with driving experience and holding an M.O.T. licence, are given a minimum of nine days' training. Conductors being trained as drivers are taught for a minimum of twenty-one days. In both cases there is some flexibility, but the prevailing view of the senior instructors appeared to be that when the minimum training time had been completed it was possible to assess whether or not a trainee would 'make a bus driver'. Up to *about* twenty-five days' training is allowed for training conductors as drivers, and up to about twelve days' training for direct entry drivers.

The driving potentialities of conductors are assessed by means of a simulator. In essence this consists of a steering wheel and accelerator, together with a rear-projected screen showing a 'street scene' which responds to movements of the wheel and accelerator. In so far as it is intended to assess steering wheel control, it appeared not un-realistic, but it must be emphasized that assessments of driving skill and potentialities are essentially subjective on the part of the

[1] An exception to this was that some conductor training was carried out at divisional offices or at garages, if the number of trainees from one locality made this feasible. The training given was in every respect similar to that at Chiswick.

[2] By agreement between the L.T.B. and the T.G.W.U., not more than 80 per cent of trainee drivers are new recruits, the remainder are taken from the Board's conductors. With the conversion of the bus fleet to one-man operation, the training of conductors as drivers is likely to become an increasing part of the Centre's task. In 1968, L.T.B. commissioned a study of the problems of retraining conductors as drivers by the Industrial Training Research Unit of University College, London. See London Transport Board, *Annual Report and Accounts, 1968* (London, H.M.S.O., 1969), p. 38. See also M. A. Pearn, 'The Industrial Training Research Unit', *Race Today* (Vol. 4, No. 2, February 1972), pp. 63–4, for a report on the work of the I.T.R.U. Its conclusions on the training problems of coloured immigrants accord closely with my own.

instructor. Normally up to three men each day 'drive' the simulator, so a trainee can expect to spend one-third of a day 'at the wheel'.[1]

Trainees are assigned to one of three categories on the strength of their simulator performance: those whom it is predicted could never be successfully trained as bus drivers, those regarded as possible drivers, and those regarded as doubtful. Conductors in the first category are rejected; those in the possible category are accepted for training, but they may have to wait a few months before this begins. As a check on the simulator assessments, 10 per cent of conductors in the doubtful category were accepted and trained, but we were told that up to the time of our visit in 1967 none had qualified as drivers.[2] Should a conductor rejected as doubtful then pass the M.O.T. test, he can return for another simulator assessment.

The buses used for training purposes are normal service types, the only modification made is the removal of the partition between the driving cab and the lower deck so that the instructor may instruct and apply the hand brake if he deems this necessary. The ideal number of trainees per bus, we were told, is three: one driving, one listening to the instructor's comments, and one on the platform to keep off potential passengers. On occasions, though, the number of trainees per bus has been up to seven, though this is most likely to happen in 'type' training. Instructors operate from garages as near as possible to those the trainees will work from on completion of their training. Familiarity with the routes they will work is considered important. Direct entry drivers train with other direct entry drivers, conductor trainees with other conductors.

The aims of this training are, first, to teach the skills of *bus* driving. London Transport buses differ from other commercial vehicles in that, for instance, they have pre-selector gear mechanisms or fully automatic transmission. The skills of bus driving differ, too, from those of other vehicles in that much bus work is 'nearside' work. The bus driver is expected to care for passenger safety and comfort, and here the training is intended not only to teach skills but also to influence behaviour and attitudes towards passengers.

The driving instructors all have experience as L.T.B. drivers. Their appointments are permanent; in contrast to the Railway Operating instructors, they are not *expected* to move on to other appointments,[3] though some do achieve promotion.

---

[1] Simulator assessments are accepted by the T.G.W.U.
[2] This practice was experimental and has since been discontinued.
[3] See below, p. 283.

As was noted earlier, there were less hard data available to us on success and failure rates than we had hoped. It was *estimated* that about one-third of direct entry driver applicants were rejected after their initial tests. No information was available on the comparative rejection rates of native and coloured applicants. The 'pass' rate for direct entry drivers was, we were told, usually in the 80 to 85 per cent range. Again there was no breakdown which distinguished between white native and coloured immigrant trainees. Nor were figures available to us on the rejection rates of the simulator. There were, however, data available on the comparative success and failure rates of trainee drivers who were in service as conductors, and these are shown in Table 14.1.

TABLE 14.1
Test Performance of Conductors Trained as Drivers, 1966, in Percentages*

	White†	Coloured	White and coloured
Passed driving course	50	18	38
Failed or discontinued driving course	50	82	62
(Number)	(524)	(294)	(818)

* Source: L.T.B. Training Centre, Chiswick.

† A simple 'white-coloured' dichotomy was used for these records. It can be assumed that most, if not all, those regarded as coloured were immigrants; and most of the whites were natives, though the latter possibly included Irish and other immigrants. This probably corresponds very closely to our 'native-immigrant' breakdowns.

The success rate of the coloured conductors was far below that of their white fellow-trainees. We do not know why any of the trainees were failed, nor do we know the relative numbers whose training was discontinued. A further unknown is the number in each group who had previous driving experience and held M.O.T. driving licences. In terms of the numbers accepted for training, the coloured conductors were slightly over-represented: they comprised 36 per cent of the trainee drivers, but 30 per cent of the total of *male* conductors.[1] I do not know the relative rejection rates of coloured and white conductors applying for driver training. It is likely that the coloured staff are over-represented in the younger

[1] See Chapter 4.

age groups who are possibly most likely to apply for driver training, but again no data were available.

In considering possible reasons why there was such a difference in the success rates of white and coloured conductors in driver training, it is useful to draw on our interview material. We asked our samples which training courses they had attended; whether they had experienced any difficulties on these courses; and how they thought the training could be improved. The data from these questions are, though, not completely reliable: self-esteem is probably important here and some were reluctant to admit that *they* had experienced any difficulties. This perceived tendency was probably more widespread amongst the immigrant than the native interviewees. On the other hand, some who had failed a training course said that the training could not be improved. The suggestions made to improve the training courses were related to the perceived difficulties. Thus if the course was said to be too short, the suggestion was that it should be longer. The answers to these questions have therefore been combined, and are summarized in Table 14.2.

TABLE 14.2
Training Difficulties Reported by Busmen, in Percentages.*

	Native	Immigrant
No difficulties	93	70
Failed driving course once	7	25
Failed driving course twice	—	3
Course too short/not enough road training	7	19
Harsh/unhelpful instructors	—	10
Nervous during test	—	4
Two or more instructors confusing	—	3
Other answers	2	3
No answer	3	—
(Sample)	(59)	(67)

* These answers are from the male samples only. The 'no difficulties' category applies to training for drivers *and* conductors, as some had been trained for both grades, but the difficulties listed apply only to training for driving. Difficulties reported in conductor training are discussed below. More than one answer was recorded and the percentage totals may therefore exceed 100.

The table must be interpreted with caution as far more of the immigrant conductors wished to be drivers,[1] far more had attempted

[1] See Chapter 6.

the driving course, and they were therefore more at risk of possible failure. (Most of those who had failed the driving course were conductors; a few had taken the course again and become drivers.) The difference in the length of service patterns, too, is likely to be relevant, in that the training experience of the immigrants is on average more recent and this possibly results in a greater recall of difficulties. It is, then, the general over-all difference between the samples that is important, rather than any precise distinctions. This general difference is, however, broadly consistent with that shown in Table 14.1.

The most frequent criticisms made, and they came mostly from the immigrants, were that the course was too short or that there was not enough road training. Both amount to the same thing: the trainees did not spend long enough at the wheel. These criticisms came mostly, but not exclusively, from those conductors who had failed the driving course.

The other major target of criticism was the behaviour of the instructors: they were thought to be 'too harsh'; 'they shout at you'; they were 'not helpful'.

There are some nice instructors, but some are like sergeant majors: they shout at you and I could never do anything right. . . . I've been told that the instructor is *told* to shout at you to see if you can stand the pressure. [West Indian Conductor.]

Some instructors are unhelpful. I went out with one and he never said a thing all day: so I didn't know whether I was [doing] right or wrong. [West Indian Driver.]

A few of the immigrants said they were nervous when taking a driving test, and others that having more than one instructor was confusing because they contradicted one another.[1]

A number of busmen, mostly coloured immigrants, clearly were critical of the driving instruction they had received. On the other hand, one or two conductors who had failed the driving course said it could not be improved.

There was not a complete consensus amongst the Training Centre staff we met on why the failure rate for coloured immigrant conductors training for driving was far higher than that for white natives. Nor can I, on the basis of this rather limited study, adequately explain why this was so, and it is to be hoped that the University

[1] The Training Centre attempts, but does not always find it possible, to ensure that each trainee has only one instructor.

College study will throw more light on the subject. Any conclusions offered are then tentative.

Cultural differences between instructors and immigrant trainees appeared to pose a problem for communicating with one another. There are differences of accent, which can be a problem if either speaks quickly. There is also a problem of colloquial expressions: one illustration given was of the use of the term 'look out!' To most native Britons it implies a warning; some West Indians were said to interpret it literally.

The West Indians' behaviour towards those in authority—that is, the instructors—was thought to pose problems. They have, we were told, a 'great desire to do things correctly and to please, and there is a desire to establish a behaviour pattern of what to do in a given situation'. The problem here, it was said, was that few driving situations are ever identical. Related to this was a perceived over-cautiousness on the part of some West Indian trainees when driving in traffic. Some of those interviewed mentioned that they had been told they were too cautious.

A London bus is said by many drivers with wide experience to be 'easy' to drive, in the sense of controlling its movements. The environment in which it is driven is, though, often one of dense traffic. There is probably an element of strangeness here for the immigrants, though this would presumably decline the longer they have been in Britain. This *relative* unfamiliarity with intense traffic is probably one factor which results in the perceived over-cautiousness of some. The reported harshness of some instructors in this context is probably unhelpful. What constitutes shouting is, of course, largely a matter of perception.

It may be that a somewhat longer training programme, by providing more time at the wheel, would compensate for some of the handicaps which some immigrants appear to suffer.[1] It will be remembered that this was the most frequent criticism made by ex-trainees, and there is some evidence to support this view. A group of garage staff, mostly West Indians, had all spent some time on the driving course, but all had been rejected after their progress had been assessed, and their training was discontinued. Each was then given one hour's individual tuition each day. (How long this training lasted is not known.) Of the ten men in the group, seven eventually passed as drivers. The experiment, though limited, does

[1] It has been pointed out to me that the criticism that a training programme is too short is one commonly made against many types of training courses.

suggest that it is possible to achieve higher 'pass' rates amongst immigrant trainees than had been attained.

Assessments of driving skills and performances, it must be re-emphasized, are essentially subjective on the part of the assessor. It may be that, intentionally or unintentionally, some instructors are more likely to fail a coloured than a white trainee. It may be, too, that some are less sympathetic or helpful to coloured than to white trainees. I have no evidence on this either way, but it is a possibility that cannot be ruled out. The reader will remember that some of the trainees quoted took care to distinguish between instructors. That some were seen as fair by coloured busmen is supported, too, by the following comment, from a West Indian driver who had previously applied *ten* times—unsuccessfully—for employment with L.T.B.:

I was sent to Chiswick for a test on the eleventh attempt, but I failed. On the twelfth attempt I went to Chiswick, saw the instructor who had previously tested me and he passed me to another instructor for a test. This was very fair.

Turning to the conductors, their training programme was as follows. Three days were spent at Chiswick, mostly in classroom learning. This covered a wide range of topics: schedules, tickets, the use of ticket machines, time cards, cash total sheets, the calculation of fares, bell signals, paying in cash, and so on. In other words, trainees were taught the uses of various documents, how to handle equipment, and some aspects of conductors' behaviour. The morning of the third day was spent playing the role of a conductor on a bus, driven by trainee drivers. Additionally, they were instructed on the duties of inspectors and the behaviour expected of conductors when they meet inspectors.

Five days were then spent on road training. This was done at the garages from which they would be working and, as far as possible, on the routes they would work when in service. For road training they were assigned to a 'conductor instructor': that is, a conductor who was paid a few shillings a day extra when he had a trainee with him. Conductor instructors were given one day's briefing on their training duties, but at the time of our study changes in the system were being considered. Whilst with the conductor instructor, the trainee carried out a conductor's duties; the instructor was available on the platform both to assist and advise him.

The final two days were spent at Chiswick, again in classroom learning. The instructors attempted to draw on the trainees' road experience, particularly of passengers' behaviour. The Central Buses *Rule Book* was used here. There was also more instruction on documents, procedures for dealing with lost property, and so on. Finally, instruction was given on conductors' behaviour in emergencies: accidents, bad weather, traffic diversions, and so on.

At the end of their training, trainees were given a verbal and practical test, that is, they were questioned on a conductor's duties in an interview situation. The test was to that extent a subjective assessment by the instructors. Similarly with the practical part of the test: the use of a ticket issuing machine, the completion of cash total sheets, and so on. The failure rate for conductors was low: 1 or 2 per cent. This rate has at times been higher for native than for immigrant trainees. This possibly reflects the higher standard that, intentionally or not, has at times been required of coloured immigrant recruits.[1] It possibly reflects, too, the self-selection by applicants: coloured applicants were thought to be often better than their white native counterparts, owing, most probably, to job discrimination elsewhere.

The only provision made for any training needs peculiar to the coloured immigrants has been for those conductors recruited in the Caribbean. They received three days' extra training: two on the geography of London; one on British currency and role-playing on a bus.

Training staff identified additional handicaps of the coloured immigrant trainees—and these were said to apply almost exclusively to direct recruits: problems of communication, difficulties with British currency, and poor knowledge of slang expressions particularly. The communications problem was said to arise largely from differences of accents. Barbados has used a decimal currency for a number of years, and initially there were difficulties over £.s.d.[2] The Barbados direct recruits were also unfamiliar with slang terms for coins: 'tanner', 'bob', and so on. Confusion could arise, too, when, for instance, a passenger tendered a half-crown and two pence for an eightpenny fare, but this was soon overcome. The pace of learning of direct recruits was said to be slower than that of the natives at the beginning of the course, but in the words of one instructor, 'they soon speed up'.

[1] See Chapter 12.
[2] See Chapter 13 on pre-recruitment training in Barbados. (This was, of course, before decimalization in Britain.)

Our interview data tend to confirm these opinions, with the reservation that problems over British currency, for example, were not confined to direct recruits. The only difficulties reported by any number concerned the use of British currency, the completion of documentary returns such as cash total sheets, and the use of a ticket machine. Such difficulties were reported by 12 per cent of the immigrant sample, and proportionately more by the women conductors.[1]

Other criticisms, made by small numbers of immigrants and to a lesser extent natives, were that the training course was too short, that there was not enough practical training, or that generally it was inadequate or misleading.

The time could be extended—there is a lot to learn. But you can't do the job as they tell you: you'd never move the bus. [West Indian Conductor.]

It is misleading—it is not as they tell you ... When you get out on the road you feel you have had no training at all. [West Indian Woman Conductor.]

The comment that 'you'd never move the bus' refers to the divergence between practice and the *Rules*. For example, to comply with the *Rules*, conductors should give the starting signal at compulsory stops from the platform only. Similarly, conductors are instructed to ask the passenger his destination and if necessary his boarding point before issuing a ticket. Most will though issue a ticket for the *value* requested. Most, clearly do not completely comply with the *Rules* and it is doubtful if these requirements are compatible with the complete collection of fares on a large, fully loaded bus.[2] In these and other ways practice departs from what is taught.

The training programme is intended to impart a great deal of *information* in a comparatively short space of time. Much of this is concerned with documentary returns and with formal procedures. A comparison of the training given to conductors and railway trainees is open to the objection that the skills of instructors vary somewhat; but, with this reservation, comparisons can be made. In railway training much more use was made of duplicated prepared material and of the blackboard. Trainees were issued with notebooks, and used them. Perhaps more important, there was far more attempt to *involve* the class in the training sessions, with constant

[1] As a number of the drivers had been trained as conductors this 12 per cent is of the total sample of 78.

[2] See Chapter 4.

questioning of individuals. By contrast, the conductors' classroom training was more of a lecture presentation. With this type of training it may well be that much of the information given is not retained.

For all trainees there is an element of strangeness in the tasks they are required to learn in a short space of time. The immigrant, particularly if he is a recent arrival, suffers the handicap that many other aspects of the environment in which he works are also strange to him. Hence the view that 'when you get out on the road you feel you've had no training at all'. Additionally, the coloured conductor is likely to meet more difficulties from passengers than is his white native colleague,[1] which has direct bearing on our next consideration: the teaching of social skills.

In the training programme there is some attempt to influence attitudes and to inculcate the value that 'the passenger is always— or nearly always—right'. In other words, a service orientation is emphasized. The skills of a conductor in his interactions with passengers, particularly those who are in any way difficult, are largely social skills. Little or no attempt is made to teach these skills, and this was seen as a defect by a few of the coloured immigrants. They wanted more guidance on action to take in difficult situations. The conductor can, by the use of his social skills, extricate himself from *some* difficult situations with passengers, and it may be that more instruction in these techniques would reduce the amount of overt passenger-conductor conflict.

In two respects, then, the coloured immigrants suffer some handicap. First there is their relative lack of familiarity with, for example, British coinage. Second, they are at a disadvantage in respect of passenger behaviour: there are a myriad of subtle cultural differences in cues, the perception of cues, and so on. Yet precisely because he is a coloured immigrant the conductor is likely to encounter more difficulties with passengers. Initially at least, he is less well equipped to handle them than is his native colleague.

RAILWAY OPERATING
The Railway Training Centre, located at White City, is housed in modern buildings. Its equipment is comprehensive, including a simulated motorman's cab, rail car bodies, a station platform, and a booking-office, together with various technical apparatus. The

[1] See Chapter 6.

average weekly intake to the Centre was seventy to eighty trainees; its capacity exceeded two hundred.

The Centre provides a wide variety of courses; most combine formal training in the classroom with practical training at a station, depot, or signal box, as appropriate. In the formal classroom training, the lesson method is used: that is, the instructor attempts to *involve* the trainees, by constantly questioning them and by, for example, gradually building up a diagram on a blackboard with their participation: 'where should the next component be placed, and why?' (If there is one word which symbolizes the work of the Centre it is 'why'.) Some use is made of duplicated notes, but mostly trainees are expected to take their own.

The length of training courses varies widely. For example, the stationmen's course lasts a total of eleven days: three days of formal training, six at a station, followed by two more days of formal training. For practical training, a number of stations situated in Central and West London are used. The course for guards lasts a total of seventeen days: ten days of formal instruction, two spent on a train working as a guard—along with a qualified guard, four days working with a motorman,[1] one day of revision at the Training Centre. (A trainee *recruited* to the guard grade has to complete both the stationman's and the guard's training courses.)

Both oral and written examinations are used for assessing trainees at the completion of their training. Stationmen are not formally examined; they are usually asked a number of questions. The aim here is to ensure that they are competent to carry out their duties with safety and particularly that they know what to do in an emergency. Guards are orally examined for a period lasting up to one day. Usually two or three are examined together in an informal discussion with an instructor. The examination has some learning content in that the trainee probably gains something from the discussion. Written examinations, as used, for example, for assessing station foremen's knowledge of rules and regulations, may last up to a day and a half. Generally, the more senior the grade for which staff are being trained, the longer the examination. Trainees are not usually assessed by their own instructors; senior staff are usually examined by the senior instructors.

The details of each training course or its method of examination need not concern us much. The important point is that there is a large subjective element in the assessment methods used, particularly

---

[1] Guards are expected to be able to move a train in an emergency.

in the informal oral examinations.[1] It is argued by the Training Centre staff that there is an *accepted* 'standard of competence' throughout the Department, and this is maintained by a number of factors. Periodic checks are made of the pass rates of the examiners, and they tend to be fairly similar. There is a constant interchange of ideas and information between the instructors. Some assessments of trainees are made by divisional inspectors.

The instructors were all railwaymen. They were expected to apply for other posts in the Railway Operating Department after they had held an instructor's post for three years,[2] though, as they may have acted as instructors for up to three years before being given a substantive appointment, the total time spent at the Centre could be as long as six years. This movement of staff in and out of the Training Centre does, it is argued by some, assist in preserving the accepted standard of competence in the Department; also it probably ensures that the training staff keep in touch with developments in the Department, and emphasizes that they are railwaymen rather than professional instructors. The Training Centre is an avenue of rapid promotion: instructors recruited from amongst the motormen or booking-office clerks, for example, may be appointed to senior supervisory posts on completion of their instruction period, and many senior supervisors and managers in the Department are ex-instructors.[3] Instructors who do not achieve promotion revert to their former grades on completion of their training appointments.

Much of the work of the Training Centre is, of course, directed to teaching technical expertise. There is, though, a considerable emphasis on influencing behaviour and attitudes in non-technical areas. With new recruits the *service* orientation of the undertaking is underlined: the importance of courtesy, punctuality, smartness, and so on. Punctual attendance at training sessions is required, and lateness is treated as quite a serious matter. Some training is carried out on Saturdays. In these ways the training staff attempt to quickly socialize the new entrants in the norms of railway work. Similarly, there is a considerable emphasis on safety: that railway tracks and equipment are potentially very dangerous.

Turning to the Centre's experiences of native and immigrant

---

[1] I am not, of course, arguing that written examinations are objective.

[2] This has since been increased to five years.

[3] It is thus *possible* to bypass the seniority requirements for promotion, as such appointments are sometimes to grades for which the seniority rules do not apply.

trainees, there were far less comparative data available than we had hoped. As we had found elsewhere in the Railway Operating Department, there was an almost rigid insistence on treating native and immigrant railwaymen equally, which in practice appeared to mean *similarly*. As a complement to this approach, there was an insistence on treating individuals as individuals with differing training needs, but these needs were not seen to be related to ethnic origins. Again we found this line of thinking, coupled with a reluctance to generalize about groups, elsewhere in the Department.

The only difference in the training programmes which related to ethnic origins was that the Barbadian direct recruits were given a few days extra, mostly on the geography of London. The training course for new entrants, it was argued, assumed no previous knowledge of railways or railway work. There was therefore no need to cater specifically for the needs of immigrants: theirs did not differ from those of other trainees. This training course did indeed begin at an elementary level by providing basic information about railways. If, though, it assumed no previous knowledge of railways, it can be argued that the trainee with some knowledge has an advantage which he possibly retains throughout his training.

The only generalization applied to the immigrant trainees by the Training Centre's staff was that they were thought to be prone to 'parrot learning': that is, they would learn and could recite a rule or a procedure to deal with a given symptom of equipment failure, for example, but without understanding *why* the rule or the procedure specified a certain course of action. With this generalization, though, there were qualifications: it was thought to apply to Asians more than West Indians, and native Britons were by no means immune. It was thought, too, that there was a communications problem with *some* immigrants.

Largely perhaps as a result of this rejection of group differences, there were very few figures available on comparative success and failure rates. It is possible, too, that those in the Railway Operating Department who did not wish coloured immigrants to be discriminated against were reluctant to have comparative statistics collected; some saw the compiling of such statistics as *in itself* a discriminatory act.

The pass rate of coloured immigrant motormen was said to be very similar to that of white natives: 57 per cent and 65 per cent, respectively.[1] It was thought, too, that the difference in the pass

---

[1] It was not clear which period of time these figures referred to.

rates had narrowed over the previous few years. Assuming that coloured immigrants are handicapped in training in relation to their white native colleagues, then this narrowing is explicable in terms of the greater length of time that more recent trainees are likely to have spent in England, compared with earlier trainees.[1] Possibly, too, the training staff have become more skilled in teaching coloured immigrants.

The only comprehensive comparative figures on pass and failure rates available to us were those for eight one-week intakes of direct recruit guards in 1967. These are shown in Table 14.3.

TABLE 14.3.
*Pass and Failure Rates of Direct Recruit Guards, in Percentages.**

Results	White†	Coloured
Completed and passed training course	53	64
Withdrew before completing training course	29 ⎫ 47	2 ⎫ 35
Completed but failed training course	18 ⎭	33 ⎭
(Number)	(160)	(42)

* Source: Railway Training Centre.
† A simple white-coloured dichotomy was used for these figures. See note to Table 14.1 above.

It will be seen that both the pass and failure rates of the coloured trainees were higher than those of the white trainees—the failure rate appreciably so. The most significant difference is, though, in the relative numbers who withdrew before completing the course. It is not known how many of these resigned from the Board's service and how many opted to become stationmen. Nor do I know why they withdrew from the guards' training course.

There are two possible explanations for the difference in with-drawal rates. Some may have decided that railway work was not for them either in terms of the work task or the hours of duty. One variable here is discrimination in the outside employment market: white natives who withdrew from training and resigned would

[1] This appeared to be the explanation accepted by the Training Centre's staff.

have found less difficulty in obtaining comparable employment than would their coloured colleagues.

A second possible explanation lies in the practices adopted in recruitment. There have been attempts at times to slow down the rate of build-up of the coloured immigrant part of the Department's workforce.[1] (In 1965, coloured guards comprised 50 per cent of the total.[2]) In so far as this was achieved, it resulted from the greater selectivity of recruitment staff in their engagement of coloured applicants.[3] *By the selection criteria* the coloured direct recruit guard trainees were, then, better than their white native colleagues, or, more accurately, the worst of the coloured recruits were better than the worst of the white recruits. If the selection process is at all related to subsequent success or failure in the training course—and I have no evidence either way—then a higher standard of recruitment should be reflected in a greater likelihood of trainees passing the training course. This appears to have happened: as I have noted, I do not know why such a relatively large number of white trainees withdrew, but it is possible that some decided that they were unlikely to complete the training course successfully.

The other source of information on training was the interview material. For reasons given above,[4] these data cannot be regarded as completely reliable, but are nevertheless indicative of the differences in training experiences of white native and coloured immigrant railwaymen. Table 14.4 summarizes the difficulties reported. (See p. 287.)

One obvious drawback to this type of comparative analysis is that it is not practical to control for the differing periods of time that have elapsed since these railwaymen were at the Training Centre, and this is likely to be a variable in the recall of training experiences. However, when the data for the native railwaymen with under fifteen years' service were analysed separately, a pattern very similar to that of the total native sample emerged, with marginally more difficulties and failures reported. (The under-fifteen years' service groups were chosen to match the length of service pattern of the immigrants.)

A further defect is that almost all of those interviewed had at least passed one training course, the trainmen possibly two or three. It tells us nothing about those who withdraw from or fail training courses and subsequently—or consequently—resign. The samples of

[1] See Chapter 7.   [2] See Chapter 7.
[3] See Chapter 12 on recruitment procedures.   [4] See p. 275.

TABLE 14.4.
Training Difficulties Reported by Operating Railwaymen,* in Percentages.

Type of difficulty	Native		Immigrant	
	Trainmen	Station staff	Trainmen	Station staff
No difficulties	79	50	58	17
Failed training course once	4	39	10	65
Failed training course twice	—	—	2	4
Training course too short	6	30	23	43
Technical information difficult to understand	8	11	23	22
Not enough practical training	4	6	23	—
Instructors unhelpful/two or more instructors disagreed	—	—	5	9
Test/exam problems	—	—	5	4
Other answers	2	6	5	4
No answer	6	6	2	4
(Sample)	(53)	(18)	(60)	(23)

* These answers are from the males samples only, as there was no direct line of promotion for women above Ticket Collector I. The patterns of answers from the female samples were in fact very similar to each other: few in either group reported any difficulties. The 'no answer' category included one or two of the station staff who said they had had no formal training. More than one answer was recorded and the percentage totals may therefore exceed 100.

station staff are small, but it is the broad over-all differences that are of interest, rather than the minute detail.

With these reservations, the data are still valuable for the over-all pattern they reveal. Across both samples it was the station staff rather than the trainmen who were more likely to report difficulties or that they had failed. This difference is explicable in terms of the promotion structure: most of those station staff who had failed had done so on the guards' course. A few had been direct recruits to the guard or station foremen grade and on failing the training course became stationmen.

Between the samples, the immigrants were both more likely than the natives to report that they had failed a training course and had experienced difficulties in training. The three main areas of criticism were that: training courses were too short; technical information was difficult to understand and learn; there was not enough practical training. A few mentioned difficulties experienced in the tests or examinations; some, again few in number, criticized the instructing staff for being unhelpful or inconsistent. (The numbers in these latter groups were small.) The criticisms made can be illustrated from the interview material. First, the criticism that the training courses were too short:

Two weeks is not long enough to learn it all—you cram it in without thinking. [West Indian Motorman.]

They are doing their best, but we—from the West Indies—come from a country without railways and should have longer. [West Indian Guard.]

That many West Indians had 'never seen a railway' before they arrived in England was a recurring theme, mentioned in other contexts as well:

Yes, the technical side of it at first [was difficult]. I'd never seen a train before I came here. [West Indian Motorman.]

You wouldn't call it difficult if you were mechanically minded. The brakes got me most—rules and regulations were not too bad ... they explain it clearly, but some minds don't work as fast as others. [U.K. Stationman who had failed Guards' course.]

It will be noted that difficulties were not confined to the coloured immigrant trainees. Criticisms were seldom complete: some who had failed said that 'they explain it clearly', or 'they do their best'. The efforts of the instructing staff were appreciated.

The last group of answers given by any number all related to a perceived emphasis on teaching theory at the cost of the practical.

It is all blackboard and notebooks, but in practice it is different. They could give you a longer spell as practical: on the job. [U.K. Station Foreman.]

Those immigrant trainmen who wanted more practical training were seldom very explicit, though one or two would have preferred more time on train equipment and less on rules and regulations. Most who spoke of a need for more practical training were motormen, or guards who had failed the motormen's course.

Finally, there were a few who complained of differences between two instructors or between instructor and examiner, or had difficulties in the test or examination.

The examination is such that they condemn any man on the oral exam. It should be more of a written exam ... [The training] is very nicely organized, but the examination should be written: then there would be *proof* if you were right or wrong. [Pakistani Ticket Collector who had failed Guards' course.]

There is perhaps a hint in this quotation at discrimination by the examiners, but this was atypical of most opinions expressed on the Training Centre staff. Far more typical was the comment of a West Indian stationman who had failed the guards' course:

They do their best as far as *we* [West Indians] are concerned.

This does not deny that West Indians who had never seen a railway before they came to the U.K. had particular problems. It does mean that most of the immigrants did not indicate any perception of discrimination by the Training Centre's instructors, and were more likely to praise them.

One other aspect of railway training is worthy of mention at this point: the voluntary classes provided by the Training Centre. Throughout the winter months a number of evening classes are run. They are held fortnightly but repeated in the intervening week— that is, the same class is held on two consecutive weeks—to ensure that staff are always able to attend each class on one of the two occasions on which it is held. Most are rostered to work a week of 'earlies' followed by a week of 'lates'. These courses are intended both for those seeking promotion and those wishing to improve their proficiency in their own grade. They are intended to supplement the full-time training courses, and not as a substitute for them. A number of subjects are covered, for example, train equipment, rules and regulations, stationmasters' responsibilities. We asked our interview samples if they had attended any of these classes; Table 14.5 shows the answers given. (See p. 290.)

Proportionately more immigrants than natives had commenced voluntary classes. I do not know how many of either group completed their courses. Many railwaymen achieve promotion during the course and some apparently then abandon it.

The data from our interview samples indicate that coloured immigrants were both more likely to experience difficulties in their training and to fail on completing the course. The information from the Training Centre on direct recruit guards is not completely consistent with our interview data: it is complicated by the high withdrawal figure amongst the white trainees, but it does show a higher failure rate for the coloured trainees amongst those who completed the course. It may be, too, that these figures are atypical

TABLE 14.5.

Attendance at Railway Operating Voluntary Classes, in Percentages.

	Native	Immigrant
Had not attended voluntary classes	65	55
Had attended voluntary classes	24	30
Had attended but had not completed course	11	13
No answer	—	1
(Sample)	(71)	(83)

* These answers are from the male samples only: none of the women in either sample had attended voluntary classes. The figures for those who had commenced but not completed a course of voluntary classes may understate the numbers who belong in this category, as we asked if they had 'attended' any of the classes and not if they had completed a course. Those in the 'not completed' category volunteered this information.

of most training courses: the hypothesis that these trainees joined when there was a restriction on the number of coloured staff recruited is a tenable one.

Most of the coloured railwaymen in the Department were West Indian, and whilst there is a strong English orientation in the education and culture of the English-speaking West Indies, it is likely that cultural differences, in perception and so on, put the West Indian trainee at a disadvantage compared with his native British counterpart. Apart, perhaps, from the Anglo-Asians, immigrants from other New Commonwealth countries are likely to be at a greater disadvantage than the West Indians. These differences do diminish the longer the coloured immigrant stays in Britain, and the handicap is reduced. It may well be, too, that cultural differences put the immigrant at a disadvantage in an oral test: possibly it is more difficult for him to convince an examiner that he is 'good enough' to be a motorman, guard, or other railwayman. I have no direct evidence on this, but it is a tenable hypothesis. There is a large area of subjectivity in the assessment procedures used. It is also possible that some examiners discriminated *deliberately*, but I have no evidence to lead me to suppose that they did and it was seldom hinted at by the railwaymen interviewed. Generally, the whole question of cultural differences as variables in learning—amongst adults as well as children—appears to merit further study.

A further handicap, confined largely or exclusively to those West

Indians from the smaller islands, including Barbados, is that many had never seen a railway before they arrived in Britain. The recruits' training courses do begin at a basic elementary level and to this extent assume no previous knowledge of railways. The point here, though, is that the immigrant, and most obviously the newly arrived immigrant, is in a society with many 'strange' aspects— railways constitute one additional area of strangeness.

The difficulties reported by the immigrant railwaymen, and their criticisms, were largely confined to three areas: training courses were too short, the understanding of various technical aspects presented problems, and, related to this, there was not enough practical training. It does not, of course, follow that a longer train- ing programme would necessarily increase the pass rate, or that better railwaymen would emerge from such a training course. Claiming no expertise in training techniques, I cannot comment on the suggestion that the courses should have a more practical slant. Nor do I know if this is possible, given the skills which it is thought necessary for railwaymen to possess. It may be, though, that greater use could be made of equipment to supplement or possibly partly substitute for blackboard teaching. Many trainees—native as much as immigrant—have presumably had few occasions for taking notes and drawing diagrams since they left school and their skills in these tasks are probably not very great.

In the training sessions observed, it was not obvious that the coloured immigrants experienced any more difficulties than the other trainees on most of the topics covered. The area in which such difficulties were apparent, and they were shared equally by immigrants from Ireland, was that of the geography of London. There was, for example, some confusion over the meaning of the term 'the City' of London. This is not, though, the most vital part of the training programme, nor did the railwaymen interviewed see it as a pressing problem. As a reservation here it ought to be added that the time available permitted us to observe relatively few training sessions. Viewing the training sessions from the standpoint of *participant* observers, the defect most readily apparent to us was the construction of blackboard diagrams: they could with advantage have been larger and hence more clearly understood.

The most important conclusion to emerge from this analysis is, then, that the learning problems experienced by the immigrants appear to be somewhat different from those of the natives and it may well be that the emphasis on equality obscures this. Equality would in any case require a recognition of these different problems, so that ethnic differences were not variables in the pass and failure rates.

This analysis has been largely concerned with the teaching of the skills of railway operations. There is, though, some attempt to influence attitudes and behaviour: for example, punctual attendance, the importance of time. I do not know how effective this is for the simple reason that I know nothing about the attitudes of the immigrants before they begin their training. When exploring the attitudes of native and immigrant railwaymen to various aspects of their employment, however, it was clear that the similarities between the two groups were more prominent than the differences, though there were some differences of emphasis.

PERMANENT WAY

Training was given to new recruits to the relayer and lengthman grades. The training course, of two weeks' duration, was held in the School located at Neasden. Its maximum capacity was sixteen trainees and the average number was ten to twelve.

The main emphasis of the training course was on teaching 'working with safety' on the track, including, for instance, the use of tools. There was some practical training provided in the technical skills of permanent-way work, both in the classroom and on the track. The former included, for example, the assembly of rail joints, the latter a wide variety of tasks: handling sleepers, rails, and so on. Given this strong emphasis on safety, there was little possibility of a trainee failing the course in the usual sense of the word. The only reason for which a trainee might be rejected was if he was thought not to have the physical ability for the heavy tasks performed by a platelayer.

The instructor thought that the abilities of the trainees varied widely, but ethnic origins were not seen as a variable in these differences.

Apart from a short visit to the training School, the other main sources of information on permanent-way training were the interview samples.

None of those who had been trained reported any difficulties in their training. Criticisms, which came almost exclusively from the native platelayers, centred on a perceived lack of practical training and, to a lesser extent, on the amount of training given, with the implication that the training period ought to be longer.

Given that the main emphasis of the training was on safety, then any evaluation would have to consider factors such as accident records which are clearly outside the scope of this study. Similarly, I cannot comment on whether or not the content of the training course was the most appropriate for the needs of the trainees or the Department. It is clear, though, that the immigrants did not experience any more difficulties in training than did the natives. Over half of the immigrants interviewed were ex-tradesmen, and it may be that their skills were under-utilized in their present grades. This background possibly gave them some advantage over ex-labourers in learning some of the skills of permanent-way work.

As in the Railway Operating Department, evening classes are provided by Permanent Way. The course is for a certificate of the Permanent Way Institute. Six of our interviewees—three natives and three immigrants—had commenced this course; all but one, a West Indian, had given up. The numbers of staff who attended these classes appeared to vary quite widely from one year to the next and it was not possible to draw any conclusions on the relative participation of the coloured immigrant staff from the data available.

Training was of interest chiefly in relation to its effects on the occupational distribution of the immigrants. The evidence indicates that coloured immigrants both experienced more difficulties and were more likely to fail than white natives. The reasons for the different failure patterns are complex, and no one simple explanation is adequate. The data suggest that various aspects of strangeness are important. In many respects the immigrant *is* a stranger. The common language of the English-speaking immigrants obscures this. Important here is a large element of uncertainty in areas which natives take for granted. Given this uncertainty, then a need to establish a 'behaviour pattern' is explicable: it provides reference points, anchors, as it were, and the area of uncertainty is reduced. The courses were designed primarily for native trainees, but the needs of the immigrants differ somewhat. It is unlikely that equality of opportunity in occupational attainment will be achieved until there is a greater recognition of these different needs, and provision made for them.

15

IMMIGRANTS AND THE TRADE UNIONS

Some indices of absorption or pluralism in industry are the extent to which coloured immigrants adapt to the prevailing norms of the native workers in relation to trade unionism and how far they are accepted by both the native trade unionists and their unions—accepted, that is, as ordinary members and as representatives and officers.

Membership of the Transport and General Workers' Union was a condition of employment for drivers and conductors in Central Buses. At the time of our fieldwork, union membership for railwaymen was voluntary, but it later became a condition of employment for them also.[1] It was widely believed that most L.T.B. railwaymen were trade unionists, and the majority of those interviewed were.

Most of the rail operating staff had a choice of two unions: the National Union of Railwaymen (N.U.R.) and the Associated Society of Locomotive Engineers and Firemen (A.S.L.E.F.). The broad distinction between the two is that the N.U.R. is an industrial union and recruits all grades; A.S.L.E.F. recruits only footplate staff and those in the line of promotion to the footplate. On L.T.B. railways this category included most of the operating grades with which we were concerned.[2] For Permanent Way and female operating staff, the N.U.R. was the appropriate union. With two unions organizing the rail operating staff, competition between them to recruit and retain members was strong. Trade union membership was new to most of the immigrants: only 17 per cent of the men interviewed, and one woman, had been trade unionists in their countries of origin. Most of these were West Indians from Barbados or Jamaica.

The trade union membership of the railwaymen[3] is shown in Table 15.1. (See p. 295.)

[1] *Locomotive Journal* (Vol. 82, No. 12, December 1969), p. 286. Existing staff were given six months to decide which of two unions to join. (This was written before the 1971 Industrial Relations Act.)

[2] See Chapter 7, p. 128, for lines of promotion.

[3] The terms 'railwaymen' and 'busmen' also include women workers in these occupations, unless otherwise stated.

TABLE 15.1.
*Trade Union Membership of Railway Operating and Permanent Way Staff, in Percentages.**

Union	Native			Immigrant		
	Train-men	Station staff	Per. Way	Train-men	Station staff	Per. Way
N.U.R.	74	73	81	73	83	100
A.S.L.E.F.	21	7	—	27	6	—
Other/uncertain as to which union	—	7	14	—	—	—
Non-member	6	17	5	—	14	—
(Sample)	(53)	(30)	(21)	(60)	(36)	(21)

* That both station staff samples total more than 100 percent is due to the fact that one man in each sample belonged to both A.S.L.E.F. and N.U.R.

To the extent that they had joined a trade union, the immigrants had conformed to the norms of the majority of native workers and their proportionate membership over-all was slightly higher.

There are, of course, several levels of participation in trade union branch activity: attendance at branch meetings, joining in branch discussions, holding a branch office such as secretary, member of the branch committee, and so on.[1] To give an indication of attendance at branch meetings, we asked both samples: 'do you go to trade union branch meetings?' Those who said 'yes' were asked 'when did you last go?' Answers to this last question were often couched in terms of 'the last strike' or 'the last overtime ban' rather than 'x weeks ago'. Further questioning revealed whether attendance at branch meetings was regular, or rare and on special occasions, such as a threat of a strike. The answers to these questions are shown in Table 15.2. (See p. 296.)

The table shows that within every occupational group the immigrants were less likely to have been to a branch meeting than were their native colleagues. Over-all, the natives were more likely to report that they attended branch meetings regularly, but in all cases, apart, perhaps, from the trainmen, the figures were relatively

[1] T.G.W.U. branches are on a garage basis: one branch for each garage. A.S.L.E.F. branch membership is on a depot basis; that of the N.U.R. is based on residence.

TABLE 15.2.

Attendance at Trade Union Branch Meetings, in Percentages.

| | Native | | | | Immigrant | | | |
	Bus-men	Train-men	Station staff	Per. Way	Bus-men	Train-men	Station staff	Per. Way
Have never been	26	8	43	48	71	58	75	67
Go rarely/to special meetings	70	77	37	38	28	38	8	33
Go regularly	4	9	3	10	1	3	3	—
Non-member	—	6	17	5	—	—	14	—
(Sample)	(70)	(53)	(30)	(21)	(78)	(60)	(36)	(21)

small. (The 10 per cent of native Permanent Way men cannot be regarded as significant in view of the smallness of the sample.)

Levels of regular branch attendance that are broadly similar to those reported by the native workers have been found by researchers in other industries.[1] These studies have shown, too, a higher than average level of participation by craftsmen and 'workers in long-established heavy industries'.[2] If the trainmen are regarded as broadly analogous to craftsmen in other industries, then the data fit the pattern found elsewhere.

Comparing the attendance patterns of the N.U.R. and A.S.L.E.F. members—A.S.L.E.F. being very much a craft-oriented organization, in contrast to the industry-wide appeal of the N.U.R.—5 per cent of N.U.R. and 10 per cent of A.S.L.E.F. members claimed to attend their branches regularly. (These figures are for trainmen and male station staff, native and immigrant.) However, the A.S.L.E.F. sample is small and little significance can be attached to this difference. Moreover, the figures for those who had never been to a branch meeting were very similar for both A.S.L.E.F. and N.U.R. members.

I do not know why railwaymen choose to belong to one trade union rather than the other. This probably depends, partly at least, on the speed and persuasiveness of union activists who recruit new employees as members. The relative distribution between N.U.R.

[1] See, for example, Goldthorpe, *et al.*, p. 99; and the works cited by Goldthorpe and his colleagues.
[2] Ibid.

and A.S.L.E.F. of the native and immigrant railwaymen samples was broadly similar.[1]

The lack of motivation of most to participate actively in formal trade union activities was confirmed by two further questions. We asked all the union members if they had ever held any trade union office; those who had not were asked if they would like to. Table 15.3 summarizes the answers to these two questions.

TABLE 15.3.
Experiences of and Aspirations to Trade Union Office, in Percentages.

	Native				Immigrant			
	Bus-men	Train-men	Station staff	Per. Way	Bus-men	Train-men	Station staff	Per. Way
Have not held office	96	89	80	95	99	98	86	100
Have held office	4	6	3	—	1	2	—	—
Not applicable (not T.U. member)	—	6	17	5	—	—	14	—
Do not want to hold office	96	87	77	90	86	77	67	67
Would like to hold office	—	2	3	5	13	22	19	33
Has held/does hold office	4	6	3	—	1	2	—	—
Not applicable (not T.U. member)	—	6	17	5	—	—	14	—
(Sample)	(70)	(53)	(30)	(21)	(78)	(60)	(36)	(21)

The great majority had neither held trade union office nor wished to. The two immigrants who had held office had both been members of branch committees. Considerably more of the immigrants than the natives indicated that they were at least interested in holding office. Before discussing the significance of this, it might be useful to report the findings from one further question addressed only to the native samples: would there be any opposition to a Commonwealth immigrant being a union representative?[2] The answers are summarized in Table 15.4. (See p. 298.)

[1] That A.S.L.E.F. had a fairly substantial coloured membership on L.T.B. railway was apparently overlooked when, during a manning dispute with British Rail, it was suggested that in its opposition to the 'third man' travelling in the locomotive rear cab, it was motivated by considerations of colour. See 'When Colour Rides the Footplate', *Sunday Times* (26 November 1967).

[2] It was made clear that the question referred to a union representative at the local level, not a full-time official.

TABLE 15.4.
Native Attitudes to Immigrant Trade Union Representatives, in Percentages.

Would there be opposition?	Busmen	Trainmen	Station staff	Per. Way
No	59	66	63	57
Yes	29	19	—	29
Don't know	13	9	20	10
Not applicable (not T.U. member)	—	6	17	5
(Sample)	(70)	(53)	(30)	(21)

Over-all, the pattern of answers from each group of workers was fairly similar.

Having sketched the outlines with the bare statistics, I can now fill out the picture. The difference between the native and immigrant samples in the numbers who had *never* been to a branch meeting, is striking. Trade unionism is new to most of the immigrants, but it is very doubtful if the differences in attendance can be explained solely in these terms. Before discussing this difference, it is necessary to introduce another: that between the busmen, on the one hand, and the railwaymen, on the other.

We did not ask direct questions on attitudes towards the unions, but nevertheless quite a number of those interviewed did offer comments. The predominant attitude to emerge from the railwaymen—white and coloured, operating and Permanent Way—was one of indifference towards their unions. There appeared to be no difference between A.S.L.E.F. and N.U.R. members in this respect.

Attitudes of the coloured busmen towards 'the union' were a compound of beliefs: it was a 'white man's' organization; it was ineffective *irrespective* of the colour or origin of the members. And some were indifferent. The attitude that the union was not *their* union appeared to be fairly widespread and can be illustrated by two quotations, both given in answer to the question on attendance at branch meetings:

No [I have not been]. I feel I would not be welcome at the branch. [West Indian Driver.]

[The branch] is not a place for coloureds: you are kept out. [West Indian Driver.]

Some detected a difference between the theory of unity and brotherhood, on the one hand, and practice, on the other:

At the branch they are all one body—but not when they are out on the road. The union is not just the officials, it is *everybody*—but there isn't much unity. The union does look after things like wages, but not only the union is concerned with wages: the Government is also concerned so you can't say the union even does that. [West Indian Driver.]

The second thread of the criticism of the T.G.W.U. was that it was ineffective as a bargaining agent.

Most workers here haven't much faith in the trade union—they are double-dealing the workers. Year by year you are doing more work—for less money. West Indians and English share this attitude. There is no co-ordination between the [union] divisions: one division will do one thing, and one another. [West Indian Driver.]

As is suggested by this last quotation, criticism of the T.G.W.U. was not confined to the coloured busmen: it appeared to be almost equally widespread amongst their white workmates.

Turning to the railwaymen, the prevailing attitude was one of indifference to the unions. Very few criticized their unions, few praised them, but a number of the immigrants cited the union as a body which would protect them from discrimination by their employer or fellow-workers. Some had had problems attended to by their union. Accident claims had been settled for others. This help was appreciated. The most critical comment by far was the following:

They are only interested when they want to get elected. The people they have are useless—they are no help. [West Indian Guard.]

One or two of the native station staff said that they had been 'let down' by the union, or that it had been 'no help' when, for example, they had wanted a transfer from one station to another.

The protective function of the unions, as it was perceived by the coloured railwaymen, can be illustrated from the interview material. The first comment quoted was made in answer to a question on hostility;[1] the second, to one on how far expectations of working in England had been realized:[2]

Yes [there has been hostility], but on the transport you have so much backing from the union they can't do much. [West Indian Lengthman.]

[1] See Chapter 8.   [2] See Chapter 16.

It's turned out very well: you have the trade unions, and no one can say 'you have got to go back.' [West Indian Motorman.]

Whilst, then, the coloured railwaymen *may* have felt excluded from their unions, few gave much indication that this was so. They were aware of the protection offered by the unions and prepared to use these facilities when they thought this necessary. The difference between the relative numbers of immigrant busmen and trainmen who had never been to a branch meeting was not very large, but is consistent with the other evidence that the immigrant railwaymen felt less excluded from their unions than did the immigrant busmen.

Part of the difference between the immigrant and native railwaymen—and busmen—in the numbers who had never been to a branch meeting can be explained by the different length of service patterns: the natives had had longer service and presumably greater opportunity to attend one or more meetings. This interpretation is supported by the fact that those natives who had never been to a branch meeting were concentrated overwhelmingly in those groups having the shortest length of service. It may be, too, that in the past branch attendance was higher and more regular than it is today.

The indifference towards the unions of both native and immigrant workers was seldom complete: some in both groups appeared apologetic that they did not attend branch meetings. They indicated that they thought they *ought* to attend, but for one reason or another were unable to do so. Home commitments, the distance between home and meeting-place, a lack of time, and sometimes specifically shift work, were all given as reasons for not attending branch meetings. 'I am ashamed to say never' was the answer of one West Indian stationwoman to the question asking when she last attended a branch meeting, and this typifies the attitude of many. A small number of natives who had never attended a branch meeting said they were 'going tonight' or 'next week'.

A number of factors appear important in explaining the different attitudes of the busmen and the railwaymen—both white and coloured—towards their unions. In the services offered to their members, there appeared to be little difference between the railway unions, on the one hand, and the T.G.W.U., on the other. In both the road and railway sections of L.T.B., there have at times been unofficial movements of members discontented with the official union leadership. Nor was there anything to distinguish between them in their attitudes and behaviour, at the official level, towards their coloured members. All have taken the view that the coloured members should be treated on the same basis as the white members, with the same rights and duties. Nothing has been done specifically for the benefit of one group.[1] We must then look elsewhere for an explanation of the differences found.

One major cause of the busmen's criticisms of the T.G.W.U. appeared to be that it was seen as being too closely identified with management, almost as though it was regarded as another arm of management authority. It is perhaps inevitable that any union organization, which is in continuous contact with management over schedules and so on, will be liable to this type of criticism. One difference between the T.G.W.U. and the railway unions was the part played by full-time officials: the rail unions had no officials concerned exclusively with their L.T.B. memberships, the T.G.W.U had four.[2] It is possible, then, that the railway unions' lay officials were *seen* by their memberships to be far more involved in negotiations than were their busmen counterparts.

The criticisms made of the T.G.W.U. may reflect, too, the fact that union membership was part of the *employment* contract, enforced by the employer. Another probable consequence of compulsory trade union membership is a number of reluctant members, who quite possibly form a source of discontent and criticism.

That two unions compete—sometimes aggressively—for substantially the same membership is one further factor which helps explain the difference between road and rail. It is not suggested that this affects the quality of service given, but it possibly makes for a greater *awareness* of union activities.

The Central Bus Committee's pronouncements on London Transport's policy of recruiting staff abroad have probably not helped its image with the coloured busmen, some of whom had attended branch meetings when white members had made critical comments of either the Board's policy or the coloured staff.

Finally, it may be that the criticisms made of their union by both white and coloured busmen reflect the more general discontent with

[1] One exception to this is that in the early 1960s the T.G.W.U. held a conference of 'coloured delegates' from the garages. At that time it was promised that a further conference would be held, but owing to a change of union officials this did not happen and there was apparently some resentment that this undertaking was broken.

[2] It should be added that the T.G.W.U. membership in L.T.B. was appreciably larger than the combined L.T.B. memberships of the N.U.R. and A.S.L.E.F.

their employment which appeared to be both more widespread and deeply felt in Central Buses than in the railway departments. Taken together, all these factors explain the differences between the attitudes of the busmen and the railwaymen.

Whilst attitudes towards the possibility of an immigrant as a union representative were far less hostile than they were towards the notion of an immigrant inspector or senior ganger, a common element appeared to underline the *hostile* attitudes to both: this was the view that it would be *wrong* for a coloured man to be in a position to instruct white men. Two quotations illustrate this point of view admirably:

I wouldn't like that colour to tell me what to do—from your own you take it. [U.K. Woman Conductor.]

It wouldn't be advisable, as even with the man we have he comes in for criticism. A coloured man in charge of whites is dodgy. [U.K. Conductor.]

They could equally have been speaking of the possibility of a coloured inspector.

Some suggested that the coloured staff lacked the requisite social skills, and this echoed some of the criticisms of their relations with passengers, particularly in respect of the coloured ticket collectors:[1]

I don't want to see it, but it's bound to come: they haven't the same way with people. [U.K. Motorman.]

The fears that a coloured man would favour the coloured staff, which were voiced in relation to a coloured supervisor, were again in evidence:

They [coloured immigrant representatives] would want to run it for themselves, and not for the whole [membership]. [U.K. Guard.]

The majority, though, thought that there would not be opposition to an immigrant trade union representative, sometimes with the qualification 'provided he was a good man', or words to that effect. A number made the point that such a representative would have to be elected, and therefore the question of opposition was less likely to arise. Others pointed out that relatively few of the white members were prepared to hold union office: if a coloured man was able and willing to do so, 'good luck to him'.

Some would [object], but I wouldn't take a trade union post so I don't see why they should object. [U.K. Station Foreman.]

[1] See Chapter 9.

A few were of the opinion that it might be advantageous if the coloured members played a more active role in trade union affairs.

Not if he's a good man and knows what he's talking about—it might be a good thing. [U.K. Guard.]

At the time of the fieldwork, I was not aware of any coloured trade unionist holding any office higher than that of branch committee member,[1] though one coloured railwayman had been a member of the staff side of a sectional council.[2] A number of the coloured staff interviewed told us that they would like to hold trade union office. However, over one half (54 per cent) of them had never been to a branch meeting, and only 5 per cent claimed to attend their branches regularly. Their enthusiasm had evidently not been translated into action. This apparent inconsistency is partly explicable in terms of the feelings of exclusion from the unions which we found mostly amongst the coloured busmen. On the other hand, this exclusion was perpetuated by the fact that there were so few coloured trade unionists holding branch or other offices. It may be, too, that another partial explanation for the divergence between expressed wishes and reported actions is a need to appear—to a white interviewer—confident that they *could* carry out the duties of a union representative. I return to this theme below in the context of promotion aspirations.[3]

With these reservations, there appeared to be a source of potential recruits for union officers which could be tapped, given the right approach. Such recruitment might do something to overcome the feeling of exclusion from the union which appeared to be most widespread amongst the coloured busmen. Should the aspirations and discontents of the coloured staff not be met by the existing trade unions, then it is possible that some would turn to other, racially or ethnically based organizations. This course could have several consequences, but from the point of view of racial harmony it is likely that it would be regressive.

It is appropriate at this point to add that throughout the fieldwork we were looking for any instances of coloured spokesmen for

[1] Sometime before the spring of 1970, a West Indian had been elected Chairman of a T.G.W.U. Central Bus branch.

[2] Sectional councils are joint negotiating and consultative bodies in the railway departments. There are several, each concerned with one or a few grades: for example trainmen have one sectional council, permanent-way staff another. See Clegg.

[3] See Chapter 17.

the coloured staff in a garage, depot, or station. No such instances were found.[1] There were, though, cases of union branch officials using immigrants—usually of long service—as intermediaries in dealing with other immigrants: those who were reluctant to join the unions, in arrears with their contributions, and the like. There have also been a few cases of coloured railwaymen using coloured advocates at disciplinary hearings, but the majority have been represented by white natives, usually sectional council representatives.

The immigrants had conformed to the norms of the native work-force to the extent of joining a trade union. This, combined with their participation in strikes and other forms of organized industrial conflict, has assisted their acceptance by the native workforce. The fears of some natives that the immigrants might form an unreliable part of the workforce have been removed. To that extent, there had been absorption.

On the other hand, participation by the immigrants in trade union affairs was minimal: a majority had never been to a branch meeting and many felt excluded from the unions. There has, though, been little evidence of separate immigrant *industrial* organization which would indicate a more overtly pluralistic situation.[2] There appeared to be fairly widespread acceptance by native trade unionists of the notion of immigrants as trade union representatives, and some of the immigrants were interested in this possibility. Their participation, as branch officers for example, would tend to reduce the widespread feelings of exclusion from the unions.[3]

---

[1] At a few garages there were, by spring 1970, coloured branch committee members who acted as 'representatives' of the coloured members.

[2] See Chapter 6, p. 103 n. on the activities of the West Indian Standing Conference.

[3] This chapter has concentrated largely on *formal* participation in trade union affairs. It is unlikely that an examination of informal activities would have revealed relatively different levels of participation as between white native and coloured immigrant trade unionists.

16

SOME ASPECTS OF ABSORPTION AND PLURALISM OUTSIDE THE WORK SITUATION

Most of this volume is inevitably concerned with the work situation, and that was the main focus of the study. To confine the analysis completely to work behaviour and attitudes would, though, present a distorted picture: men and women have other roles besides their occupational ones; in terms of the theoretical framework adopted, it is vital to know how far absorption, or pluralism, in the work situation is reflected in the non-work world. In this chapter, I will examine a number of aspects of this world, some of which are inevitably concerned with work activities: relationships between white native and coloured immigrant workmates out of working hours; relationships between the various immigrant groups; participation in sports and social activities; relationships with neighbours, white and coloured; experiences of immigrants in seeking housing accommodation; the expectations the immigrants had before they came and how far they had been realized; the likelihood that the immigrants will stay in Britain or return to their countries of origin.

RELATIONSHIPS BETWEEN NATIVES AND IMMIGRANTS OUT OF WORKING HOURS

We asked a number of questions intended to show the extent and types of contact between coloured immigrants and white natives outside the work situation. We also asked similar questions on contacts with their own groups out of working hours. Table 16.1 summarizes the answers to a number of these questions. (See p. 306.)

These data must be interpreted with some caution: the coloured immigrants *wanted* to be accepted by their white native workmates, and there was probably a loss of self-esteem involved in admitting to a white interviewer that they were not accepted outside the work situation. It appeared to us that there was some over-statement of

TABLE 16.1.

Contact with Own and Other Groups out of Working Hours, in Percentages.

Contact with other group	Busmen	Trainmen	Native Station staff	Per. Way	Total	Busmen	Trainmen	Immigrant Station staff	Per. Way	Total
None	77	85	90	86	83	65	67	64	71	66
At pubs or clubs	14	4	7	10	9	31	22	19	24	25
Other social activities	9	11	3	5	8	9	10	17	5	10
Visited homes of members of other group	19	9	10	24	15	32	22	22	19	28
Members of other group have visited own home	26	15	13	14	19	41	28	31	43	38
Never visited or been visited by member of other group (at home)	69	81	80	76	75	58	57	64	53	58
Contact with own group										
None	44	53	50	57	49	27	12	25	14	21
At pubs or clubs	16	8	13	38	16	8	—	3	5	4
Other social activities	10	9	10	—	9	5	2	6	5	4
At homes or parties	30	30	27	5	26	59	85	67	67	69
Knew some of those with whom in contact now before coming to U.K. (immigrants only)	—	—	—	—	—	24	33	25	14	29
(Sample)	(70)	(53)	(30)	(21)	(174)	(78)	(60)	(36)	(21)	(195)

the extent to which they were accepted, and that this applied with particular force to the questions on home visiting. On the other hand, the answers from the native samples are probably reliable: those who associated with, had visited or been visited by their immigrant workmates would have little reason for hiding this from a white interviewer, nor would those who had no contacts away from work.

The table shows that roundly four-fifths of the natives and two-thirds of the immigrants had no contact with workmates of the 'other group' outside the work situation.[1]

Contacts at pubs or clubs—and they were mostly pubs; clubs were only important for railwaymen who sometimes had a social club with bar facilities near the depot or station—were mostly 'for a beer' at the end of the shift. For the Permanent Way night men it would be a beer before the beginning of the shift. The greater extent of contact between busmen is explicable in terms of the greater likelihood of them living close to their workplace as compared with the railwaymen. Near most garages there appeared to be one or two public houses which were regularly patronized by busmen. We were interested here in meetings which had been arranged, rather than casual encounters, but it was often difficult to distinguish between the two categories. Those who 'had a drink together' with someone of the 'other group' were, then, included; those who merely *happened* to be in the same public house or club were not.

It will be seen, too, that roughly one half of the natives had no contact with their native workmates away from the job, and that the numbers who had a beer with other natives were relatively small. (The *relatively* high figure for the Permanent Way men in this category is compensated for by their low percentage on the index of visiting the homes of other natives.)

The immigrants were far more likely than the natives to claim that they met members of the other group out of working hours for a beer. It seems likely that the extent of interaction between members of the different groups is over-stated here, but it may also indicate a different perception of the situation: when the immigrants thought they were *part* of a group in a bar, for example, they were not seen in this light by the natives concerned.

'Other social activities' were varied and included visits to football and wrestling matches, the cinema, or bingo, and playing in a darts team together. In all the interaction in which the natives were involved, with immigrants or with other natives, it was clear that it was confined to 'one or two friends'. Immigrants appeared to be in contact with a wider circle of other immigrants, particularly at parties. Some who had no contact with members of the other

---

[1] 'Own group' as it was applied to the immigrants meant those from their own country or island. Relationships *between* immigrant groups are discussed below, pp. 312–14. Whilst this analysis treats immigrants and natives as two groups, it is an over-simplification to the extent that there were of course a number of groups.

group with whom they worked,[1] added that they had coloured friends or white friends. This did not, though, appear to alter significantly the over-all impression given by the figures in Table 16.1.

Turning to home visiting, it will be seen that over-all three-quarters of the natives and between one-half and two-thirds of the immigrants had never visited the home of a member of the other group. Moreover, it will be seen that only a quarter of the natives were on 'visiting terms' with other natives with whom they worked. The differences in reported visiting across racial and ethnic boundaries between the native and immigrant samples is partly explicable in terms of esteem and acceptance, which I have discussed earlier, but there were also different perceptions of the situation between the natives and immigrants. The natives drew a distinction between visiting 'socially' and other visits, for example, a casual 'drop in for a cup of tea' on the way home or a visit to a sick workmate. This distinction is of some importance, and was not made by the immigrants to any appreciable extent: they appeared to include casual visits in home visiting. The distinction drawn by the natives between social and casual visits can be illustrated from the interview material:

My conductor has called round, *but not socially*.[2] [U.K. Driver.]

I only see those [English workmates] who live near—we don't visit socially. [U.K. Driver.]

The distinctions that other researchers have found between friends and mates, and between work and home life, were in evidence.

Work is work. [U.K. Driver.]

Home life is at home. [U.K. Conductor.]

I have made invitations [to my immigrant workmates], but it must be when my wife is away: she doesn't like *anyone* there. [U.K. Conductor.]

That to most native workers 'home life is home life' and to that extent private and divorced from the work situation, was not apparently appreciated by the immigrants who were not aware of English working-class norms in this area.

One driver had a coloured conductor and he [the coloured conductor] went round at Christmas and everyone was embarrassed. [U.K. Conductor.]

---

[1] That is, those at the same garage, station, etc.   [2] My italics.

Most native workers do not, then, visit other natives socially, and there is very little *social* visiting across racial or cultural barriers. Most visiting between natives and immigrants appears to be when one party is sick, or for a cup of tea at the end of the shift. Broadly similar figures on the extent of home visiting between white native workers have been found by other researchers.[1]

The immigrants, in contrast, appeared to be far more gregarious outside the work situation. This was so particularly amongst the West Indians, and parties appeared to be the main vehicle of interaction. A fifth, though, reported no contact with members of their own group outside of work, and this excluded the odd one or two who said there were none at their place of work. Whilst the norm that 'work is work and home is home' was found mostly amongst the natives, it was not completely confined to them.

You work with them [other Jamaicans] but you don't want to visit them. I've never had a coloured driver. [Jamaican Woman Conductor.]

Contact between white and coloured at work is legitimized by the work situation, and there are sanctions supporting it. By contrast, outside the work situation there is not this legitimacy, and the sanctions against deviations from group norms are likely to be strongly felt. The group norms in this case are those of the neighbourhood or friends, rather than the work group—when they do not coincide, that is, and they frequently do not. Given that maintaining a social distance from coloured immigrants appears to be a cultural norm, and that there are sanctions for deviance from it, then we might expect different patterns of behaviour at work and away from work.[2] This *apparent* inconsistency—and it is only apparent, since one is dealing with two different social situations—had been noticed by the immigrants and they often commented on it. To them it *was* an inconsistency.

Some [natives] don't *see* you when they meet you outside. They can be nice at work but outside they don't want to know. [West Indian Guard.]

Some say 'hullo' at work, but then out of work they don't know you. [West Indian Woman Conductor.]

These comments referred to apparently casual encounters in the

---

[1] See Goldthorpe, *et al.*, pp. 56–9; and Ferdynand Zweig, *The Worker in an Affluent Society* (London, Heinemann, 1961), pp. 117–8.

[2] Banton, *White and Coloured*, p. 104.

streets. The sanctions against home entertaining would be greater, and again an inconsistency had been perceived by the immigrants.

They [the natives] are always willing to come to me, but they never say 'come to us'. [West Indian Relayer.]

Clearly, then, there are differences in the norms and expectations of both groups. To the native worker, home life is home life and he is unlikely to entertain his native workmates socially. There is, though, quite a lot of dropping in for a cup of tea, or to borrow a set of spanners to repair a car. The coloured immigrant is less likely to be accepted in the home: there are sanctions here, though again he might be *taken* in for a cup of tea. All out-of-work relationships in which the natives were involved were likely to be confined to one or two 'special mates', as it were. When members of the other group were away from work through sickness, they were likely to be visited: for example, by their driver or conductor, or by their ex-driver or ex-conductor. The immigrants were not aware of English working-class norms in respect of home visiting, and clearly put some considerable value on acceptance in this area. In the words of one who had visited natives, and had been visited by them, 'you feel then you are wanted'. Some clearly found the contrast between natives' behaviour at work and away from work, hurtful. There are cultural differences in norms and expectations and this is summed up in the comments of a native woman conductor who was not apparently hostile towards the immigrants:

No [I do not see immigrant workmates out of working hours], there is a kind of barrier. They are friendly, and it cuts both ways.

SPORTS AND SOCIAL ACTIVITIES

A very wide variety of sports and social activities is sponsored by clubs in London Transport: cricket, football, athletics, rifle shooting, amateur dramatics, and many others. Some are organization-wide; others cater for specific sections or departments, for example Central Buses. Additionally, a number of sports and social activities are organized on a garage or depot basis.

Evidence from the staff magazine indicated that many immigrants, particularly West Indians, participated in these activities, especially in outdoor games and athletics, where they have made a notable contribution. We asked all those interviewed if they took part in any London Transport Sports or social activities, and their answers are summarized in Table 16.2.

TABLE 16.2.
Participation in L.T. Sports and Social Activities, in Percentages.

| | Native | | | Immigrant | | |
	Bus-men	Op. railmen	Per. Way	Bus-men	Op. railmen	Per. Way
None	56	80	100	76	73	76
None now but have done so	9	7	—	1	8	19
Sports activities	6	5	—	15	18	—
Social activities	17	7	—	4	1	5
Sports and social activities	11	—	—	4	—	—
No answer	1	1	—	—	—	—
(Sample)	(70)	(83)	(21)	(78)	(96)	(21)

The majority of both natives and immigrants did not take part in sponsored sports or social activities. Those least likely to participate were the women in all samples, In so far as there was a difference between natives and immigrants, the former were more likely to join in social activities and the latter in sports. This reflects in part their different interests—the most obvious being the West Indians' interest in cricket, though this is not true of all—and possibly, too, the different age structures of the samples. However, this is not necessarily a complete answer on why there was little immigrant participation in work-based social activities. The following comment is perhaps revealing on this question:

There are Sunday trips to the seaside run by the social club, but very few West Indians go. Most West Indians have social handicaps with the English. [Jamaican Driver.]

This suggests the West Indians' perception of cultural barriers, a lack of confidence perhaps in themselves in these social situations—using the term in its accepted working-class sense—and possibly a fear of being rebuffed and not accepted. Amongst the natives the feeling that 'work is work' and that relationships born of it ought not to be carried over to non-work activities was again in evidence.

Whilst the degree to which sports or social activities can break down differences between groups can easily be exaggerated, they do appear to function in that direction and certainly they were seen to by those involved. At one of the garages visited, there had been a party when an apparently popular West Indian left to return to the Caribbean and, in the words of one of the natives invited, 'there has never been such a party'.

One other aspect of immigrant participation in locally sponsored activities can conveniently be mentioned at this point. At a number of locations, particularly garages, loan clubs are run by busmen or railwaymen. Although run by the staff, London Transport provide banking and accounting facilities for the clubs. The general arrangement of these clubs appeared to be that members could secure an advance; the maximum figure was related to their weekly contributions. West Indians in particular were reported to be enthusiastic participants in these clubs which appear to fulfil the functions of 'partners associations' or 'sou-sou' which have been found by other observers,[1] but with more security of funds than is apparently found in some of these associations.

RELATIONSHIPS BETWEEN MEMBERS OF DIFFERENT IMMIGRANT GROUPS
One naïve assumption made by many natives during the early years of post-war coloured immigration to Britain was that all coloured immigrants were the same, that the simple shared characteristic of skin colour provided a common sense of identity between the different immigrant groups. Some native informants, at the managerial and supervisory levels as much as the operatives, were clearly surprised and disconcerted to discover that not only did West Indians not necessarily get on well with Africans, but that Jamaicans, for example, did not necessarily regard Barbadians as similar in every respect to themselves. Largely, perhaps, as a result of this discovery, and possibly also to divert attention away from white native-coloured immigrant conflict, there was in many of our discussions with managers and supervisors a considerable emphasis on conflict between members of the various immigrant groups.

We asked questions of our immigrant samples on their relationships with other immigrant groups, both in and outside the work situation. This, more than any other, was an area that many were reluctant to discuss frankly with a white interviewer. Consequently, I have made no attempt to quantify the data on this topic as it is unreliable and would present a distorted picture. With these reservations, the main outlines can be sketched in.

We were, of course, mainly concerned with West Indians. Apart

---

[1] See Patterson, *Dark Strangers*, pp. 348–9.

from when they worked together in, for example, a bus or train crew, there appeared to be little interaction between the West Indians, on the one hand, and the Asians—mostly Indians and Pakistanis—on the other. In the interviews, the Asians usually were at some pains to point out that *they* were different from the West Indians, sometimes to the extent of identifying themselves with the English in relation to the West Indians.

They [the West Indians] are different to us. Normally they consider us to be the same colour, but very seldom do they mix with us. Some are O.K., but they think we are on the same level. They are more friendly than the English. [Pakistani Conductor.]

In questions on hostility, too, the Asians appeared very much to play down the hostile behaviour they had encountered from native workers or from passengers, almost as though it was only the West Indians who had these difficulties.

What the West Indians perceived as the assumed superiority on the part of the Asians was keenly resented by them:

The Indians try to claim they are not coloured and therefore superior. [Jamaican Driver.]

There is a tendency for those from the East to consider themselves superior, even to the English. [West Indian Motorman.]

It is not clear how far these references to 'Indians' were meant to apply specifically to Indians or to all Asians.

Turning to relationships between West Indians and the various African groups, I have relatively little information from the latter, as we interviewed so few and they may well be atypical. Again, from the West Indians there was some evidence of resentment against Africans:

Africans are not keen on Jamaicans. [Jamaican Driver.]

The Africans call West Indians 'slaves'. [Barbadian Woman Conductor.]

Between the various West Indian groups it appeared that the inter-island rivalries were abating somewhat as each group got to know the others better, but they were far from absent. The major differences appeared to be between the Jamaicans and Barbadians, and these were in any case numerically the largest groups. The Jamaicans' jibe of 'little islander' was apparently still applied to others, including Barbadians, and the latter also suffered the 'little Englander' label. There were still reservations about members of other West Indian groups, though most took care not to generalize.

I don't seem to fancy the Jamaicans—they are quick to lose their tempers. There are not many here, and some are very good. [Barbadian Driver.]

Apart from rivalries between West Indians springing specifically from the Caribbean situation, there was also a considerable element of strangeness among the various groups.

I study [other West Indians] as much as I study the English. Their ways are sometimes more peculiar than I imagined. Sometimes I wonder what mixture of languages brought about that way of talking. It is easier for the English to understand us than those from the smaller islands. [Jamaican Platelayer.]

These differences were dying down, and Jamaicans could say that 'some of my best friends are Barbadians' and apparently mean it. There appeared to be quite a lot of contact between West Indians outside of the work situation, at parties and so on, and some shared accommodation with others of different territorial origins. By contrast, there was little or no contact between West Indians and Asians or Africans.

In sum, the material on relationships between the immigrant groups is sparse, but it does indicate a wish on the part of the Asians to avoid being identified with the West Indians and, to that extent, to claim a superior status. This claim was both contested and resented by the West Indians. Among West Indians, antipathy was far from absent, but it appeared to be abating as each group got to know the others better, and possibly also in the face of a common antipathy from the white natives.

HOUSING DIFFICULTIES EXPERIENCED BY IMMIGRANTS

Other studies have shown the difficulties experienced by coloured immigrants in finding suitable living accommodation in England at rents they could afford. It appears useful, then, for us to collect data on the experiences of immigrant interviewees, and we asked them if they had 'had any difficulty in obtaining satisfactory housing in London'. Table 16.3 summarizes the answers given.

First a word on the coding categories used. Those who stated that they had lived with relatives or friends volunteered this information. Similarly, those who said that they had experienced difficulties but were satisfied now, did likewise. Both categories may therefore

TABLE 16.3.
Difficulties Experienced by Immigrants in Obtaining Satisfactory Housing in Percentages.*

	Busmen		Op. railmen		Per. Way		Total	
No difficulty	22		32		14		26	
No difficulty: lived with relatives or friends	23	} 45	10	} 42	5	} 19	15	} 41
Had difficulty	31		37		43		35	
Had difficulty but satisfied now	24	} 55	19	} 56	38	} 81	23	} 58
No answer	—		1		—		1	
(Sample)	(78)		(96)		(21)		(195)	

* The experiences of the Barbados direct recruits in the housing accommodation found for them are described in Chapter 13.

understate the numbers who properly belong in them: questioning on this topic was not exhaustive and depended on the time available during the interviews. With these reservations the data are useful, as the broad distinction between experiencing and not experiencing difficulties is valid.

The definition of satisfactory was, of course, a subjective one and depended on the expectations and aspirations of those interviewed. Over-all roughly two-fifths reported that they had not experienced difficulties in obtaining satisfactory housing, and the assistance provided by friends or relatives was clearly important for some. The majority reported that they had experienced difficulties, and many were clearly dissatisfied with the housing in which they were accommodated. The major difficulties reported were those of finding *any* accommodation within the limits of the rent they could afford, and of paying too much for too little—in other words, having to pay high rents for accommodation which in their eyes was inferior.

Many clearly had experienced considerable distress and hardship in their search for adequate accommodation. White and coloured landlords were condemned, as were estate agents who apparently openly discriminated. A number of those who said that they were satisfied with their present accommodation had bought houses with the aid of mortgages, sometimes from local authorities, less often from building societies, and also from finance companies which charged a relatively high interest rate for a short-term loan.

Most of the discrimination reported was in terms of colour, and a 'colour tax' appeared to be applied.

Whilst this is not the place for a detailed analysis of the housing market, and I do not know how well, in their view, the native workers were housed, it does appear that the coloured immigrants were at a considerable disadvantage in the housing market. White landlords discriminated against them, either by refusing accommodation or by charging a 'colour tax' rent. Coloured landlords similarly charged high rents. Estate agents did not show them the most desirable properties and were prepared to charge a 'colour tax'. From the data, I know little about the practices of local authorities and building societies in allocating mortgages. Some had obtained mortgages, others had been refused, but this could, of course, have been due to the condition of the prospective purchase, its price in relation to a valuation or the applicant's income and so on. Whatever the reasons, a number of coloured immigrants were virtually forced into the hands of finance companies which were prepared to provide assistance—but at a price. Finally, some had apparently fallen foul of estate agents who were prepared to accept deposits and not return them, including one coloured estate agent who had ceased business owing one of our interviewees a considerable sum of money.

A number who had experienced difficulties were now satisfied with their accommodation. Their situation had improved, and some specifically mentioned that *finding* accommodation at least was easier.

All these data were, of course, collected before the Race Relations Act of 1968. I do not know how far the situation has changed since the Act became operative.

RELATIONSHIPS WITH WHITE AND COLOURED NEIGHBOURS

One other area of interaction between white native and coloured immigrants outside of the work situation which we explored briefly was that of contacts between neighbours of the 'other group'. That is, we used a simple white native-coloured immigrant dichotomy. First it was necessary to establish the residential pattern: did the white natives have coloured immigrant neighbours and *vice versa*; were the immigrants living in streets with numbers of other immigrants? Table 16.4 shows the pattern of residence.

This analysis is admittedly very crude. Streets vary considerably in length, so, apart from those natives with immigrants living 'next door', I do not know their physical proximity. The analysis rests,

TABLE 16.4.
Proximity of Coloured Immigrant Neighbours, in Percentages.

	Native				Immigrant			
	Bus-men	Op. rail-men	Per. Way	Total	Bus-men	Op. rail-men	Per. Way	Total
None/no others in same street	36	41	43	39	5	10	5	8
Few in same street	40 ⎱	35 ⎱	14 ⎱	34 ⎱	62 ⎱	49 ⎱	43 ⎱	53 ⎱
Several in same street	23 ⎰ 63	24 ⎰ 59	33 ⎰ 47	25 ⎰ 59	27 ⎰ 89	37 ⎰ 86	53 ⎰ 96	35 ⎰ 88
Coloured immigrants next door (natives only)*	16	25	48	24	—	—	—	—
Don't know	1	—	10	2	5	3	—	4
No answer	—	—	—	—	1	—	—	1
(Sample)	(70)	(83)	(21)	(174)	(78)	(96)	(21)	(195)

* This is a double code, hence the percentage totals for the native samples exceed 100. The 'next door' category includes those living in the same building, i.e. a block of flats or multi-occupation of one dwelling.

too, on the respondents' perceptions and definitions of 'few' and 'several'. It may be that there were differences between the samples in these perceptions: the natives' definitions of 'several' might have been similar to the immigrants' perceptions of 'a few'. It is possible, too, that these perceptions would vary according to the intensity of immigrant settlement in the *area generally*: visibility is important. Few immigrants lived in streets not also inhabited by other immigrants; considerable numbers of natives are shown to live in all-white streets.

We next asked both the native and immigrant sample how they 'got on' with neighbours of the other group. The answers to this question are summarized in Table 16.5. (See p. 318.)

Again the immigrants were more likely to claim acceptance than the natives are to concede it, even to the limited extent of exchanging greetings which is the content of the 'speaking terms' category. Typical examples of helpfulness or friendliness were taking in parcels when the other was out, or lending—or being able to borrow —a pair of steps. There was, then, little contact with neighbours of the other group, other than an exchange of greetings, and amongst the natives this was fairly restricted. One problem here is that the areas in which the respondents lived varied considerably: from those of considerable multi-occupation via 'Young and Willmott' type

TABLE 16.5.

Contact with Neighbours of 'Other Group', in Percentages.

How each group got on with neighbours of other group	Native				Immigrant			
	Bus-men	Op. rail-men	Per. Way	Total	Bus-men	Op. rail-men	Per. Way	Total
No contact: no neighbours of other group	36	41	43	39	—	1	—	1
No contact	39	36	38	37	15	12	10	13
On hostile terms	—	2	10	2	—	4	—	2
On speaking terms	21	19	5	18	62	69	67	66
On helpful/friendly terms	3	—	5	2	18	6	24	13
On visiting terms	1	1	—	1	5	7	—	6
(Sample)	(70)	(83)	(21)	(174)	(78)	(96)	(21)	(195)

inner London communities[1] to the outer suburbs. In some areas anonymity was more or less complete, as was pointed out by some of those interviewed.

It is difficult, then, to know what significance to attach to the category of those who had no contact with neighbours: it may be the accepted pattern in the area, regardless of colour or ethnic origins. On the other hand, there were indications that in some cases this lack of contact was one indication of a lack of acceptance of coloured immigrants by their white neighbours. This is one area where acceptance by the white population can be granted or withheld, and the sanctions of ostracism can be very hurtful to those against whom they are directed.

In some cases children established the initial contacts with neighbours. On the other hand, children of immigrants were not always accepted by white neighbours, and white children were discouraged from being friendly.

The predominant manifestation of non-acceptance was ostracism rather than any other more overtly hostile behaviour. This, though, was perceived as, and probably often intended to be, a demonstration of hostility towards coloured neighbours.

Behaviour which *was* intended to be hostile was reported by a few natives:

The landlord has told them to move. The neighbours tried to stop them coming and have now got rid of them. Their way of life is different—they don't want to fit in at all, and they're dirty. [U.K. Guard.]

[1] Michael Young and Peter Willmott, *Family and Kinship in East London* (London, Routledge & Kegan Paul, 1957).

Of those natives who lived next door (as defined) to immigrants, nearly half were on speaking terms; also all those who were on visiting terms and most of those on friendly or helpful terms were also in the 'next door' category. On the other hand, most of the natives who reported that they did not get on with their coloured neighbours had them next door. Nearly half of the natives with coloured next-door neighbours had no contact with them, but a number of these were living in houses and streets of multi-occupation where, it may be hypothesized, anonymity is the norm and overt conflict is not absent.

The evidence from the limited data is inconclusive, but it suggests that close proximity is more likely to be followed by acceptance—though possibly limited acceptance—in traditional working-class areas. It suggests also that non-acceptance and conflict are more likely in both areas of multi-occupation and physical deprivation and in all-white or near-white suburban areas. This is, though, a very tentative conclusion. Over-all, there appeared to be relatively little contact between white and coloured neighbours; in part this appeared to be the norm of anonymity, but in part it indicated the white neighbours' non-acceptance of their coloured neighbours.

IMMIGRANTS' EXPECTATIONS OF WORKING IN ENGLAND

I never thought Englishmen worked: I thought they all wore bowler hats and lived like lords. I was never told what *ordinary* people did.

This quotation, from a Barbadian motorman, illustrates in perhaps an extreme form the West Indians' often Victorian image of the mother country. This image is clearly relevant to their expectations of their own future attainments in this country, and these expectations will in turn influence their behaviour in their new home. In order to gain some insight into these expectations and to see how they differed from reality as they had found it, we asked the immigrants, 'how does working in England compare with what you expected?'[1] One problem is, of course, that the question was asked several years or more after their arrival and the answers on expectations may have been coloured by subsequent experiences. I cannot show that this was or was not so here, but the answers given do at least appear to be credible and, to that extent, reliable. Table 16.6 summarizes the answers given. (See p. 320.)

[1] The comments of Barbadian direct recruits on the information given concerning L.T.B. employment are discussed in Chapter 13.

TABLE 16.6.

How Expectations of Working in England Compared with Subsequent Experiences, for Coloured Immigrants, in Percentages. *

	Busmen	Op. rail-men	Per. Way	Total
Easier/better than expected	17	18	19	17
Didn't know what to expect	26	27	24	26
As expected/not much difference	19	18	24	19
Surprised over hours of work and other aspects of time	10	16	10	13
Harder/worse than expected	21	8	14	14
Disappointed over job opportunities/jobs/pay	12	6	5	8
Disappointed over hostility experienced	3	4	5	4
Other answer	—	1	—	1
No answer	1	3	—	2
(Sample)	(78)	(96)	(21)	(195)

* More than one answer was recorded and the percentage totals may therefore exceed 100.

The table shows that a wide variety of answers was given, some in very general terms and some specific. With one or two minor variations, the pattern of answers was similar for all three departments.

Those who found working in England easier or better than they had expected did so for a number of reasons, all of which related to some aspect of employment. A quarter of the samples and the largest single group did not know what to expect. In marked contrast were those who said that working in England had largely measured up to what they had expected.

All the answers in the remaining categories expressed surprise and a number expressed disappointment. Some were surprised over the hours they were expected to work and over other aspects of time.

The next group of answers indicated that in some way working in England was harder or worse than had been expected. Some referred to the problems of working in a relatively cold climate; others were less specific.

It's like Dick Whittington and his cat: I thought the streets would be paved with gold. In my country a man is poor and happy; here he is rich and unhappy. [Jamaican Relayer.]

The types of employment which were open to coloured immigrants, the work content of such employment, and the financial rewards were found disappointing by some.

It's worse: I can't get the sort of work I want. [Jamaican Guard, an ex-prison warder who wished to be a prison officer in the U.K.]

Finally, there were those who said that they were disappointed over the hostility which they had encountered. Whilst relatively few mentioned this, it seems likely that this under-states the numbers who felt it.

Some drew comparisons between employment experiences here and in their countries of origin. Others without experience of working in their home countries were unable to make this comparison. Clearly, most did not have expectations that matched even approximately what they found: only one in five said that their experiences had accorded with their expectations. This indicates that there was a lack of accurate information in the countries of emigration, or at least if it was available it was not believed by many. One important point here is that many came filled with tremendous optimism about opportunities open to them in the mother country. Hence reports which painted a less optimistic picture of life in England might well have been disbelieved. Returning migrants were one possible source of information, but they were atypical in the sense that most of the immigrants have *not* gone back and, *assuming* that these returning migrants had painted a sombre picture of life in England, they might well have been disbelieved *because* in a sense they had not been successful. It is likely, too, and this is probably far more important, that the feedback of information from immigrants here to their relatives and friends back home is far from accurate. They set considerable store on being successful and on being accepted. It is painful to admit that their expectations have not always been met in both these respects.

Many, of course, had been in Britain a number of years, and it is possible that more accurate information is now available. Certainly, incidents of job discrimination against coloured workers in Britain appeared to be prominently reported in the Barbados press. At the time of my visit in 1966, the colour bar on the transfer of a West Indian British Railways worker was prominently featured.[1]

Less than one in five found working in England easier or better in some way than they had expected, and almost twice this number were either unpleasantly surprised or disappointed with what they found. Some of these comments related specifically to public transport employment, and the West Indians' problem of accepting and internalizing the various time constraints was again in evidence.

Whilst there was a considerable measure of agreement between those interviewed in the three departments, the busmen again appear to have suffered most disappointment and discontents. As on other topics, those who viewed the situation in the U.K. over a period of time concluded that, so far as they are concerned, 'things are improving'.

WILL THE IMMIGRANTS STAY IN BRITAIN?[2]

The likelihood that coloured immigrants will stay in Britain and the possible size of the coloured population have been the subject of some considerable controversy. It is not my intention here to enter this controversy, but our data do serve to throw light on the question of 'will they stay'. We asked our immigrant samples two questions which are relevant here: their intended length of stay at the time of their arrival and their intentions at the time of the interviews. Table 16.7 shows the reported intentions at the time of arrival.

TABLE 16.7.
Intended Length of Stay at Time of Arrival in England, for Immigrants, in Percentages.

	Busmen	Op. rail-men	Per. Way	Total
Not fixed	31	39	57	37
Up to 5 years	53	41	24	44
6–10 years	9	11	14	11
Over 10 years	5	3	5	4
Permanently	3	6	—	4
(Sample)	(78)	(96)	(21)	(195)

[1] *The Advocate* of Bridgetown, Barbados, (14 July 1966).
[2] The findings of this section have been reported in *Race Today* (Vol. 1, No. 5, September, 1969), pp. 132–4.

Somewhat over one-third had no firm intentions at the time of their arrival. Of the remainder, the largest single group had intended staying up to five years. The group who intended to stay permanently was composed mostly of the Anglo-Indians.

When these reported intentions are compared with the length of time the respondent had been in England, the large majority (81 per cent) had already been here five or more years, including 53 per cent who had been here seven years or more.[1] The expectations of a number of a relatively speedy return had clearly not been realized.

Next, the reported intentions at the time of the interviews. These are shown in Table 16.8.

TABLE 16.8.
Immigrants' Intended Length of Stay in England at Time of Interviews, in Percentages.

	Busmen	Op. rail-men	Per. Way	Total
Would return now if could afford to do so	1	2	10	3
Up to 5 more years	14	8	5	10
Up to 10 more years	6	3	—	4
More than another 10 years	6	3	10	5
At least until children have completed their education	3	1	19	4
No idea/indefinitely	62	70	53	65
Will not go back	8	12	5	10
(Sample)	(78)	(96)	(21)	(195)

The table shows that those with a specific length of time in mind comprised only about a quarter of the samples. A small number *hoped* to be able to move on to Canada or the United States: some had relatives in Canada and some had worked in the United States.

For the majority, going back was something they aspired to in the indefinite future, rather than an event for which they were planning and saving. To many, it was about as remote as winning the football pools. Even so, few thought that they would *never* go back to stay permanently.

Every year I say 'another five years'. [West Indian Guard.]

[1] See Chapter 3.

Several had plans to return to the Caribbean for a holiday and to 'see what it is like now' in the West Indies, but few appeared to be at all optimistic that they would stay there.

Some would only contemplate returning when they had, in their own estimation, been 'successful': either financially or in terms of obtaining formal qualifications and with them, greater earning power. Self-esteem, though obviously important here, was not the sole consideration: equally important was the esteem in which they would be held by others. When West Indians said that 'you can't go back worse than you came', they appeared to have both aspects in mind.

A number, as I have shown,[1] had hoped to be able to study for a formal qualification whilst in England. Some had begun study courses, mostly at evening classes, but few had found the demands of these courses compatible with the unusual and changing hours of work in public transport.

Some intended to stay at least until their children had completed their full-time education in England, where the educational facilities were widely regarded as superior to those of the Caribbean.

The large majority, then, had no plans or hopes of an early return. Going back was in the indefinite future. What of those two 'deviant' groups: those who wished to return immediately and those who planned to settle permanently in Britain?

Those who intended to stay here included all the Anglo-Indians. For them the push factors of migration were somewhat different from those affecting the other migrants, and they had journeyed to Britain with the intention of settling here. All were operating railwaymen, most had worked on the railways in India. Some had accepted occupational down-grading in the move from one railway undertaking to another.

An intention to settle in Britain was not, however, confined to the Anglo-Indians. Of the total number of West Indians in the samples, 7 per cent intended to settle permanently here—that is, more than twice the number who wished to return immediately to their countries of origin. The remaining 'settlers' were found amongst the relatively small groups of migrants from a large number of countries. To name their countries of origin might risk identifying individuals.

Amongst the West Indians, the Jamaicans were over-represented

[1] Chapter 3.

and the Barbadians under-represented; but given the number of settlers relative to the total sample little significance can be attached to this difference. Their occupational level of attainment had been higher than most: amongst the operating railwaymen, most were motormen or station foremen; amongst the busmen, most were drivers. All were men. Their ages were higher than those of the majority: whereas two-thirds of the male immigrants (including non-West Indians) were under 35, a similar proportion of the West Indian settlers were over 35.[1] They, too, had been in Britain longer than most: two-thirds of the male immigrant sample had been here eight years or less, whilst a similar proportion of the West Indian settlers had been here nine years or more, most of these for eleven or more years.[2] A few of the settlers—both West Indian and non-West Indian—had married European girls, as had one or two of those who intend to stay here indefinitely. The reasons given for not wishing to go back mostly had to do with the absence of anything to go back to, usually in terms of employment opportunity and, less frequently, family ties.

What of that other deviant group: those who wished to return immediately to their countries of origin? Occupationally, they were a diverse group: one driver, one guard, one stationman, two length-men. All were West Indians; all were men. In terms of age and the length of time they had been in Britain, there was no pattern to distinguish them from the total male immigrant sample. Nor were they distinguished by having experienced any more difficulties over training and promotion than had other immigrants, though their occupational level of attainment was lower than that of the settlers. In sum, there was nothing to distinguish them *as a group* from many other immigrants.

Their wish to return home appeared to be prompted largely by personal circumstances. One particularly wanted to go back to be with his parents. Another had been a skilled hand craftsman in the West Indies and had been unable to obtain a similar job here. A third obviously had more difficulty than most in adapting to the requirements of a large bureaucratic public service organization. Two were living in poor accommodation and paying high rents relative to their incomes—but so were many others. None were optimistic that they would be able to return home at an early date.

I concluded that the majority of the immigrants interviewed

---

[1] See Chapter 3.   [2] Ibid.

will in all probability not go back—they are here to stay—but it would be unwise to generalize from this sample to the immigrant population at large.

A number of disincentives to returning to their countries of origin apply in varying degrees to most Commonwealth immigrants: a relative lack of economic opportunity there for themselves and their children, the educational facilities available in Britain, the fact that many of their children have spent most of their formative years in England, and so on. Yet there are a number of factors which apply with particular force to those in our samples and the populations from which they were drawn.

The samples were comprised of workers whose occupational level of achievement has been somewhat above that of many of their fellow-immigrants. Comparing the West Indian males in the samples with the economically active males of British Caribbean birth in the Greater London area, as shown in the *Commonwealth Immigrant Tables* from the 1966 Sample Census, Socio-Economic Group 9 (skilled manual) is somewhat over-represented: 56 per cent as against 39 per cent. Confining the comparison to the Registrar General's Socio-Economic Groups 8–11 (manual), S.E.G. 9 is still somewhat over-represented in our samples: 56 per cent as against 45 per cent. For reasons related to the main focus of the study, immigrants in some grades were over-represented in our samples, notably those of motormen and drivers.[1] Those who had achieved relatively more success in terms of occupation were then over-represented.

The skills of railwaymen are largely specific to the industry and to the undertaking. A number of motormen can expect to become supervisors or train operators; numbers of guards and platform staff can expect to move up to and possibly through the motorman grade. The market for these skills elsewhere is minimal; in the Caribbean it is non-existent. The higher they move up the occupational heirarchy, the less likely they are to return to the Caribbean.

The skills of the busmen are, of course, not specific to the undertaking and those of the drivers not specific to the industry. It is somewhat unlikely, however, that there will be a substantial demand for these skills in the Caribbean.

A number of busmen and railwaymen were skilled tradesmen in their home countries. Should they wish to return to these trades after an absence of several years, they are likely to be at a disadvan-

[1] See Chapter 1.

tage compared with immigrants who have continued to follow their crafts.

It may well be that with a decrease in discriminatory practices in other industries the concentration of immigrants in public transport will be somewhat lessened; but in spite of the Race Relations Act of 1968 and the activities of the Race Relations Board, covert job discrimination is likely to remain an enduring feature of the employment scene. This, combined with those features of public transport which make it both particularly well suited for and congenial to the employment of Commonwealth immigrants, and their levels of occupational attainment, makes it likely that they will be over-represented in public transport for many years to come.

The evidence strongly suggests, therefore, that whilst many West Indians dream of eventually returning to the Caribbean, 'better off' than when they came, the majority of those in public transport at least will not do so. This probably applies also to many in other industries. Their occupational and economic achievements and prospects, coupled with a lack of employment opportunity in their home countries, conspire to keep them here.

Drawing the threads together, the evidence shows that neither the absorption nor the pluralism model is completely appropriate, though the latter fits the data more closely than does the former. The situation is one where members of groups defined as racially or ethnically different can interact *relatively* harmoniously in task-determined activities, but outside of this area there was little contact between them.

In relation to most areas of interaction between coloured immigrants and the host population the verdict of the immigrants was that 'things were getting better': hostility from white workmates was abating; some had been able to improve their housing situation, and so on.

Certainly the culture of the West Indians and their own predispositions would point towards a process of absorption. This appeared to be so for those who had migrated as adults. There were, though, indications amongst the *small* number who had travelled to England as children or teenagers which suggested that *they* were not seeking absorption in the same way as their elders. They were aware of the difficulties facing coloured immigrants to Britain, and they did not seek to be absorbed into a society which they perceived had largely rejected them. They *were not interested*.

17

SOME CONCLUSIONS

I began in Chapter 1 with a statement of the theoretical framework. Some of my concepts were drawn from immigration theory; some were from race relations theory; and some were from the sociology of industry. One question raised at an early stage was that of the immigration versus the race relations approaches to the research area. The relative importance of immigration and race variables is then something to be constantly borne in mind. In this final chapter I shall first summarize and discuss the more important conclusions to emerge from Chapters 4 to 11, that is, those concerned with relationships in the work situation. I shall then look more closely at a number of areas: acculturation of attitudes; those features of the employment situation which have assisted the absorption of coloured immigrants; management practices; the relevance of the *relative* number of immigrants in a workforce; the impact of coloured immigrants on London Transport. Finally, I consider whether the absorption or the pluralistic model is the most appropriate to the situation found.

RELATIONSHIPS AT WORK: A SUMMARY AND DISCUSSION

In all three departments white native workers voiced their opposition to and resentment of the initial employment of coloured immigrants. The passage of time has all but precluded any accurate comparison of the reported reactions of native staff in the three departments, but opposition appears to have been least in Permanent Way. Between Central Buses and Railway Operating it is difficult to say whether opposition was more widespread or intense in one than the other, but only in Central Buses was strike action threatened. This was, though, confined to one or two garages.

Colour was the most frequently mentioned reason for objections to the employment of coloured staff, followed by fears that wages, conditions, and standards would be threatened. Most of the evidence on the social significance of colour—particularly on likely reactions to coloured supervisory staff—suggests that a dark skin is associated with low status. To that extent, the data support the colour-class hypothesis.

It is probable that there would have been an adverse reaction to the employment of any *identifiable* non-traditional group, though it appears that colour made this reaction both more widespread and more intense. In Central Buses, though, the employment of women conductors is far from completely accepted by their male colleagues, and the employment of women drivers has, up to the time of writing, been successfully opposed.

In the years prior to the Second World War, employment with London Transport was seen as desirable for a number of reasons. With a relatively high level of unemployment prevailing, *any* employment was sought-after. London Transport offered a high degree of job security at a time when insecurity was the norm. It offered pay and conditions which compared favourably with those found in many other occupations and industries. These factors appear to have given employment with London Transport a relatively high status—certainly in the eyes of its employees. Some long service workers compared their situations with those of others whom they thought were at a similar status level in the pre-war era: postmen, firemen, and policemen.[1]

In the immediate post-war years, the favourable wages position of London Transport workers had been eroded somewhat, but it still offered job security—an incentive for a number who joined—when a return to pre-war levels of unemployment was apparently widely expected. By the early fifties a relatively low level of unemployment had prevailed for ten years or so, and an economic depression was not obviously just over the horizon. It was at this time that London Transport employment began to appear less attractive, and staff shortages became prevalent. The relative earnings position of London Transport workers had declined. Whilst this might have been acceptable to some as the price to be paid for job security had unemployment been high, this security probably appeared less of an advantage now that it was apparently becoming more common in the wider labour market. Security, is, though, far from unimportant now. Given this decline in the relative advantages of London Transport employment, it may be hypothesized that its status would similarly decline, and this appears

[1] Some policemen apparently joined London Transport's predecessors after the 1919 police strike.

to have happened. The opposition to the employment of coloured immigrant workers is, then, partly explicable in terms of the weakening of bargaining power which was seen to result from a reduction in the staff shortage and from the employment of a group perceived as possibly unreliable in the event of organized industrial conflict. Moreover—and this was the most important consideration—the newcomers were coloured. Apart from other antipathies arising from this fact, the already declining status of London Transport employment was seen to be further threatened.

That there was apparently least opposition in Permanent Way is consistent with the colour-class viewpoint: Permanent Way men appeared to have been least concerned with the question of status.[1] Market considerations appear to have been most important for the busmen: conflict over wages has been fairly constant in Central Buses and from time to time the question of *recruitment* overseas has been brought into this conflict. That London busmen form a discrete bargaining unit is obviously relevant here, too: the likely effects of a reduction in the staff shortage on bargaining power could most immediately be perceived. Considerations of status and, related to this, of tradition appear to have been most salient for the trainmen. The Railway Operating Department was in most respects the most tradition-bound; its beliefs and values stressed continuity and long service; its culture was one likely to be inhospitable to newcomers who were both strange and perceived as low in the status hierarchy. Whilst there were these differences between the two operating departments in the opposition to the newcomers, they are relatively small compared with the over-all common pattern.

It is not suggested that the colour-class hypothesis is the complete explanation for the widespread white British aversion to dark-skinned people. Feelings on this are obviously deeply held, and there is clearly scope for much more detailed research on the social significance of colour. Certainly, I was impressed by the *strength* of feeling of many on the question of colour. This aversion came out most strongly in the answers on the possibility of coloured supervisors. Yet a marked antipathy towards coloured people in general was at times combined with complete or near-complete acceptance of individuals.

The numbers of women in our samples were relatively small, and any conclusions on over-all differences between the sexes must

[1] This does not mean that they necessarily accepted the low status ascribed them.

thus be treated with caution. With this reservation, there were indications that the native women were both more hostile towards the immigrants than were their male colleagues, and also that they perceived a deeper and more widespread hostility amongst the natives than did the men. This hostility appeared to be directed more against coloured men than women, so the situation was complicated by sex differences.

To return to my theme, I concluded that given the existing market and status situations, there would probably have been opposition to any *identifiable* group of outsiders. That the outsiders were coloured served to make any opposition aroused both more widespread and—more importantly—more intense. In part, then, the situation was one of immigration and in part one of race relations. To state with any degree of accuracy which of these was uppermost in the native British response is difficult. Certainly, it was reported to us more in terms of colour than of any other factor, and to that extent it may be seen as a race relations response. The *ease* of identification was an important factor in relationships between white and coloured workers, particularly between bus crews on the road.[1]

It is, perhaps, useful at this point to ask how realistic the opposition of the native British workers was, in the sense of how accurately their fears were fulfilled. On the question of the relative status enjoyed by public transport workers, I can say little, since these workers were our only source of data. It appeared to be fairly widely assumed that their status had declined, but the employment of coloured workers was seen as only one of the factors contributing to this decline: market and other considerations were also important.

The fear that coloured immigrants would be unreliable in organized conflict proved to be groundless, and their reliability in this respect has been important in their acceptance by native workers.

It is not obvious that an absence of coloured recruits would have improved the pay and conditions of the existing staff: more rapid technical change or a more marked reduction of services were possible alternative reactions to a staff shortage. Certainly, it is most unlikely that a large publicly owned organization operating in the capital could have avoided employing numbers of coloured immigrants, had it wished to.[2] More important, though, it is far

---

[1] See Chapter 5.

[2] In the United States urban transit industry, public ownership has also been conducive to the recruitment of black workers. See Jeffress, pp. 49 and 93.

from self-evident that the employment of coloured immigrants has significantly reduced the staff shortage over the past fifteen years or so. I return to this topic in more detail below.[1]

One other fear reported was that standards of performance would be lowered. There was nothing to suggest that the work performance of the immigrants as a group was at all different from that of the native workers.

Whilst there were these objections to the employment of coloured immigrants, the work performance and personal characteristics of the early recruits to both Central Buses and Railway Operating encouraged their acceptance. They were good ambassadors, and to that extent allayed somewhat the fears and hostility of the native workers and smoothed the way for later coloured recruits. Possibly, the recruitment staff were more selective in the early stages of recruitment and engagement of immigrant workers, and these early recruits may have accorded more closely with the ideal type than did those engaged later. Job discrimination elsewhere was probably more widespread in the early fifties than in later years, and possibly these early recruits were more proficient or adaptable.[2] Certainly, the very first coloured workers were regarded as something of a novelty, and to that extent, had an attraction for some.

Numbers were important in that with very few coloured workers employed at any location, they had to fit in and conform to the natives' norms. The development of separate immigrant groups, in canteens, messrooms, and so on, possible when a number were employed, appears to have been the occasion of increased hostility and resentment from the native workers. To that extent, numbers were important. However, hostility between native and immigrant workers had passed its peak and was declining. This decline was in the context of a growth in the relative numbers of coloured immigrants, and in this respect numbers were unimportant.

The native workforce has, of course, changed considerably over the past few years. Those who joined before the early 1950s were accustomed to an all-white or almost all-white workforce. Many have since resigned, retired, or died. Few who have joined in more recent years can have been unaware that they would in all probability

[1] See pp. 353-4.

[2] Probably, too, their behaviour conformed more closely to the Englishman's expectation of the *deferential* black man than did that of later recruits: the 'Uncle Tom' image. There were changes in this respect over the years: some were less prepared to play this deferential role.

be working with numbers of coloured men and women. This continual change in the native workforce has quite likely had an impact on its predominant attitudes and behavioural norms. It is unlikely, though, that this was the only or even the major variable in the decline in overt hostility reported.

The following conclusions can be drawn on the size and speed of build-up of an immigrant workforce. When *very* few are employed, they *have* to fit in and conform. That a fairly continuous growth of the immigrant workforce was accompanied by an increase and then a decline in hostile attitudes and behaviour from the natives, strongly indicates that once the numbers of coloured immigrants have passed a low figure it is the *rate* of build-up which is the important variable conditioning the native response. I cannot say how small this low figure will be. It will differ according to a number of variables, the most important of which are the technical and social organization of work. There is in all probability an optimum rate for the build-up of coloured immigrants in a workforce or, rather, there is a maximum rate which, if exceeded, will cause an increase in hostile attitudes and behaviour on the part of the native workers. Again, it is not possible to say what this maximum rate is; again, it will vary between establishments. The important variables here appear to be the traditions and culture of the organization, the skills and other attributes of the immigrants, the tasks to be learned and performed, and again, the technical and social organization for these tasks. The data strongly indicate that in the London Transport situation this optimum rate was exceeded: the build-up was too rapid for smooth acceptance. In general, it would appear that, from the point of view of smooth absorption, in the sense of minimizing hostile reactions from the native workforce —including managers and supervisors— and of gaining acceptance, a slow rate is preferable to a fast one.[1]

At the time of the fieldwork, the extent of hostile behaviour was declining and the incidence of hostile actions was lessening. Moreover, *very* hostile attitudes were confined to a relatively small number of the natives. The manifestations of this hostility appeared to be largely confined to writing on the walls, to some natives ostracizing the coloured staff, to 'a rough word' now and again, and to some conflict both between and within crews. I concluded that the vast majority of the natives accepted that the coloured staff constituted a permanent part of the workforce, that they were not

[1] The relative size of the immigrant part of the workforce as a variable in acceptance is further discussed below, pp. 349–52.

a temporary expedient which would be replaced when more 'normal' times returned. There were a few who did not accept this, some whose hostility was unremitting and who it is reasonable to assume were prejudiced in the sense defined earlier.[1]

Beyond this, one must proceed with caution: a lack of hostile behaviour is not to be equated with full acceptance. It was *individuals* who were accepted, rather than the immigrants as a group or a number of groups. Task performance and other aspects of behaviour were the key variables in acceptance, task performance probably being the most important of all.

Similarly with other aspects of behaviour: the more closely the immigrants accorded with the natives' behavioural norms, the more likely they were to be accepted. One important exception here concerned acceptance of coloured immigrants in the minor supervisory roles they occupied at the time of the fieldwork. A condition of acceptance of immigrants made by some natives was that they did not fully exercise the authority content of such roles. In one respect some of the immigrants appeared to go beyond the natives' norms, as it were, in that they were seen to be 'real gentlemen' —a designation which indicated a rather Old World courtesy, and behaviour which is not widespread amongst natives in the work situation, such as handshaking.[2]

Whilst there was this acceptance of individuals *as individuals*, there was between groups a considerable extent of pluralism. This applied most markedly in situations associated with work, but not task performance: there was a tendency for mixed crews to separate for meal breaks, there were ethnically based card or domino 'schools', there was some separation in the Permanent Way cabins.[3] Outside the work situation pluralism was the norm.

I concluded that the industrial absorption of immigrants is a slow process. The majority of natives accepted that the immigrants were a permanent part of the workforce, but this acceptance was often grudging, a recognition of reality as it was perceived. Many probably wished it were otherwise. Beyond this minimal acceptance, individuals were accepted more or less as equals. Given that this

[1] See Chapter 1.

[2] This is not to suggest that natives did not regard some of their fellow-workers as gentlemen, but the behaviour of West Indians in particular in respect of these gentlemanly aspects was favourably commented on, and it was behaviour that was not seen to be widespread amongst the natives.

[3] It is possible that between the white groups, e.g. the English and the Irish, there was a considerable extent of pluralism, but it was not evident.

was an organization which had employed coloured immigrants longer than most in Britain, that its policies and tasks were in most respects favourable for the absorption of minority groups, this may appear a pessimistic conclusion, in that I emphasize the slowness of the process. It is, though, the conclusion that all the data point to.

Comparing the acceptance which the natives accorded the various immigrant groups, I can only comment on the West Indians and the Asians: the other groups were too small in number. The West Indians were the groups most fully accepted, and at the same time they were the object of most antagonism. The Indians and Pakistanis appeared to provoke relatively little antagonism: they fitted in in the sense that they were thought to be unobtrusive. The pluralistic model applied most to relationships between native British and the Indians and Pakistanis. There was little antagonism and only minimal acceptance. Other commentators have noted that Indians and Pakistanis seek only limited acceptance, but in this respect those in our samples were atypical. They all spoke good English, otherwise they would not have been engaged. Certainly, they were concerned to emphasize how well *they* were accepted and most reluctant to discuss the hostility they had encountered. Moreover, they *wanted* to be accepted: from many of their comments one might have concluded that only the West Indians experienced difficulties. Yet the Asians were less *fully* accepted by their native workmates than were *some* West Indians.

On the other hand, the West Indians were the object of most antagonism. Colour was a variable here, and it was a handicap which those who were accepted had overcome: 'we don't think of him as coloured'. Acceptance of individual West Indians was often accompanied by marked antipathy towards others. Some natives resented the exuberant gregariousness of the West Indians, and their outward enthusiasm and gusto when playing cards or dominoes, for example. Certainly, their behaviour here was some way removed from that of the more staid, reserved natives.

In so far as native workers distinguished between the West Indian groups—which was relatively rarely—it was the Jamaicans who were regarded with most disfavour. Individual Jamaicans were, though, accepted as much as were members of other groups.

Comparing the three departments, the pattern of answers to a number of questions was often very similar. Yet over-all acceptance was greatest and overt hostility least in Permanent Way; acceptance was least and overt hostility greatest in Central Buses. Railway

Operating occupied a middle position on this axis, and here I differentiate between trainmen and station staff. A number of factors lead to these conclusions.

There was far more conflict built into the organization of bus work than in either of the railway departments. Particularly important here was conflict between crews over the allocation of the work-load: there was the *actual* fiddling and the *belief* that fiddling was commonplace. I have shown, too, the possibilities of conflict between driver and conductor which arise from different expectations of performance. Relationships between crews and supervisors were a further area of conflict. Whilst the reported patterns of relationships between both bus and train crews and inspectors were fairly similar, the bus inspector was far more likely than his rail counterpart to take arbitrary actions, and hence to be accused of unfairness or favouritism.

The absence of coloured bus inspectors, coupled with a belief that this did not result from chance, legitimated the views of the native busmen who were antipathetic towards the coloured immigrants. The immigrants, on the other hand, resented, often bitterly, the fact that none had been promoted to the inspector grade. Recruitment overseas had from time to time been a live issue in Central Buses and whatever the intentions of the Central Bus Committee may have been, there is no doubt that many, both white and coloured, interpreted its actions as aimed against the employment of coloured staff *as such*. The presence of immigrants was resented by some natives because it was seen to reduce both the staff shortage —and hence weaken the case for wage increases—and the amount of overtime and rest-day work. Some drew a parallel here between the coloured immigrants and women conductors.

In the Railway Operating Department, the traditions of railway work, particularly the emphasis on long service, experience, and so on, may be seen as contributing to a culture inhospitable to outsiders, particularly coloured immigrants. There was, though, far less conflict built into the organization of train crews' work as compared with that of busmen.

That role allocation in the Railway Operating Department was largely by seniority was important: promotion was automatic and impersonal; the opportunity for discrimination inherent in a merit system was thus largely absent. It is likely that by this time the promotion of coloured immigrants to supervisory posts *by seniority* will have increased their acceptance by white staff. Promotions on this basis are far more likely to be seen as legitimate than are those made on the largely subjective basis of merit.

Conflict between coloured immigrant and white native staff was more apparent among station staff than among trainmen. Station staff interacted in face-to-face situations for a far longer part of the shift; within the relatively close confines of a station, individuals made a considerable impact on the quality of immigrant-native relationships. Conflict with passengers often intruded into these relationships.

A number of factors contributed to the greater acceptance of coloured immigrants in Permanent Way and the relative lack of overt conflict. Considerations of status were less important than in the operating departments. The task performance of individual platelayers was important to their workmates in every respect. The organization of the workforce in relatively small groups, too, was important: familiarity was more likely to be an element in the relationships between members of a small work group. Finally, numbers of coloured immigrants had been promoted, and had been *seen* to have been promoted, to minor supervisory roles in the Department. The promotion structure of Permanent Way, with its gradual 'steps', facilitated these upgradings and probably reduced the likelihood of native resentment. Compared with Central Buses, each promotion step was small.

THE ACCULTURATION OF ATTITUDES

One of my hypotheses was that the less the immigrant stands out in his new society, the more fully he is absorbed into it. This is relevant both for behaviour and attitudes. In our interviews of native and immigrant workers, we explored a number of attitudes. We were interested here in seeing how far the immigrants had acquired the attitudes of the numerically larger native workforce which were regarded as the norm.[1] The process was then seen as one of acculturation, though I know nothing about the attitudes of the immigrants before they entered the workforce. Additionally, these attitudes have some interest in their own right, as it were.

In most of the attitudes revealed it was the similarity between the native and immigrant groups which was most striking, rather than the reverse. In Central Buses and Railway Operating there was some indication that the immigrants were more conscious of the various

[1] I do not wish to imply that attitudes *should* change in a one-way direction, only that this appears to aid acceptance and reduce conflict.

time constraints, and it is likely that they had not fully internalized the time values.

In their expectations of the good supervisor, there was a broad measure of agreement between the immigrants and natives, though there were one or two differences. Across the three departments there was no consistent difference between the immigrants and the natives, and again the patterns of answers must be related as much to the specific situation as to some more general cultural factor. For example, the immigrant platelayers' greater emphasis on fairness as a quality of the good supervisor is explicable in terms of the belief of some that certain supervisors were not fair.

The immigrants' difficulty over time came out again in their expectations of reciprocity from supervisors over late bookings on, though they appeared to recognize that there were limits, set by the requirements of the task, to the amount of lateness possible.

In both the Railway Operating and Permanent Way departments, the natives showed a greater positive orientation towards various aspects of the task, and I suggested that this reflected a greater extent of self-selection amongst the natives as compared with the immigrants. The immigrant trainmen's greater stress on freedom from supervision was explained in terms of a marked reduction in the possibility of discriminatory actions from first line supervisors, as compared with other occupations, that is. That London Transport was seen as a good or fair employer by the immigrant platelayers was explained largely in terms of the formal procedures, which again reduced the likelihood of discrimination.

The pattern of dislikes was broadly similar between the native and immigrant samples, but the immigrants' difficulty over accepting some of the formal requirements of the organization was in evidence. Particularly important here was the requirement that absences from duties should be explained. Some objected to being called upon to give an explanation when this involved personal or private matters. Others reasoned that as they were not paid for a day off, they should not have to give any explanation. The contractual obligations of their employment, in other words, were seen to cover only the hours worked. There appeared to be also some resentment against having to give a *written* explanation.

It was in their expressed promotion aspirations that the natives and immigrants differed most markedly. In all the male samples, the immigrants were far more likely to say that they wished to be promoted than were the natives. There were differences between the samples, which are spelled out in the appropriate chapters, that go some way towards explaining the different patterns of promotion aspirations, but they do not appear to be the complete explanation.

One variable here may have been the fact that the interviewers were white: esteem was involved and it may have been that the coloured immigrants wished to appear confident of their own abilities. The fact of colour may be important in another way, too: studies of coloured immigrant children in Britain[1] and Negro children in the United States[2] have both shown that these children had higher aspirations than their white fellow-pupils. In so far as these children mirror their parents' aspirations for them, this may 'reflect an understanding by the Negro that in a "white world" he must aim higher and be better to get as far as his white counterpart'.[3] Similar considerations may be relevant here. A number of the immigrants appeared to be imbued with what in another context has been termed the 'American dream'; an optimism that opportunities are wide open to those who 'have what it takes'.[4] Yet this apparent confidence and optimism were held against a background of known discrimination: in employment and in housing, for example. Only in Central Buses was there widespread conviction that internal promotion was influenced by considerations of colour, and this, as I have shown, was well founded.[5]

It may, of course, be that some self-deception was present here: it is reassuring to be able to look forward to a better tomorrow, whatever the problems of today. I do not know how realistic these aspirations were, in the sense of being attainable, regardless of ethnic origins. The socialization which moulds aspirations is a subtle and complex process. It may be that the natives were unduly modest in their aspirations. Alternatively, they may have made a realistic assessment of their likely chances of rising in the occupational hierarchy.

---

[1] David Beetham, *Immigrant School Leavers and the Youth Employment Service in Birmingham* (London, Institute of Race Relations, Special Series, 1967).

[2] Martin Deutsch (ed.), *The Disadvantaged Child* (New York, 1967), quoted by Dipak Nandy, in 'Unrealistic Aspirations', *Race Today* (Vol. 1, No. 1, May 1969), pp. 9–11.

[3] Ibid.

[4] Ely Chinoy, *Automobile Workers and the American Dream* (New York, Doubleday, 1955), p. 1.

[5] See Chapter 6 above.

FEATURES OF THE EMPLOYMENT SITUATION WHICH HAVE ASSISTED THE
ABSORPTION OF COLOURED IMMIGRANTS

In this section I will draw together and summarize those aspects
of the employment situation which have assisted the absorption of
coloured immigrants in the organization. The object here is to
isolate those variables which to a greater or lesser degree are unique
to either the industry or the organization. I will argue that in many
respects the work tasks of the organization and its procedures, for
task and role allocation and so on, make it peculiarly well suited for
the absorption of minority groups. It is the combination of these
features of the employment situation, rather than any individual
aspect, which is important for absorption. These tasks and procedures existed before immigrants were employed and it is not,
therefore, a case of the organization adapting to a new element in
the labour force: such adaptation has been minimal.[1]

The work tasks performed by busmen and underground railwaymen contain an element of interdependence, though the extent and
nature of this interdependence vary somewhat. For example, it is
important to a busman that he has a good workmate, that is, a
driver or conductor. For the trainman, a similar interdependence
exists, though to varying degrees: it is of greater importance under
conditions of crisis, and such interdependence as exists under normal
service conditions is over-all less than that found amongst busmen.
Interdependence is also an element in the relationships of station
and Permanent Way staff, though it is somewhat different. In both
situations, though, the performance of individuals impinges on the
ease or difficulties of the tasks of their fellow-workers.

It may, of course, be argued that an element of interdependence
is found in many occupations in other industries and this is doubtless
so. An important difference, so far as bus and train crews are concerned, is interdependence combined with physical separation and
a lack of face-to-face contact. The extent to which a busman is
seen to measure up to a good driver or conductor is then more
important than his other characteristics, since face-to-face interaction is minimal. The same holds true for trainmen. Another
important difference from many other occupations is that the interdependence is largely between two people.

In the despatch of traffic and movement of passengers by station
staff there is an element of interdependence, but it is less than that

[1] See pp. 344–9 below.

SOME CONCLUSIONS 341

between members of a bus or train crew. This is one feature contributing to the less smooth pattern of relationships between immigrant and native station staff. In cleaning duties there is interdependence to the extent that it matters to the individual that the person who previously carried out a particular task was seen to do it properly: otherwise the task is more difficult to perform.

For Permanent Way staff, performance matters in a number of respects: in pulling one's weight in physically arduous tasks, in a concern for safety, in the quality and quantity of work done and the effect of this on bonus earnings.

In these ways, then, the performance of the individual busman, operating railwayman, or platelayer impinges on the ease or difficulty of the tasks of his fellow-workers. In so far as they are seen to measure up to the expectations of their native fellow-workers, the performance of the coloured immigrants has been a variable encouraging their acceptance. Failure to meet these expectations of performance encourages conflict and non-acceptance. A majority of native workers in each department evaluated their coloured immigrant fellow-workers as being on the whole no better or worse than the natives in the performance of their roles. It can be hypothesized, then, that interdependence between white and coloured workers in task performance encourages the acceptance of the latter by the former, provided the coloured workers are perceived to perform their roles adequately in the sense of meeting the expectations that their white fellow-workers have of them; that the greater the extent of this interdependence, the greater the likelihood of acceptance. Physical separation also appears to be a variable here in that it probably reduces the possibility of conflict over some aspects of behaviour not central to task performance, such as the expression of attitudes. This is probably more important in the early stages of immigrant absorption and also for those native busmen or trainmen who are most antipathetic towards the coloured immigrants: the latter can earn their acceptance by their task performance.

There is in the rail situation little or no potential for conflict between train crews over the allocation of the work-load. By contrast, the potential for such conflict between bus crews is considerable. I have shown the importance of this potential as a variable in immigrant-native relationships, and it can be hypothesized that the degree to which conflict between workers is built into the technical

and social organization of work is a variable in the pattern of immigrant-native relationships. The greater the potential for conflict
between roles or work teams, the greater the likelihood of white
native-coloured immigrant conflict.

The allocation of the work-load is relevant, too, in the quality
of the relationships between coloured immigrant workers and white
supervisors. Control of train crews under normal service conditions
is by an impersonal signal system. By contrast, in the bus situation,
there is a great deal of face-to-face interaction between supervisors
and busmen, which is productive of conflict. One problem here
was that the roadside point inspector did not have enough reliable
information on which to assess the performance of individual
crews and many of his actions were arbitrary. This clearly affected
his relationships with his subordinates, white and coloured. In
general terms, though, it can be hypothesized that the more task
performance is controlled by impersonal mechanisms, the less
potential there is for conflict between supervisors and subordinates. The relevance of this for the absorption of coloured immigrants is that one further potential source of conflict is minimized.
Whether supervisors *are* discriminatory in their actions is less important than whether or not they are perceived to be so by their
subordinates.

Whilst there is this important difference between the situation
of busmen and trainmen, they do, however, share one common
feature relative to many other occupations: this is their high degree
of freedom from constant interaction with supervisors. This is
important for the immigrants in that again the possibility of discriminatory behaviour is reduced. That the duties of busmen and
trainmen are allocated by an impersonal roster system is important
here, too. Again, face-to-face interaction with supervisors is minimized: 'no one tells you what to do, you read it'. This applied also
to the station staff, but to a lesser extent. In Permanent Way, on the
other hand, we saw that the perceived inequality in the distribution
of both work tasks and overtime opportunities by some supervisors was the cause of some resentment by the immigrant platelayers, and to that extent it hindered absorption. This, then, supports
my previous hypothesis on impersonal mechanisms. Freedom
from constant supervision has a wider appeal in that it is seen by
native busmen and trainmen as one of the attractive features of their
employment situation.

The tasks performed are relevant in one other respect. All

require some formal training by the organization.[1] The importance
of this training is that previous occupational skills and experience,
whilst not completely irrelevant, are of less importance than in some
other industries. Training is important, too, in the acculturation of
behaviour and attitudes.

So far in this section, I have been concerned with those features
of the employment situation most directly related to the tasks of
the individual busman or railwayman. I now turn to some aspects
of the larger organization which appear relevant.

That the organization is a bureaucratic one is important to the
extent that bureaucratic procedures *tend* not to discriminate.[2] This
has a number of aspects. First in the recruitment of staff. There are
criteria laid down for recruitment, though they are in some respects
inexact. They do not preclude discrimination in engagements, but
they make it less likely.[3] Such discrimination as we are aware of
was deliberate and at the request of the departments concerned.
That recruitment is centralized is important here, too: were it
localized, there would be more opportunities for more people to
discriminate. Centralization was important also in the distribution
of the immigrants in that those in the departments who were reluctant to accept them had little choice. This was largely but not completely so, in that the views of individual supervisors and managers
concerning the numbers of immigrants at their locations were not
ignored.

The formal and centralized recruitment system was important,
too, in maintaining standards. Task performance was important and
so, therefore, were the abilities and potential of recruits. The early
recruits were thought to have been particularly good in this respect.

Formal procedures were most important, perhaps, in two areas:
discipline and promotion. The disciplinary procedures, with their
provisions for representation and appeal are important in all respects,
but most of all in job security. They ensure that no one can be
dismissed arbitrarily by an individual. This is not unimportant for all
workers, but it is particularly relevant for the coloured immigrants

[1] More correctly, training is provided by the organization since it is *possible* that
for some grades, staff could be recruited and trained on the job by example and by
performing the tasks of the job.

[2] See Chapter 2, p. 33, for a discussion which qualifies this statement.

[3] For a very similar conclusion relating to Negroes entering employment with the
New York transit systems, see James J. McGinley, *Labour Relations in the New York
Rapid Transit Systems, 1904–1944* (New York, Columbia University Press, King's
Crown Press, 1949) p. 253, quoted in Jeffress, pp. 29–30.

as the potential for one form of discriminatory behaviour is very much reduced.[1]

The other main area where formal procedures are relevant is that of promotion. Again, I would not argue that formal promotion procedures remove the possibility of discrimination—I have shown that this was not so in respect of the promotion to the inspector grade in Central Buses. This was, though, a case where discrimination was built into the procedure. In general, formal promotion procedures appear to operate in the opposite direction.

The use of seniority as the chief criterion for role allocation is an important feature of the formal procedures, though it was found only in Railway Operating. It is an impersonal mechanism, and it can be measured. Again, there was a built-in tendency not to discriminate on grounds of other criteria.

It can then be hypothesized that the more bureaucratic and impersonal the mechanisms for recruitment, role allocation, discipline, and so on, the less likelihood there is of discrimination in these areas. This points to the conclusion that in some respects the large organization is more suited to the absorption of minority groups than is the small, though the latter may have other characteristics which are favourable in other respects.

Finally, the fact that bus and train crews are widely dispersed whilst performing their tasks aids absorption. This is important both in terms of interaction between *groups* and of the natives' perceptions of the situation. Were comparable numbers of white native and coloured immigrant workers concentrated under one roof in a manufacturing plant, the situation would be very different in both these respects. Shift work, too, reduces the numbers interacting at any one time.

MANAGEMENT PRACTICES

Throughout this study there is a strong emphasis on explaining the absorption of coloured immigrants in terms of the traditions and norms of the organization, its tasks, and so on. It is, then, pertinent to ask to what extent have management policies and practices assisted or impeded the absorptive process. Here I distinguish between those actions which were concerned with the tasks of the organization as such and those which were specifically concerned with coloured immigrants and influenced by their presence. What, in

[1] 'Reduced' is the appropriate word: I would not argue that discriminatory dismissals are impossible with this type of system, but they are less likely.

other words, had management done specifically about the coloured immigrants?

The superficial answer to this question is very little, but that requires considerable clarification. Coloured immigrants were recruited to meet a staff shortage and management practices have reflected that basic fact. It is important to emphasize here that in so far as management devised policies and developed skills to meet problems occasioned by the presence of coloured immigrants, they have been essentially self-taught and have arisen from experience. There was, in any case, no body of knowledge or expertise to which they could turn for advice, had they wished to do so. Until fairly recently, there was little published on the employment of coloured immigrants in Britain, and London Transport's managers, collectively, had more experience than most of the problems which arise. Thus in the early days they had to learn that one coloured worker did not necessarily get on harmoniously with another simply because they were both coloured, that a West African did not necessarily regard a West Indian as his brother, that Jamaicans and Barbadians regarded each other as very different.

Whilst it was then largely a process of learning by experience, there were positive aspects. For example, in the early days of the Barbadian recruitment, care was taken not to place one Barbadian in a garage by himself, but with always at least one or two. Again in this early period, a West Indian was appointed specifically to deal with the immigrants' welfare problems.[1] Resistance to the placement and promotion of coloured immigrants was mostly handled firmly.[2] As Sheila Patterson has written, 'it would appear that if upper management takes a positive and forthright line from the start over the entry and acceptance of immigrants the outcome is more likely to be successful'.[3]

At the local level, some garage managers avoided placing coloured immigrant conductors with white native drivers known to be very hostile to them. In this they appear to have been guided primarily by the need to ensure that services operated.

Generally, management's emphasis was on treating coloured

[1] When he later resigned, he was not replaced by another immigrant: management took the view that there was no longer any need for these separate provisions.
[2] The major exception here was, of course, the *anticipated* reaction from white native busmen to coloured inspectors, but this was not the only or even the most important consideration. See Chapter 6.
[3] Patterson, *Immigrants in Industry*, p. 236.

immigrant and white native workers equally, which meant similarly.[1] From the point of view of aiding acceptance of immigrants by native workers, this approach had much to commend it. I have shown the resentment occasioned by the 'more favourable' treatment of the immigrants—in a few cases real, in most imagined. Yet this emphasis on similar treatment is not without its drawbacks, in that it obscures the extent to which native and immigrant workers *are* different. These differences became most important in the area of training. By *training criteria alone*, there was a case for treating natives and immigrants differently, in other words, for treating the immigrants 'more favourably', to reduce or eliminate the handicaps that many undoubtedly suffered. Whether this was a practical proposition is another matter: any advantage gained might well be more than outweighed by the resentment caused among the native staff. Possibly this problem could to come extent be overcome by more flexible training arrangements, but in so far as these served to reduce the *inequality* of the immigrants they would be seen to *favour* them. To some extent this was a problem of the early years of immigration. Yet it is unlikely that the training problem will be confined to recent immigrants or even to the first generation. The question of unequal treatment intended to promote equality of opportunity is likely, then, to be a relatively long-enduring one.

With this reservation concerning training, the principle of similar treatment of immigrant and native workers was appropriate for harmonious absorption, or, more accurately, for a reduction of tension. Two areas where treatment was not equal were in promotion to the inspector grade in Central Buses and, on occasions, in recruitment.

On the question of promotion of coloured inspectors, little need be added to that written above.[2] An adverse reaction was expected from passengers, native busmen, and immigrant busmen of different origins. These were very real fears, and the physical safety of coloured

[1] In 1969, London Transport set up its own machinery under Schedule 2 of the Race Relations Act, 1968. This machinery dealt with eleven complaints in 1969. In no case was discrimination found. London Transport Board, *Annual Report and Accounts, 1969* (London, H.M.S.O., 1970), p. 31. In 1970, eight cases were dealt with, and in the first eight months of 1971, there were three cases. Again no discrimination was found. Source: Office of the Chief Establishment Officer, L.T.E. The operation of the 1968 Act, including the industrial machinery, has been subjected to some criticism. See *Race Today* (Vol. 3, No. 10, October 1971; and Vol. 3, No. 11, November 1971).

[2] Chapter 6, pp. 108–9.

inspectors could not be guaranteed. On balance it may be argued that London Transport was over-cautious here in that its actions impeded absorption. It certainly appeared to legitimate the views of those native busmen who were very much opposed to the possibility of coloured inspectors, and it caused much resentment among the coloured busmen. The bus inspector's supervisory role is a particularly difficult one to perform adequately, and he is exposed and vulnerable to an extent which is quite unusual. The point to emerge here which is of wider applicability is that the acceptance of coloured supervisors by white subordinates is enhanced if the first coloured workers promoted are seen to be somewhat better than the average white supervisor.

Recruitment of coloured workers has on occasions been slowed down. The motives behind these actions have been fears that the rate of build-up of numbers of immigrants was proceeding too fast, that native resentment and hostility might get out of hand, that problems of training were intensifying, and that the next generation of supervisors would not be found in the existing workforce or, more accurately, there would not be a sufficient number of the calibre required. These restrictions were largely confined to Railway Operating, though they were also made in Permanent Way when sufficient numbers of white native recruits were available. In Central Buses the rate of build-up of numbers of immigrants at individual garages was at times slowed down, usually at the request of the garage manager. Given the widespread staff shortage, coloured recruits could usually be placed in other garages.[1]

All the evidence indicated that from the point of view of smooth absorption, the rate of build-up of the relative numbers of coloured immigrants was too fast—in spite of these attempts to restrict it. Whether a *small* acceleration or deceleration in this rate made or would make much difference to native acceptance or hostility, I do not know.

In the early period of immigrant recruitment some attempt was made to disperse them and to restrict the numbers at any one location. This was done without the rigidity implied by a quota system, but some rule-of-thumb measures were adopted, most notably in Permanent Way. In practice the ability of staff to transfer locations militated against this dispersal policy, and one or two concentrations were reported. The evidence on the *speed* of build-up

[1] At times a shortage of drivers brought restrictions on the numbers of conductors who could usefully be recruited.

indicates that in so far as dispersal tended to slow this speed, it assisted absorption.

From this section so far the reader might conclude that management practices were uniform, that there was a unity of purpose. This would be misleading. Most managers appear to have been essentially task oriented in their approach to the employment of coloured immigrants: they were part of the workforce and had to be treated as such. Any problems had to be ironed out. In this respect, whether they would have preferred an all-white workforce is largely beside the point: they had to manage with the staff they had. This was the prevailing approach, but there were exceptions. A *few* would *definitely* have preferred an all-white workforce. If they had to accept immigrants, they would rather that they did not achieve promotion. They were, though, very much in the minority. Again the advantages of the large bureaucratic organization for the absorption of immigrants is emphasized: the extent to which these few managers could actively influence policies was very much constrained by the rules and by centralized procedures.

There were differences, too, over the speed with which change ought to be attempted, for example, in the promotion of coloured bus inspectors. These differences appeared to be largely related to those of personalities, though there was perhaps some tendency for line managers to be more cautious than those in the service departments.

One other area in which differences were found between managers was that of the recording of information which distinguished between native and immigrant workers. Practices were not uniform here. As a general rule it appeared that those who were most opposed to the keeping of separate records were against any form of discrimination—and the collection of such information was seen as a discriminatory act. There was also a fear that these records might be misused.

Recruitment overseas was the most significant management action concerned specifically with coloured immigrants. The evidence indicated that the Barbados scheme reduced the initial problems of the immigrants—in housing, pre-recruitment training, and so on—and to that extent it aided absorption. Against this must be weighed the resentment caused in the native workforce: overseas recruitment kept to the fore the issue of the employment of coloured immigrants *as such*. It is hardly possible to say whether on balance the over-all absorptive process was aided or impeded by overseas recruitment. The Barbadians were the immigrant group seen to conform closest to the natives in a number of respects and to that extent, they appear to have been found more acceptable. Their attributes were those of Barbadians, rather than of Barbadian direct recruits. The evidence indicated, though, that many would not have come to Britain but for the recruitment scheme.

I began this section by asking, 'what has management done specifically about the coloured immigrants?' The superficial answer given was very little. Subject to the qualifications in these pages, the answer must remain very little in that the major variables which have assisted or impeded absorption did not result from management actions occasioned specifically by the presence of immigrants.

THE RELEVANCE OF THE RELATIVE NUMBERS OF IMMIGRANTS IN A WORKFORCE

I have argued that the rate of build-up of the immigrant part of a workforce is an important variable conditioning the native response. Does its *relative size* make much difference to the quality of white native-coloured immigrant relationships? This is the question I discuss in this section.

In the literature on coloured immigrants in British industry, there is considerable evidence of the use of a 'quota' system, 'whereby the number of coloured immigrants employed by a firm is kept at or below a given percentage of the total labour force'.[1] These quotas have mostly ranged from 3 to 10 per cent.[2] Similar arrangements have also been applied to the employment of foreign European workers.[3] That there may be 'desirable limits' to the proportions of workers of different ethnic origins is acknowledged, too, by the racial balance provisions of the Race Relations Act, 1968.[4]

The coloured immigrant proportion of the total workforce varied widely between the locations included in this study, and the relative size of the coloured population was one of the most important criteria in the selection of garages for the fieldwork. Coloured

[1] Wright, p. 63.

[2] Patterson, *Dark Strangers* and *Immigrants in Industry*; Wright; and J. Egginton, *They Seek a Living* (London, Hutchinson, 1957).

[3] J. A. Tannahill, *European Volunteer Workers in Britain* (Manchester, Manchester University Press, 1958). See also J. A. C. Brown, *The Social Psychology of Industry* (London, Penguin, 1954), p. 115.

[4] Race Relations Act, 1968, Section 8, part 1, sub-section 2. See also the *Guide to the 'Racial Balance' Provisions of the Race Relations Act, 1968* (London, Race Relations Board, 1969).

staff comprised 14 per cent of the total at Eastside, 20 per cent at Westside, and 31 per cent at Southside garages. In the Railway Operating Department, Northway had a coloured immigrant population of 40 per cent and Southway one of 41 per cent. The relative numbers of coloured immigrants at stations and in Permanent Way groups and gangs also varied. With the single exception of Eastside, the garages and rail depots all had coloured immigrant populations well above the 10 per cent level which appeared to have become part of managements' 'conventional wisdom'. Did these variations between the locations affect the quality of coloured immigrant-white native relationships?

No simple answer can be given to this question, for a number of reasons. First, it is unlikely that the influence of the relative numbers of coloured immigrants would be restricted to those at any one location. Most bus routes are worked by staff from two or more garages and busmen frequently interact with those from other garages. Trainmen, too, interact with railwaymen at many locations other than their home depot. In so far as the relative number of coloured immigrants was an important variable in native attitudes and behaviour, it may well be that the proportion in the total undertaking or the locality was the most significant figure, rather than the number at the garage or depot. Second, it may be that the rate of build-up varied between the locations, but it is unlikely that there were significant differences here. Third, whilst it appeared that this rate of build-up had declined, that the relative numbers of coloured immigrants had reached a plateau, I do not know if the native busmen and railwaymen perceived it in these terms. Maybe some at least saw the numbers increasing relatively rapidly and this conditioned their response. Fourth, when I analysed the interview data according to the sex of the interviewer, there were found to be differences.

Analysis of the data in terms of responses/attitudes elicited by the interviewers showed that the most significant differences concerned the responses from the native samples. Relatively fewer reported hostility towards the immigrants to female than male interviewers. The patterns from the coloured immigrant samples were not very different between the interviewers.

Between the two rail depots there was little over-all difference in the pattern of answers from both native and immigrant railwaymen to questions on hostility and—from the natives only—in their anticipations of reactions to coloured supervisors. Both depots, it will be remembered, had very similar proportions of coloured staff.

Turning to the garages, Eastside (with a coloured immigrant population of 14 per cent) showed the highest proportion of natives reporting hostility towards the immigrants and when the 'qualified' answers[1] were taken into account, this pattern was repeated by the immigrants. Westside (with a coloured immigrant population of 20 per cent) showed the lowest proportion of natives reporting hostility towards the immigrants. The pattern from the immigrants is not consistent here: in their initial answers they did not differ very much from the other two garages, but again when the 'qualified' answers were included relatively fewer reported hostility than at Eastside or Southside. To that extent, the answers from Westside's immigrants and natives were consistent. Over-all, Southside (with a coloured immigrant population of 31 per cent) occupied a roughly mid-way position, but closer to that of Eastside than Westside.

A major complication arises from the fact that all the interviewing at Eastside was done by a male (myself) and all at Westside by a female. At Southside the interviewing was shared. It may be that the sex of the interviewer was the most important variable in these different patterns of response, and this is the conclusion I am inclined to accept. On the other hand, there were differences between the garages which *could* explain the different patterns of response.

Eastside, it appeared, had the most cohesive native workforce. Westside had a considerable number of white immigrants. Southside had been staffed with busmen—and trammen—from other garages. It may be argued that more resentment of and antagonism towards outsiders would be expressed by a cohesive workforce than by one composed of a number of groups, as at Southside, or by one in which white immigrants form a sizeable proportion, as at Westside. One further factor which could go some way towards explaining the relatively low reporting of hostility at Westside was that this was the garage with appreciably less crew pairing across ethnic boundaries than existed at the other garages, and this did not appear to result from chance. Possibly this pairing pattern was conducive to a relative lack of overtly hostile behaviour.

Between the locations the evidence is inconclusive.[2] Certainly,

---

[1] See Chapter 5.

[2] The data from other locations were not analysed separately, owing to the relatively small numbers interviewed at any one.

it has not been possible to establish a connection between the relative size of the immigrant population and the extent and intensity of native hostility.

One argument advanced for quotas has been that working skills and techniques are acquired by immigrants more quickly if their numbers are relatively small. My data throw no light on this problem, largely because skills are taught formally and there was no evidence that the relative numbers of immigrants made any difference here.

On the extent of intensity of native hostility the data are, I believe, valuable. When there are *very* few coloured immigrants employed, they have to conform largely to the natives' norms or, more accurately, the pressures to conform are great. As soon as there are sufficient numbers for separate immigrant groups to form, these pressures are lessened and their own group norms are reinforced by the presence of others from their own group. When a separate immigrant group, or groups, is formed, then there are what amounts to separate cultures. The development of these separate cultures caused some considerable resentment amongst the natives, but in so far as they were not prepared to accept the immigrants *on an equal basis*, they have helped to create them.

How large an immigrant group has to be before a separate culture develops depends on many variables, but in most situations it is likely to be small, relative to the size of the native workforce. It appears that beyond this the relative size of immigrant groups can vary widely with little or no impact on the quality of white native-coloured immigrant relationships.

In those industries or occupations where technical skills are acquired by performance, rather than formal tuition, the quota argument may have more force in that one consequence of the development of separate cultures is the retardation of the process of acculturation. Here too, though, the rate of build-up of the relative number of immigrants is probably a more crucial variable.

In the London Transport situation, the coloured immigrants were overwhelmingly West Indian. To that extent, the predominant immigrant culture was West Indian, though there were divisions within the West Indian group. When immigrant groups of very different origins are more closely matched in size, then the situation would probably be very different, particularly in terms of the potential for conflict between immigrant groups.

THE IMPACT OF COLOURED IMMIGRANTS ON THE ORGANIZATION

Coloured workers were recruited to meet a staff shortage: other recruits of the standard required were not available in sufficient numbers to meet the wastage of existing staff. It is then logical to begin by asking how far London Transport's staff shortage has been alleviated by the recruitment of coloured immigrants. Here I must proceed with caution. The wastage rate of the Barbados-recruited staff has been considerably lower than that of other staff.[1] I have no hard evidence, but it seems likely that the wastage rate of coloured immigrants has been lower than that of white native staff. The staff shortage has, though, remained fairly constant, and this applies most to Central Buses: the establishment has been reduced over the past few years, and staff shortage as a percentage of this establishment has remained fairly stable. One important consequence of a reduction of the establishment was a decrease in scheduled mileage. This decrease in mileage was accompanied by a reduction in the amount of rest-day work and overtime available. It is a tenable hypothesis that, at any given level of wages relative to those in the wider labour market, a number of busmen were only retained by the amount of rest-day work and overtime available. When the establishment was reduced, so was mileage and so, in turn, was rest-day work and overtime. A number of busmen left, and potential recruits were deterred. This analysis is crude and doubtless an over-simplification. Far more detailed data would be required to substantiate the hypothesis outlined. *Prima facie*, though, the hypothesis that there was in these terms a staff shortage built into the organization is a tenable one. This appears to have most direct relevance to the recruitment and retention of busmen, but it probably applies, though with less force, to railwaymen also.

I am not arguing that earnings were the only or even the most important factor in the recruitment and retention of busmen. Other considerations were clearly important, most notably the discontent stemming from shift work and from the organization of work: problems of bunching, fiddling, and so on which are discussed in detail in Chapters 4, 5, and 6. In economic terms, I am concerned here with the margin: it is the marginal men who leave or do not join. Other conditions, in any case, are in the short-run constant. This analysis applies to both coloured immigrant and white native workers, but most forcibly to the latter: I have argued above that

[1] See Chapter 13.

in some respects the two groups are in different labour markets, the market for the natives being more favourable for them.[1]

It can then be argued that the employment of coloured immigrants has done little to solve London Transport's staff shortage *directly* or, rather, that it is not self-evident that it has done so. Immigration has, of course, increased the capital's—and the country's—labour force, and recruitment overseas has brought a net addition which probably would not have taken place without positive action. It may well be that the employment of coloured immigrants has resulted in a more *stable* workforce, or rather, the coloured immigrants provided a relatively stable section of the labour force. The Barbadian direct recruits certainly did; other coloured immigrants probably did also. This relative stability is not without its advantages to an organization which expensively trains recruits and those seeking promotion, and which fills all supervisory and many managerial posts from existing staff.

Some might argue that but for the coloured immigrants the staff shortage would be far greater. This may be so, but the relatively constant staff shortage provides a compelling argument, though it is not conclusive. That *coloured* immigrants have been employed is in any case irrelevant to the argument: the relationship of staff shortage to establishment, earnings, and rest-day and overtime work does not depend on the ethnic origins of some of the workforce.

Aside from this postulated effect, or rather the lack of it, on the staff shortage, in what other areas has the employment of coloured immigrants made for changes in the organization? The short answer is that they are relatively few and slight. One problem here is that I cannot realistically compare the situation found with the hypothetical continuation of an all-white native workforce—I cannot, in other words, project the pre-immigrant situation to the present. I can only look at any changes which appear to have been occasioned by the presence of coloured immigrants without conjecturing what might have happened in their absence.

Beginning with the recruitment of staff, cultural differences made the selection of coloured immigrants more difficult than that of native applicants. Training too, was more difficult for similar reasons, and the failure rates of coloured immigrant trainees were generally higher than those of their white native counterparts. To that extent, it was more costly.

There is no evidence to suggest that the task performance of the

[1] See Chapter 3.

organization has been in any way affected by the presence of coloured immigrant workers. To this must be added the reservation that it has been productive of conflict, though this is mostly a question of ethnic and racial differences aggravating conflict which was potentially present. It might, perhaps, be expected that this conflict would be reflected in lower task performance, but I know of no measurable effects. Similarly, there was no evidence that the task performance of coloured immigrants was on average any different from that of white native workers.

That many public transport workers are coloured immigrants has probably increased the amount of overt staff-passenger conflict —certainly coloured staff experienced more of this kind of difficulty than did their white native colleagues.

In the culture of the organization, in its accepted ways of behaving and thinking, there has perhaps been some movement in the direction of greater latitude. I have shown that combined with absorption in some areas, notably task performance and in terms of Eisenstadt's dispersion concept, there was a considerable extent of pluralism. This development of pluralism may well ease the tensions somewhat, but in so far as there is less conformity with the natives' norms, it occasions some resentment amongst them.

Beyond this, though, adaptation by the organization has been minimal. At managerial and supervisory levels in particular there was a pronounced emphasis on the immigrants conforming to the established norms. In so far as they have been seen to do so their acceptance has been made easier.

ABSORPTION OR PLURALISM?

Eisenstadt's three indices of full absorption, it will be remembered, were '(a) acculturation; (b) satisfactory and integral personal adjustment of the immigrants; and (c) complete dispersion of the immigrants as a group.'[1] Acculturation was defined as being 'concerned principally with the extent to which the immigrant learns the various roles, norms, and customs of the absorbing society'.[2] The three indices are, of course, interrelated: the data show that the dispersion of the immigrants within the organization was assisted by their acculturation and impeded by their lack of it. On the second of the three indices, 'the satisfactory and integral personal adjustment of the immigrants', the data throw little light.

---

[1] Eisenstadt, p. 11.   [2] Ibid., p. 12.

The other two indices are applicable. They are in some respects crude or, more accurately, they require a number of more precise indicators. A further problem is that they do not adequately take account of the behaviour and attitudes of the host population: theoretically, at least, it is possible to have a situation where a high degree of absorption as measured by these indices is combined with marked antipathy from the host society.

Patterson has devised some 'indices of industrial absorption'.[1] These appear applicable to my data, but as she recognizes, the processes of absorption are essentially 'untidy' and out of step. When I fit my data to these indices, I find a situation that is in some respects one of the earlier phase of accommodation, in others one of assimilation, and yet has some characteristics of pluralistic integration. Thus, whilst these indices are useful in that they spotlight the various stages and processes of absorption, we cannot as it were plot a given situation on a scale of absorption. There are a number of dimensions and the relationship between them is not as yet sufficiently clear.

It is not my intention here to attempt to construct detailed indices of absorption or pluralism. That must await a later work. Instead, I propose to look at some of the data in terms of two of Eisenstadt's indices, and to pose the question suggested by the title of this section. I will also consider further the race relations versus the immigration approaches to the research area.

Beginning with recruitment, I have shown that a lack of acculturation, for example, a perceived weakness in spoken English, put the immigrants at a disadvantage compared with the native applicants. In this respect the situation may be seen in terms of the immigration perspective. In so far as the recruitment staff deliberately discriminated at the request of the departments in an attempt to restrict the speed of build-up of numbers of immigrants, this was a response to a situation which was seen partly in immigration and partly in race relations terms. To the extent that the departments were concerned with the relatively high failure rates of immigrants on training courses, the problem was one of immigration. In so far as the departments were responding to a perceived hostile reaction from native workers, then the race relations perspective is the most appropriate.

The immigrants' greater difficulty in learning technical skills, in so far as it impeded their dispersion, retarded their absorption.

[1] *Immigrants in Industry*, p. 206

A lack of acculturation in relation to two main areas of behaviour was also seen to impede absorption of operating staff: specifically a lack of full acceptance of the various time values and of the formal procedures of the large bureaucratic organization.

When the changes in the occupational dispersion of the coloured immigrants over the period 1965–6 to 1970 are examined, the picture that emerges is far from clear-cut. Table 17.1 shows the occupational distribution of the immigrant busmen in 1966 and 1970.

TABLE 17.1.
Drivers and Conductors in Central Buses, in Percentages.

	Drivers	Conductors	Women conductors	Total conductors	Total
As at September 1966:					
White native	91	70	87	75	83
Coloured immigrant	9	30	13	25	17
(Number)	(13,311)	(9,520)	(4,077)	(13,597)	(26,908)
As at April 1970:					
White native	92	74	84	77	85
Coloured immigrant	8	26	16	23	15
(Number)	(12,162)	(7,925)	(3,066)	(10,991)	(23,153)

It will be seen that apart from the woman conductor grade, the coloured immigrant representation has declined.[1] The total numbers of busmen—and women—have also declined. The relative decline of white native and coloured immigrant busmen is shown in Table 17.2.

TABLE 17.2.
Relative Decline in the Numbers of Busmen, 1966–1970, in Percentages.[*]

	Drivers	Conductors	Women conductors	Total conductors	Total
White native	— 8	—12	—27	—17	—12
Coloured immigrant	—18	—29	—13	—26	—24
All	— 9	—17	—25	—19	—14

[*] The decline in numbers has been expressed as percentages of the 1966 figures.

[1] The trend of Negro employment in the American urban transit industry has been in the opposite direction. See Jeffress.

The relative decline in the number of coloured immigrants was twice that of the white natives over roughly three and a half years, September 1966 to April 1970. There has, of course, been a considerable 'through-put' of busmen in this period, and the figures tell us nothing about staff wastage rates. This decline in the relative numbers of coloured busmen was probably largely a reflection—via the recruitment process—of the reduction of the numbers of coloured immigrants entering Britain and, of most immediate relevance, of direct recruitment in Barbados.[1] It may be, too, that there has been a greater dispersion of coloured immigrants in other industries. Another way of looking at these data is to compare the coloured busmen's representation in the driver and conductor grades in 1966 and 1970. In 1966, 30 per cent of the coloured male staff in Central Buses were drivers, the remainder were conductors. By 1970 the figure for drivers had risen to 34 per cent. There had then been some lessening of the concentration of coloured busmen in the conductor grade, but the shift in the direction of more accurately reflecting the occupational distribution of the native workforce had been fairly slight. Some coloured immigrants were to be found in the supervisory grades in Central Buses, and included one area traffic inspector, four garage inspectors, and eleven inspectors; but in total they comprised only 1 per cent of the supervisory grades.

Turning to the operating railwaymen, a somewhat different picture emerged. Table 17.3 shows the representation of coloured immigrants in a number of grades in September 1965 and April 1970.

Clearly, there was a considerable change in the coloured immigrant railwaymen's representation in some grades over the four and a half year period. Whilst immigrant trainmen in 1965 were mostly guards, by 1970 they were spread evenly over the motorman and guard grades. None were automatic train operators, but the seniority for this grade in the autumn of 1970 was twenty years. Seniority was an important factor in the increased representation of the coloured railwaymen in the motorman grade, and in their appearing in numbers in the inspector grade. The decline in the numbers of coloured guards again probably reflects the fall in coloured immigration to Britain.

So far as the Railway Operating Department was concerned there was then a considerable shift in the occupational distribution of the

[1] See Chapter 13.

TABLE 17.3.
Railway Operating Staff in Selected Grades, in Percentages.

	Motormen	Guards	Station foremen	Station inspectors*
As at September 1965:				
White native	87	50	72	100
Coloured immigrant	13	50	28	—
(Number)	(1,669)	(1,691)	(501)	(215)
As at April 1970:				
White native	67	67	74	83
Coloured immigrant	33	33	26	17
(Number)	(1,748)	(1,799)	(465)	(235)

* The total figure for station inspectors is as at May 1966.

immigrant part of the workforce in the direction of a more accurate mirroring of that existing amongst the native workforce.

No very recent data were available to me on the structure of the Permanent Way workforce, but one or two coloured immigrants had entered the extra ganger grade, and it is reasonable to assume that the distribution of the immigrants was moving in the direction of that of the natives.

As measured by the third of Eisenstadt's indices, that of dispersion, there had been minimal movement in Central Buses over the period 1966–70, but in Railway Operating absorption was plainly occurring, and the same is probably also true of Permanent Way.

Finally, it is useful to draw the threads together on one other problem: how far and in what respects are the absorption and pluralism models appropriate to the situation found?

In terms of two of the three indices found by Eisenstadt, the data point in the direction of absorption. There had been some consider-able acculturation, and dispersion was taking place, most notably in the railway departments. On the other hand, a number of elements of pluralism were in evidence. In canteens, messrooms, and cabins, some separation between white natives and coloured immigrants appeared to be the norm. There was relatively little contact between immigrants and natives outside of the work situation, though many natives preferred to keep separate their work and non-work roles— 'mates are not friends'—regardless of the ethnic origins of their workmates. Differences of race and ethnicity, though, added one further barrier to interaction outside their work roles. The other indicator pointing in the direction of pluralism was the relative lack of contact, and in some cases the overt conflict, reported between white and coloured neighbours.

The most important single factor determining whether relationships between coloured immigrants and the native population in the wider society move in the direction of greater absorption or pluralism is clearly the behaviour of the host population. At the present there are elements of both absorption and pluralism—race and ethnic relations are at the crossroads.

In so far as the West Indians—with whom I have been largely concerned in this volume—are able to attain their aspirations in employment, housing, acceptance *as equals* by their white fellow-citizens, then the situation will proceed towards further absorption. The orientation of the West Indians certainly points in this direction, though there are indications that some younger West Indians do not seek acceptance by a society which they feel has largely rejected them.

The situation of the Asian communities in Britain is likely to be very different from that of the West Indians. Not only are they far more culturally distinct from the native British than are the West Indians, but they are conscious of their own cultural traditions and reject some English norms and values. Moreover, their communities are far more cohesive than those of the West Indians, and they appear increasingly to be generating their own economic infra-structures. These tendencies point, then, in a pluralistic direction. Whether in the longer term this is likely to prove viable is problematical.

Official policy, as reflected for example in the activities of the Community Relations Commission, points towards an absorption or assimilationist solution—in spite of the cultural diversity doctrine propounded by Roy Jenkins when Home Secretary. Possibly the thinking of official and other bodies has at least progressed beyond the stage when the second generation were regarded as 'black Englishmen', differing from their contemporaries only in the colour of their skin—but not very far beyond: the assimilationist viewpoint still prevails. Not only is this official policy likely to be seen as irrelevant by the Asian communities, but any pressures to conform will be counter-productive.

In the short run, probably for the next two or three generations,

such absorption as takes place in the area of employment is likely
to be accompanied by elements of pluralism. Possibly there will be a
situation where members of different ethnic groups can coexist
relatively harmoniously in employment relationships, but return
to their own communities when the factory gate or office door
closes.

Pluralism has lately become one of the popular concepts of some
academics and practitioners concerned with race in Britain. Perhaps,
then, it should be emphasized that a plural society can contain
marked inequalities between the ethnic groups, that it need not
necessarily conform to the Jenkins notion of 'equal opportunity . . .
in an atmosphere of mutual tolerance'. Discrimination, particularly
in employment and housing, is likely to be relatively long-enduring;
a marked and deep-seated antipathy towards coloured people is
widespread amongst the native population. By reducing contact
between ethnic groups, the elements of pluralism in the society will
tend to lessen the chances of conflict. To that extent it might be
conducive to *relative* racial harmony; it might be seen as a half-way
stage, as it were. In so far as it contains elements of considerable
inequality between the different ethnic groups, it will be inherently
unstable.

Whether within a capitalist framework a plural society in which
race ceases to be a factor is attainable, is problematical. My own
view is that it is not. Moreover, the prospects for *cultural* pluralism
without inequalities and conflict between the constituent ethnic
groups do not appear much brighter.

APPENDIX I

Questionnaires Used in the Study[1]

A. *General Background*
    1. Age
    2. Sex
    3. Department
    4. Location
    5. (Busmen only)   Present route no. Previous route nos. (If applicable) Why did you change routes?
    6. (Immigrants only)   How long have you lived in England?
    7.   ,,   ,,   Where are you from originally?
    8.   ,,   ,,   What was your job in [country of origin]?
    9.   ,,   ,,   (If from Barbados) Were you recruited by London Transport in Barbados?
    10.   ,,   ,,   At what age did you leave school?
    11.   ,,   ,,   Is your family in England?
    12.   ,,   ,,   Did you have any other jobs in England before you joined London Transport? (If yes) What were they?

B. *London Transport Background and Present Situation*
    13. How long have you been working for London Transport?
    14. What is your present job?
    15. How long have you been a [present grade]?
    16. How long have you been at [location]?
    17. (If applicable) What other jobs have you had with London Transport?
        For how long [each previous grade]?
        (Busmen only) (If applicable) Why did you change [jobs]?
    18. Did you have any friends or relatives working for London Transport before you joined?
    19. How did you hear about a job with London Transport?
    20. Do you have any relatives working for London Transport now?
    21. Why did you join London Transport?

[1] The indented questions were asked only of the staff named in brackets before the question.

22. (Barbadian direct   Did you attend the classes run by the
     recruits only)   Barbados Government for people who
                                were joining London Transport? (If yes)
                                Were these classes useful? (If yes) How?
                                Do you think these classes could be
                                improved? (If yes) How?
23. Which courses have you been to at the training school?
24. Did you find any difficulties on these courses?
    (If yes) What sort of difficulty?
25. Do you think the training course/courses could be improved?
    (If yes) How?
26. Have you attended any evening classes on transport subjects/
    voluntary courses run by London Transport?
    (If yes) What and where?

C.   *Relations in Work Situation*

27. (Busmen and trainmen   Is your [other crew member] English or
    only)   from abroad?
                                  (If abroad) Where from?
28. (Trainmen only)   Would/do you prefer to have a per-
                                manent motorman/guard?
                                  Why/Why not?
29. (Bus drivers only)   Is your conductor a man or a woman?
                                  Which do you prefer? Why?
30. (Busmen and trainmen   How long have you worked together?
    only)
31. (Busmen and trainmen   How do you get on together?
    only)
32. (Busmen only)   Did either of you ask to work together?
                                  (If yes) Which one? Why?
33. (Busmen only)   Do you take your tea and meal breaks
                                together; do you sit at the same table?
34. (Busmen and trainmen   How can a [other crew member] help
    only)   his [own occupation] with his work?
35. (Busmen and trainmen   How can a [own occupation] help his
    only)   [other crew member] with his work?
36. (Station platform staff   How can the platform staff help the
    and trainmen only)   train crews in their work?
37. What makes a good [own occupation]?
38. What makes a good [immediate supervisor]?
39. How do you get on with your [immediate supervisor]?
40. (Permanent Way staff   How many are there in your gang?
    only)
41. (Permanent Way staff   How many of these are Commonwealth
    only)   immigrants?

42.	Permanent Way staff only)	(Immigrants) How do you get on with the English? (Natives) How do you get on with the Commonwealth immigrants?
43.	(Permanent Way staff only)	How many of the gang do you normally work with?
44.	(Permanent Way staff only)	Are these usually the same people?
45.	(Permanent Way staff only)	(If yes) Are they English or from aboard?
46.	(Permanent Way staff only)	How do you get on together?
47.	Do you like working in this garage/depot/station/gang? Why/Why not?	
48.	(Permanent Way staff only)	Have you ever worked in a day/night gang?
49.	(Permanent Way staff only)	Do you prefer days or nights? Why?

D.   *Relations in Work Situation*

50.	(Natives only)	Do Commonwealth immigrants make good [own occupation]?
51.	(Native busmen and trainmen only)	Do Commonwealth immigrants make good [other crew member's occupation]?
52.	(Natives only)	Was there any objection to the employment of Commonwealth immigrants here when they first came? (If yes) When was this? (If applicable) On what grounds?
53.	Has there been any hostility in this garage/depot/station/gang towards the Commonwealth immigrants?	
54.	Is there any hostility now?	
55.	(Immigrants only)	How do you get on with the [other immigrant groups] at work?
56.	(Natives only)	Would there be any objection if a Commonwealth immigrant was appointed [appropriate supervisory post]? (If yes) Why?
57.	(Native station staff only)	Have there been any Commonwealth immigrant station foremen here?
58.	(Native station staff only)	Have you worked under a Commonwealth immigrant station foreman?

59. (Native station staff   (If applicable) Was there any objection
    only)   to a Commonwealth immigrant becom-
                                 ing a station foreman?
60. (Busmen, trainmen, and What sort of difficulties do you have
    station staff)   with passengers?
61. (Native busmen,   Have you been present when immigrant
    trainmen, and station   staff have had difficulties with passengers?
    staff)   (If yes) What happened? What did you
                                 do?

E.   *Trade Union and Social Activities*
  62. (Not busmen)   Do you belong to a trade union?
                                 Which branch?
  63. (Immigrants only)   Did you belong to a trade union in
                                 [country of origin]?
                                 (If yes) Which?
  64. Do you go to trade union branch meetings?
  65. When did you last go?
  66. Do you take any active part in trade union branch meetings?
  67. Have you ever held any official trade union post?
      (Specify)
  68. Would you like to?
  69. (Natives only)   Would there be any opposition to a
                                 Commonwealth immigrant being a
                                 union representative?
                                 (If yes) Why?
  70. Do you take part in any London Transport sports or social
      activities?
      (If yes) Which?
  71. (Natives only)   Do you meet any of your Common-
                                 wealth immigrant workmates out of
                                 working hours?
                                 Where?
  71. (Immigrants only)   Do you meet any of your English work-
                                 mates out of working hours? Where?
  72. Have you visited their homes?
  73. Have they visited your home?
  74. (Natives only)   Do you meet any of your English work-
                                 mates out of working hours? Where?
  74. (Immigrants only)   Do you meet any of your [own group]
                                 workmates out of working hours?
                                 Where? Are they people you knew
                                 before you came to England?
  75. Where do you live?

76. (Immigrants only)   Do you meet any of the [other immigrant groups] out of working hours? Where?

78. (Immigrants only)   Are there many [own group] or other immigrants living in the street where you live?

79. (Immigrants only)   How do you get on with your English neighbours?

77. (Natives only)   Are any of your neighbours (either side or in the same house) Commonwealth immigrants?

78. (Natives only)   Are there many Commonwealth immigrants living in the street where you live?

79. (Natives only)   How do you get on with them?

F.   *Aspirations*

80. (Immigrants only)   Why did you come to England?

81. (Immigrants only)   (If previously white-collar or skilled) When you came to England did you expect to get a job as a [previous occupation]?

82. (Immigrants only)   Have you tried to get a job as a [previous occupation]?

83. (Immigrants only)   Will you try later?

84. (Immigrants only)   (If unskilled before migration and not recruited direct) What sort of a job did you expect to get in England?

85. (Immigrants only)   How long did you intend to stay in England when you came?

86. (Immigrants only)   How long do you intend to stay now?

87. (Immigrants only)   How does working in England compare with what you expected?

88. (Immigrants only)   Have you had any difficulty in obtaining satisfactory housing in London? What sort of difficulty?

89. (Immigrants only)   (If Barbados direct recruit) Did the Barbados Welfare Service find you accommodation? Was this satisfactory? (If no) Why not?

90. What do you like about working for London Transport?
91. What don't you like?
92. Why do you stay?
93. Do you want to be promoted to another job?
94. (If yes) What sort of job? Why?

95. Have you applied for promotion?
    (If yes) What job?
96. Do you intend to apply for promotion (again)?
97. (If yes) Do you think you will be promoted?
    Why/Why not?

G.   *General*
   98. (Natives only)   Have you been in the forces?
                             (If yes) Did you serve overseas?
                             (If yes) Where?
   99. (Natives only)   What was your father's occupation?
  100. Is there anything else you wish to tell me?

APPENDIX 2

DISCIPLINARY PROCEDURES

A. Disciplinary Procedure Applicable to Drivers and Conductors: Central Buses

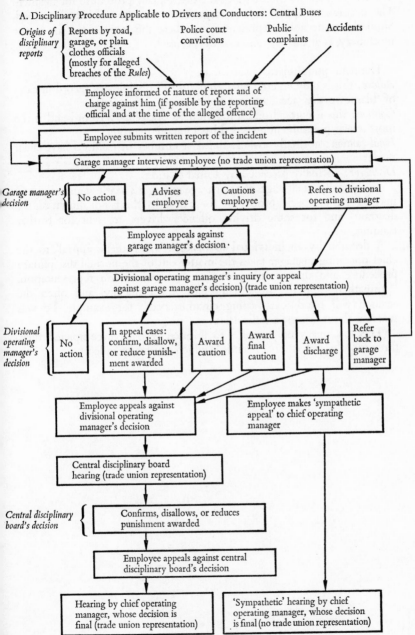

Notes on the Central Buses Disciplinary Procedure

The diagram shows the stages of the disciplinary procedure for busmen·
The decision to appeal at any stage is that of the individual accused.
Similarly, trade union representation, where this is provided for in the
machinery, is at the discretion of the accused.

The main punishments awarded are:
Advice: this is only entered on an individual's disciplinary record in cases
of 'blameworthy' accident or a police court conviction;
Caution: this is entered on an individual's disciplinary record and is the
most severe punishment awarded by a garage manager;
Final caution: normally awarded after a number of cautions have been
made;
Discharge: normally preceded by a final caution.

Additionally, at all stages above garage manager's hearings an individual
may be 'put on special probation' for x months (this is not shown on the
diagram) and for some driving offences drivers are sent for further
training.

A decision by an individual to make a 'sympathetic appeal' to the
chief operating manager takes the matter out of the normal disciplinary
procedure and there is no provision for trade union representation.
'Sympathetic appeals' are usually pleas for clemency, and often the
accused will plead 'extenuating circumstances', for example, he was
worried about domestic difficulties.

(This machinery only applies to busmen who have completed their
three months' probationary service, which can be extended.)

B. Disciplinary Procedure Applicable to Train and Station Staff:
Railway Operating

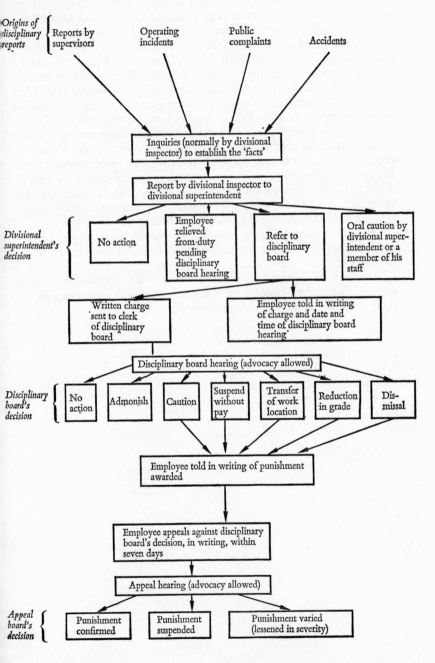

Notes on Disciplinary Procedure in Railway Operating

The diagram shows the various stages of the procedure. Employees are given at least three working days' notice of the date and time of disciplinary board hearings. The board is composed of two departmental officers, one of whom is usually the staff relations officer. The employee is charged on written evidence, he can state his defence, and can be assisted by an advocate. Such advocates are usually trade union officials or sectional council representatives. The only limitation here is that 'no member of the staff may attend as advocate or spokesman on behalf of employees over whom he has the responsibility of supervision'.

Appeals are normally heard by the assistant operating manager (staff); in his absence the chief operating manager will hear appeals. Normally, one of the officers forming the disciplinary board is in attendance. Leave to appeal may be refused in what are considered trivial cases (for example, when a charge is proved but the sentence is nominal), but such cases are apparently rare and are open to representations. Advocacy at the appeal board is similar to that at the disciplinary board.

Only in an *exceptionally* serious case' would an employee be suspended from duty (with or without pay) before a disciplinary board hearing.

Suspension as a punishment can be of varying duration, but rarely exceeds three days. Transfer of work location while remaining in the same grade is a relatively rare punishment.

C. Disciplinary Procedure Applicable to Grades up to and Including
Ganger: Permanent Way

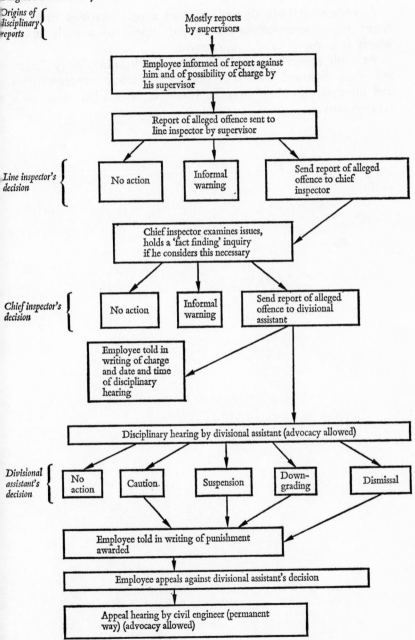

Origins of disciplinary reports

Mostly reports
by supervisors

Employee informed of report against
him and of possibility of charge by
his supervisor

Report of alleged offence sent to
line inspector by supervisor

Line inspector's decision

No action | Informal warning | Send report of alleged offence to chief inspector

Chief inspector examines issues,
holds a 'fact finding' inquiry
if he considers this necessary

Chief inspector's decision

No action | Informal warning | Send report of alleged offence to divisional assistant

Employee told in
writing of charge
and date and time
of disciplinary
hearing

Disciplinary hearing by divisional assistant (advocacy allowed)

Divisional assistant's decision

No action | Caution. | Suspension | Down-grading | Dismissal

Employee told in writing of punishment
awarded

Employee appeals against divisional assistant's decision

Appeal hearing by civil engineer (permanent
way) (advocacy allowed)

Notes on Disciplinary Procedure in Permanent Way

Advocates at both disciplinary and appeal hearings must be
either department employees or an official of a trade union
which is a party to the agreement.

At both supervisory and divisional levels, disciplinary 'cases'
are often discussed with staff (sectional council) representatives
and informal warnings may be issued in association with such
representatives.

BIBLIOGRAPHY

ABBOTT, SIMON. Defining racial discrimination. *Race*, Vol. XI, No. 4, April 1970.

ALLEN, SHEILA. Immigrants or workers, in Zubaida, Sami (ed)., *Race and racialism*. London, Tavistock Publications, for the British Sociological Association, 1970.

Associated Society of Locomotive Engineers and Firemen. *Locomotive journal*.

BAGWELL, PHILIP S. *The railwaymen: the history of the National Union of Railwaymen*. London, Allen & Unwin, 1963.

BANTON, MICHAEL. *White and coloured: the behaviour of British people towards coloured immigrants*. London, Cape, 1959.

—— *Race relations*. London, Tavistock Publications, 1967.

BARBADOS GOVERNMENT PRINTING OFFICE. *Information booklet for intending emigrants to Britain*. Bridgetown, Barbados Government Printing Office, undated.

BARKER, T. C., AND ROBBINS, MICHAEL. *A history of London Transport*, Vol. I: *The nineteenth century*. London, Allen & Unwin, 1963.

BEETHAM, DAVID. *Immigrant school leavers and the youth employment service in Birmingham*. London, Institute of Race Relations Special Series, 1967.

—— *Transport and turbans*. London, Oxford University Press, for Institute of Race Relations, 1970.

BLALOCK, HUBERT M. *Towards a theory of minority-group relations*. New York, Wiley, 1967.

BROOKS, DENNIS; DAVIES, TOM; AND FRYER, BOB. Attitudes to employment on the postal side of the G.P.O. London, Imperial College, 1968.

BROOKS, DENNIS. Commonwealth immigrants: who will go back? *Race today*. Vol. I, No. 5, September 1969.

BROWN, J. A. C. *The social psychology of industry*. London, Penguin Books, 1954.

BROWN, JOHN. *The un-melting pot*. London, Macmillan, 1970.

BROWN, RICHARD K. Research and consultancy in industrial enterprises. *Sociology*, Vol. 1, No. 1, January 1967.

SOME CENTRAL LONDON BUS BRANCHES (OF T.G.W.U.). *Bus stop*.

CENTRAL STATISTICAL OFFICE, TRINIDAD AND TOBAGO. *Barbados population census, 1960*, Vol. II: Summary Tables. Port of Spain, Central Statistical Office, 1963.

CENTRE FOR URBAN STUDIES. *London: aspects of change*. London, MacGibbon & Kee, 1964.

CHINOY, ELY. *Automobile workers and the American dream*. New York, Doubleday, 1955.

CLEGG, H. A. *Labour relations in London transport*. Oxford, Blackwell, 1950.

COLEMAN, TERRY. *The railway navvies*. London, Penguin Books, 1968.

COTTRELL, W. FRED. *The railroader*. Stanford, California, Stanford University Press; and London, Oxford University Press, 1940.

CROSS, MALCOLM (ed.), *Race and pluralism*. *Race*. Vol. XII, No. XII, No. 4, April 1971.

CUMPER, G. E. *Report on employment in Barbados*. Bridgetown, Barbados Government Printing Office, undated.

DAHRENDORF, RALF. *Class and class conflict in industrial society.* London, Routledge & Kegan Paul, 1959.

DAVISON, R. B. *West Indian migrants.* London, Oxford University Press, for Institute of Race Relations, 1962.

—— *Commonwealth immigrants.* London, Oxford University Press, for Institute of Race Relations, 1964.

—— *Black British: immigrants to England.* London, Oxford University Press, for Institute of Race Relations, 1966.

DOLL, RICHARD, AND AVERY-JONES, FRANCIS. *Occupational factors in the aetiology of gastric and duodenal ulcers with an estimate of their incidence in the general population.* London, H.M.S.O., 1951. (Medical Research Council Special Report Series, No. 276.)

EGGINTON, J. *They seek a living.* London, Hutchinson, 1957.

EISENSTADT, S. N. *The absorption of immigrants.* London, Routledge & Kegan Paul, 1954.

EMERY, F. E. (ed.). *Systems thinking.* London, Penguin Books, 1969.

FOOT, PAUL. *Immigration and race in British politics.* London, Penguin Books, 1965.

FOSTER, P. M., AND GARDNER, G. The recruitment and retention of bus drivers in central London. London, Tavistock Institute of Human Relations, 1966.

FURNIVALL, J. S. Some problems of tropical economy, in Hinden, Rita (ed.), *Fabian colonial essays.* London, Unwin, 1945.

—— *Colonial policy and practice.* Cambridge, Cambridge University Press, 1948; and New York, New York University Press, 1956.

General Registrar Office, London. *Sample census, 1966; Commonwealth Immigrant Tables.* London, H.M.S.O., 1969.

GERTH, H. H., AND MILLS, C. WRIGHT. *From Max Weber: essays in sociology.* London, Routledge & Kegan Paul, 1948.

GLASS, RUTH. *Newcomers: the West Indians in London.* London, Allen & Unwin for the Centre for Urban Studies, 1960

GLAZER, NATHAN, AND MOYNIHAN, DANIEL PATRICK. *Beyond the melting pot.* Cambridge, Massachusetts, M.I.T. Press, 1963.

GOFFMAN, ERVING. *Behavior in public places.* New York, The Free Press; and London, Collier-Macmillan, 1963.

GOLDTHORPE, JOHN H.; LOCKWOOD, DAVID; BECHHOFER, FRANK; AND PLATT, JENNIFER. *The affluent worker: industrial attitudes and behaviour.* Cambridge, Cambridge University Press, 1968.

GOULDNER, ALVIN W. *Patterns of industrial bureaucracy.* London, Routledge & Kegan Paul, 1955.

HEPPLE, BOB. *Race, jobs and the law in Britain.* London, Allen Lane, the Penguin Press, 1968.

HOLLOWELL, PETER G. *The lorry driver.* London, Routledge & Kegan Paul, 1968.

HUGHES, EVERETT CHERRINGTON, AND HUGHES, HELEN MCGILL. *Where peoples meet: racial and ethnic frontiers.* Glencoe, The Free Press, 1952.

International social science bulletin: Recent research on racial relations. Vol. X, No. 3, 1958.

Institute of Race Relations. *Coloured immigrants in Britain,* London, Oxford University Press, for Institute of Race Relations, 1960.

Institute of Race Relations. *Colour and immigration in the United Kingdom, 1968.* London, Institute of Race Relations Facts Paper, 1968.

JACKSON, ALAN A., AND CROOME, DESMOND F. *Rails through the clay*. London, Allen & Unwin, 1962.

JAQUES, ELLIOTT. *The changing culture of a factory*. London, Tavistock Publications, 1951.

JEFFRESS, PHILIP W. *The Negro in the urban transit industry*. Philadelphia, Pennsylvania, Industrial Research Unit, Department of Industry, Wharton School of Finance and Commerce, University of Pennsylvania, 1970.

JONES, JACK. Employment, in LESTER, ANTHONY, AND DEAKIN, NICHOLAS (eds.). *Policies for racial equality*. London, Fabian Society, 1967.

JONES, K., AND SMITH, A. D. *The economic impact of commonwealth immigration*. Cambridge, Cambridge University Press, for N.I.E.S.R., 1969.

KINGSFORD, P. W. *Victorian railwaymen*. London, Cass, 1970.

LITTLE, KENNETH. *Negroes in Britain*. London, Kegan Paul, 1947.

LOCKWOOD, DAVID. Race, conflict and plural society, in Zubaida, Sami (ed.), *Race and racialism*.

London Transport Board. *Annual report(s) and accounts* for the years 1963-9. London, H.M.S.O., 1964-70.

London Transport Board. *Rule book for drivers and conductors*. London, L.T.B. Central Buses, 1964.

London Transport Board. *Codes of practice for incentive bonus scheme, permanent way conciliation staff*. London, L.T.B., Department of Chief Civil Engineer, 1966.

London Transport Board. *Reshaping London's bus services*. London, L.T.B., 1966.

London Transport Board. *London Transport magazine*. London, L.T.B.

London Transport Board. *The busman*. London, L.T.B. Central Buses.

London Transport Executive. *Rules for observance by employees*. London, L.T.E., 1949.

MCKENNA, FRANK. *A glossary of railwaymen's talk*. Oxford, Ruskin College History Workshop, 1970.

MCPHERSON, KLIM, AND GAITSKELL, JULIA. *Immigrants and employment: two case studies in East London and Croydon*. London, Institute of Race Relations Special Series, 1969.

Ministry of Labour and Ministry of Transport. *Report of the committee of inquiry to review the pay and conditions of employment of the drivers and conductors of the London Transport Board's road services* (the 'Phelps Brown report'). London, H.M.S.O., 1964.

Ministry of Transport. *Transport in London* (Cmnd. 3686). London, H.M.S.O., 1968.

MISHAN, E. J., AND NEEDLEMAN, L. Immigration: long-run economic effects. *Lloyds bank review*, No. 87, January 1968.

MURPHY, C. E. *London buses: a challenge from the driver's cab*. London, Foulis, 1965.

NANDY, DIPAK. Unrealistic aspirations. *Race today*, Vol. 1, No. 1, May 1969.

National Board for Prices and Incomes. *Pay and conditions of busmen* (Cmnd. 3012). London, H.M.S.O., 1966.

——— *Productivity agreements in the bus industry* (Cmnd. 3498). London, H.M.S.O., 1967.

——— *Proposals by the London Transport Board and the British Railways Board for fare increases in the London area* (Cmnd. 3561). London, H.M.S.O., 1968.

——— *Pay of municipal busmen* (Cmnd. 3605). London, H.M.S.O., 1968.

——— *Proposals by the London Transport Board for fare increases* (Cmnd. 4036). London, H.M.S.O., 1969.

National Union of Railwaymen, *The railway review*. London, Kings Cross Publishing Co.

PATTERSON, SHEILA. *Dark strangers*. London, Tavistock Publications, 1963.

PATTERSON, SHEILA. *Immigrants in industry*. London, Oxford University Press, for Institute of Race Relations, 1968.
——— *Immigration and race relations in Britain, 1960–1967*. London, Oxford University Press, for Institute of Race Relations, 1969.
P.F.C. AND C.D. *Taking London for a ride*. London, A Group of London Busmen, 1967.
PICKWOAD, A. H. Planned entry. *The lancet*, 30 October 1965.
Political and Economic Planning and Research Services Ltd. *Racial discrimination*. London, P.E.P., 1967.
THE PRIME MINISTER. *Immigration from the Commonwealth* (Cmnd. 2739). London, H.M.S.O., 1965.
QUENNELL, PETER (ed.). *Mayhew's London*. London, Spring Books, undated. (Selections from Mayhew, Henry, *London labour and the London poor*, 1851.)
Race Relations Act 1968, Chapter 71. London, H.M.S.O., 1968.
Race Relations Board. *Guide to the 'racial balance' provisions of the Race Relations Act, 1968*. London, Race Relations Board, 1969.
Race today, Vol. 3, Nos. 10 and 11, October and November, 1971. (A number of articles and comments on the operation of the Race Relations Act 1968.)
RADCLIFFE-BROWN, A. R. *Structure and function in primitive society*. London, Cohen & West, 1952.
RADIN, BERYL. Coloured workers and British trade unions. *Race*, Vol. VIII, No. 2, 1966.
RAFFLE, ANDREW. The occupational physician as community physician. *Proceedings of the Royal Society of Medicine*, July 1970, Vol. 63, No. 7.
REES, T. B. Accommodation, integration, cultural pluralism and assimilation: their place in equilibrium theories of society. *Race*, Vol. XI. No. 4, April 1970.
REX, JOHN, AND MOORE, ROBERT. *Race, community, and conflict: a study of Sparkbrook*. London, Oxford University Press, for Institute of Race Relations, 1967.
——— The concept of race in sociological theory, in Zubaida, Sami (ed.). *Race and racialism*.
——— *Race relations in sociological theory*. London, Weidenfeld & Nicolson, 1970.
RICHMOND, ANTHONY H. *The colour problem*. London, Penguin Books, 1955.
RIMMER, MALCOLM. Race relations and job regulation: a study in a Midlands foundry. University of Warwick, M.A. dissertation 1970.
——— *Race and industrial conflict*. London, Heinemann, 1972.
RISHER, HOWARD W., JR. *The Negro in the railroad industry*. Philadelphia, Pennsylvania, Industrial Research Unit, Wharton School of Finance and Commerce, University of Pennsylvania, 1971.
ROETHLISBERGER, F. J., AND DICKSON, WILLIAM J. *Management and the worker*. Cambridge, Massachusetts, Harvard University Press, 1939.
ROSE, E. J. B., AND ASSOCIATES. *Colour and citizenship: a report on British race relations*. London, Oxford University Press, for Institute of Race Relations, 1969.
ROUTH, GUY. *Occupation and pay in Great Britain, 1906–1960*. Cambridge, Cambridge University Press, 1965.
ROY, DONALD F. 'Banana time' job satisfaction and informal interaction. *Human organization*, Vol. 18, No. 4, Winter 1959–60.
Select Committee on Nationalised Industries, London Transport. *Report and proceedings of the committee*, Vol. I. London, H.M.S.O., 1965.
Select Committee on Nationalised Industries, London Transport. *Report*, Vol. II. Minutes of evidence, appendices and index. London, H.M.S.O., 1965.

Select Committee on Nationalised Industries, London Transport. *Second special report* (observations of the London Transport Board). London, H.M.S.O., 1965.

Select Committee on Race Relations and Immigration, Session 1968-9. *Report*, Vol. IV, Appendices to the minutes of evidence. London, H.M.S.O., 1969.

Select Committee on Race Relations and Immigration, Session 1969-70. *Control of Commonwealth immigration*, Minutes of evidence, Thursday, 12 March 1970. London, H.M.S.O., 1970.

SCOTT, WILLIAM G. *The management of conflict: appeal systems in organizations*. Homewood, Illinois, Richard D. Irwin Inc. and the Dorsey Press, 1965.

SHEPPARD, HARVEY. *Dictionary of railway slang*. Somerset, Dillington House College for Adult Education, 1965.

SHETH, N. R. *The social framework of an Indian factory*. Manchester, Manchester University Press, 1968.

SILVERMAN, DAVID. *The theory of organisations*. London, Heinemann, 1970.

SIMPSON, GEORGE EATON, AND YINGER, J. MILTON. *Racial and cultural minorities*. New York, Harper, 1958.

SMITH, J. H. Social aspects of industrial change. *Occupational psychology*, Vol. 27, No. 2., April 1953.

——The changing status of the London busman. Memorandum submitted to the Phelps Brown Committee, 1964.

—— Busman's honeymoon? *New Society*, Vol. 3, No. 82, 23 April 1964.

SMITH, M. G. *The plural society in the British West Indies*. Berkeley and Los Angeles, University of California Press, 1965.

SOFER, CYRIL. Working groups in a plural society. *Industrial and labor relations review*, Vol. 8, October, 1954.

STEPHENS, LESLIE. *Employment of coloured workers in the Birmingham area*. London, Institute of Personnel Management, 1956.

TANNAHILL, J. A. *European volunteer workers in Britain*. Manchester, Manchester University Press, 1958.

THOMAS, RAY. Journeys to work. *Planning*, Vol. XXXIV, No. 504, November 1968.

TRIST, E. L.; HIGGIN, G. W.; MURRAY, H.; AND POLLOCK, A. B. *Organisational choice*. London, Tavistock Publications, 1963.

TURNER, BARRY A. *Exploring the industrial subculture*. London, Macmillan, 1971.

VAN BEINUM, HANS. *The morale of the Dublin busmen*. London, Tavistock Institute of Human Relations, undated.

VAN DEN BERGHE, PIERRE. *Race and racism*. London, Wiley, 1967.

WASON, C. R. *Busman's view*. London, Allen & Unwin, 1958.

West Indian Standing Conference (London Region). *The unsquare deal*. London, W.I.S.C., 1967.

WOODWARD, JOAN. *Management and technology*. London, H.M.S.O., 1958.

—— *Industrial organization: theory and practice*. London, Oxford University Press, 1965.

WRIGHT, PETER L. The coloured worker in British industry. University of Edinburgh Ph.D. thesis, 1965.

—— *The coloured worker in British industry*. London, Oxford University Press for Institute of Race Relations, 1968.

YOUNG, MICHAEL, AND WILLMOTT, PETER. *Family and kinship in East London*. London, Routledge & Kegan Paul, 1957.

ZWEIG, FERDYNAND. *The worker in an affluent society*. London, Heinemann, 1961.

INDEX

Abbott, Simon, 17
Absence, accounting for, 193, 195, 338
Absorption, xx, 1, 4, 8, 9–11, 13, 15–19, 25, 333; and different immigrant groups, 312–14; and employment, 340–4; and length of stay, 322–7; and management, 344–9; and pluralism, 305–27, 355–61; and relations with neighbours, 316–19; in social contact, 305–12; and work expectations, 319–22; *see also* Acceptance, Adaptation *and* Group dispersion.
Acceptance, 3–4, 14–17, 330, 333, 334, 335, 340–1, 346, 354–5; *see also* Absorption
Accommodation (concept of) *see* Absorption
Accommodation *see* Housing
Acculturation, 15–17, 337–9, 343, 355–7; *see also* Adaptation
Achievement, occupational, 325–6
Acton Society Trust, xvii
Adaptation, 3–4, 7–8, 15–19; *see also* Acculturation *and* Conformity
Africans, 60, 208, 312, 313, 314; recruitment and tests, 240–4, 247, 249, 251, 252, 253, 254
Allen, Sheila, 2–3, 6
Anglo-Asians, 290; *see also* Asians
Anglo-Indians, 34, 103, 104, 240, 268, 323, 324; *see also* Indians
Antipathy *see* Hostility
Appeal systems, 29; *see also* Discipline
Apprenticeship, 244
Armenians, 240
Asians: as busmen, 63, 103, 104; group relations, 313, 314, 335, 360; job

performance, 268; training, 284; as trainmen, 147; *see also* Anglo-Asians
Associated Society of Locomotive Engineers and Firemen (ASLEF), xviii, 294, 295, 296–7, 298, 301
Australians, 240, 241, 242, 243, 248, 252
Avery-Jones, Francis, 119

Bagwell, Philip S., 134, 203
Baltic States, immigrants from, 207
Banton, Michael, 4, 6, 13, 309
Barbados: education in, 268; unions, 294
Barbados Government, 19, 69, 70, 256, 257, 262, 263
Barbados Labour Department, 257, 260
Barbados Migrants' Liaison Service, 256, 261
Barbados recruitment scheme (1955–70), 19, 43, 238, 252, 256–70, 345, 358; absorption and, 348–9; bonus, 69, 70; British currency, familiarity with, 259, 266, 268, 269, 279; busmen, 77, 78; delays, 263; employees, views on, 265–8; English language instruction, 16, 259, 266, 269, 279; entry vouchers, 260, 263, 268; Government loan, 35, 69, 257, housing, 261–2; immigration restrictions and, xix, 258, 261, 262–3; information on Britain, 257, 258, 269, 270, 319; instructors, 40, 259–60, 267; intended length of stay, 324–5; job discrimination, 322; job performance, 263–5, 268; management views on, 264–5; medical examinations, 257, 260, 263; numbers, 34, 42, 240; previous occupations, 266;

381